# Social Change
# and Applied Anthropology

# Social Change and Applied Anthropology

## Essays in Honor of David W. Brokensha

EDITED BY
## Miriam S. Chaiken and Anne K. Fleuret

## Westview Press
BOULDER, SAN FRANCISCO, & OXFORD

*Westview Special Studies in Applied Anthropology*

Copyright © 1990 by Westview Press, Inc.

Published in 1990 in the United States of America by Westview Press, Inc., 5500 Central Avenue, Boulder, Colorado 80301, and in the United Kingdom by Westview Press, Inc., 36 Lonsdale Road, Summertown, Oxford OX2 7EW

Library of Congress Cataloging-in-Publication Data
Social change and applied anthropology : essays in honor of David W.
  Brokensha / edited by Miriam S. Chaiken and Anne K. Fleuret.
    p.  cm. — (Westview special studies in applied anthropology)
  Includes bibliographical references.
  ISBN 0-8133-7734-X
  1. Applied anthropology.  2. Social change.  3. Human geography.
4. Brokensha, David.  I. Brokensha, David.  II. Chaiken, Miriam S.
III. Fleuret, Anne Klingelhofer, 1947–    .  IV. Series.
GN397.5.S67  1990
303.4—dc20                                                    90-12092
                                                                   CIP

Printed and bound in the United States of America

The paper used in this publication meets the requirements
of the American National Standard for Permanence of Paper
for Printed Library Materials Z39.48-1984.

10    9    8    7    6    5    4    3    2    1

# Contents

PART THREE
SOCIAL CHANGE AND SOCIAL INEQUALITY

PART FOUR
NATURAL RESOURCE MANAGEMENT

# Preface

At the American Anthropological Association meetings in 1987 a group of David W. Brokensha's former students discussed our reactions to his announcement of his intention to retire in 1989. All of us were keenly aware of David's influence on our lives; we were attempting to apply our anthropological perspective to issues of economic and social equity and resource conservation and management as well as attempting to act as advocates for unempowered people, all of which parallel David Brokensha's lifelong interests. Our professional lives, and to a great extent our ethical and personal goals, have been shaped by our interaction with David Brokensha. We decided that a collection of essays in his honor, focusing on issues which had concerned him throughout his professional career, would be an appropriate tribute to his roles as anthropologist, teacher, guide, and friend.

In the following months the editors contacted a number of anthropologists who had professional connections with David Brokensha; former students, colleagues, and other applied anthropologists with similar interests. The enthusiasm for the project was overwhelming, and without exception everyone we contacted spoke of how influential David had been in their lives and their work. He is a man of tremendous sensitivity, integrity, and professional capability, and while his unassuming nature would likely make him embarrassed by such effusive expressions of sentiment, the response from other anthropologists is a fitting testimony to his influence on all of us.

David Brokensha's contributions to applied anthropology and development studies are notable. He has carried out pioneering research on several issues which have become increasingly important in recent years. He was one of the first anthropologists to focus on the consequences of social change in the era of independence in Africa, especially in his research in the newly independent Ghana (Brokensha 1966). He was also an innovator in examining the social aspects of river basin development and new lands settlement, which have continued to be major concerns both of development anthropologists and of the Institute for Development Anthropology, which he helped establish.

Long before it was commonplace, Brokensha advocated paradigms of applied anthropology which are now central to the discipline. He stressed the need for equity in development, focusing especially on the effects of development on women. He emphasized the importance of incorporating indigenous perspectives and knowledge in development planning and the need for sustainable natural resource management. These views were incorporated into the graduate courses he taught and were represented in his numerous publications.

He insisted that if applied anthropologists were to be effective they must learn the languages and concerns of other disciplines, participate in interdisciplinary research, publish in ways that would reach wider audiences rather than addressing only the anthropological community, and make their results and recommendations available to a broad constituency of development administrators, local politicians, rural villagers, and academics. Toward these ends, he has engaged in collaborative research and co-authored papers not only with other anthropologists, but also with geographers, economists, foresters, political scientists, and sociologists. He has given workshops and public addresses internationally, ranging from professional presentations at the Food and Agriculture Organization (FAO) of the United Nations, to facilitating discussions among African villagers, to providing training on social forestry to foresters in Malawi and middle-level bureaucrats in India. He has consistently tried to bring anthropological awareness and the concerns of those at "the bottom" to those at the top.

David Brokensha is interested in many geographic regions and has participated in research or consulted around the world, but his most important contributions have dealt with sub-Saharan Africa, the area of his most enduring interest. His roots in South Africa, and his explicit rejection of his patrimony of racial inequality, have caused him much personal anguish in his lifetime, but rather than distancing himself from the area, he has never ceased to champion the potentials of independent, autonomous African countries. Though mindful of growing social inequality and critical of the formation of indigenous elites in independent African nations, he has consistently admired the richness and diversity of African cultures and the capabilities of Africa's indigenous peoples.

David Brokensha's career has been a model of how to be an effective applied anthropologist, and his personal integrity and selflessness have been an inspiration to many. We can be grateful as anthropologists for his enormous contributions to the field of applied anthropology, just as we are grateful as individuals for having had the opportunity to work with and learn from him. It is with affection and admiration that we dedicate this book to David W. Brokensha.

*Miriam S. Chaiken*
*Anne K. Fleuret*

# Acknowledgments

Many people have helped make this book possible—most especially all of the contributors, who viewed the project with enthusiasm and were conscientious in providing manuscripts and revisions in a timely manner. Vivian Carlip, of the Institute for Development Anthropology, passed along a number of bits of helpful advice on manuscript preparation based on her extensive experience. Tom Conelly advised on the electronic wizardry necessary to convert computer diskettes in multiple formats into a common denominator, and at the eleventh hour he provided a keen eye for proofreading tables and figures. At Indiana University of Pennsylvania (IUP), Beth McHenry and Sharon Richwine helped retype several chapters into the computer, and Cynthia Cronk and Evelyn Mutchnick helped us gain access to a laser printer for preparing the tables. Illustrations were capably prepared by John Henry and Doug Shumar of IUP's Media Resources, and the Graduate School provided some additional funds for the photocopying expenses the manuscript required. To all our heartfelt thanks.

*M.S.C.*
*A.K.F.*

# Selected Publications of
# David W. Brokensha

1960 (edited jointly with P.T.W. Baxter) Egya Survey. Accra, Ghana: University of Ghana, Institute of Education.

1960 The District Commissioner as an Agent of Social Change in Tanganyika. *In* Research in Progress. H. C. Taylor, ed. Bellingham, Washington: Western Washington College of Education.

1961 Christianity and Change. Pittsburgh, Pennsylvania: Duquesne University. Institute of African Affairs.

1962 Volta Resettlement. Ethnographic Notes of Southern Areas. Accra, Ghana: University of Ghana.

1963 Resettlement and Anthropological Research. Human Organization. 22(4):286–290.

1966 Social Change at Larteh, Ghana. Oxford: The Clarendon Press.

1966 Applied Anthropology in English-speaking Africa. Lexington, Kentucky: Monograph No. 8. Society for Applied Anthropology.

1967 Development Administration in Africa. Rural Africana. 4 (December):3–11.

1969 (edited with Marion Pearsall) The Anthropology of Development in Sub-Saharan Africa. Lexington, Kentucky: Monograph No. 10. Society for Applied Anthropology.

1971 Handeni Revisited. African Affairs. 70(279):159–168.

1972 (with others) Akwapim Handbook. Accra, Ghana: State Publishing Corporation.

1973 (with Jack Glazier) Land Reform among the Mbeere of Central Kenya. Africa. 43(3):182–206.

1974 Africa, Whither Now? Journal of African Studies. 1(1):101–112.

1977 (with Michael Horowitz and Thayer Scudder) The Anthropology of Rural Development in the Sahel. Binghamton, New York: Institute for Development Anthropology.

1979 (with Peter Moock and Bernard Riley) Kenya Rural Access Roads. Consultants' First Annual Report. Washington, D.C.: Devres for Agency for International Development, Kenya.

1980 (edited with D.M. Warren and Oswald Werner) Indigenous Knowledge Systems and Development. Lanham, Maryland: University Press of America.

1981    (with A.P. Castro and Thomas Hakansson) Indicators of Rural Inequality. World Development. 9(5):401–427.

1983    (with Bernard Riley and A.H. Peter Castro) Reforestation in Kenya. Washington, D.C.: Agency for International Development.

1984    Part-time Subsistence and Traditional Inland Fisheries. Report for the Food and Agriculture Organization of the United Nations. Binghamton, New York: Institute for Development Anthropology.

1987    Inequality in Rural Africa: Fallers Reconsidered. Manchester University Papers on Development. III(2):1–21.

1988    (with Bernard Riley) The Mbeere in Kenya (2 volumes). Lanham, Maryland: University Press of America.

1988    (edited with Peter Little) Anthropology of Development and Change in East Africa. Boulder, Colorado: Westview Press.

# PART ONE

# Introduction

# The Participant Observer Observed: A Companion's Reflections on David W. Brokensha

*Bernard Riley*

D.W.B. first swam, quite literally, into my ken at the Tanga Yacht Club in July 1954, when our paths (or perhaps more accurately our wakes) crossed during our colonial service experience, when we overlapped for the first time. This meeting may have been to his surprise, but not to mine. I had acted on a mutual University friend's prior suggestion, that I might look him up should opportunity present itself, as he had preceded me by a year to Tanganyika Territory. In the interim, between leaving graduate year at London University and making his acquaintance, I had visited Southern Africa for the first time. Rhodesia and South Africa were both then still integral parts of the British Commonwealth, with their checkered administrative history and traditions. Since this initial contact, our collaborative efforts have been influenced by his social and geographic origins and our adoption of common interests. This casual meeting initiated opportunity for me to observe tenets of social anthropology put into action. I had read already some studies by well-known practitioners, such as Max Gluckman (who arrived at Manchester University in my first undergraduate year), Evans-Pritchard, and Godfrey and Monica Wilson. I was to witness, through several decades, their teachings put into perspective and practice by a gifted and dedicated administrator, researcher, and teacher.

D.W.B.'s long interest in social inequality stems initially from his exposure to inequalities of acceptance and opportunity in his own background; they were cemented in teen-age and young adult years by his first-hand experience at the receiving end, so to speak, of rejection processes. First, because he was not sports-minded or athletically adept within his native milieu. Second, because he was a prisoner of war in Italian, German, and finally Russian bureaucratic incarceration during his most impressionable years. It took many years, plus his wide variety of experience to develop his intellectual proficiencies to understand the complex interacting causes of social inequality. But man-

*3*

ifestations of inequality occurring throughout the development process have remained his underlying concentration within social adjustment and change. My close, continuous observation of D.W.B. through three decades convinces me that privilege never had attraction for him. This character facet alone probably accounts for his effectiveness with many people while conducting investigative fieldwork research. Indeed this came to light during our very first rural journey together.

We drove along scattered tracks through the coastal bush of Tanga Province to distribute supplies to village clinic staff of additional medicine from the Provincial Dispensary. At our approach, small children fled at first sight. The contrast with the usual jubilant rush to greet casual visitors to isolated fishing villages was telling. His subsequent enquiries yielded tales of missing children that coincided with passage of a mysterious unmarked four-wheel drive vehicle. It raised the whole specter of slave-raiding along mangrove-fringed lagoons, although it was never proved. "Master-servant" distinctions, and how these continue, or reinforce their impact during critical periods of economic, social, and political stress, have always occupied his attention.

It was dissatisfaction, perhaps, with official insensitivities while an administrator of the Tanganyika Colonial Service, in terms of carrying out government development projects, policies and procedures, that led to his resignation. To a young district officer trying to stimulate local acceptance of a wattle-bark scheme, the inability of many forest service officers either to comprehend traditional priorities, or understand the validity of indigenous knowledge or ecology with regard to natural vegetation (of which they were only transient observers) was irksome. This was so because a strong, subtle "master-servant" attitude pervaded its basic concept, yet remained unquestioned.

When D.W.B. relocated to urban-township administration in Bulawayo (then Rhodesia), the move brought his professional attention to more entrenched, sophisticated forms of social inequality. Only after sustained and bitter administrative battles had the white government of the day, at both municipal and national levels, accepted any concept of African home ownership in settler areas. Hugh Ashton, then Director of African Administration and Housing in Bulawayo, was to become an inspiration and model for tenacity of purpose in the face of abrasive resistance. During this period D.W.B.'s army dispatch rider training—brief as it had been in North Africa before capture—enabled casual, informal contact with Mpopoma residents. He rode around the home-ownership scheme he was employed to supervise by motorbike; enjoying the increased accessibility. Not all his colleagues were quite so unconcerned with status! But, the greatest value of the change was its opportunity for pioneering experience; to oversee practical implementation of a new concept.

In addition, he was able to add further innovations as their niches became apparent. One of these was a popular and successful "charladies" school and diploma; a prototype certificate of competence. It attempted to bridge the mistress-to-domestic-employee slough of despond that floundered, usually from lack of any mutual comprehension. Tales soon went their round. Increased employability of women graduates was predicated on trying realistically to reduce origins of social friction. It enhanced respect and greater harmony within the home between customary protagonists. In the wage-earning urban economy, both parties acquired sophistication derived from mutually acceptable standards of behavior; chasms can be bridged when both sides observe behavior patterns that are domestically advantageous. D.W.B. gained insights which considerably smoothed his work with wives of growers and migrant workers a decade later, among Anglo and Mexican-American women's groups in Patterson, California.

When it became apparent there was little hope for the success of a multiracial government in Rhodesia, D.W.B. applied for an academic post—"Lecturer in Social Administration" in the Department of Sociology—at the University of Ghana. Here his expertise to cope with social change problems in a rapidly modernizing milieu provided an opportunity to choose a base for an intensive, longitudinal study for his Oxford D. Phil. Paul Baxter, a valued friend, in his perpetual wisdom, urged selection of a strategic location accessible to the Legon campus. My own modest input augmented Paul's assessment with an additional geographical priority; choice of location where ecological and environmental impacts would be manifest earliest and paramount. D.W.B. chose Larteh, where two milieu were rapidly intermingling. Accessibility was assured with two (then) all-weather roads to Accra, via Dodowa and Aburi that permitted growing incursions of acquired sophistication radiating from the capital into the indigenous local scene.

But the increasing *"wabenzi"*[1] sub-culture stimulated stratification that cut across traditional layers. It was a complex mix that challenged criteria differentiating rural and urban sectors. His first book showed the validity of small rural towns acting as refracting cultural lenses, focusing social change through several spectra simultaneously. It contained the seeds of our on-going professional collaboration. We each made the other aware of ecological and sociological interdependencies—a blend of physical and cultural factors and processes. We did not set out to examine this interchange deliberately; there were no hypotheses waiting to be tested, but we found almost by default an attractive and accessible location to study social change in depth over a protracted period of time.

We went to Mbeere Division of Eastern Province, Kenya, mostly as a result of the dramatic events in the period when D.W.B. was chairperson (well it was quite unashamedly "chairMAN" in those balmy days) of the Anthropology Department at U.C.S.B. Without peering too closely into the well of hindsight, a ferocious storm of social protest centered on academic institutions marked the tenor of those days; it stimulated him to request the first sabbatical leave of his career. This was not really surprising; he had been identified by campus protest ringleaders as the villain of the piece in not having recommended for tenure a largely incompetent junior colleague who was popular with the student lunatic fringe. Evaluating government development plans is far more rewarding than trying to find the relevance of vituperative graffiti, when you are the object of the expressed vehemence and have no redress. So, off to Kenya we went; D.W.B. as official evaluator of the Mbeere Division Special Rural Development Plan then taking place, one in each of the six provinces of the country. It was an escape into an area about to plunge into a miasma of social development and change; it could not have been better timed. During our first three months I tried to come to grips with ethnobotanical criteria important to the local people, mostly as a result of realizing I knew nothing about savanna vegetation as a traditional resource base. However, most of that resource base was becoming subject to unprecedented forces of change that had not been faced before. During our first period of fieldwork, in 1970–71, Mbeere changed as we sought to observe and understand—virtually week by week as our investigative forays traversing the district's nether reaches from our Ena House headquarters clearly demonstrated. Ecological and environmental erosion surrounded us, even as we recruited local informants to help us survey and assess the conditions and make an inventory of resources. Then significant winds of change arrived; in effect ecological tornadoes.

Drought years in succession resulted in crop failures both of subsistence and cash sources. These, in turn, triggered a spreading fuelwood crisis, in all its guises. There was in addition another vector; the inception of fuelwood commercialization, linked to urban scenarios. All this occurred under the penumbra of provincial administration's insistence on "concluding" land adjudication and demarcation, while Byzantine convolutions of litigation disputes were thrown in for good measure. Each and every change was ripe for evaluation of social stratification and inequalities of consequences. Our own great good fortune lay in repeated visits; each was an opportunity for in-depth investigation at first hand, yet all were cemented by continuity of informants with their altered destinies. Follow up visits provided opportunities to fill in oversights and link "then"; with "now" and to gain insights of altered perception among Mbeere people themselves. Testing hypotheses would have functioned as harness blinkers; we were lucky to not be so encumbered.

This period provided incomparable experience for us both. It was particularly true for D.W.B. who was able, again and again, to observe and document growing gaps between "haves" and "have nots" in a significantly fluid situation of drastic cultural adjustment and sociopolitical change. In this local maelstrom, few other participant observers appeared to give those who were down and farther behind any particular concern. Our very length of involvement permitted us to evaluate interactions between social ingredients not manifest at the outset of the period. We came to recognize many irreversible forces with unrealized inequality vectors built-in.

While in Ghana in the late fifties and early sixties, D.W.B. had been involved with Volta Resettlement, in surveys brought about by the creation of Akosombo Dam and Lake Volta during the Nkrumah administration. This occurred long before the advent of mandatory social-impact analysis, now required by many international agencies before funding commences.

Volta Lake was not strictly visible from Larteh on the Akwapim Ridge, nor yet disturbed unduly its arcadian tranquility. But, even then, D.W.B. had concern for forces leading to detachment of people from their traditions and stabilizing resource base. Would those to be relocated "grieve for a lost home"; was his recognition of these symptoms in others the psychic echo of personal experiences in POW camps? Yet that was the beginning of his professional involvement; since then he has pursued similar examples. All of them focus on examining strains in the social fabric and dislocations of traditional networks on the peripheries of several ethnic groups. At U.C.S.B. his "minorities" class consistently functioned as his major academic thrust and concern with his graduate students; the apogee of his "Anthropology of Development" focus.

So it continues, today in Mbeere Division, Kenya, where its eastern boundary corresponds to the Tana river valley. Here enforced Government Resettlement Schemes have drastically accelerated environmental changes and development has become a fact of life. The building of the fifth hydroelectric power dam at Kiambere will mean the uprooting of some 5,000 people, over half of them Mbeere, for whom no adequate compensation has been forthcoming from the central government. He will be participating in further environmental impact evaluation for some time to come.

Underneath all this has lain a facet of character few academic colleagues or friends of D.W.B. have been fortunate to witness; quiet courage in the face of sudden unexpected adversity, particularly on two occasions when unjustified raw authority was used against him that were flagrant breaches of administrative sensibilities. Both were calamitous brushes; both potentially threatened his career. In the face of derisive reaction and criticism, he championed in the late sixties the sudden flowering of Shona sculpture in (then) Rhodesia, using a paternal legacy to purchase the core of a collection, and brought it to America. This he did overseas quite unaware of an U.S. Executive Order of Rhodesian trade sanctions passed by the Johnson Administration. Federal policy and practice brought the full weight (eleven burley bodies conveyed in four gas-guzzling Detroit products to be precise) of F.B.I. approbation out of the blue to seal of his escape from the driveway of our tranquil abode. The operation was intended to confiscate African artisan art objects he had "illegally" imported, even though purchased from a sovereign state's National Art Gallery and fully documented.

It was the combined thrust of his colleagues' and friends' opinion of his character and worth which eventually quashed all the felony charges—and canceled his hurt at the ridiculous way in which the arrest was made. Few other people had the privilege to witness his quiet, steely strength of conviction that was maintained throughout a protracted period; of his outrage at misplaced, unbridled abuse of authority. Only when the total removal, from every official record, of all traces of this incident was completed was he able to expunge its memory from his mind and be free of the taint that he had lied to anyone, official or otherwise.

A similar, but less widely known brush with official power occurred in Mbeere Division, where he was accused by an advantaged (and misguidedly authoritarian) rival of obstructing the course of local "democratic" elections for office. He was accused of being the dupe of a local power-hungry parliamentary figure. The conflicting circumstances of this charge, with his earlier exercise of administrative authority as Colonial District Officer and his vulnerability to remain neutral under such an accusation was at stake. He regarded the threat of being declared "persona non grata" as an unwarranted attack on maintaining impartiality. Yet, a personal interview with the powerful Provincial Commissioner, a very senior Kenyan administrator of Kenyatta's generation and appointment, solved the impasse. The august figure declared that D.W.B. was so patently honest he could not possibly be guilty of duplicity—a conclusion, had I been asked, I could have supported on numerous prior occasions. It was a relief on my return from a frantic, secret journey to acquaint the central government in Nairobi with warning of this adverse turn of events (I had witnessed the arrest on the Ena House verandah) to learn that the charges had been so eloquently, speedily, and sensibly dismissed. Championing our champion of the underdog when the chips were down was not really necessary after all.

## Notes

1. The term *wabenzi* is Swahili slang which literally means "the people who are owners of Mercedes Benzes". This term is casually used to refer to the emerging political and economic elites in urban Africa.

# The Making of an
# Applied Anthropologist

*Thayer Scudder*

It is a pleasure and a privilege to write this foreword to a book in honor of one of my closest friends. David Brokensha and I met in the 1960s because of our mutual interest in the involuntary resettlement of over 80,000 people that was then underway in connection with construction of Ghana's Volta Dam at Akosombo. His 1962 "Volta Resettlement, Ethnographic Notes of Southern Areas" was one of the first publications dealing with people who have subsequently been called "development refugees". The next year in an article in *Human Organization* on "Volta Resettlement and Anthropological Research" he called for a sociology of resettlement hence anticipating a field of enquiry that has since become a major thrust in anthropology.

With his usual modesty, David does not consider himself a major player in resettlement studies, although recently, as a World Bank consultant, he critiqued the resettlement program carried out during the 1980s in connection with the World Bank-assisted Kiambere Dam. Furthermore, with Della McMillan as Deputy Director, currently he is directing a large-scale 18 month Institute for Development Anthropology (IDA) contract funded by the United Nations Development Programme, and executed by the World Bank, that will recommend options for development in the eleven West African countries participating in the WHO-executed Onchocerciasis (river blindness) Control Program (OCP).

OCP may well be the largest public health program carried out within a single geographical area (as opposed to such global efforts as the successful smallpox program). How the eleven countries deal with the development of their oncho zones will have a major impact on their future, so that the IDA study under David's direction could have a major impact on raising the living standards of millions of people during the remainder of this century. I also anticipate that the final report will make a significant contribution to our understanding of the dynamics of pioneer settlement of new lands since it will include the results of detailed comparative research carried out by IDA teams in four of the eleven countries. Especially interesting will be the research ten years later on settler households studied in the late 1970s by Della McMillan and Josette Murphy.

When David Brokensha and I were traveling together to Binghamton, New York, recently for a meeting of David's oncho team with World Bank officials, I asked him what he considered to be his major contributions to anthropology. His answer was his Larteh and Mbeere studies (the second being a collaborative effort with Bernard Riley), his teaching, and the Institute for Development Anthropology. As with his resettlement research, David's Larteh study was a pioneering effort. Initiated in the early 1960s, it was one of the first ethnographies by an anthropologist of an African town. Located in the Akwapim Hills overlooking the Accra Plain, Larteh was close to the University of Ghana where David was teaching at the time, so that he could easily carry out research for his Oxford dissertation during weekends and academic holidays. Since publishing his 1966 *Social Change at Larteh, Ghana*, David has periodically gone back to visit Larteh. I accompanied him on such a visit in June, 1989, and was impressed by the close friendship that he has maintained with the senior chief and his family. He has also encouraged Alfredo Varela, a graduate student in anthropology at UC Santa Barbara, in his plans for making a study of market-women's networks, based at Larteh. Following up on an shorter initial visit, Alfredo will be leaving for an extended stay in Larteh this December.

Mbeere David also considers his most interesting research, in part because of close collaboration with Bernard Riley—collaboration that resulted in their two volume 1988 *The Mbeere in Kenya*. The origins of that research go back to the late 1960s when David was chairman of the Department of Anthropology at Santa Barbara. Wearied by turmoil within the university at that time, he accepted an invitation from James Coleman to come to Kenya as a Rockefeller Senior Research Fellow in connection with the foundation-assisted Special Rural Development Programme of the Kenya Government. This dealt with six districts, including Mbeere. As with colleagues Robert Chambers and John Nellis, David's appointment was a joint one with the Institute for Development Studies (IDS) at Nairobi University.

While Chambers and Nellis were based at IDS, David wanted to be in the field during most of his 15 month assignment. He choose Mbeere, spending 12 months there in 1970–71. Bernard Riley, on joining David, quickly saw the research potential of the area, with the two returning for further research, now funded by the National Science Foundation, in 1974 and 1976–78, and shorter visits thereafter.

David believes that the value of his Larteh and his and Bernard's Mbeere work lies in the sound descriptive analysis that characterizes the resulting ethnographies. In this era when research proposals must be replete with testable hypotheses, David remains comfortable with the anthropological role of ethnographer. While some may consider this role anachronistic, I would disagree. Though anthropological methodologies are becoming more rigorous, and testable hypotheses are increasingly emerging, I believe that much of the value of Elizabeth Colson's, Jonathan Habarad's, M.E.D. Scudder's and my long-term study of the Gwembe Tonga in Central Africa lies in the rich data on many, many topics that we have gathered over a 33 year period. When we commenced gathering such data, we did so not so much because we knew what we were going to do with all of it. Rather that was the sort of broad-based data anthropologists were supposed to collect as specified in Murdock's HRAF headings and the British *Notes and Queries in Social Anthropology*. Today I believe we still have that responsibility. Where problems arise is not with data collection as such, but with the failure of anthropologists to define their categories carefully enough, and to collect time series data from various research sites around the world for comparative analysis—a failing which the recently formed Linkages: World Development Research Council hopes to correct.

This book is witness to David's success as a teacher, both editors being colleagues who were former students. As a teacher, he has tried both as an individual, and through the Institute for Development Anthropology, to bring out student qualities through encouragement, and through facilitation of their research and careers. David's commitment to teaching includes a sense of obligation to help students become aware of, and develop their own ideas about, issues about which David feels strongly. Born in South Africa, his rejection of apartheid played a major role in the development of a course dealing with ethnic conflict and minorities, while concern about environmental issues (and especially with the global fuel wood crisis) led to courses with Bernard Riley in environmental studies. In the field, Bernard and David pioneered the use of secondary students in anthropological research, the two of them using approximately one hundred in their Mbeere research. One, now Dr. E.H.N. Njeru of University of Nairobi, became sufficiently interested in the work that he eventually came to UC Santa Barbara to study anthropology with David.

David's collaboration with Michael Horowitz and myself in the founding of the Institute for Development Anthropology in the late 1970s, has been the capstone to his longstanding interest in what is now called development anthropology. I do not know the origin of this interest and perhaps David himself does not know. Certainly it dates back to his undergraduate years at Rhodes University when the influence of Monica Wilson directed him both toward anthropology and toward using anthropology for the betterment of people. Pursuing those anthropological interests first at Cambridge, and then at Oxford, he joined the Colonial Service as a way in which to link interests in administration and development anthropology. After he resigned from the colonial service—having anticipated the "Winds of Change" that led to national independence, his deepening interest in working with Africans toward a multi-ethnic society, and in policy oriented research, stimulated him to take a job working with Hugh Ashton as Bulawayo urban affairs officer in the newly formed Central African Federation. Unfortunately, that experiment failed completely, so that David moved on to newly independent Ghana where, as a lecturer in social administration, he could help hone the administration skills of Ghanaian government officials.

Now over ten years old, the Institute for Development Anthropology still has the same three founding directors, showing the extent to which we share the same principles as they relate to sustainable development with equity for low-income populations, and the same hope that IDA can help such populations raise their living standards. Though a number of colleagues predicted that our collaboration would be short-lived, in fact it has been strengthened by our very different backgrounds, with David bringing to IDA at its founding knowledge of British development institutions, Michael of USAID, and myself of various UN agencies and the World Bank. While this is not the proper place to commend IDA, it is appropriate to note that IDA contracts have involved over 400 anthropologists in policy oriented research relating to IDA goals. And it is appropriate to thank David for taking on the directorship of our onchocerciasis project at a time when he and Bernard were looking forward to travel and to a more leisurely life style after David's retirement from UC Santa Barbara in June, 1989.

I have noted David Brokensha as a pioneer of resettlement anthropology, small town studies (Larteh followed by Patterson in the central valley of California), and of development anthropology. In addition he has done pioneering work dealing with indigenous knowledge, Brokensha, Warren, and Werner's 1980 *Indigenous Knowledge Systems and Development* still being the best edited collection in the field. This interest also dates back to Ghana days, where, incidentally, David met Michael Warren when he was training Peace Corps Volunteers (of whom Warren was one).

This preface would be incomplete without adding some words about David Brokensha as a human being. More than any other anthropologist that I know, David has struck up enduring friendships throughout his career so that he and Bernard can literally stay with friends in different countries around the world. While too many of us lead lifestyles which preclude strengthening ties with friends and colleagues, David and Bernard not only make a special effort to build visits with friends into practically all of their travel plans, but they also travel especially to see friends. As I write this, for example, David is in England, making the long trip from Santa Barbara to London for the sole purpose of attending a godson's wedding. That David has at least six godchildren is just one indicator of the affection and respect with which he is held.

I personally know what a pleasure it is to have David as a close friend. Recently we spent a month together in the field in Burkina Faso. One of my most pleasurable trips was when we traveled together over a 48 hour period down Lake Volta in the Buipe Queen—a relatively new tug and barge owned by Volta Lake Transport which picks up people and cargo along the way. Another most pleasurable occasion was when I visited David and Bernard at their Mbeere field site in Kenya. While there they not only introduced me to the people and showed me the different agro-ecological zones that extended from the Tana River to the slopes of Mount Kenya, but they also took me for bird and game watching in a nearby national park. I look forward to future such trips.

PART TWO

# Social Change, Applied Anthropology, and Solutions to Contemporary Problems

Until the early 1960s, anthropology was primarily an academic discipline, in which the role of anthropologist was identified as a professor/researcher affiliated with a university. Application of anthropology to contemporary issues was uncommon, with a few notable exceptions such as the work of anthropologists in the Bureau of American Ethnology, in various defense support capacities during World War II. (such as the War Relocation Authority, and the development of national character studies), and a few early and remarkable efforts at "action anthropology" or "participant intervention" such as the Fox and Cornell-Peru Vicos Projects (Erasmus 1961; Holmberg 1958; 1962; Partridge and Eddy 1987; Spicer 1979; Tax 1958; 1975). As Partridge has noted, while application of anthropology certainly occurred, it was not considered the primary focus of most anthropological research, and traditional teaching posts in universities were considered the appropriate forms of employment for "bona fide anthropologists" (Partridge 1987: 214).

The past three decades, however, have witnessed a change in the nature of applied anthropology, as it has shifted from an activity performed by a small minority, or a task which was relegated to a secondary position within a major research project, to being the primary focus of many anthropologists. The "new" applied anthropologists have sought both to define new methodological specialties, particularly the development of technical applications, such as river basin development, forestry, or nutrition intervention (Scudder 1987), and to develop new paradigms of planned social intervention. In particular anthropologists have been critical of the traditional top-down approaches and centralized planning which have characterized most projects of planned social change, and the emphasis on capital-intensive development projects. Greater incorporation of anthropological concerns in development planning, and more frequent use of social scientists in the design, implementation, and monitoring of development projects has been partly responsible for a shift away from assumptions that benefits would indeed "trickle-down"

13

to the rural masses, and towards a new emphasis on local participation in all phases of the development process.

Participatory development is often the approach now adopted by development agencies, including national governments and multilateral international organizations such as the World Bank and UNICEF (see Cernea 1985; Chambers 1983; Gran 1983). One aspect of participatory development which has been most effectively advocated by anthropologists is the incorporation of indigenous knowledge into development planning (see Brokensha et al. 1980). Traditional anthropological research included collection of local peoples' perspectives on social and political issues, and this practice is logically continued in contemporary applied and development anthropology, with the incorporation of indigenous knowledge into development programs.

The articles included in this section of the book are all linked to David Brokensha's continuing interest in bringing anthropological perspectives into development and planned social change. In particular, these articles all deal with understanding indigenous peoples' perspectives and the relations between the theory and practice of participatory development. The first three articles, by Murphy, Luce, and Hewlett, examine paradigms of participatory development or incorporation of knowledge of cultural systems into development plans. Josette Murphy analyzes the views of both anthropologist and development planner, and identifies ways in which agencies must respond to the realities that anthropologists have long recognized, in particular that indigenous knowledge systems are grounded in the real and the practical. Randall Luce's article examines how various types of private, humanitarian aid agencies adopt different paradigms of development, and how the relationship of the private voluntary organization (PVO) to its funding source, and its need for political neutrality often present dilemmas for effective development policy. He argues that the most effective PVOs will incorporate greater levels of indigenous perception and information sharing. Barry Hewlett's article examines mechanisms for the transmission of cultural knowledge, and argues that planned social interventions have failed to understand the influence of traditional modes of cultural transmission on the acceptance of innovations. He argues that understanding indigenous social structure and mechanisms of cultural transmission will lead planners to anticipate responses to their intervention designs.

The remaining articles in this section deal not with the paradigms of applied anthropology and participatory development, but are case examples of how these ideas have and have not been incorporated into specific projects. Thomas Painter's article is an historical analysis of cooperatives in West Africa in which he notes that the failure of cooperatives can often be attributed to the failure to incorporate indigenous needs and perspectives. He expresses concern that some current attempts at participatory development may reflect budgetary constraints rather than representing a sincere commitment to empowerment of rural people.

Dolores Koenig and Michael Horowitz examine a contemporary West African case involving mandatory relocation as part of a river basin development project. They note the discrepancies between the project objectives and concerns of the local population, and describe the applied anthropologist as being perceived by project officials solely as a trouble shooter, rather than as a full participant in the development administration. Their case study clearly illustrates the often conflicting objectives of social scientists, national officials, rural people, and representatives of the international donor community.

Finally Miriam Chaiken's paper discusses an East African case in which an expressed paradigm of participatory development was in effect only selectively implemented, as the recent history of social changes created obstacles to full participation of women by dissolving the natural support networks between rural women. She argues that expressed willingness to facilitate participatory development by planners is insufficient, and that fundamental anthropological sensitivity to local social and historical changes are necessary to ensure that all members of the recipient group have an opportunity to be participants in development interventions.

The articles in this section are unified by a common theme; the continuing contribution anthropology can make to understanding and improving the process of planned social change. Although anthropologists have clearly had an impact on the processes of development, notably with the adoption of paradigms of participatory development, there is need for continued advocacy and redoubled efforts to bring anthropological perceptions into development planning.

## References Cited

Brokensha, David W., D.M. Warren, and Oswald Werner.
    1980    Indigenous Knowledge Systems and Development. Lanham, MD: University Press of America.

Cernea, Michael M., ed.
    1985    Putting People First. Sociological Variables in Rural Development. New York: Oxford University Press.

Chambers, Robert.
    1983    Rural Development: Putting the Last First. London: Longman Press.

Erasmus, Charles J.
    1961    Man Takes Control: Cultural Development and American Aid. Indianapolis: Bobbs-Merrill Publishing Co.

Gran, Guy.
    1983    Development By People. Citizen Construction of a Just World. New York: Praeger Press.

Holmberg, Allan R.
    1958    Research and Development Approach to the Study of Change. Human Organization. 17:12–16.
    1962    Community and Regional Development: The Joint Cornell-Peru Experiment. Human Organization. 21:107–124.

Partridge, William L.
    1987    Toward a Theory of Practice. *In* Applied Anthropology in America. Elizabeth
            M. Eddy and William L. Partridge, eds. pp. 211–236. New York: Columbia
            University Press.
Partridge, William L. and Elizabeth M. Eddy.
    1987    The Development of Applied Anthropology in America. *In* Applied An-
            thropology in America. Elizabeth M. Eddy and William L. Partridge, eds.
            pp. 3–58. New York: Columbia University Press.
Scudder, Thayer.
    1987    Opportunities, Issues, and Achievements in Development Anthropology
            since the Mid-1960s: A Personal View. *In* Applied Anthropology in
            America.Elizabeth M. Eddy and William L. Partridge, eds. pp. 184–210.
            New York: Columbia University Press.
Tax, Sol.
    1958    The Fox Project. Human Organization. 17:17–19.
    1975    Action Anthropology. Current Anthropology. 16 (4).

# 1

# Farmers' Systems and Technological Change in Agriculture

*Josette Murphy*

## Trends

African agencies and development practitioners now understand better than in the past that the planning and implementation of sustainable agricultural development will be facilitated if indigenous knowledge and objectives are understood and taken into account. It is also more systematically accepted that development agencies (in-country institutions as well as any external funding agencies involved) should seek the participation of local population and should increase their knowledge of location-specific situations at an early stage of the identification of a program, so that the information can influence its objectives as well as implementation plans and procedures.

Taking local knowledge and objectives into consideration is likely to improve the relations between the population and local development authorities, but its significance goes well beyond this. It is a recognition that indigenous knowledge and objectives are valid, relevant, and useful to the design of development programs, and that technological change cannot occur satisfactorily on a long term basis if that change is not absorbed into the internal processes and mores of the local communities and of individual farming households.

Several recent publications, notably *Putting People First* (Cernea 1985), emphasize that the social factors should be an integral part of every phase of development planning and implementation, and this from the very first step, before the identification of specific projects or activities begins. Specifically, agents of change (whether authorities and staff in local institutions or in development assistance agencies) are now more frequently willing to accept that they need to know, understand, and take into account at every stage, (1) who are the people they want to reach, not just as a general category of all people involved in farming in a given region, but as differentiated socioeconomic categories within their community, and, (2) what these people know, what their objectives are, what their rights and obligations are within their household and their community, and under what constraints, of any kind, they operate.

This conceptual evolution has yet to result in a systematic integration of local participation into program and project identification, design and implementation, but there have been enough positive experiences and evidences of real, if incremental, changes in the way development agencies operate, to warrant cautious optimism. The shift has been strongly influenced by the work of social scientists and of technical and managerial staff who are sensitive to social issues, and who worked with the development agencies to slowly influence the way in which they operate.

Professor Brokensha was a pioneer among these agents of change through his own research, through his direct contributions to numerous development projects as a social scientist and an environmentalist, through his leadership in creating a consulting firm which emphasizes the importance of the social sciences, and of course through his teaching and advisory role for many undergraduate and graduate students. Indeed, Professor Brokensha's experience with development anthropology in Africa was a key factor in my decision to study at the University of California-Santa Barbara, at a time when "development anthropology" was not yet an established part of the anthropological curriculum.

While his formal seminars were always interesting and instructive, what I will remember most upon his retirement is his unfailing support and advice during the stressful periods of fieldwork and dissertation writing and, for years afterwards, his help and advice in identifying and securing appropriate positions in development agencies. In his own words, he encouraged his students to identify "an unoccupied niche" in which they would have an opportunity to develop a blend of social science and technical skills, which would put them at a comparative advantage over other young professionals with a more restricted background. My first development position led me to build such a niche around the monitoring and evaluation of agricultural development; the topic covers all activities which help managers (in both national institutions and development agencies) answer some basic questions during the implementation of a development program and integrate the answers into future programs; what do the people expect from us? What are the agricultural potentials and constraints? Are we providing the services for which we are responsible? Are the people informed of our services, do they take advantage of them, do they find them useful and appropriate to their needs? Are we achieving the results we expected, why or why not and what should we do about it? Monitoring and evaluation activities range from good record keeping to quantitative and qualitative surveys of the so-called target populations. While they are undertaken by the implementing institutions as part of the routine management of their program, development agencies often provide technical advice and training to local staff. This is a topic which calls for agricultural, sociological and management skills, one which requires an interdisciplinary and holistic approach for which the anthropological perspective is particularly appropriate.

## · Difficult Words: Farm, Farmers, Household

While anthropologists have long understood that seemingly simple words can obscure complex concepts, agricultural experts have met with difficulties when they attempted to define and analyze a farm or a household in traditional agriculture, according to the Western tradition from which the agricultural and economic sciences evolved.

Research or extension experts are likely to think of "a farm" in terms of the land controlled and managed by the head of household. Yet a traditional farm in most parts of Africa does not coincide with a single production unit or with a household, itself a complex socioeconomic system. Other individuals within the household control some plots of their own, including the wife (and eventually co-wives) as well as the young unmarried adults who are residing with the household for that cropping season. Among the Mossi of Burkina Faso and other ethnic groups in West Africa, each individual is expected to provide labor on the household's main fields, which are managed by the head of household, but each individual will also spend time in his or her own field in the early morning or after work is completed on the main fields. In other regions, each adult may have its own farm, managed as a separate entity. The traditional structure is changing in some countries (such as Kenya and Malawi) where many men work in towns or on plantations for a good part of the year, and the women are de facto heads of households and agricultural decision-makers.

Although there may be more of an overlap between the nuclear family and the farm in other parts of the world, agricultural households in the less developed countries almost always have other income-producing activities, such as paid agricultural labor, petty trade, or some craft production. In turn, each member must provide for the household well-being in some way; usually the head of household is responsible for providing the bulk of the major cereals consumed, while the women provide supplementary feedings for the children as well as condiments for the main meals. We see that each individual in a household has obligations towards the household as well as some rights to his/her own source of income.

Differentiating among individuals active in agricultural and related activities is particularly relevant in regard to women farmers, who play a significant, sometimes primary, role in food production. Programs for technology transfer have sometimes failed, or have had unexpected negative consequences on part of the population, because agricultural services, such as those providing extension advice, credit, or fertilizer and other inputs, dealt only with the head of household. Unexpected negative effects occurred when a change in technology created some opportunities for income not specifically covered by traditional rules, and the male head of household, because of his control over household productive assets, asserted his right to that new source of income. Often, when new opportunities were presented to increase production and marketing of a crop, such as rice, previously limited to small scale cultivation for household use, what had traditionally been a sideline production for the women became a cash crop, managed and controlled by the men (Dey 1983).

Such unexpected changes can have negative effects on the nutritional status of the children and on their access to education, two domains in which the women play a predominant role. This is because women usually reserve the food they grow for extra feeding for their children, and channel their resources in cash or kind to pay school fees and health costs. In addition, women make great efforts to substitute their own labor for that of their schoolage children, so that they can stay in school.

The increased understanding of the relevance of indigenous knowledge benefited from but now goes beyond the "farming system perspective", (described in numerous sources, for example Norman, Simmons, and Hays 1982) developed in the late 1960s and 1970s as a reaction to a number of disappointments and failures in technology transfer. At first, the focus under a farming system perspective had been limited to the technical side of the agricultural production system, with people brought into the picture only insofar as they provided labor for several crops, and labor availability might become a constraint. When research and extension agencies first attempted to take the household composition into account, it was primarily to assess its productive capacity in terms of land, labor, and equipment. The household was identified as a labor pool, a field crew which happened to eat from the same pot, so to speak. Often, the age and sex of the "workers" were taken into account to calculate a theoretical labor index, but the diverse obligations of individual members in regard to agricultural and other activities were still not taken into account. This was found to be too narrowly focused for development planning, leading to a shift towards attempts to analyze what I will call the "farmers' system" rather than the technical problems in isolation.

Working at this broader level of analysis for problems which were already immensely complex present great difficulties. We see that decisions regarding agricultural change in a region are made by a diversity of farmers (i.e. all individuals active in farming, not just the heads of household), within the broad context of their overall income and production goals, as well as the consumption needs of their households. Individual decisions are best understood by looking at the household as a complex network of rights and obligations in which several individuals interact, and by placing these decisions in the context in which farmers operate (such as infrastructure, support services, pricing and marketing policies). The next section introduces the various categories which need to be considered in this context.

## Factors Which Influence the Farmers' Decisions
## Related to Technological Change

In order to discuss the various entry points through which indigenous knowledge and objectives should be integrated into the design of agricultural programs, it is necessary to review the various categories of factors that individual farmers take into consideration when deciding on their production strategies for a given crop season.[1] These categories relate to the agro-ecological conditions at the local level, the farmers' knowledge of production alternatives, the resource base available at the household level, the physical and sociocultural conditions at the community level, and the economic and policy conditions at the regional and national levels.

### Agro-ecological Conditions at the Local Level

Agro-ecological conditions can vary tremendously, often within short distances. Farmers are well aware of local soil characteristics and conditions, and detailed taxonomies of soil and plants have developed over generations in the local languages. In dryland agriculture, and especially in the Sahel region, the farmers are also well aware of the range of yearly fluctuations in amount and distribution of rainfall, and of their consequences for plant health and growth. In a given year, they are keen observers of climatic patterns, and act not in function of an hypothetical average but according to the likelihood of extreme conditions. Innovations (whether in new plant material or "improved" cultural practices) may not be biologically viable in diverse micro-environments, even within a rather small area for which they were deemed appropriate, or they may not be dependable in years with poor or erratic rainfall. In other words, in a good year they will produce much more than the traditional varieties, but in a bad year they may produce less. This is a risk which may be seen as unreasonable in rural households with low stocks or little means to buy food in case of a crop failure.

Experience with on-farm research has shown that researchers and farmers can hold a constructive dialogue, to identify pertinent problems for research as well as to sort among possible solutions for those most likely to be usable in real farming conditions. For example, a team of agronomists and plant breeders from the International Crop Research Institute for the Semi-arid Tropics (ICRISAT) working in the Sahel held a series of lively discussions with farmers to identify the plant characteristics of interest to the farmers and to locate plots which would be appropriate for field testing. During the course of such discussion, a systematic comparability became obvious between the scientific and local typologies for plants and soils.

### Awareness and Knowledge of Production Strategies and Technological Alternatives

One can only select among technologies one is aware of, and use correctly those one understands. A farming household's knowledge of alternative production strategies is a blend from several sources, of which the formal extension service is only one. Agricultural knowledge among the farmers is dynamic, even in the absence of exogenous development activities, as farmers the world around observe and discuss various techniques in use in their area or noticed by one of them in the course of travel. This pool of knowledge is much greater than the technologies and practices in actual use at any point in time, as it includes the body of accumulated experiences passed on through generations at the local level. It forms an essential repository, well adapted to local agro-ecological conditions in a given land/labor ratio, yet it has sometimes been ignored or only superficially understood by researchers. Farmers undertake constant testing and observations of their fields as well as those of their neighbors, and observations of practices in other regions are brought in by travelers (often together with some seeds). This has lead to adjustments and innovations quite independently from research or extension activities. Results from formal research are disseminated through extension, radio programs, posters or other sources, and if found appropriate, they can spread among all farmers quite rapidly.

## Resource Base at the Household Level

This includes the means of production available to the household, in terms of land, labor, capital, and equipment. It is not a static, fixed amount of resources; again it is more flexible than what development officials tend to believe, because the household can activate various intra- and interhousehold mechanisms to modify its resource base, temporarily, or for the long term. In many cultures, individuals can be "borrowed" between households, for a day, a crop season, or longer; mutual labor exchanges are prevalent, and group labor remains common. The right to cultivate a plot of land can be obtained through a number of tenure or lease arrangements, for a season or over several years. Capital can be borrowed, a long term exchange of gifts can be arranged, or a partnership established. Equipment can be exchanged, rented, or shared. Households can be rather creative in making use of various combinations of these alternatives. In a resettlement program in Burkina Faso, where land had been allocated, in good western fashion, to the male head of household on the basis of the number of workers officially resettling with him, a number of these coping mechanisms were quickly activated; the women and young unmarried adults opened unofficial plots in the forest, family members were sent from the home village for the cropping season, strangers who became neighbors reorganized the traditional labor groups on the basis of ethnic origin or new neighborhood relations, and some enterprising farmers bought a plow and a team of oxen and worked for a fee in their neighbors' fields as well as their own (Murphy and Sprey 1980; McMillan 1983). However, this flexibility in access to resources has its limits, and is more likely to become unequal to the task if many households see their requirements change at the same time, or if an increased population on a finite amount of land hampers it.

## Sociocultural Mores of the Community

The sets of obligations within and among households discussed earlier, the social hierarchy of households in the community, and the rules and regulations regarding group activities all intervene to determine if a technology is socially feasible and desirable. Here we come back to the notion of network. Any household is likely to be part of several networks of interactive obligations, on the basis of ethnic group, neighborhood, lineages through blood and marriage, production focus, and economic status. Often, an individual differentiating himself or herself from others in the group would endanger the security offered by group membership. This would be an unreasonably risky strategy in a resource-poor environment, thus adoption of a new technology will be influenced by the opinions and actions of other farmers in the group. In the extreme dislocation of traditional social ties associated with resettlement, these traditional networks are revised to incorporate new and old occupants of the land. For example, in the resettlement program discussed above, the settlers made sure that gifts were exchanged with the local farmers who had previous claim on the land, and they asked the indigenous authorities to continue holding the traditional ceremonies at planting time (McMillan 1983).

## *Economic and Policy Conditions at the Regional and National Levels*

Farmers take into consideration many factors related to economic and policy conditions when deciding whether to modify their cropping pattern or cultural practices. This is an important aspect for development projects, which usually encourages an increasing use of inputs as well as a greater production to be marketed. Farmers look at a number of factors, over which they have no control. The more obvious factors would include:

- the availability or reliability of recommended inputs and necessary services, such as credit and transportation,
- the relative prices of various commodities, required inputs, and other production or income alternatives
- the availability and cost (financial and social) of land and agricultural labor, as well as the relative wages or benefits from alternative production strategies,
- marketing opportunities and restrictions (including storage, transportation and processing requirements) for each crop, and
- the availability of alternate income-generating opportunities, for agricultural and for off-farm labor, whether in the village or elsewhere.

The reliability of the key inputs in a newly recommended technology can be determinant to the acceptability of that technology. For example, in Nepal, agricultural researchers were puzzled by the low use of fertilizer on newly introduced wheat crops. Farmers were well aware of the high increase in production which could be obtained from a correct (linked to irrigation) fertilizer application on this irrigated crop. However, they knew too well that the electricity supply was highly unreliable, and that the irrigation pumps could not function without electricity. Since the irrigation schedule was uncertain and out of their control, they did not buy fertilizer which they could not be sure of applying under proper conditions (Simmons et al. 1982).

In some countries, labor opportunities in town or on plantations, or even in neighboring countries, are much higher than the extra income which could be derived from improved agricultural practices. This leads to an increase in households which are for all practical purposes headed by women, with the constraints this entails in term of labor availability and access to inputs and services such as credit and extension. The poorer women, who have very little land under their control and are drastically short of cash, may be obliged to sell their labor (working for cash on a neighbor's farm for example) at the time where work is most needed for intensive cultivation of their small plots. Often, they cannot do both because the peak labor demand is the same for everyone in the area. The result is that their own-produced food supply remains lower than it could be with good husbandry (see Swanson 1986 for an African example).

These various factors interact to determine step by step whether a proposed practice or technological change is biologically possible (can it work here?), economically viable (will it pay off overall?), technically feasible (have I got the resources required?) and socially desirable (is it worth the potentially negative impact on my network of relationships? will it better my individual situation? will it run counter to our intrahousehold obligations?). Adoption problems may arise if a constraint at any of these levels makes the technology unattractive.

This review of the factors involved in the farmers' decisions should not be interpreted as presenting a closed social and technological system, for which agricultural research can do no more than suggest incremental improvements in existing practices. Dramatic changes in agricultural technology have taken place, quite rapidly, whenever the new technology offered a significant improvement. The label "the green revolution" has been rightly used to characterize the pace of change in rice and wheat cultivation in Asia in the 1970s (see for example Chandler 1979). This summary does suggest that an agency seeking to improve agricultural productivity needs to test the reasoning underlying each technological recommendation in order to identify constraints or bottlenecks likely to hamper adoption of the technology. In each case, it will be necessary to analyze alternate solutions to remove or work around the potential constraint, or eventually to adapt the technology to the constraint. If this were done systematically, there is no doubt that some "technically feasible" or "biologically possible" breakthroughs would have to be rejected, but that other solutions may be found within the indigenous knowledge of the farmers.

## Implications for Program Planning, Implementation and Evaluation

Identifying and designing a program to increase the productivity and income of farming households requires a review of the overall agricultural system, including identification and assessment of the contextual factors involved, and identification of the various categories of farmers (categories of individuals, not just households), whom the program will attempt to reach. Most importantly, it will be essential to monitor, throughout implementation of the program, the reactions of the farmers and other individuals (traders, entrepreneurs, input suppliers) who are expected to modify their behavior. Being able to diagnose on short notice the reasons for any bottleneck in implementation, any problem with the continued use of the services provided, or any change in the adoption of some new technology, will be a key to a successful, sustainable program. Finally, some institutional changes within the local and donor agencies may be necessary. This section will elaborate on those three levels of implications.

## From Farming System to Farmers' System

The concept of land management and land use planning has grown together with the increasing social and environmental concerns. This concept combines the technical and social elements of agricultural production, as well as concerns for environmentally sound, long term sustainability of production and the multiple uses of property managed by households as well as that managed by a community. The concept is particularly important in Africa, at a time when population pressure is bringing an increasing utilization of marginal lands and shortening of the traditional long fallow periods, and in a social context where group activities at the community level are better accepted than individual differentiation. Changes in land use of the tropical forests are also an issue of concern worldwide.

In most projects today, emphasis is placed on giving responsibility to the local community (or to the appropriate subgroup in the population) for various aspects of implementation and for maintenance of equipment and common resources. This can range from pastoral associations, which control and organize access to common pastures and water, to village groups which elect a few individuals for training and subsequent maintenance of a well, or which oversee maintenance and repairs as well as the collection of water charges. It is particularly appropriate in irrigated agriculture, where users' associations are rooted in a long tradition, and where top-down approaches to maintenance and regulation of the system have consistently failed (see Uphoff 1986 for examples). Local participation is also encouraged in projects through which the communal land tenure system is being formalized, while at the same time land conservation measures are introduced and implemented by the community, with a full concept of communal responsibility and common property.

Similarly, the concerns raised in the past decade by most funding agencies on gender-related issues reflect a better understanding of the importance of indigenous knowledge and social mores. Systematic efforts to take "women in development" into account in project design and implementation are sometimes derided as a politically motivated tokenism, but when an effort is explicitly made to integrate gender-related issues into routine projects (and not to fund special "women's" projects), it is a clear indication that what the people—men and women—know, think and do are recognized as legitimate factors which must be taken into consideration when identifying development problems and potential solutions. It is a sign that the level of analysis used for development planning as been extended from that of an economic and technical system to one in which people are the beginning and the end of development.

## Changing Patterns in Information Needs

The design of a "farmers' system" agricultural program implies information needs that are different from straightforward infrastructure programs. It becomes necessary, at the earliest stage of project identification, to have both descriptive and explanatory information on the people the project is to benefit. For example, the number of households and the regional data on marketed crops are useful but not sufficient. Information about division of labor within the households, relative proportion of time allocated to food versus cash crops, the channels from crop production to storage, processing, and marketing, and consumption becomes necessary.

This evolution means that development planners cannot expect routine statistical reports to provide the necessary data. Additional information about why people assign priority to one crop or one task over another will be necessary, as well as information on the constraints people encounter as they attempt to modify their previous technological package. Qualitative analyses are recognized as fully relevant sources of information, before, during and after a program is being designed and implemented, on the same level of importance as statistical data. This means that a diversity of methods for data collection is called for, including qualitative interviews with both individuals and groups, and participant-observation. Major international agencies such as the Food and Agriculture Organization, the World Bank, the International Fund for Agricultural Development have been very explicit in that regard in their recent technical publications (see for example Casley and Kumar 1987; Murphy and Marchant 1988; and Salmen 1987). This is a domain in which sociologists and anthropologists have made significant contributions, particularly in the methods used in agricultural research to identify research problems and technical recommendation domains (see for examples Horton 1984; ISNAR and Rockefeller 1985; Rhoades 1984 and 1986).

## Institutional Changes Within Local and Donor Agencies

The evolution described in this chapter could not be occurring without some institutional changes within local and donor agencies. Until now, these changes have been mostly reactive, and may seem slow to come, but they have been steady and very real. In the mid-70s, the U.S. Agency for International Development had made social impact assessments and environmental assessments an administrative requirement. While not all donors have been as explicit, the social science perspective is more and more playing a significant role within normal planning and implementation activities in donor agencies. This influence should not be measured by the narrow administrative criterion of the number of positions earmarked for social scientists, but it is best reflected in the type of areas of concern which agencies are addressing; social forestry, the social aspects of resettlement, household food security, women in development, family planning, safe motherhood and child survival, land tenure and management, and the social dimensions of macro-economic adjustment, to name but the most obvious, are all key components of current assistance which cannot be addressed without integrating social factors into design and implementation.

In a recent article in the Anthropology Newsletter, Cernea (1988) gives a detailed review of the increasing role of anthropologists at the World Bank in involuntary population resettlement projects. This "unprecedented progress" (Cernea 1988:1) has been reached through the ongoing involvement of a small number of staff anthropologists and long-term consultants in policy work as well as for project design, supervision and evaluation. But the rising concern with the sociological dimension extends into the general population of development experts. A series of sociological roundtables on Agriculture and Natural Resources Management: Sociological Dimensions, while organized by the World Bank's sociological advisor, are attracting a large number of technical specialists with no formal background in the social sciences.

## How Social Scientists are Facilitating This Evolution

The evolution described in this paper was influenced by development anthropologists and other social and biological scientists, and in return it gives a more constructive role to anthropologists and rural sociologists. In the past, their role has often been restricted to either impact assessment during project preparation, or to project evaluation after implementation was completed. Now, they are likely to be full members of the research or implementation team, albeit not necessarily with a title openly stating their social science background. The broadening of interdisciplinary agricultural research is an interesting example of these new opportunities. In agricultural research institutions, a significant step was taken when the (technology) users' perspective was highlighted as a key factor not only in technology adoption, but as one factor relevant to researchers when establishing research priorities and selecting possible technological strategies for research and development. Several of the International Agricultural Research Centers have evolved the focus of their socioeconomic work, broadening the factors which they identify as relevant for research to include not only every phase of agricultural production per se but also related activities, such as crop storage, processing, marketing, and consumption habits (for examples, see Rhoades 1984 and ISNAR/Rockefeller Foundation 1985).

However, in order to be most effective, individuals trained in the social sciences need to work within research and development agencies, not necessarily as social scientists, but in positions where they can be fully involved in—and have influence on—the identification, design and supervision of projects. In a career which involved working for a U.S. university, a bilateral donor agency, an international research center and an international funding agency, I have never been directly employed as a social scientist, yet my training has always influenced both my activities as a technical specialist and my interactions with my colleagues. Indeed, social scientists who work in development agencies can play a dual role, because in addition to providing their technical expertise to various tasks and projects, they do influence their colleagues in a general way, by highlighting the social dimensions of development during meetings, by asking pertinent questions, by explaining why farmers react the way they do (and by emphasizing that statements such as "they are risk averse" or "they are bound by tradition" are neither correct nor useful explanations). It is essential however that these social scientists be fully cognizant of the administrative and political factors which constrain any national or international agency, and that they demonstrate in their actions that they are cooperative and capable of working as a team with other disciplines.

## Conclusions

Just as the farming system perspective represented a significant step in the analytical framework within which development programs are designed, the emphasis on "farmers' system" described here, with its recognition of farmers as actors of change, whose diversity needs to be taken into account, represents an additional potential for development. Rural sociologists and anthropologists have the opportunity to contribute to sustainable development activities, which benefit men and women farmers in the less developed countries, without seeking to impose foreign values on them; they can do so if they are able to cooperate constructively with other disciplines and with senior management in national institutions as well as in funding agencies.

## Acknowledgments

The views presented in this chapter are those of the author only and should not be attributed to the World Bank or its affiliated organizations. The detailed comments of Joan Atherton are gratefully acknowledged.

## Notes

1. This section uses a framework expanded and adapted from Zandstra et al. 1981. A first version was presented at a USAID workshop (Murphy 1983).

## References Cited

Casley, Dennis J. and Krishna Kumar.
    1987    Monitoring and Evaluation in Agriculture. A joint World Bank, FAO and
            IFAD publication. Baltimore, MD: John Hopkins University Press.

Cernea, Michael.
 1988 Development Anthropology at Work. Anthropology Newsletter, 29(6). September.
Cernea, Michael, ed.
 1985 Putting People First. Sociological Variables in Rural Development. A World Bank Publication. New York: Oxford University Press.
Chandler, Robert F.
 1979 Rice in the Tropics: a Guide to the Development of National Programs. Boulder, CO: Westview Press.
Dey, Jennifer.
 1983 Women in African Rice Farming Systems. Paper presented at the IRRI Conference on Women in Rice Farming Systems. Los Banos, Laguna, The Philippines.
Horton, Douglas E.
 1984 Social Scientists in Agricultural Research. Lessons from the Mantaro Valley Project, Peru. Ottawa, Canada: International Development Research Center.
International Service for National Agricultural Research (ISNAR) and the Rockefeller Foundation.
 1985 Women and Agricultural Technology. Proceedings of a CGIAR Inter-Center Seminar. Bellagio, Italy. March 25–29.
McMillan, Della.
 1983 A Resettlement Project in Upper Volta. unpublished Ph.D. Dissertation. Department of Anthropology. Northwestern University.
Murphy, Josette and Leendert Sprey.
 1980 The Volta Valley Authority: Socio-economic evaluation of a resettlement project in Upper Volta. Lafayette, Indiana: Dept. of Agricultural Economics. Purdue University.
Murphy, Josette.
 1983 Farming Households' Perception of Alternate Production Strategies. A paper presented at the USAID Workshop on Dryland Agriculture. Washington, DC. November 21–22.
Murphy, Josette, and Timothy J. Marchant.
 1988 Monitoring and Evaluation in Extension Agencies. Technical Paper No. 79. Washington, DC: The World Bank.
Norman, David W., Emmy B. Simmons, and Henry M. Hays.
 1982 Farming Systems in the Nigerian Savanna: Research and Strategies for Development. Boulder, Colorado: Westview Press.
Rhoades, Robert E.
 1984 Breaking New Ground: Agricultural Anthropology. Lima, Peru: International Potato Center.
 1986 Using Anthropology in Improving Food Production: Problems and Prospects. Agricultural Administration. 22:57–78.
Salmen, Larry.
 1987 Listen to the People: Participant Observer Evaluation of Development Projects. Washington, D.C.: The World Bank.
Simmons, Emmy, Joseph W. Beausoliel, Gary Ender, Gregory Heist, and Josette Murphy.
 1982 Food Grain Technology: Agricultural Research in Nepal. Project Impact Evaluation No. 33. Washington, DC: U.S. Agency for International Development.

Swanson, Burton E. and INTERPAKS.
   1986   An INTERPAKS case study of the agricultural technology system in Malawi.
          Urbana, Ill.: INTERPAKS, University of Illinois.
Uphoff, Norman.
   1986   Improving Irrigation Management with Farmer Participation: Getting the
          Process Right. Boulder, Co.: Westview Press.
Zandstra, Hubert G., E.C. Price, James A. Littsinger, and R.A. Morris.
   1981   A Methodology for On-Farm Cropping Systems Research. Los Banos, The
          Philippines: International Rice Research Institute.

# 2

## Anthropologists and
## Private, Humanitarian Aid Agencies

### Randall C. Luce

David Brokensha could be extremely frustrating when teaching develop-ment. That was not his intention, but his lectures often made me question prospects of "planned development". He had no grand theory, no paradigm that promised success. He had us consider the mundane, "unscientific" dilemmas of development (for example, how does one deal with a pig-headed official?) and exposed the human frailties that all too often doomed the best intentioned programs.

Development, Brokensha implied, was not a science (though social science can, and should, be applied) or a technical application, but a human process, a difficult art. Development was immersed in politics, from capital to village, and the expert, no matter how technical his field, could not escape that fact. For the expert, development became a humbling discipline. There was much to view critically, including the effects of one's own efforts.

This paper reviews the different orientations toward international devel-opment found in private, humanitarian aid agencies in the United States. These agencies, as a group, are in a rare period of reassessment. Experts discuss new ways of "doing" development, and even of defining it. Many positive things are being said, at least from the view of anthropologists. I hope to highlight these new insights, but also point out weaknesses, and consider what insights anthropologists can bring to these agencies. Like Brokensha, I will emphasize politics, and thus the problematic nature of development that precludes any final "social scientific" answer to the problems we confront.

### Private Aid Agencies in the United States

Private, non-profit, humanitarian aid agencies are a varied lot. Indeed, it is difficult to speak of a single, homogeneous "world" of Private Voluntary Organizations (PVOs)[1] because such a world does not exist. Some PVOs are disaster relief oriented agencies that follow the headlines, bringing aid to the site of one emergency, and then another, but which have few if any long term programs of rehabilitation or development. Others are solely development oriented agencies. Most do some of both.

Even among agencies of one type are differences in style and operation. Development agencies can have widely different operational definitions of "development". Development can mean supplying the infrastructure needed for an immunization program, or teaching villagers preventive health measures, or forming village credit and advocacy groups designed to increase and equalize the village's resource base. Each of these examples reveal more than just differences of approach to a common problem (poor health), but also differences of defining the source of the problem.

Anthropologists working with or for a PVO should be aware of this extreme diversity, but also of the common history PVOs, as a group, share. If anthropologists are to have any understanding of what anthropology can bring to PVOs, they must know both that common history and the peculiar history of the particular agencies with which they work.

PVO social history, for our purposes, can be broken down into two stages of evolution and a third stage, so far primarily a theoretical ideal. Each is characterized by a specific concept of mission. These three stages, or "generations" as one analyst calls them, of PVO evolution can be termed; (1) the first generation of aid as "relief and welfare", (2) the second generation of aid as "local self-reliance", and (3) the third generation of aid as "sustainable systems development" (Korten 1987:147; also see Broadhead 1987:2–3; and Elliott 1987:57–59).

To many analysts of the PVO world today, understanding what each of these three generations mean involves a sense of progressive refinement or clarity of mission. The term "generation" is meant to convey not so much the passage of time, but a growing maturity. This paper will critically evaluate "third generation" strategies and the prospect that most real life PVOs ever will become "third generation" PVOs.

Part of that analysis will address the political world in which PVOs live, which like most political worlds is very complex and often frustrating. Most PVOs regard themselves as "nonpolitical", but implicit in the third generation analysis is the recognition that development is politics far more than it is economics or, especially, acts of mercy.

## Two Generations of Aid

David Korten has drawn upon his extensive experience in Asia to arrive at the three generation typology. Though all three now co-exist, they were developed sequentially, the succeeding following as a response to the deficiencies of the previous. Thus, each generation corresponds roughly to a historical period of the PVO world.

### Relief and Welfare

Development, when it first became an issue, was thought to be a matter of capital inequities and technology gaps. Developed nations had capital and new technologies; undeveloped nations lacked both. Large scale aid involved capital and technology transfers from "Northern" governments to those of the "South".[2] Small scale aid was focused on individuals or families. In both approaches underdevelopment was thought to be a simple lack of money or materials. The solution was to simply give, or loan, what was lacking (Korten 1987:146–148; also see Elliott 1987:57–58).

This orientation developed as governments and PVOs responded to the relief needs of post-World War II Europe, and to disasters in other parts of the world. In these situations resource transfers seemed a just and fitting response. But as aid shifted to newer, more problematic areas in Southern nations, the deficiencies of this approach became apparent. Certain transfers, especially of technical inputs, were not accepted, or not used as the donors envisioned, or were used and then put aside. Immediate needs were being met, but a sustained solution was missing (Korten 1987:148).

## Local Self-Reliance

The second generation emphases on local self-reliance came in response to a perceived inertia on the part of PVOs beneficiaries. Aid must not simply be given, it must be promoted to it's "backward" recipients. Analysts argued that, to accept aid programs, the beneficiaries must first be made to see the positive effects of such programs. The focus of aid switched from the individual and family to the community.

This was the early, naive period of the second generation of aid. The paternalistic aspect of this orientation gradually gave way to an orientation critical of the manner in which aid was given rather than blaming local inertia for failed programs. Beneficiaries must now be the ones who decide what they need and what projects should be instigated, while PVOs have become facilitators of local initiatives.

The stress is on the adjective "local". Such projects usually replicated government services found in more developed areas of the country. PVOs could not, and would not, pretend to supplant civil government duties on a regional or nation-wide scale. Their small base of resources and their sense of political propriety narrowed their scope to a small number of select, local villages (Korten 1987:148; also see Robertson 1984:203–204; and Elliott 1987:58).

## The Third Generation of Aid

Local self-reliance has had its successes. But these have been few and limited. Development only goes so far with this approach, and the limitations are built into its basic, localized orientation. The successes that occur are due to the favored position of the community which has access to the resources and talents of the PVO and its personnel. Other communities without such resources rarely benefit from this approach (Korten 1987:149). More fundamentally, success rarely occurs if national or regional government policies are in opposition to the PVO's goals. Even if a local success is achieved, success often breeds failure as successful, progressive projects increasingly run afoul regressive, and sometimes even repressive, national governments (Robertson 1984:203–204; Elliott 1987:58).

Advocates of "sustainable systems development" define the issue of development as an institutional problem whose locus is neither the needy individual nor the inert village, but the regional or national economic and political system. PVOs must focus their efforts on these areas. Development experts have slowly learned that villages do not exist separately from their national governments, nor from the international economic systems of which their governments are a part (Korten 1987:149; Broadhead 1987:3–4).

This emerging awareness is related to another development. Indigenous NGOs are now advocating a larger role for themselves relative to that taken by American PVOs. Southern NGOs claim that they should do the bulk of direct community organizing and development. After all, those are "their" communities. The PVO contribution should be limited to advocacy and institutional support. In short, analysts argue that PVOs should seek to develop the capacities of indigenous NGOs rather than communities (Korten 1987:149, Drabek 1987:x).

Thus, a third generation approach is to limit one's input to that of a catalyst, attempting to influence, through indigenous NGOs or government agencies, regional and national development policies, regulations, and institutions. Specific NGOs capable of building social institutions required for natural, sustained development are supported by PVOs, usually with informational—both networking and technical—inputs rather than cash or material resources. And PVOs act as policy advocates and educators in the United States to promote international policies conducive to sustained development policies in Southern nations (Korten 1987:149; Garilo 1987a:118–119; Davies 1987).

Proponents of this approach note several implications for PVOs. Examples include increased professional expertise in select development fields, such as health or agricultural production, long term country assignments, and an in-depth knowledge of local conditions (Korten 1987:153).

The political implications of this approach are clear. In some Southern countries an effort is underway to de-centralize development planning, which provides indigenous NGOs opportunities for greater influence in development planning than they enjoyed in the past. Alliances of NGOs, especially, can create power centers of advocacy for specific development strategies (Garilo 1987a:116). As facilitators of particular NGOs, American PVOs would become identified, though indirectly, with specific development policies that would benefit specific political blocs. And, as policy advocates in the United States, PVOs would assume a greater political role than they traditionally have taken.

## Prospects for a "Systems" Approach

The rationale and strategy of this approach should sound familiar to anyone who has taken a graduate course in the anthropology of development.

Anthropologists, of course, have long advocated increased incorporation of local expertise, (Brokensha et al. 1980) a more sophisticated view of "isolated" or "backward" villages and peoples, increased reliance on indigenous institutions and cultural norms, and an increased awareness of the political aspects of development. Still, anthropologists interested in working with PVOs should view systemic, or third generation, approaches critically. To what extent can PVOs be expected to conform to a systems approach? And does this approach actually solve the unresolved dilemmas of the welfare and local self-sufficiency approaches?

## Prospects of Implementation

Two considerations should give one pause: money and politics. Is a third generation approach fundable? Can PVOs become political actors, and, indeed, would they ever want to be?

PVOs often pride themselves on their flexibility, meaning that when new opportunities of service arise, the agency has the ability to engage itself. Too often, this is a rationalization necessitated by an insecure funding base, which nearly always is built on mass mailing lists. Flexibility then means going where the current, popular interest (and therefore money) is. Systems approaches require that PVOs limit their activities to areas—geographical and topical—where they demonstrate expertise, experience, and long-term commitment. This approach demands that PVOs do not diversify, even if their area of competence is of little interest to the donor public, and even if donors are questioning why the agency does not "do something" about conditions in more highly publicized or more deeply troubled areas.

A second problem arises in regard to money. Donors expect PVOs to "do something". Most PVOs proudly advertise their hands-on programs. Advocating policy changes, or facilitating the work of NGOs through information exchanges rather than through cash grants would represent quite a departure from this norm. Concrete accomplishments (a new vaccination program, or wells dug to provide a sanitary water supply) would give way to more abstract achievements. This would not go well with most PVO's fundraising departments.

The political implications of a systems approach also would represent problems for most PVOs. The PVO community is virtually unanimous in its adherence to taking a non-political stance. Not only should beneficiaries receive aid regardless of political affiliation, but PVOs should not seek to advance political agendas.

There is an increased awareness of the complex interrelationships between politics and aid. This issue undoubtedly poses the greatest dilemma for PVOs today, particularly with the effect armed conflict has had on exacerbating famines and other emergency conditions (see for example Minear 1988). Anthropologists certainly see the merit of PVOs refraining from dictating development policies to their host nations. But what should be the response of PVOs working in countries with governments that clearly use "development" policies to consolidate power, or serve an elite, rather than to provide for the poor? Deciding how to play the advocate's role, and in what forum, are difficult decisions indeed.

Systems approaches require that such advocacy, albeit indirectly through indigenous NGOs, be a normal part of PVO programing. When working with a government agency a PVO would be even more directly involved. As Korten (1987:149) acknowledges, such a PVO role would be very problematic "given the mutual suspicion, if not outright hostility" often found between host governments and PVOs.

Just how problematic is indicated by the current controversy over GOBI (Growth monitoring, Oral rehydration, Breast feeding, Immunization) policies, now gaining popularity within primary health programs. GOBI is scaled-back primary health care (PHC), focusing on the four most vital and easily implemented interventions. Advocates say that in a world of limited resources, functioning GOBI policies are preferable over unworkable, comprehensive primary health programs. Critics say that substituting a policy of technical interventions for the empowering qualities of PHC denies the fundamental concept of primary health. PHC, these critics say, defines health care as primarily a political problem (see Werner 1988).

Primary health, as originally envisioned, approaches health care with a systems approach. The major "health problem" is not disease, malnutrition, nor unsanitary conditions, but the economic and political systems, usually out of the people's control, that determine their quality of life. As David Werner wrote, "[N]on-governmental community health programmes and workers have often become the focal points of community awareness and organization, which has helped both to foster and to strengthen popular movements for social transformation" (1988:3). "Social transformation" is not just a beneficial by-product of PHC, but it's ultimate goal. Taking control of the community council, formerly controlled by local elites, becomes just as much a part of health care (even more, some would say) as dispensing medicines (see Werner 1988:7–8).

GOBI, Werner charges, is a politically neutral policy that betrays the central premise of PHC, and this is precisely why GOBI is now so popular. Most governments that implement PHC programs do so through health care "packages" tightly controlled by government agencies. GOBI is well suited for this centralized, nonparticipatory approach. Thus, even progressive organizations such as WHO and UNICEF, in Werner's view, have backed away from the original political premise of PHC (Werner 1988).

Werner recognizes that reform is not easily achieved, and that furthermore, in many countries, the logical outcome of empowerment would not be reform but revolution. Werner says that true empowerment is too fundamental a goal to abandon. His critics could easily say that the concrete benefits of GOBI are too important to defer to unrealistic political aspirations. Both parties have valid points.

The controversy over GOBI shows that political advocacy in development is extremely problematic. It poses real and acute dilemmas not just for conservative, "pro-Western" agencies put off by populist, leftist rhetoric, but also for progressive, international agencies, such as UNICEF and WHO.

Thus, it is not surprising that PVOs traditionally have rejected advocacy roles. Not only was advocacy regarded as too controversial in the field, but also with donors. Recently, through the formation of the umbrella group InterAction, PVOs have taken a more visible advocacy role, especially concerning US foreign aid. But a true systems approach, as I understand it, would require a far greater involvement, which few PVOs would consider desirable or proper (see Broadhead 1987:3).

## Prospects of Success

Quite apart from issues of implementation remains the question of whether a systems approach would be successful if implemented. There are some PVOs capable of and willing to become third generation agencies. As they do, will they succeed? A critical view of the systems approach should give anthropologists valuable insights to offer PVOs.

A systems approach has much to recommend it, especially from an anthropologist's viewpoint. However, significant problems remain, such as, an assumption that government agencies will allow outside "catalysts" to influence policy change; and insufficient attention (at least in most of the presentations I have heard and read) to the reality of competing interest groups within beneficiary populations.

## Receptiveness of Government Agencies

Korten (1987:152–153) provides "a prototype strategy", for a would-be catalyst PVO, which begs the question of the political openness of the system to be reformed. After identifying government and NGO agencies that "dominate the policy and program environment" in the PVO's area of concern (eg. health care or agricultural policy) important individuals within these agencies are found who advocate community based approaches to managing development resources. These people are used as channels through which funds are provided to the agency for critical studies on existing local development resource management practices and the agency's impact on them. These studies then provide the basis for "workshops" and "working groups" composed of agency representatives committed to "the institutional change effort". Pilot projects are designed, implemented, and monitored (Korten 1987:152–153).

Such studies, and follow up analysis and implementation, would be fraught with political controversy. Most agencies are not very receptive to meaningful internal review and reform. And government advocates of "community based approaches" are only to be found in the policy setting circles of the most progressive or democratic of governments. As Garilo admits (1987b) NGOs will have political clout only in the most open, or democratic, governments (also, see Frantz 1987:123–124).

Korten's prototype strategy treats underdevelopment primarily as a problem of agency expertise. Once the proper studies are concluded, and the working groups formed, reform of the system and government agency will proceed apace. But if development is a "process of democratization" (Korten 1987:146), an explicitly political strategy is required. So the question remains, how does one democratize a closed system?

To be fair, that question probably has no answer, at least for PVOs. But if systems approaches are workable only to the degree that the recipient society is open, this limitation should be acknowledged.

One answer may lie with the mainline church groups,[3]—particularly Roman Catholic, but also Protestant—which are taking a leading role in supporting local empowerment movements. NGOs in Latin America, for example, often were formed to facilitate local initiatives by the poor during periods of intense government centralization and repression. During these periods of "closed political space" NGOs developed close ties with the Catholic Church, which acted as their protector and provided their only avenue of expression (Landim 1987:31–32, also see Elliott 1987:59 for an example of Protestant activism in Africa). This illustrates the importance, not often acknowledged, of mainline church groups for empowerment movements.

*Competing Groups*

Robertson has summarized the ideologies and assumptions common to most planned development programs. Development is commonly perceived in populist terms, thus the primary ideological assumption is that development can only succeed through the active cooperation of the people (1984:222). The dismal rate of program acceptance demonstrates that the recipient-oriented approach is rarely achieved outside of the theoretical, or planning, stage of programs. The political dilemmas mentioned above play a large role in this, but Robertson notes other difficulties caused by unexamined assumptions commonly held by development agencies.

Populist ideology takes the community as both the object to be developed and the goal for which development strives. As goal, the community is thought to be simple and unspoiled, a place of cooperation between like-minded fellows. These assumptions of simplicity and homogeneity are contradicted by the actual complexity and diversity of village life, and allow for an assumption that recipients will react uniformly to proposed development projects (Robertson 1984:142–146, and 224).

Even when proposed by villagers, the purpose of a project will be interpreted differently by the village elites and the poor. Both will compete for the project's benefits. Elites have the education and experience needed to successfully deal with both the outsiders (whether nationals or expatriates) who bring the project's resources into the village, and with the regulations and requirements the project imposes on its participants. The poor, generally, are less able to do so. Thus, even grass root projects, designed to benefit the poor, often do not successfully "reach" their targeted beneficiaries (see for example, Robertson on cooperatives, 1984:167–169).

Regardless of the input—food, money, or expertise on institution building— if it is offered to an illusionary, homogeneous and cooperative community, it will only benefit a particular faction of the community—usually those least in need. Newly created institutions will not represent the interests of the poor, those on whose behalf we supposedly act, unless local inequality is specifically addressed.

As facilitators, PVOs also must not assume that their partner NGO agencies have interests identical to those of their beneficiaries. NGOs often are founded and administered by urban, middle or upper class elites, who no matter how well intentioned, and better informed than their PVO counterparts on local conditions, still will likely have different agendas than those of their beneficiaries. This is especially important for those PVOs that choose not to work directly with their beneficiary communities, but indirectly through an implementing NGO. And neither should PVOs assume homogeneity within an NGO.

This does not contradict the basic assumptions of the systems approach. Social homogeneity is not a basic principle necessary for third generation strategies. Indeed, their stress on "in-depth country knowledge" could lead to an acknowledgement of complexity and diversity. But so far as I know, the assumption of homogeneity is rarely critiqued by advocates of the systems approach (Elliott 1987:66 is a notable exception).

## An Example of the Systems Approach to Aid

Such criticism notwithstanding, anthropologists can offer PVOs valuable insights by bringing a systems perspective to their programs. Even relief aid, thought to be a relatively simple matter of headline hunting and shipping logistics, if properly done with regard to the social system under crisis as well as the people, acquires a complexity best approached with a systemic perspective.

The Eritrean Relief Association's (ERA) response to the continuing famine in Eritrea illustrates a systemic approach to relief aid. ERA, through the University of Leeds, conducted a sophisticated needs assessment on which to base their appeals for commodities and funds. The study did not just estimate crop shortages, but addressed shortages within the context of existing food markets (both local and international), and expected cooperative endeavors. Thus the following systemic factors were considered:

- the estimated final size of the harvest,
- what non-agricultural jobs were available, and expected income,
- estimated availability of food in traditional regional markets,
- whether the better-off peasants and herders will help the poor, and
- the estimated relative price levels for grain and livestock (Anon. 1987).

Eritrean herders often sell livestock for grain during periods of food shortages. ERA recognized that a major purpose of food relief was to prevent catastrophic increases in the price of grain relative to livestock. Conversely, too much food relief would depress food prices, lowering incentives for farmers to produce. Given the heavy traffic in livestock for grain, ERA decided that those prices should be monitored throughout the relief effort as a rough regulator on the flow of aid (Anon. 1987:1 and 4).

Not only must the value of livestock be protected, but herd sizes must be calculated. Herders must not be forced to reduce their herds below a critical, minimal number under which recovery to normal size becomes excessively difficult. Thus, herders' relief needs are represented by a complex calculation of herd size and value (Anon. 1987:6).

Cash to buy grain in traditional markets, including neighboring Sudan, is ERA's favored medium of relief aid. Thus, the estimated availability of grain in regional markets is a crucial determinant of the amount of actual food aid needed to supplement ERA's cash transfers. This involves not just knowledge of Ertirean agricultural conditions, but also of Sudanese, which are complicated by a separate famine (Anon. 1987:6).

This systemic approach protects markets and resources as well as people. It minimizes the possibility of relief induced distortions of the economic system, and thus the possibility of induced dependence. Such an approach requires field work, close relations with local populations and community leaders (to conduct the survey), and most likely support from an academic institution. Long term staff presence, in-depth knowledge of local conditions, and close relations with NGOs with strong grass roots support are all important if not essential for such an effort. Each of these third generation qualities are such that an anthropologist could advocate within a PVO.

Though much expanded from the traditional emergency relief effort, this approach remains limited to the technical aspects of aid. In Eritrea this is not enough. A war, now past its twenty-fifth year, between nationalist Eritreans and Ethiopia causes famine conditions and hinders delivery of aid to affected areas. The ERA study includes a political message—that international pressure be brought to bear on the combatants to allow free, independent access of aid, without military escort, to all areas of need (Anon. 1987:6–7).

## Anthropologists and PVOs

Anthropologists should bring to PVOs a systemic, political awareness of the aid and development environment. Technical insights should not be neglected. Indeed, the technical knowledge an anthropologist provides should focus attention on the systemic aspects of the problem. The systems approach provides us a fundamental insight: planned development is an outside intervention changing a system of allocations. As such, it is a political process requiring political knowledge. But such knowledge should not be limited to large-scale political problems, such as trade imbalances and the politics of starvation, but should also include small-scale problems concerning local inequalities within recipient communities, and the different perspectives to be found between and within indigenous agencies, both governmental and private.

Anthropologists also should bring a critical eye to the PVO itself. PVO administrators commonly assume that their staffs approach their development projects with common, uniform perceptions, purposes and interests. But, especially with larger PVOs that employ national staffs in their host countries as well as expatriates, this is an exceptionally naive assumption. Though this message is disconcerting, anthropologists should tell it as diplomatically as possible.

Simply put, anthropologists can best offer PVOs increased awareness— of international politics, their recipients, partner agencies, and themselves— and a cautionary note as well. There is no final solution to many of the problems that beset planned development programs. Brokensha's most enduring legacy, for me, is the recognition of the political or, if you will, human dilemmas of development. These rarely are solved merely by the application of a technique or a theory of action.

Even though the systems approach recognizes the importance of politics in development, it is itself a technique. As such it assumes that development is an impartial, rational process wherein success is achieved by the "correct" entry, with the "appropriate" inputs, given to the "proper" recipients. But when influenced by politics, development policies are not always made impartially, or even rationally.

Still, PVOs should make use of the insights this technique provides. All development programs are applications of a technique, and the systems approach is in many ways the best available. But as PVOs begin to incorporate a systems approach, their staffs would do well to acquire the personal qualities of perseverance and humility—qualities that have typified David Brokensha's career.

## Notes

1. United States agencies are commonly called private, voluntary organizations (PVOs) while elsewhere humanitarian aid agencies are called non-governmental organizations (NGOs). American agencies are sometimes called NGOs but European and Southern agencies are never called PVOs. In this paper, to distinguish between the two, PVO is used to refer to American agencies, and NGO for Southern, indigenous agencies.

2. The First, Second and Third Worlds are no longer in vogue in development literature. The South, referring to underdeveloped and undeveloped countries, and the North, referring to the developed world—the West and the Socialist bloc—are used instead.

3. By "mainline church groups" I mean those, like the Roman Catholic Church and Protestant denominations such as the Episcopal, Lutheran, Methodist and Presbyterian Churches, that have strong national denominational structures and established linkages between denominations. These do not include the more conservative, fundamentalist churches, or groups, that generally are more decentralized and more dependent on charismatic individuals.

## References Cited

Anonymous.
  1987   Eritrea Food and Agricultural Production Assessment Study: Preliminary Report. Agricultural and Rural Development Unit Centre for Development Studies, University of Leeds, England.

Broadhead, Tim.
    1987    NGOs: In One Year, Out the Other? *In* Development Alternatives: The
            Challenge for NGOs. Anne Gordon Drabek, ed. World Development. 15:1–
            6.
Brokensha, David W., D.M. Warren, and Oswald Werner.
    1980    Indigenous Knowledge Systems and Development. Lanham, MD: University
            Press of America.
Davies, Peter.
    1987    Address given to participants in the InterAction workshop, Strategic Planning
            for Non-Profits. December 10–11. New York.
Drabek, Anne Gordon.
    1987    Development Alternatives: The Challenge for NGOs—An Overview of the
            Issues. *In* Development Alternatives: The Challenge for NGOs. Anne Gordon
            Drabek, ed. World Development. 15:ix–xv.
Elliott, Charles.
    1987    Some Aspects of Relations Between the North and South in the NGO
            Sector. *In* Development Alternatives: The Challenge for NGOs. Anne Gordon
            Drabek, ed. World Development. 15:57–68.
Frantz, Telmo Rudi.
    1987    The Role of NGOs in the Strengthening of Civil Society. *In* Development
            Alternatives: The Challenge for NGOs. Anne Gordon Drabek, ed. World
            Development. 15:121–127.
Garilo, Ernesto D.
    1987a   Indigenous NGOs as Strategic Institutions: Managing the Relationship with
            Government and Resource Agencies. *In* Development Alternatives: The
            Challenge for NGOs. Anne Gordon Drabek, ed. World Development.
            15:113–120.
    1987b   Address given to participants in the InterAction workshop, Strategic Planning
            for Non-Profits. December 10–11. New York.
Korten, David C.
    1987    Third Generation NGO Strategies: A Key to People-centered Development.
            *In* Development Alternatives: The Challenge for NGOs. Anne Gordon
            Drabek, ed. World Development. 15:145–159.
Landim, Leilah.
    1987    Non-governmental Organizations in Latin America. *In* Development Al-
            ternatives: The Challenge for NGOs. Anne Gordon Drabek, ed. World
            Development. 15:29–38.
Minear, Larry.
    1988    Helping People in an Age of Conflict: Toward a New Professionalism in
            U.S. Voluntary Humanitarian Assistance. New York: InterAction, American
            Council for Voluntary International Action
Robertson, A. F.
    1984    People and the State: An Anthropology of Planned Development. Cambridge,
            England: Cambridge University Press
Werner, David.
    1988    Empowerment and Health. Contact. 102: Christian Medical Commission,
            World Council of Churches

# 3

## Cultural Transmission and Development in Sub-Saharan Africa

*Barry S. Hewlett*

David Brokensha's contributions to development anthropology have been numerous and diverse. This paper extends a perspective in development anthropology that he has emphasized during his professional career—the use of the anthropological perspective to solve contemporary social problems. Just what is the anthropological perspective is less clear today than it was 30 years ago, but, typically, cultural anthropology focuses on understanding culture and how culture filters reality, and emphasizes the use of field methods that necessitate learning the local language and living and participating in the culture for a lengthy period. From this cross-cultural experience anthropologists often come away with a great appreciation and respect for the peoples' detailed cultural knowledge and have a better understanding of how culture filters reality and influences human behavior. Brokensha's contributions to development are consistent with the anthropological perspective; he has emphasized decisions from below rather from above, and how indigenous knowledge systems can be useful in development projects. His approach has been influential in international development because it provided a positive rather than a negative connotation to "culture". In many development circles indigenous "culture" is perceived as a problem or a hindrance to be overcome, rather than as an asset that can contribute to development.

Consistent with Brokensha's emphasis on the utility of the anthropological perspective, this chapter considers recent contributions to the study of cultural transmission and applies them to development anthropology. Specifically, the chapter focuses on why some cultural traits or individuals with a particular cultural heritage may change rapidly while other cultural traits or individuals with a different cultural heritage may be more conservative.

Culture in this chapter refers to the complex whole which humans collectively create; the creations or products include not only material products but social, behavioral and mental products (Mukhopadhay 1985: 20). Culture has a number of characteristic features; it is learned and transmitted generation to generation, shared, dynamic, cumulative, integrated, symbolic, psycho-

Table 3.1 - Four Mechanisms of Cultural Transmission

| | Cultural Transmission Mechanisms | | | |
|---|---|---|---|---|
| | Vertical/ Parent- to-child | Horizontal /Contagious | One-to-Many | Concerted or Many-to-one |
| Transmitter | Parent(s) | Unrelated | Teacher/leader /media | Older members of social group |
| Receptor | Child | Unrelated | Pupils/ Citizens/ Audience | Younger members of social group |
| Acceptance of Innovation | Intermed. Difficulty | Easy | Easy | Very Difficult |
| Variation between Individuals | High | Can be High | Low | Lowest |
| Variation between Groups | High | Can be High | Can be High | Smallest |
| Culture Change | Slow | Can be Rapid | Most rapid | Most Conservative |

logically real, pervasive and conservative. This chapter extends our understanding of the transmission process and the dynamic and conservative features of culture.

## Cultural Transmission Mechanisms

Cavalli-Sforza and Feldman (1981) and Boyd and Richardson (1985) have identified and described different types of cultural transmission and their general features and cultural evolution. A brief overview of four of the primary mechanisms of cultural transmission identified and described by Cavalli-Sforza and Feldman and elaborated on by Boyd and Richardson will be provided before considering their applicability to understanding development projects Africa.

Cultural transmission from parent-to-child is called *vertical* and is the closest to biological transmission (see Table 3.1), it is highly conservative and may maintain the status quo, including all the individual variation in existence. Within this mode of transmission there is little difficulty accepting an innovation at the individual level; children are especially receptive, but the innovation will be very slow to spread to others in the population unless other modes of transmission are employed along with parent-to-child transmission.

A more typically "cultural" mechanism of transmission is *horizontal* or contagious, in which transmission is between any two individuals irrespective of their relationship. This is very similar to the transmission of infectious diseases. The spread can be fast if contacts with transmitters and acceptance by receptor are frequent. Cavalli-Sforza and Feldman make a distinction between horizontal and oblique, the first referring to transmission within and the second between generations, but both are called "horizontal" in this discussion. If transmission is *one-to-many*, communication is highly efficient and if acceptance follows communication, cultural change may be very rapid. In *many-toward-one* transmission every recipient is assumed to be influenced by many transmitters, and that all transmitters act in concert so that the influence is reciprocally reinforced. Consequently, change in the frequency of a trait over time and space should be slow and variation within and between populations low. This mechanism tends to generate the highest uniformity within the group. Of course, no single cultural trait is transmitted by only one mechanism, a pattern of transmission mechanisms is more likely, where one of the types of transmission predominates.

All of the above cultural transmission mechanisms involve two stages; communication and adoption of a cultural trait. In vertical transmission and many to one transmission there may be no conscious choice in whether to adopt the cultural trait or not because the trait is transmitted at a very young age. Horizontal and one-to-many transmission are more likely to involve conscious choice as they occur later in life, i.e., they come from friends or teachers late in childhood or early adulthood. The reasons why a particular cultural trait is or is not adopted will not be considered in detail in this chapter. An extensive literature already exists on this topic (e.g., Foster 1962), but here the emphasis is placed on the consequences of the different types of cultural transmission.

## The Persistent and Pervasive Nature of Culture

While most of the attention in anthropology of development focuses on the nature of culture change, there is strong evidence to suggest that cultures and cultural traits have a greater tendency towards the opposite—conservation. Archaeologists are probably most aware of this conservation. Most stone tool traditions in African prehistory, for instance, last thousands of years (e.g., Acheulian, Sangoan, Sebilian), and ethnoarchaeologists in Africa (Yellen 1977) have identified similarities between the subsistence and settlement patterns of the hunting-gathering !Kung San of today and prehistoric hunter-gatherers of 10,000 years ago.

Some aspects of culture may be conserved more than others. Many who have worked on development projects in Africa have described dramatic changes in material culture—clothing, cars, bikes, house type, etc—while also noting the conservative nature of kinship rules, family structure and religion. One recent survey of 277 African societies from Murdock's ethnographic atlas (1967) found that family and kinship traits were statistically

Table 3.2  - Correlations between Cultural Traits and Language or
Ecology

| Trait Groups | Number of Traits in Group | Correlations with: Language | | Ecology | |
|---|---|---|---|---|---|
| | | # | % | # | % |
| Family and kinship | 13 | 10 | 77 | 0 | 0 |
| Socioeconomic | 16 | 7 | 44 | 6 | 37 |
| House building | 5 | 4 | 80 | 3 | 60 |
| Other | 6 | 0 | 0 | 0 | 0 |

Table gives the number of traits correlating significantly (at
P=.001) with language or with ecology. Correlation is tested by
chi-square. Data from Matessi et al. 1983.

more related to the linguistic family of the group than to the environment
(Table 3.2) (Matessi et al. 1983). For instance, mode of marriage, family
organization and marital residence in Africa were all statistically related to
language but not ecology (see Matessi et al. 1983 for description of language
and ecological categories). This suggests that these traits were highly conserved
during the migrations of these populations. Other cultural trait groups, such
as traits dealing with economy, social stratification, and division of labor by
sex, were not correlated more often with language or environment. Specific
traits were correlated with language (e.g., segregation of adolescent boys)
or environment (e.g., types of games) or both (e.g., caste stratification).
Cultural traits that correlated with environment, alone or in combination
with language, probably had some adaptive advantage.

Why does culture tend to be conservative? The model described above
indicates that the vertical and many-to-one types of cultural transmission
described above favor cultural conservation of cultural traits. The vertical
or parent-to-child type of transmission is probably the most common in
human history; only with increasing population density and social stratification, which appears rather late in human history, does the one-to-many
mechanism play a substantial role in cultural transmission. Today, changes
in dress and material possessions may occur rapidly as they are usually
transmitted by one-to-many mechanisms, i.e., the mass media.

The significance of cultural transmission mechanisms on culture is often
overlooked by anthropologists. In order to explain why people behave the
way they do, economic, environmental and other functional explanations are
utilized. The basic assumption is that human behavior is adaptive. In contrast,
cultural transmission models suggest that the persistence of many traits can
be attributed to the lack of adaptive or selective forces which would facilitate
change. The cultural trait may have been adaptive in the past, and in the
absence of alternative selective pressures, it prevails. A recent debate in African
hunter-gatherer studies illustrates this point. A number of anthropologists
have attempted to explain why one group of African Pygmies uses nets
(Mbuti) and the other (Efe) bows and arrows. Early descriptive studies (e.g.,
Turnbull 1965b) indicated that net hunting was more efficient than bow

and arrow hunting. As cultural ecology gained strength in anthropology, researchers began to ask why the Efe archers did not take up net hunting if it was more efficient? Turnbull (1965a) indicated that the forest was so rich that any hunting technique could be used. He disagreed with Putnam (1948:328) who suggested that the diversity had to do with proximity and economics; the differences were related to the prevailing villager custom, as the villagers supplied the Pygmies with both nets and arrowheads.

But other studies suggested that the Efe and Mbuti lived in different forest environments (Abruzzi 1979, Milton 1985, Tanno 1976). Abruzzi suggested that the northern Ituri forest was rather abundant in large game and had a lower population density than the south, so the Efe were hunting less intensely than the Mbuti net hunters who lived in an environment with greater population density and less abundant game. Since Tanno (1976) described the northern part of the forest as faunistically more diverse than the southwest, Milton suggested that the Mbuti net hunted because there was more seasonality, more severe annual low points, less diversity in fauna, and had poorer soils, which from her South American experience suggested less wildlife. Neither Abruzzi or Milton had conducted fieldwork with Pygmies, so neither had the quantitative data to support their ecological hypotheses. Bailey and Aunger (in press) now have good quantitative data on the forest environments of the two groups, and report that there are no significant differences in the Mbuti and Efe forest environments. Ichikawa (1983) reconsidered the original assumption about net hunting efficiency and quantitatively demonstrated that while net hunting had a greater yield, bow and arrow hunting was just as efficient as net hunting. There were more people on the net hunt, including women, therefore more meat was acquired, but the bow and arrow hunt provided just as much per person hour as net hunting. The net hunters traded their surplus meat for manioc and other carbohydrates, while the Efe women worked for village women to get their manioc and carbohydrates. More recently Bailey and Aunger (in press) have suggested that Efe women do not participate in the hunt because they can earn more calories per unit of time by working in agriculturalists' fields than by participating on the hunt. They indicate that Mbuti live in areas where there is a market for meat, therefore it is beneficial for Mbuti women to help on the hunt to get meat rather than working in the agriculturalists' fields. Bailey's and Aunger's hypothesis may be correct today, but Mbuti women participated in net-hunting long before a market for meat existed (e.g., when Turnbull did his fieldwork).

The above hypotheses offer "adaptive" explanations for the existence of net-hunters and archers. But if there is no adaptive advantage to one technique over the other (Ichikawa 1983) and the forest is similar in the Efe and Mbuti areas (Bailey and Aunger, in press), why the differences? Bahuchet (1987), who is interested in linguistics and ecology, suggests that the differences are a consequence of different culture histories of the two groups of Pygmies. The Efe have had a long association with Lese and other Sudanic speakers and are Sudanic-speakers themselves, while the Mbuti generally live in association with Bantu-speakers and speak a Bantu language. The Aka of the Central African Republic are also Bantu speakers and use nets to hunt rather than the bow and arrow. The word for collective bow hunting of the Efe is also Bantu. Mbuti and Efe, then, use hunting techniques that they enjoy and feel comfortable with because these are the techniques that were transmitted to them. Anthropologists realize that culture is by nature ethnocentric. Once you learn a particular way of doing things and relating to people, you come to think and feel that it is the natural and best way. Since there does not appear to be an "adaptive" advantage to net-hunting, the Efe continue to use the bow and arrow.

The point here is that culture is very pervasive, primarily because of the ways it is transmitted. Some cultural traits persist even when they may have a negative effect on reproductive fitness, or when it should be selected against (e.g, smoking, female and male circumcision). Once culture has been transmitted vertically or many-to-one, it is a powerful factor in determining physical, psychological and social reality. It patterns how we feel about and respond to the world.

### Intracultural Variability in Cultural Knowledge

Brokensha (1974:105) has pointed out the importance of identifying individual variation within ethnic populations:

> Until recently, it was common to speak of the "the Masai", "the Hausa" or "the Kikuyu" to imply uniform values and personalities. Now, I hope most of us are more keenly aware of the range of behavior and attitudes *within* a single group, however defined. (italics mine)

The cultural transmission model can help one to better understand the variability in individuals' cultural knowledge and behavior. Individual differences in cultural knowledge were especially pronounced among an Aka Pygmy population I worked with in the Central African Republic. In trying to identify basic Aka social structure, it was nearly impossible to get consistent answers on basic questions about taboo foods, the existence of forest spirit(s), the origin myth, etc. Individual variability was the pattern when it came to these and many other topics. In order to better understand this variability in relation to cultural transmission I interviewed 40 adults, 16 adolescents and 16 children (7–12 years old) about how they learned 50 subsistence, childcare and social skills (Hewlett and Cavalli-Sforza 1986). As Table 3.3 demonstrates, the Aka acquired much from their parents which allowed almost perfect conservation of individual variation and like biological transmission was also exclusively parent-to-child. The Aka also learned some traits (e.g. elephant hunting and social skills like dancing and singing) by many-to-one transmission which favored not only conservation but also uniformity. No traits were transmitted one-to-many. The study also demonstrated that women knew most skills earlier than men and that women contributed substantially to the cultural knowledge of both sons and daughters.

Table 3.3 - Contributors to Aka Cultural Transmission (Adults, N=40)

| TRAITS | Parent/s | Grand-parent | Other Family | Friend | Villager | Others | Self |
|---|---|---|---|---|---|---|---|
| | | | Percentages | | | | |
| All Traits | 80.7 | 3.8 | 1.4 | 0.7 | 1.6 | 10.0 | 0.9 |
| Net Hunt | 84.5 | 3.6 | 0.4 | 0.4 | 0.4 | 9.5 | 0.9 |
| Other Hunt | 70.7 | 4.9 | 2.4 | 0.0 | 0.0 | 19.5 | 2.4 |
| Gathering | 89.3 | 4.6 | 0.3 | 0.8 | 0.0 | 3.8 | 1.1 |
| Food Prep. | 76.3 | 2.3 | 1.3 | 2.3 | 11.8 | 5.3 | 0.0 |
| Maintenance | 86.5 | 1.8 | 1.8 | 0.0 | 7.1 | 2.9 | 0.0 |
| Infant Care | 85.6 | 3.9 | 0.9 | 0.3 | 1.5 | 6.9 | 0.9 |
| Mating | 77.5 | 6.2 | 5.0 | 1.2 | 0.0 | 6.2 | 3.7 |
| Sharing | 83.9 | 3.6 | 4.5 | 0.0 | 0.0 | 7.1 | 0.9 |
| Healing | 58.2 | 3.8 | 2.5 | 0.0 | 0.0 | 35.4 | 0.0 |
| Dance/Sing | 51.9 | 3.1 | 0.8 | 2.3 | 0.0 | 41.9 | 0.0 |

Percents represent reports of adult informants of the person(s) responsible for transmitting a given skill.

One conclusion seems inescapable on the basis of the Aka data: vertical transmission is by far the most important mechanism, accounting for about 80 percent of the cases studied. This is, according to the model, a conservative mode of transmission; it assures slow evolution while allowing individual variation. Such variation is indeed observed; variation in the length and condition of nets made by single individuals, heights of women's digging sticks, preferences for investing time in one or another activity and individual strategies observed during the net hunts. The study also points out the significance of women in the transmission of cultural skills and knowledge.

## Intercultural Variability in
## Cultural Persistence and Change

The previous section examined intracultural variability in the persistence or change of specific cultural traits. This section provides a cross-cultural examination of persistence and change in Sub-Saharan Africa as it applies to the cultural transmission model.

Intracultural variability is expected in all human populations as many cultural traits, even in highly stratified societies, are transmitted vertically. But it is also reasonable to expect cross-cultural variability as different cultures have different social structures, which influence the ways in which the culture is transmitted.

While no cultural transmission studies have been attempted with African rural farmers or urban populations, the model would predict differences from the Aka pattern, which is predominantly vertical. The Aka live in small groups of 25–30 individuals, do not have sibling caretakers, do not have age sets or intensive puberty rites and do not have strong unilineal descent groups. Rural African farmers often have the opposite: they live in relatively large groups of 100–500 individuals, have sibling caretakers, many have age sets, intensive puberty rites and strong unilineal descent groups. While many cultural traits among rural farmers would be transmitted vertically, they would also be likely to exhibit the many-to-one (descent groups and intensive puberty initiation) and horizontal types (peers and siblings) of cultural transmission. Urban Africans are likely to have more of the one-to-many types of cultural transmission (schools, TV and other mass media).

Strong unilineal descent groups, age-sets, sibling caretaking and intensive puberty initiation all promote the many-to-one type of cultural transmission, which is the most conservative form of cultural transmission and results in cultural uniformity. With these cultural patterns an older group (clan or lineage elders or older brothers and sisters) makes a concerted effort to transmit the culture. The respect and deference towards elders, a common value among rural African farmers, is consistent with the many-to-one type of transmission. The elders have special status and transmit knowledge to the youth in a concerted fashion. The communal type religion, described by Wallace (1966), is found in most of Sub-Saharan Africa, and also reflects the many-to-one type of transmission. A communal religion is where a lay group (generally elders) is responsible for calendrical, puberty, death and secret society rituals. These cultural practices and values associated with elders are not found among the Aka and other African hunter-gatherers.

The role of cultural transmission in cultural persistence and change can also be demonstrated in African history. Jack Goody (1971), for instance, offers a cultural ecological hypothesis to explain why precolonial Africans did not adopt the plow, the wheel, the gun and other technologies, even though Africa had regular trade with Eurasia, which had the technology. He suggests Africans did not adopt the technologies because land was plentiful and population density low, whereas in Eurasia the reverse was true. Unlike the discussion of hunting techniques where there was no difference in the efficiency of the competing technologies, the plow and wheel, in most cases, are far more efficient than farming with a hoe. Goody's explanation is reasonable as the generalized ecological differences between the two areas did exist. But not all areas of precolonial African had low population density and abundance of land. The West and East African kingdoms, for instance, had intensive agriculture and might have benefited from more efficient technologies. It would take extensive data and space to critique Goody's work, but the cultural transmission patterns found among farming Africans are not common in Eurasia (Goody 1976), which suggests that the conservative mechanisms may have contributed to the persistence of indigenous technologies. Eurasia also had more centralized systems, writing and formal education in the precolonial period, so innovations could potentially spread much faster with these one-to-many mechanisms.

The history of the European colonization of Africa also demonstrates the variability in how different cultures respond to culture change. Europeans entered sub-Saharan Africa as colonial imperial states, and were far more stratified and technologically developed than the bands, tribes and chiefdoms of sub-Saharan Africa. The band level societies were easily displaced (e.g., the Dutch displacing the San in Southern Africa) or manipulated; tribal level societies exerted a substantial resistance to the Europeans (e.g., the violent Maji Maji uprising of the Chagga, Hehe, and Nyamwezi tribes of Tanzania or the Ndebele rebellion in Zimbabwe), and the kingdoms were usually quickly brought under control by their own leaders or were given the some guarantee of political autonomy by the colonial administrators (e.g., Buganda and Swazi kingdoms). The impact of cultural heritage continues today as the African peoples from a band level societies are much worse off than individuals from a chiefdom heritage. The Aka, Mbuti, Efe, Hadza, !Kung, Okiek, Twa and other African hunter-gathers are politically impotent even though they have formidable weapons. They have not been able to mount much of a resistance to Europeans or their farming or pastoral African neighbors. In all of Africa hunter-gatherers are the lowest class/caste in the community. Band societies are egalitarian and have a difficult time forming large, powerful and cohesive organizations to resist intrusion or manipulation. They live in small groups, do not have authoritarian leaders, tend to lack or have weak clans and lineages or any other type of society-wide organization. Their response to imperialism has generally been flight rather than fight.

Agricultural and pastoral tribal societies tended to be more resistant to colonial intrusions. The 1902 Maji Maji uprising in Tanzania, the Kikuyu Mau Mau rebellion in Kenya, and 1904 Herero uprising against the Germans are just a few of the extremely violent responses of pastoral and farming peoples to the intrusion and manipulations by Europeans. These societies had strong had society-wide organizations based on religion, initiation rites, age sets or warfare. While they could organize, their political leadership was not absolute so a leader could not control or act on the part of all. When referring to the Shona and Ndebele, Bennett (1975:173) suggests that:

> Neither African people had a unified political leadership to direct their war effort. The Ndebele system had split into fractions following the disappearance of Lobengula after the 1893 campaign, while the Shona never had possessed centralized institutions. But as in the Maji Maji rising, religious leaders emerged to help supplying effective direction.

The indigenous political systems of agricultural and pastoral peoples of Africa were often segmentary lineages, and consequently did not have strong tribal-level leaders. But they did have the cross-cutting social organization which allowed them to respond to European intrusions. The pastoral and tribal level populations of sub-Saharan Africa are doing much better economically today than peoples from band level societies.

The kingdoms changed rapidly as most were given some form of political power and authority by the early European colonizers. They were able to change rapidly because they had highly stratified hierarchical cultures which had a powerful, often absolute king or chief. Many of the kingdoms resisted European imperialism violently in early contacts, but were often the first populations to brought under colonial control (e.g, the Buganda, Yoruba,

Swazi). Once the king signed an agreement with the colonials the other members of the culture accepted the change. This was not possible with the band and tribal societies. The colonials tended to give preferential treatment to people from stratified systems like their own. The Buganda in Uganda, the Yoruba in Nigeria, and the Ashanti in Ghana all received better treatment than other ethnic populations within their respective countries.

There are certainly exceptions to these general patterns, and cultural heritage is certainly not the only factor influencing the history of European-African relations. The culture's population size and density and the cultural heritage of the colonial invaders are also important considerations. Yoruba and Ashanti populations were large and more dense than the band level Aka and Hadza or the pastoral Maasai. Also, the British and Germans tended to be more separatist in their relations with Africans, whereas the French assumed the Africans would eventually assimilate the French way of life so were less likely to spatially and socially separate themselves from the Africans. The French were more likely to marry Africans, incorporate Africans into the clergy and colonial administration. Since the French were more humane, their relations with Africans were less violent.

The discussion of cultural transmission mechanisms is relevant to cultural heritage. Vertical transmission predominates in band-level societies, which generates tremendous intracultural variability and conservative cultural evolution as change would have to take place at the individual level. There would be a diversity of opinions as to what to do with the invading neighbors, and if one or a group of individuals accepted the colonial conditions, the others in the culture would not be compelled to follow their lead. Tribal level societies have more of the many-to-one types of cultural transmission discussed above which generate greater uniformity of cultural traits, but is even more conservative than vertical transmission. Consequently, they would be more likely to be able to reach a consensus to mount a resistance to intrusive neighbors and the nature of the resistance would be much stronger as there would be a concerted effort to maintain the culture. Since tribal populations have no or few of the one-to-many types of transmission, it would be difficult for the colonial administrators to communicate cultural change or peace agreements with all members of the culture. Kingdoms have at least some one-to-many types of cultural transmission along with the many-to-one types, so would be even more likely to be able to reach a consensus on how to respond to European invaders and have mechanisms to accept and transmit conditions of agreements made with the Europeans.

Although the kingdoms and tribes do not function as they did 80 years ago, the language and culture continue to be transmitted. Those in development tend to neglect the cultural heritage of individuals, especially if the individuals being influenced by the development project are in an urban setting. Individuals from a kingdom heritage are more familiar with the values, attitudes and ideology of stratification, inequality and specialization. Consequently, they would be more likely to do better than individuals from band or tribal populations in the city, in relations with government officials, in producing profits to increase status and prestige, etc.

## Cultural Transmission
## and Contemporary Social Problems

How can these cultural transmission mechanisms help one understand and solve contemporary social problems in sub-Saharan Africa? If one examines how *individuals* learned particular cultural traits one should be able to identify who is transmitting what cultural knowledge. One may be able to identify the role of women, elders or siblings in the transmission process, and therefore be in a better position to understand and possibly predict how innovative techniques (e.g., tractors, fish ponds) and ideas (e.g., birth control, hygiene) might be received, and how one might want to transmit the techniques and ideas. Also, if the development anthropologist understands the primary mechanisms of transmission in the culture, s/he should be better able to understand why s/he is getting uniformity or diversity in particular cultural traits. For instance, Brokensha and Riley (1980) describe how indigenous knowledge of trees can be useful for implementing reforestation projects. But it would be useful to know how the knowledge of trees is transmitted generation to generation. If the knowledge was transmitted vertically, the development anthropologist should expect to get a number of different uses and beliefs about particular trees, but if this knowledge is transmitted by a group of elders or as part of an initiation ceremony, the development anthropologist would expect greater uniformity in the responses from informants. Many cultural traits in Africa are transmitted parent-to-child, but in cultures where clans, lineages, or age sets are important, one would expect to find more of the many-to-one type of transmission, which is even more conservative and promotes cultural uniformity of those traits.

Most development anthropologists are socialized in environments where formal education, social stratification and hierarchy and mass media are commonplace. Since knowledge was transmitted in this way we may feel that it is natural to utilize these one-to-many types of mechanisms to transmit new technologies or ideas. But rarely do you find the one-to-many type of transmission in rural African populations (except where you find schools and TV). This is not to say that one should never use this technique, but it does suggest that people may not feel comfortable in those learning contexts. Also, as professionals in media and communications are well aware, the status and charisma of the individual transmitting the innovation one-to-many is vitally important in the acceptance or rejection of the innovation.

Finally, this discussion of cultural transmission mechanisms does not imply that sub-Saharan Africans are conservative in their economic endeavors and that they are slow to change due to tradition. Anyone who has been to Africa knows that Africans take risks, want to get ahead, and are willing to put up with enormous hardships to do so (e.g., the husband living away from village most of the year). When a cultural trait will better enhance reproductive fitness if modified, then changes may occur rapidly, regardless of how it was transmitted. This chapter suggests that it is important to understand the mechanisms of cultural transmission. Euroamericans are making rapid technological changes, in part, due to the pervasive one-to-many mechanisms (i.e., formal education and mass media) that exist in those societies. Africans are not conservative by nature, but are exposed to different modes of cultural transmission, which may influence they ways in which they respond to development projects.

## Conclusions

This discussion suggests several principles which might assist anthropologists in their understanding of the process of cultural change, and contribute to planned development by predicting the likely response to innovations.

1. Cultural transmission mechanisms can help one understand both intracultural and intercultural patterns of cultural persistence and change.
2. Development anthropologists could benefit from taking the time to examine cultural transmission mechanisms in target populations. They might better understand and predict responses to innovative technologies and ideas, and might be able to build upon existing transmission mechanisms to bring about effective change.
3. There may not always be ecological or other functional explanations for human behavior. Culture is often transmitted in conservative ways and many cultural traits may not enhance "fitness". Culture then, comes to dramatically influence how an individual feels about, perceives, and takes action in the environment.
4. Cultural heritage can influence how one adapts to cross-cultural contact, innovative technology, urbanization, stratification and the modernization process. It is important to understand the cultural heritage of the individual, even though s/he may be in an environment (e.g., urban) dramatically different from the one s/he was socialized.

## References Cited

Abruzzi, W.S.
   1977   Population Pressure and Subsistence Strategies Among the Mbuti Pygmies. Human Ecology 7:183–189.
Bailey, Robert C. and Robert Aunger Jr.
   in press   Subsistence Strategies Among Bambuti Pygmies: Net-Hunters and Archers. Human Ecology.
Bahuchet, Serge.
   1987   Historical Perspectives on the Aka and Baka Pygmies in the Western Congo Basin. Paper delivered at the American Anthropological Association Meetings. Chicago. November.
Bennett, Norman R.
   1975   Africa and Europe: From Roman Times to the Present. New York: Africana Publishing Co.
Boyd. Robert and Peter J. Richardson.
   1985   Culture and the Evolutionary Process. Chicago: University of Chicago Press.

Brokensha, David W.
1974    Africa, Whither Now? Journal of African Studies 1(1):101-112.
Brokensha, David and Bernard W. Riley.
1980    Mbeere Knowledge of Their Vegetation, and it's Relevance for Development (Kenya). *In* Indigenous Knowledge Systems and Development. David Brokensha, D.M. Warren and Oswald Werner, eds. Pp.111-128. Washington D.C.: University Press of America.
Cavalli-Sforza, L.L. and M.W. Feldman.
1981    Cultural Transmission and Evolution: A Quantitative Approach. Princeton, NJ: Princeton University Press.
Foster, George M.
1962    Traditional Cultures and the Impact of Technological Change. New York: Harper and Row.
Goody, Jack.
1971    Technology, Tradition and the State in Africa. Cambridge, England: Cambridge University Press.
1976    Production and Reproduction. Cambridge, England: Cambridge University Press.
Hewlett, Barry S. and L.L. Cavalli-Sforza.
1986    Cultural Transmission Among Aka Pygmies. American Anthropologist 88:922-934.
Ichikawa, M.
1983    An Examination of the Hunting-Dependent Life of the Mbuti Pygmies, Eastern Zaire. African Study Monographs, Supplemental 4:55-76.
Matessi, C.R. Guglielmino, C. Viganotti, and L.L. Cavalli-Sforza.
1983    Spatial Distributions and Correlation of Cultural Traits in Africa. Pavia, Italy: Instituto di Analisi Numerica del Consiglio Nazionale delle Richerce.
Milton, Katherine
1985    Ecological Foundations for Subsistence Strategies Among the Mbuti Pygmies. Human Ecology 13(1):71-78.
Mukhopadhay, Carol C.
1985    Introducing the Concept of Culture. *In* Integrating Multicultural Perspectives Into Teacher Education. Chico, CA: California State University, Chico.
Murdock, George P.
1967    Ethnographic Atlas. Pittsburgh: University of Pittsburgh Press.
Putnam, Patrick.
1948    The Pygmies of the Ituri Forest. *In* A Reader in General Anthropology. Carleton Coon, ed. Pp. 322-342. New York: Holt.
Tanno, T.
1976    The Mbuti Net-Hunters of the Ituri Forest, Eastern Zaire—Their Hunting Activities and Band Composition. Kyoto University African Studies. 10:101-135.
Turnbull, Colin M.
1965a   Wayward Servants: The Two Worlds of the African Pygmies. New York: Natural History Press.
1965b   The Mbuti Pygmies: An Ethnographic Survey. Anthropological Papers of the American Museum of Natural History 50(3):141-282.

Wallace, Anthony F.C.
  1966     Religion: An Anthropological View. New York: Random House.
Yellen, John.
  1977     Archaeological Approaches to the Present: Models for Reconstructing the
            Past. New York: Academic Press.

# 4

## Cooperatives, Empowerment, and Rural Development in Africa

*Thomas M. Painter*

A major challenge to anthropologists and sociologists of rural development consists of linking understandings of agrarian social structures and socio-economic change with interventions that at once promote rural development and enhance the role of smallholders as viable decision makers in the rural development process. David Brokensha's career provides ample evidence of a scholar's concern with understanding how rural dwellers perceive agrarian realities, and with ways in which these shared perceptions and the resultant systems of indigenous knowledge can be described and ascribed the eth-noscientific status they rightfully deserve. Brokensha's work also bespeaks a long-standing interest in discovering ways in which the indigenous knowledge of agrarian populations, once recognized, can be tapped by those from the outside who seek to work at the grassroots in promoting rural development (Brokensha et al. 1980). Among the topics that he has written about from this perspective are participation, the impact of land reform and land adjudication, local knowledge about and management of natural resources and their implications for rural development, and social and community forestry.

In this chapter, I will explore issues related to participation and empow-erment in rural development, a topic of considerable interest to Brokensha and to the Institute for Development Anthropology, of which David Brokensha is a cofounder and codirector. This will consist of an overview of the history, impact, and potential of efforts to organize rural cooperatives in Africa during the colonial and post-colonial periods. This is a report on work in progress and proposes preliminary generalizations concerning several points relative to cooperative organization in Africa: the depth and breadth of cooperative organizational efforts, the most common aims of those who have organized cooperatives, the distribution of power and the nature of partic-ipation in cooperatives, the performance of cooperative organizations in empowering rural populations, and the linkage between sociological under-standing of the political economy of agrarian Africa and endeavors to promote

rural cooperatives for development. The chapter closes on a critical note
concerning the relationship between "participation" and empowerment in
African cooperatives.

The issues addressed open multiple possibilities for theoretical and empirical
contributions by anthropologists and sociologists who seek better to understand African agrarian structures and social change and, in addition, share
an interest in *applying* their insights to the realities of agrarian Africa and
contributing thereby to strategies for empowering local populations and
promoting sustainable rural development.

## Cooperatives in Africa

The history in Africa of efforts to organize local cooperative organizations
is long and covers the entire continent. It spans nearly a century, and a
variety of rural cooperatives have been organized for marketing, credit and
other services, and less frequently for agricultural production, in every African
country. As early as 1910, for example, the French colonial government
promoted what some observers have very generously termed "proto-coop-
eratives" among peasants in Senegal. These *Societes Indigenes de Prevoyance,
de Secours et de Prets Mutuels Agricoles* (often referred to as SIPs) were
modeled in part on organizations introduced in Algeria in 1894 and in
Tunisia in 1907 (Gagnon 1976:108–110; Laville 1972:23, 31; cf. Lazreg
1976). From the mid-1920s through the late 1930s, the SIP model was
applied in French colonies in western, central and eastern Africa (Laville
1972:33). Cooperatives had their debut in British colonial Africa in 1913
when cooperative marketing associations were organized in Uganda. In 1933,
cooperatives were organized in Tanganyika, and were modeled after organizations introduced earlier in Punjab State, India (Hyden 1973:6–8). Cocoa
marketing cooperatives were organized in Ghana beginning in the late 1920s
(Beckman 1976:91), and in 1936, marketing cooperatives were introduced
in Nigeria (Hyden 1973:8). This list is far from exhaustive, but indicates
the range of cooperative efforts undertaken in Africa during the past century.

The major concern of those who organized rural cooperatives (or proto-
cooperatives) in Africa, be they government administrators during the colonial
or postcolonial periods, or groups that represented indigenous class interests,
was to create organizational structures to facilitate the production, collection
and marketing of agricultural commodities destined primarily for export—
principal among them, coffee, cocoa, cotton and groundnuts. Groundnuts
were the marketed commodity in Senegal, where the French colonial administration had been promoting production by Senegalese peasants through
a combination of force and incentives since the 1840s (Painter 1978:2–3).
Cooperatives in Uganda and Tanganyika marketed *Arabica* coffee, produced
by smallholders since being introduced by Catholic missionaries around 1900
(Hyden 1973:6–8). In Nigeria, cooperatives were engaged in marketing
groundnuts and cotton; in Ghana, they marketed cocoa. Again, this brief
list is only illustrative of the focus on export commodities.

This emphasis on organizing the collection and marketing, and occasionally, the production of crops for export, continues to characterize the vast majority of African cooperatives. The goal of improving the production and marketing of staple crops was, and remains to this day, of secondary importance. In some cases, staple crops were not even considered in the cooperative scheme of things, and occasionally, the impact over time of state strategies to increase export crop production through rural cooperatives resulted in a *decline* in areas cultivated in food crops (Laville 1972:78, 281; cf. Raynaut 1975). While it is true, for example, that groundnuts had long been consumed as a condiment prior to the era of French *mise-en valeur* policies and the promotion of rural cooperatives in Senegal, the spectacular growth of groundnut production was driven by external demand, not an internal market. From 1840 to 1900, Senegalese groundnut exports to France increased from 722 kilograms to 123,000 metric tons; by 1968, annual exports exceeded 800,000 metric tons (Painter 1978:2). Some shifts in this orientation occurred during the postcolonial period as African governments attempted to use rural marketing cooperatives as part of a strategy for securing low-priced staple foods for growing urban populations.

Thus cooperative organizations, particularly when they were the instruments of colonial "development" policy, as they very frequently were, (1) promoted the production and marketing of agricultural commodities that often were of secondary importance to peasant smallholders as domestic consumption items; (2) promoted thereby the integration of African smallholders in a global capitalist economy on terms that made their livelihoods increasingly dependent on returns from agricultural commodity production, which depended in turn on prices set in Paris, London, and New York; and (3) occasionally, as in the case of Senegal, so increased export crop production that production of local food crops suffered, necessitating the substitution of imported food grains (for example, Indochinese rice in Senegal).

The history of rural cooperatives in Africa, often erroneously referred to as the history of the "cooperative movement", has been one almost exclusively of unilateral (and, as they would be termed today, "top-down") state interventions. The colonial state was acting on behalf of mercantile and industrial fractions of metropolitan bourgeoisies. Colonial strategies aimed to facilitate metropolitan access to primary products needed by European industry to satisfy growing consumer demand for inexpensive edible oils and stimulant beverages, ensure colonial administrations continuing access to revenues (through head taxes on producers, taxes on exports, etc.), and promote integration of precapitalist productive organization into wider (regional and global) circuits of commodity exchange (Apthorpe 1972; Gentil 1984:5f.). In practical terms, this was accomplished by state marketing boards which mediated the linkage between smallholder producers and the world commodity market. The exceptions to this pattern are cases where an emerging African middle class—be it a planter or mercantile bourgeoisie—formed cooperative organizations (and political parties) as part of a struggle against the hegemony of foreign capital, be it European, Asian or Levantine (Beckman

1976:92; Hyden 1973:5f.; Morgenthau 1964:176–178; Painter 1985:516–523).

During the postcolonial period, independent African states often simply replaced the non-African mercantile interests that preceded them. Postcolonial governments also promoted rural cooperatives in a top-down manner, but now their task was to ensure state access to revenues in one of the few loci of accumulation available in their nominally independent national economies, i.e., the sphere of exchange. This situation was the result of decades of colonial policies that promoted highly uneven development within individual colonies or groups of colonies. The agrarian base for development inherited by many newly independent African countries consisted of nearly monocrop economies based on the production of agricultural commodities for export rather than for consumption by internal or even regional markets. The basis of commodity production was overwhelmingly dependent upon household or kin-mobilized labor[1] which was oriented in the first instance toward subsistence production and in which the productive forces consisted principally of human labor and, in exceptional cases, some animal draught power. State accumulation strategies during the postcolonial period followed the colonial patterns and have revolved around the operation of quasi-monopsonistic state and parastatal marketing boards to which rural cooperatives have been obliged and occasionally forced to sell their production (Koenig 1986).

It is necessary to make explicit what is implicit in the remarks above. Aside from instances of a strident mercantile or planter middle-class elements (Uganda, the Ivory Coast, Ghana), the history of cooperative development in Africa has been characterized by the absence of an active voice and decision-making power by smallholder populations. Referred to by administrators and planners over the years as "natives", "*indigenes*", or "*autochtones,*" "target populations", and most recently, "beneficiaries", and often forced to join cooperatives (despite the Rochedale principles of voluntary membership; cf. Hyden 1973:75; Gentil 1984:8–10), they had no say in defining the objectives of cooperative organization or the means to realize the objectives.[2]

The history of cooperatives as mechanisms for assisting and empowering disadvantaged rural populations in their attempts to gain greater access to and control over productive resources, and thus improving their livelihoods, is a history of disappointment (Apthorpe 1972; Bager 1980; Painter 1986; UNRISD 1975:45–51). While I believe this pessimistic conclusion is accurate and representative of multiple assessments of African cooperatives, a caveat is in order. We should be careful not to criticize African cooperatives for not accomplishing goals which in most cases were not intended by those who organized them—appearances to the contrary notwithstanding.

Despite a widespread state ideology, particularly during the postcolonial period, in which rural cooperatives have been promoted as instruments for expressing local initiatives and satisfying local needs, their function for the state, be it socialist (e.g., Tanzania, Ethiopia) or more liberal, free-market oriented (e.g., Nigeria, Niger or the Ivory Coast), has been very different.

In effect rural cooperatives have been key instruments in efforts by resource-poor postcolonial states to penetrate their rural economies. As mentioned above, they were organized initially to promote the production of agricultural commodities for export, and increasingly, have been promoted by African governments to ensure adequate supplies of staple food crops. This more recent role for rural cooperatives has reflected state aims of promoting national self-sufficiency in food, reducing foreign exchange losses, keeping urban populations supplied with relatively cheap food, and increasing state capture (hence profit-taking and taxation) of produce sales (Belloncle 1982:63–73; Bratton 1978:20–30; Dejene 1987:66–87; Gagnon 1976; Goussault 1973, 1976; Laville 1973). The "grass roots" contribution to cooperative development in Africa has been the exception.

Finally, the history of induced cooperation in Africa has been marked by repeated instances on the part of government planners and their foreign advisors and financiers, of a poor understanding of, lack of interest in, and frequent disdain for, the nature of local-level social organization among the agrarian populations repeatedly selected for rural development interventions, and invited or obliged to join rural cooperatives. There has been a remarkable lack of attention to indigenous forms of cooperation, their internal dynamics and relationships between locally significant social units of production and distribution, be their basis the household, co-residential extended kin groups, more distant kin having affinal ties, age-groups, collective labor organizations, or community.

National planners become "cultural dopes" with impressive regularity as they undergo professional socialization during formal education and are subjected to processes of class-biased enculturation within state bureaucracies where "official"perspectives on development "problems" and "solutions" are an integral part of organizational culture. As they become attuned to the shared and normative perceptions of "social reality", development "needs", "problems", and "solutions", that are the stock and trade of international development assistance agencies, they often lose contact with local, regional, and wider-ranging processes of change that affect the viability of indigenous ("traditional") structures of cooperation as well as the potential for viably linking them with introduced forms of cooperation (Painter 1986; cf. Putterman 1986:250f.). The result has often been an attempt to "link up with" or "build upon" poorly understood indigenous social forms in a manner that highlights the incompatibility of "modern" and "traditional" forms of social organization and cooperation (Bingen 1985:5).

## Discussion

The foregoing points may be of interest to anthropologists and sociologists of rural development, especially African colleagues in these key disciplines, who are particularly well-placed to examine (1) the specific nature and political economic "environment" of spontaneous forms of rural cooperation; (2) the potential that introduced forms of cooperative organization have for empowering a broad base of peasant smallholders; and (3) their potential contribution to sustainable rural development (Belloncle 1982:27–53; cf. Hyden 1973). It is noteworthy that endeavors to establish cooperative organizations for development continue to suffer from a lack of insightful sociological analysis of *existing* as well as planned local organizations. The results are often unsatisfactory organizational scenarios for promoting a range of local interests and responding to local needs. In an earlier attempt to examine possible links between spontaneous and introduced forms of cooperation for development in Niger, I argued that the possibilities were limited and the sociology of indigenous cooperation was impoverished (Painter 1986). Indeed, for Niger, and for most of West Africa, it was—and remains so (but cf. Beckman 1976; Charlick 1974; Ernst 1976; Schumacher 1975; Seibel and Massing 1974). An important comparative literature exists, however, thanks to descriptions of experiences with cooperatives in Eastern and Southern Africa. This literature is particularly useful because in contrast to materials on West African cooperatives, it is more likely to address the surrounding political-economy which shapes the opportunities and constraints of cooperative development.

Belloncle's work on cooperatives in French-speaking countries is an exception to the perspectives mentioned above on West African cooperatives and may also be the best long-term source on the theory and practice of cooperative organization in West Africa (see, among others, Belloncle 1978, 1979a, 1979b, 1982; Belloncle and Gentil 1968). His work is also important because of his concern with promoting rural empowerment. Despite its grounding in the experience of a long series of efforts to promote cooperatives and village organizations, however, Belloncle's writing, which is rich in description and personal reflections on his work, has not given sufficient analytical attention to issues such as intracommunity differentiation and the obstacles this poses to broad-based empowerment and participation. Postcolonial state strategies for development and accumulation and their implications for viable local participation in local-level organizations for rural development have also been neglected until recently (see below). He has been reluctant to move beyond images of local social organizations in which socioeconomic "homogeneity" and the "democratic" nature of participation in the "typical" African village are repeatedly asserted rather than taken as problematic and worthy of investigation. Whether we are concerned with existing forms of social organization or spontaneous forms of cooperative action with a view toward their role in promoting broad-based rural development, we must address such critical issues as intra- and intervillage differentiation. It is also important to consider the often immobilizing impact of intracommunity and intracooperative struggles involving individuals with allegiances to a variety of social groupings based on kinship, patronage, coresidence, age and seniority, or other locally significant social categories such as gender, caste and class (Charlick 1974; Hyden 1973; 1983:115–118).

These intracommunity and potentially intracooperative tensions and conflicts occur as individuals and groups seek to optimize scarce resources in ways that are opposed to the formal principles of rural cooperative organization, and which, as a result, often hinder cooperative functions and growth (Hyden 1973). These scarce resources include privileged access to the state through local-level representatives of line ministries (agriculture, rural development, etc.), market boards and government agencies having control over rural cooperatives, party officials, and government administrators. They also include the (albeit limited) power that cooperative officers have in allocating resources such as credit, capital, and access to farm implements and other inputs, and to training and other services (Belloncle 1978; 1982:75–84; Gentil 1984).

The consequences have become a leitmotif in assessments of African cooperatives: effective control of cooperative functions by individuals who are members of local elites, be these wealthier peasants having linkages to kin-based structures (e.g. chieftaincies) that often serve to control access to productive resources and/or individuals who are involved in lucrative commercial activities (trade, bulking, and transport). Another frequent consequence is a wide-spread skepticism and a shared perception among cooperative members that the benefits of membership are meager or nonexistent. Finally, all of these contribute to another widespread pattern among cooperatives in Africa: apathy, nonparticipation and resistance among members to cooperative ends-means schema that are at variance with their own needs and interests.

There is a need to continue with a critical reexamination of basic units of African agrarian social structure and cooperation with a view toward better understanding their features and internal dynamics as well as the larger political economy of uneven development which shapes their existence. This is necessary in order to clarify the potential, *if any*, for forming linkages between preexisting, yet clearly no longer "traditional" structures and introduced structures that are at once cooperative in nature and empowering. However tempting it may be to envision links between indigenous and introduced forms of cooperation, the two are very different and the search for the "peasant connection" is no easy matter (Cliffe 1970:60; Migot-Adholla 1970:36f.; Young et al. 1981:14–17; cf. Painter 1986).

Clearly, engaged, critical perspectives from anthropology and sociology have an important contribution to make. In part, the task consists of theorizing the fundamental units of rural social organization and cooperation with a view toward clarifying their relevance and potential roles in rural empowerment and improvement.

A recent example is Belloncle's rereading of the Marx-Zasulitch correspondence concerning the potential role of the peasant commune in the transition to socialism in Russia. His reanalysis followed a long and influential experience in organizing rural cooperatives in francophone Africa, and was an initial effort to conceptualize the development potential of local forms of social organization. Belloncle concludes that Marx's self-conscious analysis of the Russian commune fits the situation of the African village community, hence that they both agree on the centrality of the village as a social unit for development. Unfortunately, more than this is needed. He—*and we*—

must get on with the task of attending to the internal dynamics and external relations that have such an important and often limiting impact on the social life of villages in Africa, and the even more significant subunits of social organization, decision-making and resource allocation (e.g., households) that constitute village communities (Painter 1981; 1986; cf. Bingen 1985:16; Collier et al. 1986:2f.; Gentil 1984:5–6; Peters and Guyer 1987).

The second aspect of the sociological task is careful analysis of the socioeconomic "environment" of spontaneous and introduced cooperation. This consists of examining the structure of opportunities and constraints that affect cooperative organization and which result from intercommunity and intraregional differentiation and the impact of state policy options. These are often the result of continuing external constraints on decision-making, including relations of dependence with former colonial powers and pressure from foreign development assistance agencies (Collier et al. 1986).

The political economy of efforts in Africa to promote local initiatives through empowerment of rural producers has changed considerably during the nearly three decades of the postcolonial period. There has been a movement away from early postindependence efforts, particularly in francophone countries (Charlick 1984; Goussault 1970), to inform local populations about possible options and to facilitate local initiatives. Currently there appears to be a tendency among African states, hard-hit by the fiscal crisis of the 1980s, to look at "grass roots" organizations less with a view toward promoting participation or enhancing the decision-making power of rural populations than as structures to absorb investment and recurrent costs connected with development interventions in rural areas. "Participation" often consists of paying users fees for services formerly provided by the state or providing free labor for infrastructural maintenance that can no longer be provided due to government austerity measures (Painter et al. 1985; cf. Wisner 1988).

This strategy by African states and the international development organizations which fund rural development projects and pressure governments to cut recurrent costs aims to provide a semblance of coverage of rural areas in basic services such as agricultural extension, primary health care, potable water supplies, and even education while cutting costs. In many cases, this downward shift of responsibility if not the resources to handle the increased burden of "local level decision-making" has the appearance of devolution. In fact, the apparent revival of interest by state planners and international development assistance agencies in the potential development role of local organizations is driven more by a quest for cheaper conduits for service delivery than by a concern with according local populations an active role in defining the goals of local organizations or in specifying the nature and quality of support to be delivered. Under these conditions, the possibilities for rural empowerment may be limited.

## Notes

1. In Senegal, The Gambia, the Ivory Coast and Ghana, the production of groundnuts, coffee, and cocoa during the 19th and 20th centuries entailed a massive

mobilization of extrahousehold labor from hinterland areas through a combination of force and "incentives" to areas of commodity production in the form of migrants and "strange" farmers. See, among others, Diarassouba 1968; Gregory and Piché 1978; Hill 1963; 1986; Painter 1985:188–207, 503–525; Skinner 1965; Swindell 1978.

2. The literature on participation and control in rural cooperatives in Latin America is large and generally couched in a more systematic analysis of the political economic context and class forces that have limited empowerment of rural smallholders. See, among others, Collins 1988:156–159; Goodman and Redclift 1982:118–127; Perez-Crespo 1986; and Quijano 1982.

## References Cited

Apthorpe, Raymond.
  1972   Rural Cooperatives and Planned Change in Africa: An Analytical Overview. Geneva: United Nations Research Institute for Social Development.

Bager, Torban.
  1980   Marketing Cooperatives and Peasants in Kenya. Uppsala: Scandinavian Institute of African Studies.

Beckman, Bjorn.
  1976   Organizing the Peasants: Cocoa Politics and National Development in Ghana. Uppsala: The Scandinavian Institute of African Studies.

Belloncle, Guy.
  1978   Coopératives et développement en Afrique noire sahelienne. Sherbrooke, Quebec: Université de Sherbrooke.

  1979a   Développement par la participation ou liberalisme sauvage? Réponse à Albert Meister. Esprit 3(29):146–154.

  1979b   Quel développement rural pour l'Afrique noire? Dakar, Sénégal: Nouvelles Editions Africaines.

  1982   La Question paysanne en Afrique noire. Paris: Editions Karthala.

Belloncle, Guy and Dominique Gentil.
  1968   Pédagogie de l'implantation du mouvement coopératif au Niger. Niamey, Niger: Institut de Recherche et d'Application des Méthodes du Développement.

Bingen, James R.
  1985   Food Production and Rural Development in the Sahel: Lessons from Mali's Operation Riz-Segou. Boulder, CO: Westview Press.

Bratton, Michael.
  1978   Beyond Community Development: The Political Economy of Rural Administration in Zimbabwe. Gwelo, Zimbabwe: Mambo Press.

Brokensha, David W., D.M. Warren, and Oswald Werner.
  1980   Indigenous Knowledge Systems and Development. Lanham, MD: University Press of America.

Charlick, Robert B.
  1974   Power and Participation in the Modernization of Rural Hausa Communities. Ph.D. dissertation, Political Science Department, University of California, Los Angeles.

  1984   Animation Rurale Revisited: Participatory Techniques for Improving Agriculture and Social Services in Five Francophone Nations. Ithaca, NY: Rural Development Committee, Cornell University.

Cliffe, Lionel.
    1970    Traditional Ujamaa and Modern Producer Cooperatives in Tanzania. *In*
            Cooperatives and Rural Development in East Africa. Carl G. Widstrand,
            ed. Pp. 38–60. Uppsala: The Scandinavian Institute of African Studies.

Collier, Paul, Samir Radwan, Samuel Wangwe, and Albert Wagner.
    1986    Labour and Poverty in Rural Tanzania: Ujamaa and Rural Development
            in the United Republic of Tanzania. Oxford: Clarendon Press.

Collins, Jane L.
    1988    Unseasonal Migrations: The Effects of Rural Labor Scarcity in Peru. Prince-
            ton: Princeton University Press.

Dejene, Alemneh.
    1987    Peasants, Agrarian Socialism, and Rural Development in Ethiopia. Boulder,
            CO: Westview Press.

Diarassouba, Valery C.
    1968    L'Evolution des structures agricoles du Sénégal. Destruction et restructur-
            ation de l'économie rurale. Paris: Editions Cujas.

Ernst, Klaus.
    1976    Tradition and Progress in the African Village: Non-Capitalist Transformation
            of Rural Communities in Mali. New York: St. Martin's Press.

Gagnon, Gabriel.
    1976    Coopératives ou autogestion: Sénégal, Cuba et Tunisie. Montréal: Les Presses
            de l'Université de Montréal.

Gentil, Dominique.
    1984    Les Pratiques coopératives en milieu rural africain. Paris: Editions l'Har-
            mattan.

Goodman, David and Michael Redclift.
    1982    From Peasant to Proletarian: Capitalist Development and Agrarian Trans-
            formation. New York: St. Martin's Press.

Goussault, Yves.
    1970    L'Animation rurale dans les pays de l'Afrique francophone. Geneva: Inter-
            national Labor Office.

    1973    Stratification sociales et coopération agricole. Revue Tiers Monde 14(54):281–
            294.

    1976    L'Etat et le développement de l'agriculture: Le Concept d'intervention.
            Revue Tiers Monde 17(67):615–633.

Gregory, Joel W. and Victor Piché.
    1981    The Demographic Process of Peripheral Capitalism. Montreal: Centre for
            Developing Area Studies, McGill University, Working Paper 29.

Hill, Polly.
    1963    The Migrant Cocoa Farmers of Southern Ghana: A Study in Rural Capitalism.
            Cambridge: Cambridge University Press.

    1986    Development Economics on Trial: The Anthropological Case for a Prose-
            cution. Cambridge: Cambridge University Press.

Hyden, Goran.
    1973    Efficiency versus Distribution in East African Cooperatives: A Study of
            Organizational Conflicts. Nairobi: East African Literature Bureau.

    1983    No Shortcuts to Progress: African Development Management in Perspective.
            London: Heinemann.

Koenig, Dolores.
1986    Research for Rural Development: Experiences of an Anthropologist in Rural Mali. *In* Anthropology and Rural Development in West Africa. Michael M Horowitz and Thomas M. Painter, eds. Pp. 27–60. Boulder, CO: Westview Press.
Laville, Pierre.
1972    Associations rurales et socialisme contractuel en Afrique occidentale. Etude de cas: Le Sénégal. Paris: Editions Cujas.
Lazreg, Marina.
1976    The Emergence of Classes in Algeria. A Study of Colonialism and Socio-political Change. Boulder, CO: Westview Press.
Migot-Adholla, Shem E.
1970    Traditional Society and Co-operatives. *In* Cooperatives and Rural Development in East Africa. Carl G. Widstrand, ed. Pp. 17–37. Uppsala: The Scandinavian Institute of African Studies.
Morgenthau, Ruth S.
1964    Political Parties in French-Speaking West Africa. Oxford: Clarendon Press.
Painter, Thomas M.
1978    Changes in Senegalese Agrarian Structures Induced by the Peanut Economy: A Case of Colonial "Development". Unpublished manuscript, Department of Sociology, State University of New York, Binghamton.
1981    Quel avenir pour le Sahel?—A Response to Guy Belloncle. Unpublished manuscript. Files of the author.
1985    Peasant Migrations and Rural Transformations in Niger: A Study of Incorporation within a West African Capitalist Regional Economy, c. 1875 to c. 1982. Ph.D. dissertation, Department of Sociology, State University of New York, Binghamton.
1986    In Search of the Peasant Connection: Spontaneous Cooperation, Introduced Cooperatives, and Agricultural Development in Southwestern Niger. *In* Anthropology and Rural Development in West Africa. Michael M Horowitz and Thomas M. Painter, eds. Pp. 197–219. Boulder, CO: Westview Press.
Painter, Thomas M., Philip Boyle, and Hadiza Djibo.
1985    La fourniture des services publics dans les zones rurales du Niger. Une étude des coûts récurrents et des aspects sociologiques du fonctionnement des dispensaires ruraux, des écoles primaires et des l'hydraulique villageoise. Niamey, Niger: Institute for Development Anthropology.
Perez-Crespo, Carlos A.
1986    Agricultural Cooperatives: Perspectives from the Aymara and the Bolivian State. Ph.D. dissertation, Department of Anthropology, State University of New York, Binghamton.
Peters, Pauline and Jane Guyer, eds.
1987    Conceptualizing the Household: Issues of Theory and Policy in Africa. Special Issue of Development and Change 18(2). The Hague: Sage Publications.
Putterman, Louis.
1986    Peasants, Collectives and Choice: Economic Theory and Tanzania's Villages. Greenwich, Conn.: JAI Press.
Quijano, Aníbal.
1982    Imperialism and the Peasantry: The Current Situation in Peru. Latin American Perspectives 9(3):46–61.

Raynaut, Claude.
  1975    Le Cas de la région de Maradi (Niger). *In* Secheresses et famines du Sahel.
          Jean Copans, ed. Pp. 5–43. Paris: François Maspero.
Schumacher, Edward.
  1975    Politics, Bureaucracy and Rural Development in Senegal. Berkeley: University
          of California Press.
Seibel, Hans D. and Andreas Massing.
  1974    Traditional Organizations and Economic Development: Studies of Indigenous
          Cooperation in Liberia. New York: Praeger.
Skinner, Elliott P.
  1965    Labor Migration among the Mossi of Upper Volta. *In* Urbanization and
          Migration in West Africa. Hilda Kuper, ed. Pp. 60–84. Berkeley and Los
          Angeles: University of California Press.
Swindell, Ken.
  1978    Family Farms and Migrant Labour: The Strange Farmers of The Gambia.
          Revue canadienne des études africaines 12(1):3–17.
UNRISD (United Nations Research Institute for Social Development).
  1975    Rural Cooperatives as Agents of Change: A Research Report and Debate.
          Geneva: United Nations Research Institute for Social Development.
Wisner, Ben.
  1988    Gobi versus PHC? Some Dangers of Selective Primary Health Care. Social
          Science and Medicine 26(9):963–969.
Young, Crawford, Neal P. Sherman, and Tim H. Rose.
  1981    Cooperatives and Development: Agricultural Politics in Ghana and Uganda.
          Madison, WI: University of Wisconsin Press.

# 5

## Involuntary Resettlement
## at Manantali, Mali

*Dolores Koenig and Michael M Horowitz*

David Brokensha was the first anthropologist in West Africa to look at involuntary resettlement as a consequence of large dam construction. In a series of articles (1962, 1963–64, 1968), Brokensha defined the basic anthropological approach to relocation analysis, an approach that continues to enlighten. In writing this analysis we have been continually informed by Brokensha's notions of the need for effective participation of the populations involved, both host and resettled, in the entire resettlement process.

This paper reports on the relocation of some 10,000 persons in western Mali whose former villages and productive lands have been flooded out in the impoundment of waters by the Manantali Dam (see map, Figure 5.1). Since the relocation began in 1986, and the dam was first closed in 1987, it is too early for a definitive evaluation of the impacts of resettlement on the ecology, society, and economy of the region. We would like, however, to offer some preliminary assessments of the process, and to suggest some ways in which it might have been improved. Although the United States Agency for International Development (USAID), which funded both the resettlement and our research, does not have a formal relocation policy as does the World Bank (Cernea 1988), the project was based on a formal review of relocation theory, especially as developed by Thayer Scudder (1981). Rejecting an earlier European proposal to agglomerate relocatees in a few large towns whose size justified establishing schools and health facilities, the project sought to resettle villages as units, to involve the people in the choice of new locations, and to reestablish existing production systems. A project socioeconomic monitoring unit was created in association with an American rural-development research institution.

Despite its admirable intentions, the project suffers from (1) the lack of a coherent development plan for relocatees and host communities; (2) lack of adequate settler and host population participation in all phases of project planning and implementation; and (3) inadequate land over the long term to sustain local needs for fallowing and pasture. (The project also seemed

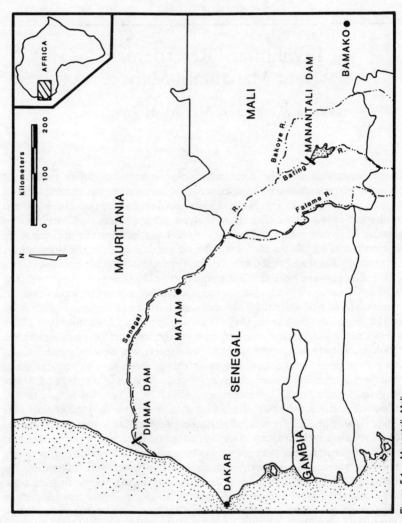

Figure 5.1 – Manantali, Mali

to suffer from government and donor inability to provide timely and quality site construction, but we do not have sufficient systematic data to explore this observation further.)

## Background

The Manantali Dam was completed in 1988 as part of an overall program planned and coordinated by the Senegal River-Basin Authority (OMVS)[1] to regulate the flow of the Senegal River, for the following objectives:

- irrigation of 375,000 hectares downstream, of which 240,000 will be in Senegal
- riverine navigation throughout the year from St. Louis at the mouth of the river to Kayes, giving landlocked Mali direct access to the sea; and
- annual generation of an average of up to 800 gigawatt hours of electricity (if priority is given to energy production).

Current cost of the infrastructure, totaling more than $500 million (of the $800 million anticipated), was loaned by a consortium of Arab (Saudi Arabia, Kuwait, Abu Dhabi, the Islamic Development Bank, and Iraq) and European (Germany, EEC, Italy, and France) donors, the African Development Bank, Canada, and the UNDP. The United States Government (USAID) agreed to fund the Manantali resettlement for approximately $18 million, with an additional $5 million from the World Food Program, and $3 million from the Government of Mali.

The impoundment reservoir at Manantali extends some 70 kilometers south of the dam, and has forced the removal of approximately 10,000 people from thirty-one nucleated villages, the largest of which had about 900 inhabitants and the average about 350. The original European proposal for resettlement (Groupement Manantali 1978) envisaged the creation of eleven new villages, all but one of which were to be substantially larger than the average village, and four of them from about 30 to 200 percent larger than the largest existing village.

Preliminary field studies done for USAID and the Government of the Republic of Mali (GRM) indicated that most people opposed being agglomerated with persons from other villages in the new settlements. No preexisting village opted to join with any other, and several fragmented during the relocation, perhaps accelerating the normal process of village segmentation. On the other hand, several hamlets did join villages rather than remain discrete. As of this writing, there are now twenty-nine official new sites and some five unofficial ones, whereas there had been forty-four sites recognized prior to the moves.

USAID (1984:16–17) explored various scenarios for compensating the relocatees:

The alternative ultimately adopted . . . is to keep the amount of physical labor required of settlers at a reasonable level while at the same time asking people to participate in both the planning and execution, including village reconstruction of the relocation. Thus, the Resettlement Project Unit (RPU) will contract (with the exception of the technical assistance) for services and materials to clear new village sites and cultivated fields; to provide access tracks, water points, warehousing, and replacement social and administrative infrastructure; to train villagers in pump maintenance and assist with the reconstruction of their homes; to transport people and their possessions to the new villages; to transport WFP [World Food Program] commodities; and to build the offices and lodgings needed by project staff. At the same time, the RPU will request villagers to assist with the reconstruction of their sleeping quarters. Villagers will be provided with materials to build granaries, latrines, corrals, chicken houses, compound walls, garden fences, mosques, and market places, but will be required to do the actual building.[2] The project will clear brush and large, non-productive trees from new fields, but farmers will be expected to do whatever is necessary for planting new fields in traditional ways.

As the research organization selected, the Institute for Development Anthropology (IDA) worked with the Malian Government's resettlement agency, the *Projet pour la Réinstallation des Populations de Manantali* (PRM). Particular emphasis was on monitoring the relocation and resettlement of the populations in the reservoir area.

IDA's linkage to the project was through the Social and Monitoring Section (SSS, *Section Sociale et du Suivi*) of the PRM. Headed by a Malian sociologist, Yacouba Konate, the SSS was in charge of all social aspects of the resettlement, including social services (liaison between the population and other project personnel, and food aid administration) as well as monitoring. IDA's involvement was principally with the monitoring component of the SSS, although in terms of daily on-the-ground administration, social services and monitoring often merged. For example, in the land distribution program, people requested the PRM to distribute fields to avoid intravillage conflict. IDA staff both participated in the distribution and monitored the effects.[3]

The goals of involvement were multiple. In terms of the project, short-term and long-term impact monitoring were both important. Short-term monitoring was oriented around the discovery of any acute problems that appeared during the resettlement phase, e.g., human or livestock diseases, nutritional crises. Long-term monitoring was focused on the question of whether people were able to reestablish their preproject production systems and quality of life, the explicit goals of the resettlement activity. IDA had a further objective: to improve understanding of the involuntary resettlement process in order sustainably to enhance the income, productivity, and well-being of future relocatees.

To fulfill these goals, three separate monitoring tasks were undertaken. First, the SSS collected a series of socioeconomic indicators on a regular basis from a sample of resettled villages and households. IDA staff provided technical assistance in the design, collection, and analysis of these data. Second, a participant observation study on land tenure and other resettlement conflict was planned and carried out by the IDA researcher, Grimm, who also served as a general counterpart to the director of the SSS. Third, a

Malian research organization, *Institut des Sciences Humaines* (ISH), is carrying out a series of short-term studies on the reestablishment of the production system in Manantali. IDA worked with USAID to prepare the terms of reference for this study and to evaluate project proposals, and IDA field teams collegially offered informal technical assistance to ISH, although no formal relationship was entered into between the two institutions.

## Successes and Failures

The success of a resettlement project can be judged by the ability of the resettled population productively to assume control over its own future. As Scudder (1981) suggests, this long process requires many years and many antecedent actions. It is too early, therefore, to make that kind of assessment of the Manantali Resettlement Project. We can, however, indicate whether the necessary antecedents are being put into place.

Three points are important for a short-term assessment of the resettlement project:

1. Are resources in the resettlement area adequate for the reestablishment of the prior standard of living?
2. What kinds of autonomy have the relocated and the host populations in directing the resettlement process to their own advantage?
3. What kind of development infrastructure has been put in place to facilitate sustainable and equitable economic growth?

### Necessary Resources

The people of Manantali, the Malinké of the Bafing river (or Bafingois),[4] formerly lived in one of the most isolated areas of Mali, with an overall population density of less than five per square kilometer (USAID 1984, Annex 7.4:6), though rising to approximately twelve per square kilometer in certain villages along the river (Groupement Manantali 1978). Their isolation was associated with an economy that combined subsistence with some commercial production. The people exploited a wide range of local resources for food and crafts, pursued semicommercialized dryland agriculture, and raised some livestock. These resources would be necessary in the resettlement sites if people were to "reestablish" their previous mode of life.

To be sure, replication of existing resources is not the only way to "sustain their current standard of living" (USAID 1984, Annex 8.4:2). New resources can substitute for old, but that strategy requires some plans for substitution, normally in the context of a development project. The Manantali Resettlement Project performed no feasibility studies to analyze which resources might be lost and how they might be replaced, and only rarely were new resources explicitly planned (for example, new water points and pumps were installed in the resettlement village sites).[5]

USAID explicitly decided not to introduce any development program during the resettlement: "[it was decided to avoid] the introduction of any

new or innovative economic activity, particularly in crop or livestock production, until at least two years after the transfer had been accomplished"
(USAID 1984:12), and, as far as we know, is not contemplating such
development for the future. USAID has contacted a private voluntary organization about operating in the region, however, and has offered startup
costs from remaining project funds. A Peace Corps volunteer working on
community development has also been assigned to the area. The underlying
assumption of the Manantali Resettlement Project was uniquely the *replacement*
of existing resources and reduplication of the previous standard of living.

The availability of land and water for the reestablishment of the production
system was addressed by the project, but other resources were given much
less attention.

*Land.* The major resettlement area, directly downstream from the dam,
is sparsely populated, an unusually favorable situation in which competition
for land between relocatees and host villagers was expected to be modest.
But the sparse population also raises basic questions: what accounts for the
low density, especially as soils appear to be fertile and rainfall attractive?

One reason for sparse settlement has been the intense presence of disease
vectors: schistosomiasis, malaria, trypanosomiasis, and, especially, onchocerciasis, as the shallow, rapidly flowing waters of the Bafing River provide ideal
breeding grounds for the larvae of *Simulidae spp.*, the blackfly whose bites
transmit the microfilaria that cause river blindness. While the disease is also
common above the dam site, there are far more breeding locations below
it. The Bafing has been included in the blackfly spraying activity of the
World Health Organization's Onchocerciasis Control Program, and it is hoped
that the incidence of the disease will decline.

The reservoir zone contained mainly alluvial soils, as the river twisted
its way between high cliffs, creating a flood plain well suited to shifting
cultivation. Below the dam site, the cliffs give out within a few kilometers,
and the soil characteristics are less attractive for farming, and therefore for
settlement.

Below the dam site, the land of the Malinké Bafing quickly ends and
that of the more hierarchic and Muslim Khassonké Bambouk, with its
prominent village mosques, begins (Samake et al. 1987). Thus expansion
northward would have meant leaving the familiar political region and assuming
a subordinated position in an alien one. For these reasons—sanitation, soil
productivity, and politics—we suspect that the fringe borders between Bafing
and Bambouk were not as attractive for settlement as the region further
upstream.

PRM attempted an equitable allocation of new farmlands by lot, based
on the number of persons aged eight years and older in a household. While
project management initially assumed that residents would be responsible
for their own division, once the overall assignment of village lands was made
in the new locations, they acceded to the requests of villagers who otherwise
feared an inequitable distribution favoring more influential households. And
indeed, prominent villagers with large families or the ability to hire labor

are already beginning to stake out claims on unallocated bushlands in close proximity to the villages, leaving the others with either inadequate lands over the full cropping-fallow cycle of about 14 years, or having to anticipate travel of considerable distances from village to field. A relatively high demographic growth rate of about 2.5 percent annually will intensify this problem, and the likelihood of shortened fallow periods will, in the absence of improved affordable technology, lead to declining soil fertility.

Because there is no development project promoting new crops or agricultural technology as part of the resettlement, there are no formal constraints on farming.[6] Farmers make their own decisions about allocation of fields among household members, and retain a good deal of autonomy in other farm-level decisions. While women are not treated more equitably than in the pre-move villages, they retain their rights to plots for cultivating groundnuts, maize, fonio, and vegetables.

*Water.* Villages relocated downstream from the dam are at some distance from the river, because the riverine lands are being reserved for a possible 9,000-hectare gravity-feed irrigation scheme, and because of a concern for water-related diseases. Preproject villages met their domestic water needs directly from the river or from shallow dug wells that frequently went dry.

PRM provided all the new villages with boreholes and handpumps, and all villages will also receive cisterns to store water to use when pumps are inoperable. While the pumps have experienced certain problems (see Note 5), these are being addressed, and a pump-maintenance training program has been carried out.

The provisioning of improved points for relatively safe and continuously available water along with the construction of roads are perhaps the major benefits, indeed, the only enduring benefits of relocation thus far received by the people.

*Bush Resources.* Harvesting of wild resources through hunting and foraging constituted an important economic activity in the Bafing, supplementing agriculture and herding. No survey of the presence of these resources in the resettlement region below the dam was made, and it may be that wild game, shea nut trees, palm trees, and bamboo groves are less common here than upstream. Wild resources added both to the quality of the local diet and to local income, for there was an active trade in these products. Preliminary analysis of monitoring data suggests that foraging has declined from 40 percent to only 16 percent of reported non-agricultural activities in the resettlement sites. Insofar as the decline is due to unfamiliarity with the new terrain, we can anticipate a reversal over time. But a good deal of it seems to derive from a reduced presence of useful fauna and flora, indicating a secular deterioration both of diet and income. Increased population density below the dam and the pressure to clear lands for farms and pastures will further reduce the environment supporting desirable wild game and plants.

Whether these activities will create a significant loss over the next few years is being monitored by SSS, but the project has thus far considered no alternative actions in compensation.

Dam construction has led to an increased presence of fish in the reservoir and a spectacular growth of spontaneous fishing. Although much of the fishing is done by migrants to the region from traditional fishing groups (Bozo, Somono), some of the younger Bafingois have also begun to fish. While this self-initiated entrepreneurial activity is surely beneficial, there has been no official attempt to develop the resource or to train local people in its exploitation. The organized development of this new bush resource might have better compensated for the loss of old ones.

*New Resources.* Dam construction brought new resources to Manantali by increasing employment and entrepreneurial activity and by decreasing its isolation. A small urban center emerged, with about 15,000 inhabitants, many of whom were wage earners dependent on the local market to buy food. Both host and resettling villagers responded to the new economic activities, selling charcoal, game, foodstuffs, and a variety of goods. As most of the wage laborers have departed with completion of the major construction work, market activity and opportunities for employment have also declined. Paid labor in building the new villages is also at an end, and there are no on-going development activities that could provide continuing sources of employment and income for the local population.

Both the project and construction company built roads, improving access to this remote area. There will be some maintenance by OMVS on the main road connecting the dam site with the railroad, some 80 kilometers down-stream, but it is doubtful that the Malian government will be interested in maintaining the other roads. The region will remain isolated, not as much as before the dam, but still more than most other populated areas of Mali. Isolation negatively affects income, putting Manantali at a comparative disadvantage. With high transport costs, it will be difficult if not impossible to market fresh fish and vegetables outside the area.

The comparative virtues of the PRM derive from the decision to resettle people as communities in a region where the environment permits the reestablishment of the major component--bush fallow cultivation—of the prior production system. Its principal shortcomings are the lack of a coherent development program both to provide a basis for self-sustaining growth and to compensate for the herding, hunting, and foraging components of the production systems that were compromised.

## Autonomy and Participation

Although resettlement following dam construction is by definition in-voluntary, the success of the relocation depends in large part on active participation of the settlers. Not only does participation facilitate identification with the move and lessen the dependency so common in these projects, it provides the project with sound information critical to management. The PRM sought local participation, but only partially achieved it. Local participation was significantly greater in planning than in implementation.

Participation in planning was relatively high. Villagers were consulted about where they wanted to live, and when potential sites had adequate land

and water and did not cause conflict with hosts or other settlers, their wishes were followed, even where disputes within a village meant that several new sites had to be found and developed. Villagers were consulted about the forms of compensation. Representatives from each village were bused to the site of the Selingué dam in southern Mali to visualize what would actually occur. This site visit to Selingué was extremely successful in persuading people that their homes and fields would indeed be lost to the deep lake that will form in the valley of what was once a free-flowing river.

The degree of participation declined markedly during implementation, in large part because of the very tight time frame within which the construction of new villages and clearing of new fields needed to be accomplished. Although USAID had agreed in principle to fund the resettlement as early as 1979, the project paper was not released until 1984, and further time elapsed while a contractor was selected and installed at Manantali, about a year later than planned. Meanwhile, dam construction proceeded according to schedule, the construction consortium receiving bonuses for timely completion of work. USAID, GRM, and PRM being therefore under great pressure to make up for lost time, decisions were made quickly with only partial information and very limited local participation, despite the excellent intentions lining all paths to Manantali. In addition, USAID appeared from time to time to regret its agreement to provide for the resettlement, and was wary of any act that could be interpreted as deepening its commitment to so remote a region of Mali. This may have resulted in a more "hands-off" oversight than is customary for the Agency. A diminution of local participation may have been one of the costs of USAID's management style. The highly authoritarian top-down management style of the GRM received minimal donor challenge. Indeed, it was only the SSS that tried to maintain local involvement throughout the project.

Yet the people took their participation during the planning stage seriously and insisted on playing important roles during implementation. This was encouraged by the SSS, which kept open communication and liaison with the population throughout the resettlement. SSS personnel lived in the villages and in direct contact with the people, and village representatives showed up regularly at SSS headquarters and were received by its director. The strategy led to a certain ad hoc negotiated quality of some of the implementation decisions and was later regretted by some project administrators who wanted more consistent policies. But, on the whole, the attitude of the PRM was clearly preferable to that shown by some of the central Malian administration who felt that the relocatees should simply follow orders they were given.

The people attempted to manipulate the government political system in their favor. In 1979 for the first time since the 1968 military coup, Mali reestablished a political party, and a national assembly followed several years later. Elected representatives as well as party officials were interested in building local constituencies in typical electoral fashion (even in this one-party state). For reasons beyond the scope of this paper, there is a rivalry between the political (the party, its officials and delegates) and administrative branches of the Malian government (the bureaucracy). In Manantali, people tried to use the party to ameliorate the deleterious effects of the resettlement project, which they viewed as caused by the administrators. The party, anxious to build a loyal constituency, held meetings in the region and listened to complaints, but acted in Bamako, the capital, in the interests of a variety of constituencies. Ultimately, many Bafingois decided that the actions taken in the capital were not particularly in their interests, but what is noteworthy is that they themselves remained participants at heart. Excluded from formal access to project implementation, they did what they could to influence it in their behalf. This was deeply resented by project administrators who felt betrayed, since they had assessed themselves as acting always in the interests of the relocatees. They did not appreciate that the *process* of participation was evaluated by the people to be at least equal to the material benefits provided by PRM. It was a measure of the project's early effects in showing people that the administration would listen that led them to approach their political representatives.

The findings from Manantali suggest the desirability of maximum local participation in resettlement projects. Open lines of communication and willing administrators are not sufficient. Participation takes time, time to build consensus, and time to make clear and consistent policy decisions. Manantali did not have time, in part because bureaucratic procedures took precedence over the goals of participation and smooth resettlement. The delays caused by cumbersome bureaucratic requirements of both the donor and the host government resulted in a panicked implementation phase. In a frantic race against the rising waters people were moved into only partially and often poorly constructed housing. Experience at Manantali reaffirms the importance of adequate lead time for resettlement planning and implementation based on genuine local participation.

### Development Infrastructure

Infrastructure adequate for economic development is largely absent in Manantali. Although OMVS and its member states are committed to large-scale development of the Senegal Valley, little of that is planned for Manantali. The benefits of the dam—irrigation, navigation, and hydropower—if they occur, will involve areas far downstream and areas, like Dakar, outside the Valley altogether. The transmission lines may begin at Manantali, but none of its residents are likely to enjoy electricity.[7] Manantali's isolation, the readiness of some donors to argue that the Selingué dam generates enough electricity to serve the capital city of Bamako, and the fact that the Niger Valley and the area south and east of the capital are preferred for development by donors and the GRM, render it a very low priority backwater for investment. USAID conceived its resettlement project as a humanitarian action, with welfare rather than development the objective. In the competition for donor attention, Manantali is not seen as having a persuasive case, though the GRM, in pursuit of its desire to dredge the river and build port facilities at Kayes, is now asking donors to investigate the possibility of mineral exploitation in western Mali. Should commercially exploitable quantities of minerals be discovered, some attention would focus on the region of the Bafing. Donors might also invest in gravity-fed irrigation, just downstream of the Manantali Dam.

Funding decisions by both AID and the GRM are informed in large part by the relatively small amounts of money each controls for development, and they have decided to invest those funds elsewhere. In the absence of important mineral discoveries, the prospects for development in the Manantali region are remote. The region is marginal to the OMVS, marginal to its own national government, and marginal to the donors. The losses endured by the people involuntarily resettled from the reservoir area of the Manantali Dam appear unlikely, at present, ever to be adequately compensated.

## Conclusions

Brokensha (1962; 1968), Scudder (1981; 1988) and Cernea (1987; 1988) have defined the conditions under which involuntary resettlement can be carried out compassionately and can be associated with sustainable development leading to improved income and living standards for relocated populations. The Manantali project illustrates the aptness of their findings.

### Planning

The Manantali Resettlement Project shows the need for holistic planning of resettlement projects, requiring changes in planning strategy at both local and national-regional levels.

At the local level, resettlement planners should have a greater appreciation of the diversity of productive resources. Although they considered major resources in Manantali, they ignored supplementary resources, which meant that "women's" resources (e.g., gathered foods, kitchen gardens) were often ignored. Livestock were also considered peripheral in the region as planners defined the people as "farmers", not herders. An understanding of production should take many resources into account and should be based on field investigations and extended discussions with all groups of the local population.

More explicit consideration should be given to which specific opportunities might be lost, and to how those losses might be compensated by new opportunities.

The PRM was highly planned, almost to the last brick. Some have suggested that it was overplanned. But what was needed was planning of a different kind. The project's concern for relocation concentrated on the material conditions of the new villages, and included very little concern with conditions of economic production. Resettlement was seen more as the technical problem of rebuilding than as the process of maintaining and improving a standard of living. The people could have been given more responsibility for building their own homes, or at least given the choice of either building themselves or having them built by the project, whereas the project relied on external contractors for the work, the quality of which was questioned in the project midterm evaluation (USAID 1987). Preproject studies that revealed the complex nature of the existing production system were slighted, and only the more visible agricultural component of the system was understood by the donor and by project administration. Even the agricultural component is likely to suffer from inadequate allocation of land, and, as we have noted, lands in close proximity to the new villages are being colonized by affluent families.

The need for holistic analysis was even greater at the regional and national levels. Planners gave little consideration to the role Manantali might play in the larger economy, seemingly in the hopes that some as yet unidentified donor would assume responsibility for its development.

A recognition of the region's low national and regional priority should have led to resettlement planning specifically geared around local self-sufficiency. Despite reference to Scudder's work in the Project Paper, no economic development activity was considered, although the newly productive fishery was an obvious arena for planning, as were new agricultural activities, including recession cultivation during the reservoir drawdown in upstream villages.

## Implementation

When time becomes a constraint, local participation is sacrificed. It is too late to begin planning for resettlement when dam completion is imminent.

The greater time span must be accompanied by a more explicitly "process oriented" rather than a blueprint approach to implementation. Not only does this allow the local population more continuous input into project decision making, but it also allows the project to adapt to changing circumstances. The contingencies in resettlement projects are high, and both project administrators and the local population must be free to adapt. An ad hoc quality to decisions is probably unavoidable.

Finally, project administrators should recognize that people will participate (or attempt to participate) in ways unforeseen, often in ways seen by project administrators as counter-productive. The nature of resettlement is so traumatic that even with a high degree of participation, people are likely to feel that they have lost control of their world (as in reality they have). Even a sympathetic project administration is likely to be perceived with hostility by those who are losing their homes. While we appreciate the sense of "betrayal" felt by those who have worked hard on behalf of the local population, they should understand that the seeking of alternative instruments to increase what little control people have is a healthy and natural response, to be encouraged and celebrated rather than attacked.

In the spectrum of recent resettlement efforts associated with river-basin development, Manantali probably ranks among the best because the people had to move relatively short distances (from a few to perhaps 60 kilometers), in village units, within their own political, cultural, and ecological region. While we predict land shortages will become important in the next decade (due both to population increase and to greater density in much of the resettlement zone), land is at present adequate for the reestablishment of bush fallowing, although it lacks adequate resources for animal husbandry, hunting, and foraging.

We fault the project for its insufficient attention to participation during implementation and to the lack of a coherent development program that would compensate for lost resources and improve the income and conditions of life of the largest number of settlers, both host and relocatees.

## Acknowledgments

Through the USAID-funded Cooperative Agreement in Settlement and Resource Systems Analysis (SARSA), the Institute carried out research on the resettlement effort at Manantali. The authors wish to acknowledge the continuing interest in the inquiry from Mr. Yacouba Konate, then head of the Project's social and monitoring office, now a graduate student in development anthropology at SUNY Binghamton. Views expressed herein are those of the authors, and not of AID or any individual acting on its behalf.

The authors gratefully acknowledge Mr. Curt Grimm, who assisted in the preparation of the paper, and Mr. Jean LeBloas, who provided good critical commentary.

## Notes

1. The following list summarizes the acronyms used in this chapter.

| | |
|---|---|
| ECBM | Entreprise de Construction du Barrage de Manantali |
| EEC | European Economic Community |
| GRM | Government of the Republic of Mali (Gouvernement de la République de Mali) |
| IDA | Institute for Development Anthropology |
| ISH | Institut des Sciences Humaines |
| OMVS | Organisation pour la Mise en Valeur du Fleuve Sénégal (Senegal River-Basin Authority) |
| PRM | Projet pour la Réinstallation des Populations de Manantali. Also known as MRP (Manantali Resettlement Project.) |
| RPU | Resettlement Project Unit |
| SARSA | Settlement and Resource Systems Analysis Cooperative Agreement between Clark University and IDA |
| SSS | Section Sociale et du Suivi (Social and Monitoring Section) of the PRM |
| UNDP | United Nations Development Programme |
| USAID | United States Agency for International Development |
| WFP | World Food Program |

2. In fact, villagers were not provided with materials by the project. They were given cash compensation for lost granaries and latrines, and had to provide their own materials and construction for corrals and chicken coops.

3. A variety of IDA personnel were involved in the Manantali Resettlement Project, supervision and coordination of which were done jointly by the authors who made regular visits to Mali through the course of the project. In addition, IDA codirector Thayer Scudder offered the benefit of his river-basin-development and resettlement experience on several visits to the project under the auspices of SARSA/IDA's African River-Basin Project, as did Muneera Salem-Murdock, the Institute's senior research associate with extensive settlement experience in Sudan and Tunisia. IDA field researcher Curt Grimm was in Manantali for 22 months during the major resettlement activities. Finally, the Institute provided two experts in computerized information management to assist the SSS in appropriate technology for handling data for monitoring and eventual evaluation.

4. Before the construction of the dam, Malinké comprised some 95 percent of the population of the region. Something less than 3 percent were FulBe, often hired by Malinké villagers as herders, occasionally as Q'oranic teachers. The remainder were a few Bambara, Khassonké, and Soninké. The construction phase brought in large numbers of outsiders, some hired by ECBM (Entreprise de Construction du Barrage de Manantali) charged with building the dam, some national and international civil servants and development specialists, and others, like Mauritanian shopkeepers and a large number of prostitutes, coming in as independent entrepreneurs. As the reservoir fills, and many of the officials and foreign construction workers leave, Bozo and Somono fishermen from other parts of Mali, some with experience in the Selingué reservoir, are settling upstream of the dam to exploit the new resource. There has been very little systematic examination of the socioeconomic impacts of this kind of spontaneous resettlement in association with involuntary relocation.

5. The first group of pumps installed were quickly corroded by the high mineral content of water in some of the villages, and stainless steel cores had to be imported from France.

6. Agricultural resettlement projects frequently require settlers to farm a specific inventory of crops, utilizing defined techniques, and even monopsonistic marketing institutions. (For a detailed description of this kind of directed settlement, see Salem-Murdock [1989].)

7. Indeed, if the recommendations of the World Bank (Anderson 1987) are followed, electricity will be the single product of Manantali, whose waters are deemed too precious to be used even for downstream irrigation let alone flood recession cultivation, and the sole consumers of that power will be residents of Dakar, Senegal.

## References Cited

Anderson, Dennis.
    1987    Scope of Tariff and Project Justification Studies. Prepared by the World Bank (WAPDR) for the OMVS.
Brokensha, David W.
    1962    Volta Resettlement. Legon, Ghana (mimeo).
    1963–4  Volta Resettlement and Anthropological Research. Human Organization 22(4):286–290.
    1968    Resettlement. *In* Dams in Africa: An Interdisciplinary Study of Man-Made Lakes in Africa. N. Rubin and W. W. Warren, eds. New York: Augustus M. Kelley Publishers.

Cernea, Michael.
1987 Social Issues in Involuntary Resettlement Processes: Policy Guidelines and Operational Procedures in World Bank-Financed Projects. Washington, DC: The World Bank.
1988 Involuntary Resettlement in Development Projects: Policy Guidelines in World Bank-Financed Projects. Technical Paper No. 80. Washington, DC: The World Bank.
Groupement Manantali.
1978 Etude d'Exécution du Barrage et de l'Usine Hydroélectrique de Manantali. Rapport Final. Mission A.1.14 Recasement des Populations. OMVS: Dakar, Senegal.
Salem-Murdock, Muneera.
1989 Arabs and Nubians in New Halfa: A Study of Settlement and Irrigation. Salt Lake City: University of Utah Press.
Samake, Maximin, M. Sow, M. Sarr, F. Maiga, and B. Camara.
1987 Etude de l'Economie Domestique dans la Zone du Barrage de Manantali. Phase IV et V. Bamako: Institut des Sciences Humaines.
Scudder, Thayer.
1981 The Development Potential of New Lands Settlement in the Tropics and Subtropics: A Global State of the Art Evaluation with Specific Emphasis on Policy Implications. Binghamton, NY: Institute for Development Anthropology.
1988 The African Experience with River-Basin Development: Achievements to Date, the Role of Institutions, and Strategies for the Future. Binghamton, NY: Institute for Development Anthropology.
USAID (United States Agency for International Development).
1984 Project Paper: Mali Manantali Resettlement Project (625-0955). Washington, DC: USAID.
1987 Manantali Resettlement Project: Mid-Term Evaluation Draft Report, March 1987. Bamako: USAID.

# 6

## Participatory Development and African Women: A Case Study from Western Kenya

*Miriam S. Chaiken*

In much recent development related research and program design, planners have failed to adequately recognize the degree of social and economic heterogeneity in rural populations, and have assumed, incorrectly I believe, that rural people are uniformly cooperative. Many social scientists identify institutions or behaviors (e.g. leveling mechanisms), or an ideology or "moral economy" (Scott 1976) which results in cooperation among rural peasants. This assumption of cooperation can be problematic if it results in development programs that depend upon tight community cohesion and consistent participation of the whole population.

This problem persists despite efforts by anthropologists to emphasize the diversity of rural communities, the complexities of indigenous social structure, and the existence of economic, social, and gender-based inequality in seemingly homogeneous populations (see Castro, Hakansson, and Brokensha 1981; Eder 1982; Hay 1976; Price 1984). The problem is particularly true of development efforts in Africa, a continent which is characterized by marked differences between ethnic groups, and which has been the primary target of development activities in the past decade. Yet the classic anthropological studies of earlier in the 20th century, notably the works of E.E. Evans-Pritchard (1940; 1950), Monica Wilson (1951), Max Gluckman (1956), Aidan Southall (1952), and Meyer Fortes (1949) all attempted to illustrate both the divisive and cohesive aspects of indigenous social structure in Africa. More recently, the development oriented anthropological research of David Brokensha (Brokensha et al. 1980; Riley and Brokensha 1988; Brokensha and Little 1988), Thayer Scudder (1981), Elizabeth Colson (1971), and many others has examined how traditional institutions and social structure are changing as societies are incorporated into the world market economy, and as a result of national development policies.

This paper examines the context of community cooperation and the ways in which it is changing, and the importance of understanding indigenous social structure for successful rural development planning in Africa. Specifically, I argue that assumptions of cooperation among rural people, especially as they are applied to women, do not reflect the social reality. The social obstacles to cooperation among rural women in East Africa have not often been recognized, and the implications of this for programs of participatory development are profound.

## Background to the Research Project

This case study is based on research conducted among the Nilotic Luo people of Western Kenya, who live along the shores of Lake Victoria. The conclusions are based on three years' research on issues of economic development in western Kenya, including a recent series of key informant interviews which specifically focused on the networks between and support for women.[1]

Although the traditional Luo were primarily a cattle keeping people, in the past century rainfed hoe agriculture has become the main subsistence activity, with most of the labor provided by women. A gender-based division of labor has continued, even though the economic activities have changed; women continue to bear the primary responsibility for subsistence agriculture, while men have moved from herding to other economic activities. The viability of livestock herding has declined as grazing lands have diminished, in part due to increased population density and land adjudication. Now few families have more than five cattle (Conelly n.d.; Conelly and Chaiken 1987), and the great herds which once characterized the Luo are all but gone. In response, many Luo men have turned to small-scale commercial fishing and wage labor as an alternate source of employment (Hay 1976).

Most of the recent research among the Luo has focused on issues of health care delivery or agricultural development (Chaiken 1987; 1988a; 1988b; Conelly 1987; 1988; n.d.; Johnson 1980; Pala Okeyo 1979a; 1979b; Rubin 1986; 1988; Shipton 1988) as the area is one of the least developed in Kenya outside the arid and semi-arid zones (CBS 1983). Other related research, has addressed the position of women and the functioning of women's groups, (Carroll n.d.; Hay 1976; Muzaale and Leonard 1982) and suggests that initial efforts to increase agricultural production or local incomes through the medium of women's groups has had limited success. I argue that the ineffectiveness of women's groups noted by other social scientists, is in part due to the lack of understanding by development planners of community heterogeneity and social dynamics. The complexity of social relations and social inequality in Luo villages can be attributed to the rapid changes of recent decades and to their system of post-marital patrilocal residence which results in the dispersal of women and the dissolution of cooperative bonds between them. I argue that this has created obstacles to the effective functioning of women's groups and prospects for participatory development among the Luo.

## Traditions of Self-Help and Cooperation
## Between Women

Among the Luo, as with most patrilineal groups in East Africa, when women marry they leave their natal homes and take up residence with their husband's family. In the postmarital community, the couple reside in the compound of the husband's father and are surrounded by comparable households of patrilineally related kin termed a *gweng*. A *gweng* was described by Southall (1952:25) as a corporate landholding patrilineage (generally consisting of about 300 people), as well as the piece of land they occupied. Traditionally the *gweng* was governed by a council of elders who were able to influence major decisions such as marriages and land allocation. Social inequality was based on age, gender, and accumulation of wealth (both cattle and wives), and the council of elders was composed exclusively of senior men who had amassed substantial resources and status.

Recent reductions in clan authority have not altered the tendency for Luo women to change residence after marriage.[2] Women spend most of their lives as members of their husband's community, whether or not the husband is resident for most of these years. Frequent migration of men to urban centers for employment has resulted in many women acting as *de facto* farm and household managers in the absence of their husbands (Conelly and Chaiken 1987; Hay 1976; Moock 1976).

Women provide most of the labor for agriculture and are central to production in these rural areas. It is no surprise, then, that development programs intended to improve agricultural productivity and incomes are increasingly, and appropriately, directed towards women in Western Kenya. These projects have generally taken the form of financial endowments bestowed upon women's groups to allow them to initiate an income generating activity. Occasionally projects involve selecting representatives from various women's groups and training them on appropriate topics (nutrition and child feeding practices, construction of fuel saving devices, etc.), with the expectation that these women will serve as "trainers" for the rest of the group. The probability of success in these types of assistance programs is diminished by assumptions of consistent cooperation between women in rural areas. My evidence suggests that the patterns of cooperation and support between Luo women are minimal, and perhaps declining, and that this has contributed to the marginal functioning of women's groups and other forms of participatory development.

For example, in a survey of participation in twenty women's groups which I conducted in South Nyanza District in 1985, several recurrent problems emerged in the analysis of women's groups as vehicles for development (Chaiken 1985:28ff). First, most of the women's groups which are found among the Luo are newly established (less than five years old), and although they have long membership rosters, they have only a few active members. Second, the history of their efforts at income generation have not been successful. Typical reports of the history of women's groups financial ventures include the following:

(1) two different women's groups have tried to begin bee keeping. The first group has apparently harvested only four bottles of honey in the past three years. The second group reported variously that the bees had refused to take up residence in the hives, or that someone had poisoned the bees.

(2) A third group received a gift of a sewing machine which they intended to use to start manufacturing and selling clothes. Now, several years later the machine sits idle and few members know how to use it. Reportedly when visitors from the donor organization arrive, the women borrow clothes made by a local tailor and have him sit at their machine to give the impression that it is actively being used.

(3) A fourth group received a large donation over two years ago to establish a poultry keeping project. The poultry shed has been completed, but there has yet to be a chicken placed in the coop. Problems which this group has encountered include concern about access to and funds for chicken feed, difficulty in accounting for the money to the sponsoring organization, internal conflicts between members, and interference from local administrators unhappy with the women's actions and decisions (Chaiken 1985:29–30).

It is no wonder that when women in this survey were asked whether they expected their women's group to improve their lives, most voiced doubts.[3]

Finally, most of the women who participate in women's groups, including the officers, have little formal education, little entrepreneurial experience, and little experience outside their own home areas. They have heard reports of successful women's group projects in other places, but know little of the failure of projects, nor do they know about the dynamics of successful groups. They have no experience with managing a cooperative venture, few skills which will allow them to assess the feasibility of a project, and little internal cohesion.

More recently a series of key informant interviews (N=10) elicited information from selected women in Siaya District on the history of their participation in cooperative labor groups.[4] When asked whether they were participating in any form of labor exchange or cooperative labor group at the present time, nine of the ten said no and one participated in a newly formed group (only a few months old) which is intended to rotate around to do weeding in different members' fields.

The sample women unanimously reported a decline in mutual assistance between women for agricultural tasks, though most said that at some time in the past they had participated in a cooperative group.[5] They noted that in the past a woman could provide a meal, which would be sufficient incentive to encourage lineage members to come and assist in the fields. Now they report that other people, even members of their husband's kin group, will not assist in agricultural labor unless they are paid in cash; reciprocal obligation is insufficient to attract labor.

Informants report a similar perception of declining mutual assistance among members of a clan. When asked what influence the clan currently has on their life or their work, four women replied that the clan had no influence, and four said that clan members could be expected to assist with funeral expenses, but nothing more.[6] Eight of the ten women reported that forms of mutual assistance between clan members had declined significantly in their lifetimes, most notably reporting that in the past clan members would contribute towards the bridewealth of a young man who wished to marry, that they would contribute money or food for needed expenses (e.g. school fees), that they would freely give labor, and that they allowed unrestricted grazing on communally held lands. These forms of assistance have largely disappeared, with only the residual responsibilities in cases of death remaining.

The two dissenting women who felt that clan support had either remained the same or increased in their lifetimes implied that poverty had forced them to become more interdependent. To paraphrase one woman, "the clan has come together more because we need to assist each other more, we do not have the resources to be independent."

Although it would be nice to assume that difficult conditions will bring people together, most women do not seem to hold this view of the current situation. Those respondents who were able to posit an explanation for declining mutual assistance linked this change with the growing importance of cash. They said that people now need cash to survive, and thus they must refuse to provide assistance unless a cash remuneration is received. One woman reported, "Money has spoiled people, everyone just wants their own things and does not want to share, and people are jealous of those who have more than they do".

This pattern of minimal intragroup support is significant when we consider that many current strategies for development rely on self-help and mutual assistance (Cernea 1985; Chambers 1983; Gran 1983). Many participatory development programs involve local people identifying targets for improvement, defining means of achieving specified goals, and then receiving financial assistance to implement the projects they design. In particular, many current programs aimed at improving agriculture, afforestation, or nutrition rely on organizations such as women's groups to implement these programs.[7] Many agencies have made a naive assumption that rural people always cooperate with each other—yet the conditions among the Luo suggest that the factors which formerly facilitated cooperation between women have largely disappeared due to the rapid social change of recent decades. The discrepancy between the goal of participatory development programs and the social realities have gone unnoticed. Simply put, there is little ground upon which cooperative relationships can be built, and in fact the recent changes are more likely to create competition between people rather than cooperation.

### Historical Patterns and Declining Mutual Assistance Between Women

There is some evidence to suggest that recent social structural changes have contributed to the low levels of cooperation among Luo women. In the past, there appear to have been frequent inter-marriages between affiliated residential clans, which would have contributed to maintaining the kinship linkages between women following marriage. In this segmentary lineage system each descent group (*gweng*) had especially strong ties with a few comparable groups, which were reinforced by intermarriage, while other groups stood in opposition and intermarriage was prohibited (Ayot 1979; Southall 1952).

This pattern could be termed a type of wife exchange, in that affiliated clans might be perceived as wife-givers or wife-takers, but it should not be assumed that women were chattel without volition and without a voice in these arrangements. A structural feature often overlooked in androcentric views of such traditional marriage practices is that in addition to creating ties among men, they also perpetuate kin-based ties among women. In this case, if a number of women from one *gweng* married into another, although their residence would change after marriage, they would be living among their own female kin (especially aunts and nieces), members of their natal descent group in their post-marital community. This may be the key to understanding the integration of traditional cooperative groups, especially women's reciprocal agricultural labor groups, as the nucleus would be female consanguines who all married into the same residential descent group.

Support for this hypothesis comes from data collected in the series of key informant interviews conducted in Siaya District. Ten women reported the history of their marriage arrangements, and ranged in age from mid-twenties to early sixties (though eight were over 40, and thus had sufficient experience to have observed changes in their lifetimes). Seven of the ten women reportedly met their husbands through relatives; either the husband was visiting a female relative who had married into the woman's area, or the woman was visiting an aunt, cousin, or sister who had married into the husband's group. After the meeting, the young couple then discussed the possibility of marriage and an older relative, (usually the one who was responsible for the initial introduction) then acted as an intermediary between the parents of the couple to negotiate agreement and bridewealth payments.

The three cases which did not follow this pattern included the youngest two women in the sample, who met their husbands in a neutral area (Nairobi in one case, and at a sports festival in another), and a third woman, non-Luo and originally from Tanzania, who met her husband when he worked in Tanzania for the East African Railways. Although the sample size is small, these data suggest that a common marriage arrangement for women over forty years of age was to meet a man through previous marriage connections between the two families, and for the arrangements to be confirmed with the assistance of an intermediary who was related to one of the two parties.

When the key informants were asked whether there were any women already living in their post-marital residence who had come from the woman's natal descent group, the results confirm the importance of kin ties between women. The two women under forty had no female relatives living in the area when they arrived, nor did any female relatives later marry into the same *gweng* after they became established. But the women over 40 (N=8) had between them a total of sixteen female relatives (sisters, aunts, nieces, and cousins) who had previously married into their husbands' *gweng*, and they were followed in the successive years by another twelve female relatives who later married into the area.

The significance of this structural pattern for relations among women has gone unrecognized. These networks between women may be the key to understanding the efficacy of traditional cooperative labor groups among the Luo, especially for agricultural labor which is predominantly performed by women.

This pattern of systematic inter-group marriages appears to have diminished in recent decades, with increased commercialization of labor and increased labor mobility of young men. It has become common for young men to spend a good portion of their youth living away from their natal families, either while pursuing a secondary or trade school education or while working in cities and towns. As a consequence of their wage employment, many young men enjoy substantial financial independence from the older generation.

During traditional times a young man worked at the behest of his father and only married with the permission and assistance of his father and close patrilineal relatives, as normally it would have been impossible for a young man to mobilize sufficient reserves to make bridewealth contributions without the support of his extended family. Today it is common for young people to marry without the express permission of the older generation, and often bridewealth payments do not precede marriage, are lower than in the past, and are primarily the responsibility of the young men, rather than the extended patrilineal group.[8]

The mobility of young people and the financial independence which has permitted the establishment of marriages which are not arranged by the extended family has the result that the young wives in any residential descent group originate from many different areas. Rather than marriages being established due to long-term inter-*gweng* relationships, modern brides now rarely find women from their own natal groups in their post-marital communities, and instead are among strangers when they move to their husbands' village.

When discussing changes in marriage practices, key informants unanimously reported that in the past it was common for several women from one natal group to marry into another, thus maintaining the kinship links between women. They also unanimously agreed that this rarely occurs any longer, that women find themselves among strangers after marriage. When asked to explain this change, most women cited the increased mobility of young men and women due to education and jobs, they said that the "girls meet husbands on their own", and they cited a loss of trust between people as contributing to this phenomenon. Their assessments of this include statements such as:

> Now boys and girls meet at school and decide to get married, they are not looking at what the family has [the wealth of the husband's family], which was important to older people.

> These marriages [in which a relative acts as an intermediary] are not common because people do not want the responsibility of being an intermediary. What

if you recommend a man but when he is in Nairobi he is a drunkard, you may not know this side of his character. If you introduce a girl to him she will blame you for her bad marriage.

People are not honest any more, a woman may try to persuade a girl to marry a certain man in her [post-marital] home, but she [the intermediary] may try to hide character flaws of the man, maybe he drinks or maybe he will not pay the bridewealth even if he says he will.

The linkages between women have declined at the same time that clans have lost their power to influence marriage arrangements, bridewealth negotiations, or land use rights. The mobility of the younger generation, the increasing importance of cash, land adjudication, and individual titling of land holdings have all undermined the traditional influence of the patrilineage elders. This may also have contributed to a decline in the systems of mutual support and assistance between women, the kin-based relationships between women, and the traditional cooperative labor arrangements.

## Participatory Development: Realities and Ideals

The stagnation and low productivity of agriculture in Luo areas may in part be explained by the shift in patterns of labor allocation described above. Certainly this factor alone is not sufficient to account for all of the problems in agriculture and nutrition among the Luo; they must also contend with marginal agricultural potential, declining viability of cattle-keeping (and consequently less milk), and the effects of overpopulation resulting in shorter fallow periods and declining soil fertility (Conelly and Chaiken 1987; Jaetzold and Schmidt 1982). But the ability to mobilize cooperative labor is not insignificant, and the assumption of cooperation between people is implicit in many programs of rural development.

To some extent alternate forms of social cooperation have replaced the traditional kin-based systems, but it is questionable whether they are as effective as the traditional groups. When asked whether they participated in any type of women's group, clan based cooperative group, church group, or other cooperative association, the key informants report only minor reliance on these forms of assistance. Most of the women do not currently belong to any cooperative group, although two of them had belonged to women's groups which had "collapsed". The first group reportedly collapsed due to the financial mismanagement of the chairwoman, the second group was established by CARE to promote afforestation, but reportedly ceased functioning when CARE ended its financial commitment.

Of the four key informants who do currently participate in some form of cooperative group, all of them belong to a church based group which requires members to make contributions to a pool which is used to offset funeral expenses.[9] Two women also participate in informal women's groups, the first is a well established rotating credit association with seven members (two of whom are members of her own natal *gweng*) which does not require any labor contribution, but only a weekly cash commitment of thirty shillings (slightly less than two dollars). The second group has only been functioning a few months and is composed of six women who are all married into a single *gweng* who plan to help each other with weeding in their fields. While not wanting to appear cynical, the past history of women's groups in Western Kenya suggests that it is too soon to count this group as a success.

## Prospects for Participatory Development

This discussion is not meant to imply that there is no future in participatory development in western Kenya. However such development programs must address the social realities and recognize that the social implications of contemporary patrilineal postmarital residence patterns means that women are not likely to forge strong bonds between them. Luo women have all of the responsibilities that they have always had (providing subsistence for their children, contributing the majority of the agricultural labor, maintaining a household), but they increasingly lack the means to fulfill these responsibilities. They have less land available, many fewer traditional foods (most notably milk and blood), the land which they do farm is not allowed sufficient time to fallow, and they no longer have some of the cooperative labor groups which eased the burden of work and provided social support. Women have become more socially isolated, and thus should be perceived as having less opportunity to have a united voice in programs of participatory development.

Development agencies, whether national social service agencies, international donor organizations, multilateral organizations such as UNICEF, or private volunteer organizations have all viewed the establishment of women's groups as the panacea for development problems in western Kenya. They have generally assumed that once a group is established, it should be able to initiate and manage cooperative income generation and education programs if external sources of seed money are provided. Their concern with reaching women and assisting in their efforts to be better providers for their families is laudable, but the means they have selected to achieve this goal is perhaps misguided.

Programs of participatory development will not succeed if they fail to recognize the constraints which limit participation of local people. In this example, the changes in social structure resulting in the decline of support networks between women, the increasing commercialization of labor, the limitations of farm size and productivity, and the limited education of most rural women combine to explain the history of failure of women's groups and women's participation in development. If programs of participatory development are sincere in their wish to incorporate women into the process, and to specifically target women as recipients of development assistance, then several modifications in approach will be required.

First, programs must be cognizant of the fact that rural populations are not homogeneous, nor are they inherently cooperative. Thus programs must seek either to build new systems of support and mutual interdependence between participants, or conversely, abandon the group approach and develop opportunities which can be capitalized upon by individuals rather than depending upon group action. The first approach might be accomplished by providing management training for women, to teach members of women's groups the skills necessary for conducting a feasibility study, and implementing and managing a project. It is important to provide all women access to such knowledge and skills, not just a representative of the group charged with transmitting this information to others, as is common in the "Training of Trainers" approach.

Women's group projects would have to be designed to have built in fall back arrangements to compensate for nonparticipation by some members (or "free riders", see Erasmus 1977), and project benefits should accrue to members in proportion to their level of contribution. For example, rather than promoting projects in which women collectively manage an income generation activity (like poultry keeping), projects would first concentrate on helping women help each other, by establishing rotating credit organizations, rotating agricultural labor pools, etc. If these early efforts to rebuild cooperation between women are successful, then more ambitious plans for collective management of entrepreneurial activities can be explored.

Conversely, development assistance could acknowledge the declining interdependence of women and seek to provide opportunities equally to individuals, ignoring the group as a vehicle for development assistance. This approach might be more in keeping with current capitalist oriented notions of development through individual initiative and competition, but it would be likely to exacerbate already serious levels of economic and social inequality— as certain individuals are more able to capitalize upon these opportunities. Such individualized approaches to development assistance might utilize groups simply as purchasing cooperatives, to obtain inputs (fertilizer, chicken feed, improved seed, etc.) at a lower cost, while allowing each individual to manage their resources independently. The failure of one individual would not then necessarily have a deleterious impact on the rest of the group.

Anthropologists have long argued that development plans must be tailored to local conditions, to vary according to local needs, and programs of participatory development to some extent reflect this growing concern within development agencies. However, the implementation of participatory development has sometimes failed to acknowledge variation between groups or divisiveness and inequality within a group. If women are to be included in development planning and assistance in a meaningful way, recognition of factors which constrain their participation and their ability to take advantage of such programs must be acknowledged. While the conditions described among the Luo may not apply to all patrilineal groups in East Africa, the situation warrants further examination, and greater anthropological sensitivity among the planners of development assistance.

## Acknowledgments

Many people contributed to this article, either through their support of the field research upon which it is based, or through their insightful comments on earlier drafts of this work. The ideas expressed in this article were first formulated while I was conducting a baseline socioeconomic survey for UNICEF in South Nyanza, and these themes were explored in more detail during research made possible by a Pennsylvania State System of Higher Education Faculty Development Grant and the a faculty research grant from Indiana University of Pennsylvania. The research was conducted in collaboration with the Title XII Small Ruminant Collaborative Research Support Program under Grant No. AID/DSN/SII-G-0049 and special thanks are due to the SR-CRSP staff in Kenya, Drs. Moses Onim, Patterson Semenye, and Nkonge Mbabu, and at the University of Missouri, the Department of Rural Sociology and Dr. Michael Nolan.

Actual field work was carried out with the invaluable assistance of Mrs. Joyce Ouma, Mrs. Karen Atieno Odede, Mr. George Okoth Ambogo, and most especially, Miss Gawdensia Juma Odhiambo. For their assistance in providing comments on drafts of this paper or participating in the stimulating discussions which preceded it, I would like to thank Peter Castro, Thomas Conelly, Anne Fleuret, Thomas Hakansson, and Deborah Rubin.

## Notes

1. My initial research was conducted for UNICEF in South Nyanza district, followed by a year's residence in the town of Kisumu, while I conducted several short-term research projects. I first became aware of the relationship between changes in the social structure and impact on women's groups while working in South Nyanza, but did not systematically examine this issue until recently. Supplemental research was conducted in Siaya district, the northernmost reaches of Luoland in which I conducted a series of in-depth key informant interviews in conjunction with the long term research project of the SR-CRSP farming systems program. While my sample of key informants is small, I think these women are reporting trends and patterns which prevail throughout Luoland.

2. An interesting example of the viability of Luo clans and the nature of funeral obligations comes from the recent dispute over the burial of a prominent Luo lawyer, S.M. Otieno. Although Otieno had largely divorced himself from traditional Luo culture and lived exclusively in Nairobi, his death precipitated a bitter legal battle between members of his patrilineage and his widow (a non-Luo) over the choice of burial location. The clan was ultimately successful in their suit to have him buried on family land in his Luo homeland, and raised hundreds of thousands of shillings to cover the court costs and subsequent burial services. His funeral and visitation in Kisumu town (before his body was transferred to the clan home at Nyalgunga) were attended by thousands of mourners.

3. This pessimism expressed by Luo women contrasts with the situation elsewhere in Kenya, as evidenced in the article by Monica Udvardy in this volume. The situation reported for Luoland is not necessarily true elsewhere in Kenya, where many long established women's groups have experienced notable success (see Mwaniki 1986).

4. The key informants were selected from a larger, randomly chosen research population who had been participating in farming systems research undertaken as part of the Small Ruminant CRSP. The key informants were selected because of their history of cooperativeness and communicativeness, but care was taken to ensure that they fairly represented the total population by comparing previously collected data

on household economic status, domestic cycle, and current economic activities. My sense is that these women do represent the experiences of the majority in the community.

5. Johnson (1980) includes a wealth of information about the various levels of kin-based social organization and the segmentary lineage structure among the Luo and Abasuba. He identifies two kin-based groups which provide various types of mutual assistance, the *gwenge* and the *anyuola* (1980:72ff), and he notes that mutual assistance could take on many forms, but generally it involved assistance in agricultural labor in the fields of all members, or mobilizing funds or support for some member's needs (funeral, school fees, etc.).

6. One woman said that the other clan members would help with labor if she was very ill, and a second reported that her husband was old and infirm and that other men in the clan occasionally helped him, but only one woman reported that she received any regular or predictable assistance from clan members.

7. A separate question, which I will not examine here, is whether women really do have an opportunity to participate in planning "participatory" development programs. In my experience, most of these planning sessions are held at public meetings called by the local Chief or District Officer (both government appointed bureaucrats), and the women who attend such meetings are generally substantially outnumbered by men. Under such circumstances, given the prevailing gender-based inequality, women tend to remain passive participants and rarely express opinions or contradict the man who chairs the meeting.

8. The increasing self reliance and financial independence of young men has historically occurred at the same time the clans have declined in influence. It is difficult to say whether one of these phenomena precipitated the other, or whether they were both by-products of more sweeping processes of social change. Whatever the causal relationship, the net effect on the marriage patterns and subsequent status of women remains the same.

9. These are not burial societies in which members arrange for their own funerals, but rather help with financial support for any member who has experienced a death in the family. Luo funerals can be very expensive, as food must be offered to all mourners who attend the burial or the days of mourning which follow. Many families find the expense of feeding several hundred visitors difficult to bear, and these cooperative activities center on contributing toward these expenses.

## References Cited

Ayot, Henry Okello.
  1979   A History of the Luo-Abasuba of Western Kenya from A.D. 1760–1940. Kenya Literature Bureau: Nairobi.
Brokensha, David W., D.M. Warren, and Oswald Werner, eds.
  1980   Indigenous Knowledge Systems and Development. Lanham, MD: University Press of America.
Brokensha, David W. and Peter D. Little, eds.
  1988   Anthropology of Development and Change in East Africa. Boulder, CO: Westview Press.
Carroll, Helen.
  n.d.      personal communication.
Castro, Alfonso Peter, N. Thomas Hakansson, and David Brokensha.
  1981   Indicators of Rural Inequality. *In* World Development. 9(5):401–427.

Central Bureau of Statistics (CBS).
 1983    Third Rural Child Nutrition Survey. Nairobi: UNICEF and the Ministry
         of Finance and Planning. Republic of Kenya
Cernea, Michael M. ed.
 1985    Putting People First: Sociological Variables in Rural Development. published
         for the World Bank. New York: Oxford University Press.
Chaiken, Miriam S.
 1987    Community Based Development: Potential and Obstacles to Implementation
         in Western Kenya. Working Paper No. 447. Institute for Development
         Studies. University of Nairobi.
 1988a   Anthropology, Nutritional Surveillance, and the Design of Health Inter-
         ventions in Western Kenya. *In* Anthropology of Development and Change
         in East Africa. D.B. Brokensha and P.D. Little, eds. Pp. 237–250. Boulder:
         Westview Press.
 1988b   Household Resource Allocation and Food Security in Western Kenya. paper
         presented at the American Anthropological Association Meetings. Phoenix,
         AZ.
Chambers, Robert.
 1983    Rural Development: Putting the Last First. London: Longman Press.
Colson, Elizabeth.
 1971    The Social Consequences of Resettlement. Manchester, England: Manchester
         University Press.
Conelly, W. Thomas.
 1987    Perception and Management of Crop Pests Among Subsistence Farmers,
         South Nyanza District, Kenya. *In* Management of Pests and Pesticides:
         Farmers Perceptions and Practices. Joyce Tait and Banpot Napompeth, eds.
         Pp. 198–209. Boulder: Westview Press.
 1988    Insect and Weed Control in Subsistence Farming Systems: Western Kenya.
         *In* The Anthropology of Development and Change in East Africa. D. W.
         Brokensha and P. D. Little, eds. Pp. 121–136. Boulder: Westview Press.
 in prep Population Pressure and Changing Crop/Livestock Management Strategies
         in Western Kenya. *In* Plants, Animals, and People: Crop/Livestock Systems
         Research in the SR-CRSP Rural Sociology Program. Constance McCorkle,
         ed.
Conelly, W. Thomas and Miriam S. Chaiken.
 1987    Land, Labor, and Livestock: Impact of Intense Population Pressure on
         Nutrition in Western Kenya. paper presented at the American Anthropo-
         logical Association Meetings. Chicago, Ill.
Eder, James F.
 1982    Who Shall Succeed? Cambridge: Cambridge University Press.
Erasmus, Charles J.
 1977    In Search of the Common Good: Utopian Experiments Past and Future.
         New York: The Free Press.
Evans-Pritchard, E.E.
 1940    The Nuer. New York: Oxford University Press.
 1950    Kinship and the Local Community Among the Nuer. *In* African Systems
         of Kinship and Marriage. A.R. Radcliffe-Brown and Daryll Forde, eds. Pp.
         360–392. London: Oxford University Press.
Fortes, Meyer.
 1949    The Web of Kinship among the Tallensi. London: Oxford University Press.

Gluckman, Max.
1969    Custom and Conflict in Africa. New York: Barnes and Noble, Inc.
Gran, Guy.
1983    Development by People: Citizen Construction of a Just World. New York: Praeger Publishers.
Hay, Margaret Jean.
1976    Luo Women and Economic Change During the Colonial Period. *In* Women in Africa. Nancy J. Hafkin and Edna G. Bay, eds. Pp. 87–109. Stanford, CA: Stanford University Press.
Jaetzold, R. and H. Schmidt.
1982    Farm Management Handbook of Kenya. Vol. IIA (Nyanza and Western Provinces). Nairobi: Ministry of Agriculture, Republic of Kenya in cooperation with the German Agency for Technical Cooperation.
Johnson, Steven Lee.
1980    Production, Exchange, and Economic Development among the Luo-Abasuba of Southwestern Kenya. unpublished Ph.D. dissertation. Bloomington, ID: Dept. of Anthropology. Indiana University.
Moock, Peter.
1976    The Efficiency of Women as Farm Managers: Kenya. American Journal of Agricultural Economics. 58(5).
Muzaale, Patrick J. with David Leonard.
1982    Women's Groups and Extension in Kenya: Their Impact on Food Production and Malnutrition in Baringo, Busia, and Taita-Taveta. mimeo. Berkeley: Project on Managing Decentralization, University of California.
Mwaniki, Nyaga.
1986    Against Many Odds: The Dilemmas of Women's Self-Help Groups in Mbeere, Kenya. Africa. 56(2):210–227.
Pala Okeyo, Achola.
1978    Women's Access to Land and Their Role in Agriculture and Decision Making on the Farm: Experiences of the Joluo of Kenya. Discussion Paper No. 263. Institute for Development Studies. University of Nairobi.
1979    Women in the Household Economy: Managing Multiple Roles. Studies in Family Planning. 10(11/12).
1980    Daughters of the Lakes and Rivers. *In* Women and Colonization. Mona Etienne and Eleanor Leacock, eds. Pp. 186–213. New York: Praeger Press.
Price, Sally.
1984    Co-wives and Calabashes. Ann Arbor: University of Michigan Press.
Riley, Bernard and David W. Brokensha.
1988    The Mbeere in Kenya. (2 volumes). Lanham, MD: University Press of America.
Rubin, Deborah S.
1986    Interdisciplinary Research on Intercropping Sugarcane and Food Crops in South Nyanza, Kenya. paper presented at IIMI-Rockefeller Foundation Workshop on Social Science Perspectives on Managing Agricultural Technology. Lahore, Pakistan.
1988    Changing Production Practices in a Sugarcane Growing Community in Kenya. Final Report. Washington, D.C.: International Food Policy Research Institute.

Scott, James C.
   1976    The Moral Economy of the Peasant: Rebellion and Subsistence in Southeast
           Asia. New Haven and London: Yale University Press.
Scudder, Thayer.
   1981    The Development Potential of New Lands Settlement in the Tropics and
           Subtropics: A Global State-of-the Art Evaluation with specific Emphasis on
           Policy Implications. Binghamton, NY: Institute for Development Anthro-
           pology.
Shipton, Parker.
   1988    The Kenyan Land Tenure Reform: Misunderstandings in the Public Creation
           of Private Property. *In* Land and Contemporary Society in Africa. R.E.
           Downs and S.P. Reyna, eds. Hanover and London: University Press of New
           England.
Southall, Aidan.
   1952    Lineage Formation Among the Luo. International African Institute Mem-
           orandum XXVI. London: Oxford University Press for the International
           African Institute.
Wilson, Monica.
   1951    Good Company: A Study of Nyakyusa Age-Villages. London: Oxford
           University Press for the International African Institute.

# PART THREE

# Social Change
# and Social Inequality

In the past twenty years, much of the work produced by anthropologists, whether explicitly applied or not, has documented the process of social and cultural change. In part this concentration is a response to the functionalism of earlier anthropology which viewed traditional cultures as static and homeostatic. Now the perception more commonly emphasizes the processes of change, examining both internal pressures for change within a cultural system, as well as those impinging on a culture from outside. With the growing recognition of the importance of change comes a debate about whether change, often termed "modernization" or "development", is inherently positive or negative. Obviously there is no single answer which is applicable in all instances, and the articles in this section of the book all deal with the impact of change on cultural groups. Building on the work of David Brokensha (1987; Castro, Hakansson, and Brokensha 1981), these articles examine issues of inequality from both a macro-level, within the context of regional economics and politics; and at a local level, examining how social change parallels changes in social, economic, or gender-based differentiation in traditional communities.

The first two articles, by Carlos and Glazier, deal with the issues of inequality and population migration. Manuel Carlos' article on migrant farm laborers in California demonstrates that the expansion of large scale commercial agriculture in the United States has resulted in the formation of a class of landless laborers who reside permanently in Mexico and commute into the United States for employment. The class of laborers is distinguished from that of the employers both by ethnicity and economic status, and the impoverished migrant laborer class has little opportunity for upward economic or social mobility, but rather supports the profitable agribusinesses with their inexpensive labor.

Jack Glazier's paper also deals with migration and social inequality, but focuses on the historical case of Jewish migration to the United States in the early twentieth century. In this instance, anti-Semitism toward the Jewish enclaves in eastern cities and discriminatory immigration policies, in combination with the Jewish tradition of community-focused charitable organizations, produced an organized movement of secondary migration to smaller communities in the interior of the United States. Social inequality between different Jewish groups generated tensions and perhaps diluted the effectiveness of the organization, but the mobilization to influence national immigration policy has clear parallels with contemporary immigration issues.

The remaining articles in this section of the book deal with the impact of rapid social and economic change and the degree of inequality in traditional communities, and include two case studies from the Philippines and three from Kenya. James Eder's article examines the sustainability of intensive smallholder commercial vegetable farming and concludes that the system in the community of San Jose has not resulted in polarization of economic or social status. He argues that the intense labor demands and the unfeasibility of large scale vegetable cropping in this area have protected the smallholders from competition from large landholders and have resulted in an increasingly strong middle class in this rural community. This case contrasts with Carlos' earlier point that the consolidation of landholdings in US agribusiness has effectively created a permanent underclass of landless laborers.

Thomas Conelly's paper also discusses economic inequality in the Philippines, and documents the differential economic status of families in the community of Napsaan. Conelly argues that while differential economic status tends to follow ethnic boundaries, ethnicity does not determine the lower economic status of the minority group. Differential economic status can be explained by differential allocation of time; the supplemental economic activities which are pursued by the ethnic minority group (in this case exploitation of forest resources) impair their ability to compete effectively as agricultural producers, while the diverse economic pursuits of the lowland, Christian farmers (e.g. fishing) are more complementary to the labor demands of farming. He argues that labor and resource allocation strategies, not ethnicity, are the factors implicated in socioeconomic inequality.

Thomas Hakansson's paper on bridewealth in a contemporary context argues that contrary to expectations, bridewealth does not decrease in importance among Gusii families with higher economic and social status, but rather becomes increasingly important. He illustrates how bridewealth has become part of the system of social and economic differentiation, and that elite families perpetuate their status through use of the bridewealth system.

The second paper dealing with inequality in Kenya is by Monica Udvardy and discusses the efficacy of women's groups in fostering development in rural areas. Udvardy demonstrates that while the "success" of women's groups in achieving their expressed goals is questionable, the participation and enthusiasm of women for these programs is undiminished. She argues that they provide an important opportunity for social support and adult learning within the existing system of gender-based inequality, regardless of the improvements to income which are the explicit purpose of such groups.

Anne Fleuret's paper examines the impact of labor migration on socioeconomic differentiation in Taita-Taveta, Kenya. Systematic out-migration of men for labor has often been perceived as symptomatic of economic stress, but in this instance she presents data which indicate that migrants' families have significantly better economic and nutritional status than households in which both spouses are resident.

Taken together, these articles illustrate the complicated relationship between economic and social change and consequent inequality. These issues will continue to be of importance as planned economic development programs and population relocation affect the lives of greater numbers of people, and the role of anthropologists in designing programs to encourage social equity is imperative.

## References Cited

Brokensha, David W.
1987    Inequality in Rural Africa, Fallers Reconsidered. Manchester University Papers on Development. III.(2):1–21.
Castro, A. Peter, N. Thomas Hakansson, and David W. Brokensha.
1981    Indicators of Rural Inequality. World Development. 9(5):401–427.

# 7

## Inequalities and an International Poverty Group in California's Developed Agriculture: The Case of Mexicali's Border Commuter Workers

### Manuel L. Carlos

Poverty groups of agricultural wage earning workers are part of the social order of both industrialized and developing societies. In many instances these groups include people who traverse international borders, for various periods of time, to work in the centers or poles of agricultural development in adjacent nations with higher levels of development (Tupper 1978; Chaney 1979; Kritz et al. 1981; Standing 1985).

The agricultural wage earning workers in this study are an excellent example of how international borders and development can generate different forms of poverty groups, in this case an international poverty group, while it accentuates inequalities in society. Certain kinds of development, for example capital intensive development in agriculture, especially agriculture based on the use of large tracts of land and intensive hand harvesting and planting methods, in fact appears to close possible options for remedying the inequalities present in the distribution of wealth, status, and occupation in agricultural societies in industrialized nations (Brokensha 1969; Galarza 1964). In these circumstances, poverty takes on a persistent or long-term condition which appears almost irreversible, despite ongoing development trends and increased agricultural production (in terms of area planted, volume and value). In a word, agricultural development in capital intensive settings, accompanied by such innovation as the use of improved technology, and the application of cost-benefit management practices, and the construction and expansion of irrigation systems, does not lead to a minimization of the presence of poverty groups or inequalities. Rather such groups simply change form or persist in a modified form and indeed seem to persist and become a necessary part of modern agriculture (Wells 1988).

This is a problem addressed by only a few anthropologists working with the agricultural populations (Goldschmidt 1947; Kearny and Nagengast 1988).

In the U.S., after an initial interest in the poverty and inequalities in advanced agriculture in the 1940s, little was done by anthropologists until some 20 years ago when David Brokensha called our attention to these issues as they revealed themselves in California's large-scale and capital intensive agriculture (Brokensha 1969) followed a few years later by Carlos and Brokensha (1971). More recently Juan Vicente Palerm, has begun to systematically examine the generation of poverty groups and enclaves in California's advanced agriculture (Palerm 1981; 1989), while Miriam Wells has analyzed attempts by such groups to develop cooperative farming systems in order to break out of their poverty states (Wells 1980; 1988). Michael Kearny and Carole Nagengast have recently begun to study issues related to empowerment, ethnic stratification, and public policy choices in impoverished Mexican and Chicano farm worker populations (migrants and non-migrants) in California's agricultural towns (1988).

These scholars, Goldschmidt (1943), Brokensha (1969), Carlos and Brokensha (1971), Wells (1980) Kearny and Nagengast (1988), and Palerm (1989), have correctly called our attention to the inequalities which develop and persist in the most prosperous and developed agriculture possible, namely California's agriculture. Each has shown us that certain forms of poverty are the direct result of agricultural development in industrial societies and that the latter do not seem to be any better equipped or determined to deal with such inequalities than are most developing countries. The case analyzed herein provides another example of this social reality.

This is a study of the agricultural commuter workers of Mexicali, Baja California, Mexico. These Mexican-born workers reside in the city of Mexicali, Baja California, Mexico, adjacent to the U.S.-Mexican border (see Figure 7.1). They commute daily during certain seasons of the year to work in the agricultural fields of the Imperial Valley.

The border commuters are part of the large underclass which makes up more than half of Mexicali's 600,000 inhabitants. They live in the *barrios pupulares* (poor neighborhoods) of the *cintas de miseria* or residential belts of misery which are characteristic of all the over-populated and densely settled Mexican cities along the U.S.-Mexican border (Hansen 1981). Border commuters are called "green carders" by local immigration officials, and others because they originally had a green card (pass) or border crossing identity card (U.S. Government form I-151). The card is now blue, but the name remains. According to U.S. immigration law, the border crossing identity card gives them the status of a foreign immigrant worker with the right to permanent residence in the United States, but for personal or economic reasons the border commuters have decided to live in Mexican territory and commute on a regular basis to their place of work in the United States (Rungeling 1969).

These agricultural workers form part of a larger pool of several hundred thousand, some say half a million documented ("legal") and undocumented ("illegal") workers who migrate on a regular basis from various border towns and from the interior of Mexico, to work in California's highly developed

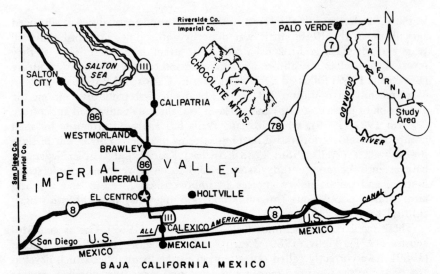

Figure 7.1 – Imperial County, California

and productive irrigation agriculture zones, where there is a high demand
for their labor. Officials at Calexico-Mexicali border believe (on the basis of
their records and daily counts) that there are between 15,000 and 18,000
such workers in Mexicali who cross the border daily into the Imperial Valley
(INS 1982). It is easy to believe these numbers if one witnesses the steady
stream of workers crossing the border starting at 2:00 a.m. each morning
and ending at about 5:00 a.m.

The purpose of this paper is to analyze the inequalities which large-scale
agriculture has produced in Imperial Valley-Mexicali area. I also examine
the manner in which these groups of workers are structurally linked to
international labor transfer processes which have moved these workers to the
border area and created the employment conditions for their reproduction.
I argue that large-scale agriculture in California and the U.S. creates and
perpetuates this international poverty group. I also analyze local level processes
of historical and social change, employment conditions, labor union ties,
and general sociocultural characteristics of this population.

## Approach

I use a theoretical framework to analyze local level inequalities which is
derived from an international labor transfer and recruitment approach for
the creation of localized labor markets in the world economic system (Portes
and Walton 1981; Frobel, et al. 1980). This approach states that labor
reserves or forces are either stationed or moved to various poles of development
or parts of the globe according to the needs and logic of international capital
(Sassen-Koob 1978; Wolf 1982). It suggests that when analyzing local-level,

large-scale, and capital-intensive enterprises such as the Imperial Valley's agriculture, it is best to view these as part of a broader multinational phenomena directly tied to worldwide capitalist investment and labor transfer patterns, aimed at creating profit or capital producing activities with low labor costs. The approach further asserts that large-scale capital-intensive enterprises, regardless of where they are located, will seek cheap labor sources even if it must import that labor force from another country and displace local labor supplies (Sassen-Koob 1978; 1988). Finally the approach maintains that international labor forces are produced, reproduced, and transferred through interpersonal networks, contract labor agreements and the like (Kearny and Nagengast 1988). When large-scale enterprises are agricultural and require large supplies of seasonal labor, the international labor transfer process, produces the creation of dependent labor pools of readily available, and cheap labor in strategic points throughout the world, including the Mexican-U.S. nexus (Buroway 1976; Standing 1985; Hansen 1981; Mines and Anzaldua 1982).

It is important to note that political boundaries do not provide effective obstacles to the international movement of labor supplies to areas of developed agriculture. Instead, countries like Mexico and the United States find legal formulas, such as border identity cards, temporary guest worker permits (e.g. the U.S. Bracero Program),[1] temporary border crossing permits and the like facilitate the process of the international labor transfers to important industrial and agricultural production zones (Petras 1980, Briggs 1982). Even the most recent U.S. Immigration Reform Act of 1986 acknowledges this reality, especially in agriculture, creating a special category for such workers wishing to enter the U.S. temporarily.

This research takes the perspective that the best way to understand the world economic system's labor transfer patterns and the resulting poverty groups it produces, as well as the relationships between developed and underdeveloped poles of economic activity and prosperity, is through case studies rather than macro analysis (Portes and Walton 1981; Brokensha and Little 1988). The present paper is, therefore, a contribution to local case studies of larger phenomena, and of the inequalities and poverty groups generated by large-scale capital intensive economic production and development.

The research methodology employed is consistent with that traditionally used by anthropologists who do first-hand field participant observation studies to understand the objective realities of different social change and impoverishment processes effecting the populations of developing societies. To accomplish these goals, I spent eight months in the area, during which time I conducted in-depth interviews and administered a survey questionnaire which was carried out by the author and a research team of five interviewers over a period of several weeks. A total of 400 workers, 350 men and 50 women were interviewed. The population was interviewed in Calexico, California, at staging areas where workers gather in the morning to be contracted and/or transported to the work areas. In addition I obtained and analyzed official documents and literature from different government agencies.

## Ecology, Transformation, Economy, and Inequalities Affecting Agricultural Labor

Agriculture in the Imperial Valley is a model case of the growth of large-scale agricultural development in the state of California (Galarza 1977). It epitomizes the application of green revolution technology, cost-benefit analysis, excellent business management, ownership of agriculture by agribusiness companies, and the use of cheap labor, particularly Mexican and Mexican American workers (McWilliams 1968; Brokensha 1969).

In its basic technology and in its corporate and land tenure ownership patterns, the Imperial Valley resembles many of the other prosperous agricultural zones in California which have been developed largely by Mexican and Mexican-American labor. The inequalities produced by capital intensive agricultural are evident. The land belongs largely to Anglo-Americans and to Anglo-American owned agribusiness enterprises. The same group owns most of the businesses and residential and business-related real estate in the valley, though legally immigrated Mexicans and their descendants have lived in the valley longer than the Anglo-Americans.

The economic and ecological transformation of the Imperial Valley, as an area of high capital investment, began in 1942, when the All American Canal was built to bring irrigation water a distance of 50 miles from the Colorado River which divides California and Arizona (see Figure 7.1). Large agricultural tracts of land in this part of the great Sonoran desert were opened up to farming, and investors from other parts of California and the United States began to arrive from the 1940s on. Later, during the years 1950–1970, the area was almost totally bought out by American agri-industry and agribusiness interests. From the very beginning, the economy of the Valley relied on imported and cheap labor, namely documented and un-documented Mexicans who crossed the border seasonally and who settled in small California towns. In recent years, with the abolition of the U.S. Government's Bracero Program of contract labor in 1964, (See Note 1 and Galarza 1968), and with the upward mobility and outward migration of local Mexican-American populations, the valley has drawn almost exclusively on Mexicali's readily accessible commuter workers as its major source of labor.

The nearly total control of the area's economy by agribusiness interests is readily observable. The most significant companies include Sun Harvest, Irvine Co., Abatti Produce, Bud Antle, Gourmet Farms and Bruce Church, Inc. Some of them have linkages to other international corporations (see Table 7.1) and nearly all operate in other areas of California, as well as of the United States. The value of their production represents the largest portion of agricultural sales (measured in dollars) in the valley. Their management staff is comprised entirely of Anglo-Americans.

Table 7.1 - Agribusiness Corporations Operating in Imperial Valley
and other California Counties, 1980

| FARM OPERATOR | CROPLAND (acres) | TOTAL LAND (acres) | COUNTY |
|---|---|---|---|
| Irvine Company | 28,257 | 82,344 | Imperial & Orange |
| Sun Harvest Inc. | 15,754 | 18,358 | Imperial & Monterey |
| Sam Andrew's Sons | 14,210 | 15,519 | Imperial & Kern |
| Elmore Company | 13,690 | 14,795 | Imperial |
| John Norton Farms | 9,948 | 12,139 | Imperial |
| Abatti Bros. | 9,516 | 10,892 | Imperial |
| Gourmet Farms | 5,692 | 6,543 | Imperial |
| Maggio Inc. | 5,601 | 6,014 | Imperial & Monterey |
| Bud Antle Inc. | 5,426 | 6,026 | Imperial, Monterey, Riverside & Ventura |

Source:  Don Villarejo, Getting Bigger (1980)

Local agribusinesses and the growers who produce for them, and other corporations in the Imperial Valley obtain their labor force through the efforts of their own labor contractors, independent private labor contractors, or through the local office of the United Farm Workers (U.F.W.). As discussed later, most of the agricultural workers, including the ones interviewed for this study, are either contracted directly by the various agribusinesses and growers, by the U.F.W., or by independent labor contractors who make a profit from providing their services to the firms and growers by charging workers a percentage of their wages. Unionized workers are in the minority (about 25 percent of the work force). Most of these labor contractors, and nearly all the union representatives, are of Mexican descent. They handle all the negotiations with the commuter workers in Spanish. Indeed Spanish is the most widely spoken language in the valley, including in the retail stores and businesses. The presence of hundreds of these workers and their spoken sounds on the streets of Calexico, California, make it appear to be an extension of Mexico into California.

The valley's towns, large and small, are populated largely by Mexican-Americans and immigrant Mexicans. The valley's 1980 population of 92,100 includes 65,266 inhabitants distributed into seven small towns (see Tables 7.2, 7.3), including the border city of Calexico which has 14,545 inhabitants. The larger ones, including El Centro, the county seat, have a sizeable minority (about 20 percent) of Anglo-Americans. They comprise most of the elected officials, professional classes, merchants, and management level personnel of the agribusiness and related commerce in the valley. The social and ethnic structure resembles that of Central California agricultural valleys and their

Table 7.2 - Population of Selected Cities of
the Imperial Valley

| Cities | 1970 | 1980 | % CHANGE |
|---|---|---|---|
| Brawley | 13,746 | 14,753 | 7.3 |
| Calexico | 10,625 | 14,545 | 36.9 |
| El Centro | 19,272 | 24,015 | 24.6 |
| Holtville | 3,496 | 4,355 | 24.6 |
| Imperial | 3,094 | 3,440 | 11.2 |
| Calipatria | 1,824 | 2,586 | 41.8 |
| Westmoreland | 1,175 | 1,572 | 33.8 |
| Totals | 53,232 | 65,266 | |

Source: Annual Planning Information Imperial
County 1981-1982; State of California Health
and Welfare Agency May, 1981. Employment
Development Department.

Table 7.3 - Hispanic Surname Population in Imperial
County, California*

| Community | (1980) Total Population | Number Hispanic Surname | % Hispanic Surname |
|---|---|---|---|
| Brawley | 14,946 | 8,683 | 58 |
| Calipatria | 2,656 | 1,760 | 67 |
| Calexico | 14,412 | 13,561 | 94 |
| Holtville | 4,399 | 2,094 | 48 |
| Seely | 1,058 | 491 | 46 |
| Westmoreland | 1,590 | 1,051 | 66 |

Source: Palerm 1989:151
* Hispanic Surname is the U.S. Census Bureau
  designation; the population is in reality of Mexican
  origin.

towns (Goldschmidt 1947; Brokensha 1969; Carlos and Brokensha 1971).
Most of the wealth and high status occupations are held by Anglo-Americans.
The latter have higher levels of education and their children tend to move
on to professional careers and highly-paid jobs either locally or other areas
of the U.S.

There are 835 agricultural production units in the Imperial Valley, averaging
an area of 600 acres (U.S. Department of Commerce, 1980). A number of
companies operate units with as many as 15,000 acres, and, as we mentioned
earlier, almost all of these large enterprises have operations in other agricultural
zones in the state. The Imperial Valley is the fifth largest producer of

agricultural commodities (measured in dollars) of the 35 agricultural counties in the State of California. In 1981, production in the valley totaled 765 million dollars (Agricultural Commission Office 1981). Crops cultivated in the valley included both mechanized crops such as alfalfa, wheat, sugar beets, and semimechanized labor-intensive crops such as lettuce, melons, asparagus, onions, and broccoli. The latter predominate in terms of the total land area and value of crops. All, however require heavy labor use to manage the irrigation of the land.

Given the characteristics of select size, texture, maturity and physical presentation required by buyers and consumers of labor-intensive crops, their production has created the need for a large seasonal work force that flows in from Mexicali at various peak periods required for irrigating, planting, weeding and harvesting. This has led to a nearly constant demand for a dependent labor reserve willing to be employed and laid off according to the different seasons of the agricultural cycle.

The months of November through March are the ones during which the greatest number of workers are required—about 18,000 people. At other times the daily commuting work force declines to about 5,000 to 8,000 workers. The excess labor force migrates north to other agricultural zones to work in similar activities during the local off season, leaving their families behind in the city of Mexicali. Others survive by saving their money and drawing unemployment benefits and by drawing on family incomes earned in local employment on the Mexicali side of the border. During the peak labor period between November and March, agricultural workers who have been working farther north in California return to Mexicali and join the community labor market of the Imperial Valley at a time when labor demands are at the highest point.

A number of our informants in government agencies claimed that green-card holder commuters from Mexicali represented 85–95 percent of the agricultural labor force in the Imperial Valley. The remainder of the labor force is comprised of almost entirely undocumented Mexican workers and a few Mexican-Americans who cannot find other employment, and who are descendants of Mexican immigrants who settled in the Valley in the last 75 years and have failed to gain upward mobility. Mexican-American and long-term Mexican immigrants in the Imperial Valley hold better jobs than the group of green-card commuters. These include such jobs as foremen and farm machinery operators, which receive higher wages and have greater stability than the seasonal employment of the commuter workers.

## Social Origins, Occupational Composition, and Size of the Agricultural Labor Force

Mexicali's poverty group of agricultural commuter workers has two originating sources. One is to be found in the exodus of rural, agricultural peoples from peasant communities in the central states of Mexico to the border towns which took place in the early and mid twentieth century (Cross and Sandos 1981). The other is in the reproduction of this labor force in the impoverished border cities of Northern Mexico in the past four decades. This study is the first to identify the reproduction of this commuter agricultural labor force in border cities as a cheap and accessible labor pool.

What are the social and economic characteristics of these commuter workers? The group we interviewed is composed primarily of males (87 percent) most of them married (63 percent). Ages ranged between 18 and 65 years, with an average age of 37 years. All come from extended households of six to ten persons including parents, children and related kin. All have worked most of their lives in agriculture in either Mexico or the U.S. The women tended to be younger than the men (an average of 18 years) and most were single (nearly 75 percent). Many of the young single women explained that they would not have such jobs if they did not need to help their families, and if they had a husband. The level of educational achievement is quite low, with 40 percent of those interviewed never having finished primary school and 20 percent never attending school at any level. The majority had lived in Mexicali most of their lives and all considered Mexicali their permanent area of residence, regardless of their migratory patterns.

The majority of the workers interviewed live in six of the most densely populated and impoverished working class neighborhoods or *Colonias* in Mexicali, including the Colonia Baja California (17.3 percent), Colonia Pueblo Nuevo (14.3 percent), Colonia Nueva Esperanza (7.0 percent), Colonia Orizaba (5.5 percent), Colonia Coachtemoc (4.3 percent), and Colonia Pro-Hogar (4.3 percent). The rest are scattered in adjacent poor neighborhoods and shanty towns. Most live in poorly constructed structures with no insulation against the extreme heat and cold of the desert area where Mexicali is located. The group blends in with the other impoverished working classes in the dusty and cluttered neighborhoods of Mexicali, but its income in U.S. dollars, though extremely seasonal, allows them certain material advantages at the household level. For example it is important to note that 87.5 percent live in homes with running water and indoor plumbing, (the rest have outhouses) and that 99.3 percent have electricity. There are 91.8 percent who have television sets, 92.5% have refrigerators and 95.5% have a gas (as opposed to kerosene) stove.

Possession of these manufactured goods place the commuter workers among the materially better-off poor of Mexicali. A popular idea exists among other residents of Mexicali that they are a "privileged group" because they earn dollars. In actuality, their possessions are hard won through a very difficult life of heavy and demanding labor under difficult climactic and working conditions, and the additional burden of labor contractor and union fee payments. Moreover, their children go to the same schools as the poorest of the poor in the city and their families lack many of the social services and recreational facilities available to the middle and upper classes of the city.

Almost 70 percent of those interviewed lived and worked as farm workers a year or more in various parts of California and the Western United States before settling in Mexicali. It is these experiences and the low cost of living that eventually attracted most of them to settle in the Mexicali area.

In 1982, the majority (72.0 percent) earned a yearly average of less than $100.00 (U.S.) a week, or between $50.00 to $75.00 per week during employed periods of six-day work-weeks of 10 to 12 hours per day. Many of those interviewed reported that when they worked on piece-work contracts, they could earn between $100.00 and $150.00 a week during hand-harvesting seasons which lasts several months a year. Most reported that their combined income was barely enough to meet their household expenses, spending nearly all of it on such items as rent, food, and public utilities. Many also shared their incomes with less fortunate relatives in the interior of Mexico, sending remittances to them on a regular basis. Moreover, because they are accustomed to U.S. goods, they tend to spend money of their earnings on commodities purchased on the U.S. side where their dollars do not stretch nearly as far, despite the fact that they tend to buy second-hand clothing and other basic staple items of low cost value.

As far as geographic place of origin, the interviews revealed that 54 percent of those questioned were natives of the State of Baja California. The other principal states of origin, in order of importance, included the three of the largest sending states of migrants to the U.S: Jalisco (13.7 percent), Michoacan (8.5 percent), and Guanajuato (5.8 percent). Other sending states are Sonora (5.3 percent), Sinaloa (19.5 percent), and Zacatecas (4.5 percent). Agricultural commuter workers report that they live in Mexicali in order to save money on housing and public utilities for their families. Some said they didn't want their children to become Americanized. Others indicated that they preferred to live in Mexicali because they liked the "customs" of the people better. Others said that they felt that in Mexicali they are among their "own people", and life was more agreeable or culturally compatible to them.

As far as the socioeconomic origins of the agricultural commuter workers who were not natives of Baja California, more than half had worked as wage-earning farm workers in their place of origin. Others had been part of agricultural household units involved in substantial farming. Among this number, 8 percent were also *ejidatarios* (communal land-grant recipients), and 7.5 percent were small farmers who had left their small holdings to become full-time wage-earners. Significantly, 81 percent said that their fathers had worked or were currently working as agricultural wage-earning laborers, whether in Mexico, the United States, or both countries, indicating that the migrant labor stream is reproducing itself through generations in the same families.

The number of informants (81 percent) who have their social origins in families of agricultural workers reveals that, as argued in the beginning of this paper, this group is genuinely a labor pool reproducing itself in the national territory of Mexico, and transferred systematically into California's agricultural labor market. Similarly, the migration from the center of the country to the border area reveals geographic labor transfers reported in other studies of the process of internationalization of the Mexican agricultural labor (Cross and Sandos 1981; Palerm 1981). Interestingly, as stated above, the interview data also reveals that there is a significant new or emergent generation of commuter workers, some 54 percent in the border area that are native to the State of Baja California.

When describing the kind of agricultural work they do, the majority (men and women) reported that their principal occupations involved the seeding of fields or hand-planting of seedlings (35 percent), and as hand-pickers, and hand-harvesters during harvest time (39 percent). A minority have higher-status and better paid occupations such as machine operators (10 percent), drivers (4 percent), irrigation workers (8 percent), or packer (4 percent), the latter largely comprised of women. Those with more specialized occupations earned more per hour, tended to be men, and had larger annual incomes.

## The Labor Market and Worker Linkages with Agribusiness

Within the "advanced" or high capital investment organization of crop production of the Valley, there are two basic modes for the contracting of labor. The first of them is through labor contracts established with the United Farm Workers (U.F.W.). Of the 400 agricultural commuter workers interviewed, 96 of them, or less than a quarter (24 percent), said that they were members of this farm workers organization. These workers meet in the early morning hours at the offices of the U.F.W. in the city of Calexico. From there they are transported by buses belonging to agricultural companies to their places of work in the Imperial Valley. The union arranges directly for their hiring and can generally guarantee employment to a worker for the life of a contract. In general, the workers under union contracts are the best paid and have stable work resulting from terms specified by their contract. The union group is considered to be the best protected and has more labor rights than the group which contracts directly with the labor contractors. There would be more workers in this category, but intimidations by the growers, and the preference given to non-union labor contractors, have successfully stopped the U.F.W. from increasing its membership (Martin et al. 1988).

The second mechanism of recruitment, and the most common, is the independent labor contractor, through which approximately 76 percent of the agricultural labor force is hired. The contractor, generally, is a person of Mexican origin, whose principal functions are to recruit, transport, supervise and pay the workers. The workers are either paid daily or, depending upon the contract, by hour or by piece.

The contracting of workers is carried out by work crew foremen and individual contractors daily. The work crew foreman have the authority to accept or reject the job applicants at the point of contract according to his personal knowledge of their abilities, perceived willingness to carry out the required work and also on the basis of previously established friendship and patronage ties either with the worker directly, or indirectly with their friends and relatives. This makes the process highly arbitrary and personal.

There is no legal nor formal obligation on the part of the foreman to hire the worker on any particular day, other than personal ties, which is why the worker comes daily to look for employment without any guarantee of it on any given day. Foremen say they can't make such guarantees because their contracts, and/or those of the contractors they represent, are subject to considerable uncertainty with growers.

On the basis of services rendered, the contractor obtains from the agribusiness firm a commission of between 31 and 34 percent of the total salaried paid to the workers. This system of contracting allows the employer to avoid a direct contract with the workers, and in this way avoids any kind of binding labor agreement with the work force he uses. It also prevents labor unions from attempting to organize the employees of an agribusiness, since the workers technically work for the labor contractor.

Many of our informants said during the open interviews that they were very unhappy with the contracting system. They declared that the contractors did not allow them sufficient rest periods and exacted excessive work quotas (at piece-work rates) from them. Many were also fearful of joining the unions because they felt it would label them as trouble makers and interfere with their future job prospects.

## Conclusions

This case study of an international poverty group and the inequalities in California's developed agriculture has yielded several important findings. First, it is obvious that the farm workers represent an essential complement to the labor force required for the labor-intensive crops produced in the Imperial Valley, and which are the foundation of its current economic prosperity. Furthermore, the workers, not just heavy capital investments and operations, have contributed to the historic economic development and prosperity of the Valley. As various informants told us, without them, the profitable labor-intensive cropping patterns and the agricultural work of the Valley could not be carried out. Many informants believe that Anglo-American populations would not endure the hardships of farm labor in the valley's severe climate.

Second, as stated in the theoretical parts of the introduction to this paper, the migratory and family data in the sample reveals in some detail that these agricultural commuter workers form part of a larger process involving the international transfer of labor wherein developing countries (in this case, Mexico) increasingly biologically and socially reproduce a reserve pool of labor in their own national territory which then circulates or is transferred to countries and poles of development (in this case the advanced agricultural zones in California).

Third, these workers are structurally linked to the system of agribusiness in other counties of California, through a labor recruitment pattern which operates seasonally from the California-Mexico border to hundreds of miles into California. At the same time, all of the above elements of the system produces a permanent underclass of poor farm labor workers. Participating in agricultural development has not led to their own economic prosperity. It is obvious that these commuter workers, (even with what they earn, compared to other impoverished border groups), continue to be as disadvantaged in their material welfare, in their quality of life, in their residential locations, and in their incomes and work conditions.

Agricultural border commuter workers have a work life which exacts from them great sacrifices, both in daily isolation from their societies and families, (up to 16 hours daily including travel time), and in terms of physical hardships of work and climate. Additionally, they have no work security and no idea of how long they will be employed on any given crop cycle. In most instances they have to move for varying seasonal periods to other areas and leave their family behind. If they are not members of the United Farm Workers, and only very few are, they do not enjoy labor protection rights and worker benefits. This places them completely at the mercy of the independent labor contractors, and the shifting and uncertain needs of the larger agribusiness companies and their subcontractors.

It is obvious that so long as California agriculture continues to require a cheap labor force, because of the profitability of labor-intensive crops it harvests, the probability of the continued reproduction and hiring of future generations of commuter workers is very high (Kearny and Nagengast 1988). Similarly, given Mexico's current economic problems, the economic patterns of past decades, the steady demand for the food products raised in the Imperial Valley, and the special status given to agricultural workers by the Immigration Reform Act of 1986, there is no reason to believe that the labor transfer process from Mexicali to Calexico will end in the immediate future.

The U.S., as a country with one of the most technologically advanced and modern agricultural systems, will continue to need a large cheap labor force from Mexico. The presence of a migratory poverty group from Mexico in the central valleys of California, and their working and living conditions was one of the contradictions of advanced agriculture in the U.S. which initially attracted the scholarly interests of the anthropologist Walter Goldschmidt and subsequently of my friend and colleague, David Brokensha, a student of African development, to the Californian agricultural scene (Brokensha 1969; Carlos and Brokensha 1971). He frequently compared the circumstances of the Mexican farm labor groups he knew from first-hand field research, to migratory farm workers in other parts of the world, including black laborers in South Africa, long before others had made similar observations (Buroway 1976). His interests in their plight and in the social and historical processes that create and sustain these poverty groups helped motivate me to take an interest in studying the same population along the U.S. Mexican border. Hopefully, other anthropologists who study development in the Third World will follow his example and the work of other such scholars (e.g.

Palerm, Kearny and Nagengast, Wells, etc.) calling attention to anomalies and pockets of poverty in the areas of developed agriculture in advanced countries which rely on foreign or imported labor.

Perhaps together we can discover solutions to some of their socioeconomic problems, their ongoing marginalization, and identify further the structural dynamics and international and local circumstances which create these international poverty groups in both developed and underdeveloped countries. For now these border agricultural migrant workers will continue along established patterns of occupational segregation and suffer from poor working conditions and economic disadvantages on both sides of the border. As noted by David Brokensha in 1969, "The social problems associated with migrant farm labor (and its relationship to California agriculture) are well-known, yet they are rediscovered every few years. In the years 1930 to 1950, at least 46 reports were published on migrant labor in California. In 1968 and 1969, [at the height of the farm worker movement in California], there has been a renewed output of reports, yet no drastic changes have occurred" (Brokensha 1969). The study presented here and other recent works (Palerm 1989; Kearny 1988), affirms this observation for other areas of California some twenty years later.

## Acknowledgments

I wish to thank the Ford Foundation and the Tinker Foundation for postdoctoral support. I also wish to recognize the valuable help given to me by a team of interviewers from the Institute of Social Research of the Autonomous University of Baja California (UABC), in Mexicali. I particularly wish to thank Frida Espinoza for assistance in the preparation of an early version of this paper. During the period of planning and implementing this research (1981–82), I was associated with the Institute for Social Research at UABC. For eight months (January to August 1982) I lived in the city of Mexicali, B.C.

## Notes

1. The Bracero Program was a Mexican labor contracting system initiated by the U.S. during World War II. when there was a labor shortage in U.S. factories and in agriculture. The program lasted from 1941 to 1952, through the Korean War and the post-World War II economic recovery period. Its effects on California agriculture are discussed in Ernesto Galarza's book *Merchants of Labor: The Mexican Bracero Story* (1964).

## References Cited

Agricultural Commission Office.
    1981    Summary of County Agricultural Commissioner's Report. State of California, Imperial County.

Briggs, Vernon.
   1982    Foreign Labor Programs as an Alternative to Illegal Immigration. *In* The
           Border That Joins: Mexican Migrants and U.S. Responsibility. Peter Brown
           and Henry Shue, eds. Totowa N.J.: Rowman and Littlefield.
Brokensha, David.
   1969    The Harvest: San Joaquin Valley, California. unpublished manuscript.
           Department of Anthropology. University of California, Santa Barbara.
Brokensha, David and Peter Little, eds.
   1988    Anthropology of Development and Change in East Africa. Boulder: Westview
           Press.
Buroway, Michael.
   1976    The Functions and Reproduction of Migrant Labor: Comparative material
           from Southern Africa and the United States. American Journal of Sociology.
           81(5):1050–1087.
Carlos, Manuel L. and David Brokensha.
   1972    Agencies, Goals, and Clients: A Cross-Cultural Analysis. Studies in Com-
           parative International Development. 7(2):130–156.
Chaney, Elsa.
   1979    The World Economy and Contemporary Migration. International Migration
           Review. 13(2):204–213.
Cross, Harry and James Sandos.
   1981    Across the Border, Rural Development in Mexico and Recent Migration to
           the United States. Berkeley: Institute of Governmental Studies. University
           of California.
Frobel, Folker, Jurgen Heinrichs, and Otto Kreye.
   1980    The New International Division of Labor. New York: Cambridge University
           Press.
Galarza, Ernesto.
   1964    Merchants of Labor: The Mexican Bracero Story. Santa Barbara, CA: McNally
           and Loftin Publishers.
   1977    Farm Workers and Agribusiness in California, 1947–1960. Notre Dame,
           Indiana: University of Notre Dame Press.
Goldschmidt, Walter.
   1947    As You Sow: Three Studies in the Social Consequences of Agribusiness.
           New York: Harcourt, Brace and Co.
Hansen, Niles.
   1981    The Border Economy, Regional Development in the Southwest. Austin:
           University of Texas Press.
Immigration and Naturalization Service (INS).
   1982    Monthly Report of Permanent Resident Alien Commuter and Seasonal
           Workers. Calexico, California: Immigration and Naturalization Service.
Kearny, Michael and Carole Nagengast.
   1988    Anthropological Perspectives on Transnational Communities in Rural Cal-
           ifornia. Davis, CA: California Institute for Rural Studies.
Kritz, Mary M. et al.
   1981    Global Trends in Migration, Theory and Research on International Population
           Movements. New York: Center for Migration Studies.
Martin, Phillip, Suzanne Vaupel, and Daniel Egan.
   1988    Unfulfilled Promise: Collective Bargaining in California Agriculture. Boul-
           der: Westview Press.

McWilliams, Cary.
    1968    North From Mexico, The Spanish Speaking People in the United States. Westport, CT: Greenwood Publishers, Inc.

Mines, Richard and Ricardo Anzaldna.
    1982    New Migrants and Old Migrants, Alternative Labor Market Structures in California's Citrus Industry. La Jolla, CA: Center for U.S. Mexican Studies. University of California, San Diego.

Palerm, Juan Vicente.
    1981    Mexican Peasants and Seasonal Migration. University of California, San Diego.
    1989    Latino Settlements in California. *In* Advisory Committee on Senate Resolution 43: The Challenge, Latinos in a Changing California. Pp. 125–172. Riverside, CA: University of California Consortium on Mexico and the United States (UC Mexus).

Petras, Elizabeth.
    1980    The Role of National Boundaries in a Cross National Labor Market. International Journal of Urban and Regional Research. 4(2):157–194.

Portes, Alejandro and John Walton.
    1981    Labor, Class and the International System. New York: Academic Press.

Rungeling, Brian.
    1969    Impact of the Mexican Alien Commuter on the Apparel Industry of El Paso, Texas. Ph.D. Dissertation. Dept. of Economics. University of Kentucky.

Sassen-Koob, Saskia.
    1978    The International Circulation of Resources and Development: The Case of Migrant Labor. Development and Change. 9(4):509–545.
    1988    The Mobility of Labor and Capital: A Study in International Investment and Labor Flow. New York: Cambridge University Press.

Standing, Gary, ed.
    1985    Labor Circulation and the Labor Process. London: Croom Helm Publishers.

Tuppen, J.N.
    1978    A Geographical Appraisal of Transfrontier Commuting in Western Europe: The Example of Alsace. International Migration. 12(3):140–165.

United States Department of Commerce.
    1980    Census of Agriculture: Preliminary Report for 1980. Imperial County.

Villarejo, Don.
    1980    Getting Bigger. Davis, CA: California Institute for Rural Studies, Inc.

Wells, Miriam.
    1980    Success in Whose Terms? Evaluations of a Cooperative Farm. Paper presented at the 40th Annual Meeting of the Society for Applied Anthropology. Denver, CO.
    1988    Political Mediation and Agricultural Cooperation: Strawberry Farms In California. Economic Development and Cultural Change. 30(2):413–432.

Wolf, Eric.
    1982    Europe and the People Without History. Berkeley: University of California Press.

# 8

## Secondary Migration and the Industrial Removal Office: The Politics of Jewish Immigrant Dispersion in the United States

*Jack Glazier*

Throughout his distinguished career, David Brokensha has addressed important problems in the broad areas of social change and migration. His pioneering research in Larteh, Ghana was innovative in its investigation of a small African town caught up in varied processes of social change. The migration of Larteh residents to various farming villages represents a notable dimension of their economic organization, and these migrations accelerated as cocoa production gained momentum. But although such movements of people have defined much of Larteh life since the nineteenth century, the migrants consider themselves residents of Larteh, where they return for part of the year. Cultural and social continuity thus marks the relationship between Larteh and its various satellite farming villages (Brokensha 1966:42–43).

In examining international migration, the present article confronts a pattern of population movement very different in scope and consequence since it looks at a massive population shift and an adaptation resulting in severe discontinuities in the migrants' lives. Studies of international migration have usually scrutinized the movement of people from one country to another without considering the process of internal resettlement once people have landed in a new territory. This latter process I term "secondary migration", which can be defined as the resettlement of individuals within an adopted country following an initial migration from their homelands. Although I shall examine a very specific case of secondary migration, the factors precipitating this general process are as varied as its consequences and no single configuration of circumstances or motivations defines the term. I use it only in the general sense of resettlement following migration between countries. It is thus distinct from what many writers term "internal migration", which concerns population movement within a country rather than an initial international migration and subsequent resettlement (Richmond and Kubat

1976; Brown and Neuberger 1977). The concept of secondary migration is particularly useful in refining understandings of the dynamics of international migration since the processes at work in spurring the initial population shift may differ markedly from those motivating subsequent relocation.

In the case of immigrant Jews to the United States during the great wave of immigration from Eastern and Southern Europe in the years between 1881 and 1924, political and economic discrimination and religious oppression stimulated the massive movement of people to American shores. Once here the new immigrants sought economic opportunity but the terms on which they attempted to climb upward were in part constrained by a Jewish leadership influenced by domestic political concerns and their own sense of individual and corporate Jewish self-interest. That is, the Jewish leadership exhorted immigrants to leave their points of disembarkation, particularly New York, in favor of towns and cities in the interior, and it is this process and the forces underlying it which inform the present article.

During the first two decades of this century the systematic, directed dispersion throughout the United States and Canada of Jewish immigrants represented the strategy of a segment of the American Jewish establishment which was descended from an earlier but smaller and culturally distinct group of German-Jewish immigrants. The religious liberalism of the latter was closely bound to their strongly held values on cultural assimilation into the American mainstream—an assimilation which they were achieving with remarkable success. Their efforts took shape in the Industrial Removal Office (IRO), founded in 1901 as a unique experiment in protecting the welfare of immigrants, while responding to the influential voices of a broad range of American opinion seeking to restrict immigration. A dramatic curtailment of further immigration, restrictionists argued, would mitigate the increasing social distress of large urban centers where immigrants had clustered. The IRO was extremely sensitive to this argument and, while strongly opposed to immigration restriction, found its *raison d'être* in sponsoring the movement of Jewish immigrants out of New York. At the same time, in less obvious fashion, the organizers of the IRO thought that they could also protect the corporate and individual positions of established American Jews believed to be in danger of suffering the repercussions of "guilt by association". If, in other words, the Jewish leadership could effectively answer the most compelling criticisms of liberal immigration, then it was believed any danger they too might face from anti-Jewish feeling could be averted. At the turn of the twentieth century, a specter of nativism and religious discrimination, rooted in midwestern populism, eugenics, and anti-immigrant sentiment among patrician Anglo-Saxons on the eastern seaboard (Higham 1955), loomed above immigrants and American Jews alike, and organized Jewish groups committed themselves to systematic campaigns to diminish the peril.

Accordingly, the records of this organized relocation address a host of critical issues in early twentieth century American history, thus providing a window on both Jewish preoccupations in the years up to and just after World War I and the manner in which Jewish communities around the country responded to the plight of the immigrants. This article briefly examines the short-lived IRO in this important formative period in American ethnic history. Particular attention is directed to the aspirations of the IRO and the relationship of its resettlement program not only to traditional Jewish ideas of communal responsibility but also to self-interested efforts to safeguard the hard-won position of established American Jewish citizens. For the anthropologist, such an excursion into the ethnic past can bring to light the broader processes underlying assimilation, (which has shaped much of the ethnic history of immigrants from Europe) in an era when minorities were waging a defensive and ultimately unsuccessful battle to maintain a liberal national policy on immigration. The present examination concentrates on the IRO in light of its stated policies and goals as articulated by its leadership and occasionally refers to the specific operation of the organization in relationship to the movement of Jewish immigrants to Indianapolis and environs. Research for this article is part of a continuing anthropological investigation of the Jewish community of that city since 1900.

## The IRO: An Historical Overview

At its founding in 1901, and over the course of its twenty-one year existence, the IRO gained impetus from the unprecedented wave of Jewish immigration beginning in the 1880s. The work of the IRO was curtailed and eventually foreclosed by the choking off of immigration during World War I and by the Congressional action in 1924 radically restricting it. The IRO primarily sought to resettle Jewish immigrants (potential "removals") landing in the large cities of the East. Foremost among these disembarkation points was of course New York City. The organizers of the IRO expressed deep concern about the impoverished mass of immigrants, especially on New York's Lower East Side, and the many problems such crowding precipitated among the new arrivals. IRO officials also worried about the strain such large numbers of deprived Jewish newcomers would create for various Jewish charities attempting to cope with these difficulties. The leaders of the IRO further discussed problems of wider scope which the Jewish immigration might portend, both for the future prospects of Jewish settlement in the United States and for settled American Jews.

Despite its oft stated goal, the IRO in its resettlement efforts made only a small dent in the massive wall of Jewish immigration. By 1910, after a decade of work, David Bressler, a guiding hand in the IRO, reported that the organization had succeeded in relocating only 50,000 immigrants to interior communities of the United States and Canada, and this pattern did not change in the ensuing twelve years of IRO activity. He went on to place this figure in appropriate perspective when he noted that the Jewish population of New York in that year was 900,000 and that an additional 100,000 Jewish immigrants might arrive in the city in any single year (1910:12). Additionally, in comparing the 1910 figure to the General Manager's report of 70,000 people resettled by 1912 thus indicating an average of 10,000 cases of relocation in 1911 and 1912, it is thus very clear that the great majority of Jewish immigrants who made their way out of New York did so independently of any formal assistance from the IRO and relied instead on kinsmen or friends who had already begun to establish themselves in an interior community. But its limited success does not gainsay the IRO's highly organized operation, requiring coordination with hundreds of host towns and cities of the interior.

Given the relatively small number of Jewish immigrants actually assisted by the IRO, the historical record of this organization thus does not compel attention for the successes it scored. The IRO simply did not effect in the immigrant Jewish population the major demographic shift it had sought, but the records of this organization nonetheless document an important period of ferment in American ethnic history. The new immigrants and the urban problems linked to them, in the opinion of some observers, jeopardized the prospects of future immigration since a considerable segment of public opinion and American political leadership leaned toward increasing restrictions as a countermeasure to the many social pathologies of urban life. The IRO set the tone for secondary migration, emphasizing both the economic opportunities available in interior communities and the extremely high stakes at risk for immigrants and settled American Jews alike, should Jewish immigrants exacerbate further the burgeoning urban problems of New York. The IRO argued strenuously that its program of redistribution could blunt these several dangers. And although its very limited success up to 1910 was well-recognized, the Organization included within its mission the dissemination of the "idea of general distribution" so that out-migration from New York would become "an automatic movement independent of any directing agency or institutional assistance" (Bressler 1910:12).

The IRO maintained very lofty ideals, as revealed in its many circulars and policy statements. By contrast, letters exchanged between the main New York office and local agents throughout the country often reveal the troublesome problems arising from the day to day efforts to assist immigrants confronting the wholly alien world of the American hinterland. These problems stemmed from misunderstandings between the New York office and local IRO agents, the conflict between long term goals of the former and shorter term concerns of the latter, and, sometimes, outright misrepresentations and duplicity by the immigrants themselves. Through it all, some very dedicated officials of the IRO at both the local and national levels remained committed to the ideal of assisting individuals, in accord with cultural values, in becoming independent and productive as soon as possible.

Shortly after the beginning of the mass immigration of Jews from Eastern Europe, American Jews became acutely aware of the urban problems developing in the dense centers of Jewish settlement and the need for grappling with this growing challenge. At first, the Baron de Hirsch Fund assisted individual immigrants wishing to find employment outside of New York or else hoping to join already established relatives in towns or cities of the interior. The Baron de Hirsch Fund also supported "removal" work aimed at assisting agricultural efforts by immigrant Jews, particularly in the East (Brandes 1971). But by the turn of the century, the sheer weight of immigrant numbers demanded a more formal approach to the question of resettlement in particular and the overall problem of aiding immigrant adjustment in general. Consequently, the effort to resettle Jewish immigrants across the country was formalized through the creation of the Industrial Removal Office. The formation of the IRO represented one of many moves to reshape earlier individual efforts at relief centered in synagogues and other highly informal, local groups into more centralized, formal and large scale organizations better suited to coping with the greatly increased scale of immigration (Glazier 1988:55).

Participants in the second meeting of the Conference of Jewish Charities in 1902, addressed these problems both in their magnitude and in their specifically human dimension. The Chairman of the Executive Committee of B'Nai B'Rith, gave an impassioned speech about the scope of the problem of anti-Semitism in Europe as a force driving Jews to the United States. He also outlined the appalling conditions among the new arrivals in New York, where Jewish communal attention was essential. Emblematic of these problems was his description of a young immigrant girl selling newspapers on Canal Street at 11:00 P.M. because she had to work far into the night in order to help support her family. This problem, he added, could be multiplied by thousands (JCUS 1902:71–72).

This meeting outlined a program for educating immigrants about the work of the IRO and for connecting the national office in New York to local receiving communities. In each city, a local person, often an employee in a fledgling Jewish Federation of Charities or equivalent community organization, would act as an agent of the IRO, which would pay a portion of his salary. In smaller towns, a rabbi or a Jewish businessman would assume responsibility for the work of resettlement. The agent in turn would inform the New York office about labor conditions in his town and the prospects for employing various categories of Jewish workers, whom the New York office might send out. An explicit understanding thus obtained between local communities and the New York headquarters regarding the importance of close coordination in the process of sending out immigrants. The latter would be closely checked in New York as to their skills and occupational suitability for the receiving community, which in turn would assume responsibility for arranging jobs, housing, and the like. When a breach in this understanding occurred, which was not unusual, some very animated and at times angry exchanges occurred between local agents and the New York Office.

In order to comprehend fully the activities of the IRO and the problems the organization faced, it is essential to go beyond records such as those of the formal proceedings of the Conferences of Jewish Charities, when IRO reports were issued, often in optimistic terms. I can only note in passing the disparity between official pronouncements and the daily reality of matching immigrants with new communities, which is especially apparent in the correspondence between particular towns and the New York office. At the local level, IRO records of particular "removals" present a highly realistic picture of the mundane operation of an overworked organization and the difficulties of receiving immigrants who were unqualified for the jobs they sought, or had misrepresented themselves to the New York office, or were simply unwilling to accept the jobs offered. The correspondence between such communities as Indianapolis and the New York office was at times highly contentious, yet very revealing of the disparity between the aspirations of the IRO and the daily problems of dealing with new arrivals of distinct culture facing variable conditions of employment and isolation across the country.

The IRO hoped that the resettlement of Jews throughout the United States not only would relieve the congestion of the eastern ghettos but also would create a kind of chain migration. That is, once resettled, immigrants would attract others to their adopted communities by of ties of friendship or kinship from the old country. Once immigrants applied to the New York office for resettlement, information regarding their employment history and skills was gathered and then forwarded to the local agents in communities where the New York office felt the immigrant would be a good prospect. An agent would then decide about the acceptability of the applicant and, should the latter prove a likely candidate for successful resettlement, the agent would contact the New York office. The latter, in turn, would provide transportation and expenses for the immigrant and inform the agent of the immigrant's arrival time by train so that arrangements could be completed for room and board and, most importantly, employment. Job opportunities, in addition to personal bonds, would thus provide another attachment for the chain of migration.

Since the major charge of the IRO was the settlement of European Jews throughout the United States and Canada, IRO officials in New York needed to know if labor and working conditions in particular communities were congenial or inimical to Jewish relocation. The New York Office in reiterating its need to be apprised of local conditions noted:

> In distributing our people into interior communities, we have to bear in mind many details and we must know local conditions. It is our business to see that the removals sent, accord with local conditions. It therefore becomes necessary that those who so kindly volunteer cooperation with us, keep us informed, at regular periods, of all the particular and peculiar conditions obtaining in given localities. The importance of these data cannot be overestimated. It makes our distribution rational and systematic and after all, while ideals are ennobling, still, in order to translate them into correlate action, organized action is necessary (IRO Records. November 9, 1912. Letter from General Manager to Isaac Baer, Lafayette, Indiana).

Accordingly, the IRO became a kind of clearing house for detailed information about industrial conditions in the hundreds of towns and cities to which Jews were directed.

## Self-Interest and Communal Responsibility

The leadership of the IRO and indeed of the nascent Jewish Federations of which the local IRO office was usually a part lay in the hands of Reform Jews. In Indianapolis, as in so many other American cities, these descendants of an earlier nineteenth century immigration of mostly German-speaking liberal Jews represented examples of an ethos of successful assimilation and social change at work. They generally lived in prosperous neighborhoods, distanced by both class and culture from the poor locales inhabited by the immigrants (Glazier 1988:50). Although they shared little in common with the Eastern Europeans newcomers and practiced a version of Judaism which had self-consciously purged itself of ancient and medieval practice regarded as inappropriate in the modern world, they still formed a variety of organizations to assist the immigrants. Looking back to the first years of the century, the Executive Director of the Jewish Federation of Indianapolis in a 1928 report emphasized the differences between the two groups but found a motive for assistance in common religious tradition:

> In Indianapolis, as in other interior communities, the newer settlers were not yet numerous, and they naturally looked to their co-religionists for succor and guidance. These co-religionists . . . were no closer socially or in experience or attitude to the newcomers, than were the other alien peoples who completely surrounded them. But the religious bond and the ancient heritage was [sic] enough to establish some degree of sympathy and understanding (Rabinoff 1926:3).

Simply put, Rabinoff regarded charitable assistance as derivative of shared values, borne of common religious heritage and obligation.

Likewise, Boris Bogen, an activist in Jewish communal matters and certainly not a proponent of restricting immigration, described the newcomers in terms further stressing the cultural differences separating them from their American Jewish supporters:

> Uncouth and unpleasant in their appearance though picturesque, foreign in speech and manners, different even in their everyday religious practices, they were complete strangers to those who befriended them. It was natural that they should settle in separate districts, and form congested neighborhoods, which since have become popularly known as the Jewish Ghettos of American cities (1917:226).

Bogen's characterization is mild in comparison to numerous other depictions of Eastern European Jews (Wirth 1928:265-267). Such unflattering portraits of the newcomers were not unusual among some long established American Jews, who felt more at home in the mainstream of American life than they did among the odd strangers with whom they shared only the barest threads of a common religious tradition.

From the outset of IRO activity, various spokesmen emphasized that the challenge of massive Jewish immigration was not simply a New York problem. Rather it was represented as an issue of fundamental interest, beyond common values, to the entire Jewish community of the United States, since the debate about immigration was a national concern. Moreover, IRO officials also warned American Jews about complacency borne of wealth or social position. At the third biennial conference of Jewish Charities, the President of B'Nai B'Rith thus admonished American Jews to take an active role in assisting in the work of distributing the new immigrants:

> No amount of labor, or sacrifice, must be too great, for in their welfare in their happiness lies our welfare and our happiness. He who for a moment believes that his or her future as an American citizen is assured by virtue of his wealth or his social condition, and ignores this great responsibility, will be woefully and sadly awakened by finding the Jewish question injected into the turmoil of American politics . . . something that we must under no circumstances permit, for its admission would be not only fatal to those who are unfortunate, but equally disastrous to those whose lives have been cast in more pleasant places (Jewish Charities in the United States 1904:140–141).

These concerns early in the century were well-placed in view of the force of anti-immigration opinion among politicians, pundits, and social scientists persuaded by nativist, populist, or eugenic arguments.

The fundamental interests of established American Jews which helped to shape their positive public response to the Eastern European immigrants include both material and status concerns. That is, the much feared "Jewish question" informing the lives of Jews in Eastern Europe would threaten the standing of American Jews as citizens with full constitutional rights and would endanger their economic position should it appear in American politics. The possibility that it might emerge as a factor in American political life loomed ever larger as public attention and the negative opinions of the restrictionists came to focus on the alarming conditions in large, dense centers of immigrant life. Additionally, the question of their social position or status loomed very large for established American Jews, who came to believe that they could be tainted by the least admirable immigrants among them. The increasing visibility of Eastern European Jews in American life and the putative danger they posed thus provoked inner conflicts among the earlier German-speaking Jewish settlers and their descendants alienated from the poor and culturally divergent Jews in their midst. As Wirth pointed out long ago in his classic study of the ghetto, the earlier settlers sometimes rationalized prejudice against the immigrants as a reaction to the alleged crudeness of the newcomers (1928:265–267).

The alarm about a "Jewish question" enhanced already well-developed feelings of Jewish corporate responsibility, while promoting a feeling of defensiveness. Jewish communities could not afford in their view to let down their collective guard against possible assaults against their legitimate American rights. At the same time, paradoxically, defensiveness and the sense that any individual failings would reflect badly on the community at large and therefore jeopardize its position and security, also grew out of an underlying feeling of optimism and rationality regarding the nature of anti-Jewish prejudice and discrimination. That is, if Jews did not give their detractors sufficient cause for hatred or exclusion, so the reasoning went, then they would have no rational grounds for working against Jews and Jewish interests. Bogen put the matter quite simply at the time:

> The immigrant after he is naturalized, in addition to the duties of an American citizen, carries the responsibility of maintaining the reputation of the Jewish foreigner; upon his conduct depends the attitude toward the newcomer; his individual wrongdoings are usually interpreted as an organic fault of the entire class to which he belongs (1917:285).

Often unhappily, many American Jews of liberal religious practice and assimilationist leanings came to see themselves as bound to this "class". For this reason, Jewish communities made strong efforts to police themselves, so to speak, to work against any expression of "bad behavior" or any acts which would make Jews as a group suffer criticism and thus either limit their future opportunities or jeopardize the position they had already attained (Glazier 1988:48). Thus organized Jewry, especially through the IRO, felt it incumbent on American Jews to respond actively to the warnings issuing from many quarters about the social dislocations of the immigrant settlements in crowded urban centers and what those problems might presage for the American Jewish future. Whatever negative attitudes they may have expressed privately and sometimes disclosed publicly about the Eastern European Jewish immigrants, the American Jewish leadership found that the religious value placed on aid and support also served their more immediate material, status, and political interests.

## The National Debate on Immigration:
## Further Impetus to the IRO

The wave of southern and eastern European immigration to the United States spawned, especially after the turn of the century, a contentious national debate about the consequences of such a massive movement of foreigners to these shores. Older Jewish organizations such as the B'Nai B'Rith and newer groups including the National Liberal Immigration League founded in 1905 lobbied extensively against restrictions. Jewish groups particularly argued that the anti-Jewish policies of Czarist Russia and periodic pogroms such as those in Kishniev in 1905 necessitated that European Jews be able to find a safe haven in the United States. Arrayed against the proponents of immigration were groups such as the Immigration Restriction League which rationalized its position through arguments ranging from "race pollution" to "race suicide" (immigrant birth rates exceeded those of native Americans) to the threat of job loss to American citizens. The large numbers of immigrants from outside of Western Europe also provoked a prominent nativist sentiment emboldening the restrictionists. Influential anti-immigration forces mustered powerful, often emotional arguments against immigration, including the frequent claim that the swell of immigrants contributed to the teeming growth of Eastern cities and to their many vices including crime, prostitution, and delinquency. In response to this kind of criticism, the IRO believed that the assistance it rendered to immigrant Jews in leaving New York for less congested towns and cities would mitigate the anti-immigration claims about the sources of urban problems.

The General Manager of the IRO in letters from the New York Office to various local communities noted how the issue was affecting national politics. In writing to the Chairman of a recently formed distribution committee in Lafayette, Indiana, the General Manager thanked the community at large and the committee in particular for responding "to the needs of the biggest problem confronting American Jewry, namely distribution of Jewish immigration". He went on to point out how the Presidential candidates of the two major parties in 1912 had each expressed sympathetic understanding of the scope of the problem while endorsing immigrant distribution over the country. The General Manager then observed:

> It can readily be seen . . . that the work of the American Jews in anticipating the action of the Government by a full 12 years, in pointing out the proper methods to guide distribution and in inaugurating the practical work which has resulted in so much good to almost 70,000 of our co-religionists, not to speak of their many dependents who have followed without our assistance . . . (October 15, 1912. IRO Records. Letter from General Manager to Arthur A. Zinkin, Chairman, and Isaac Baer, Secretary, Lafayette, Indiana).

In a subsequent letter, quoted earlier, from the New York Office to the secretary in Lafayette, the IRO manager noted in explicit terms the concerted effort of American Jewish organizations in combating moves toward tightening immigration:

> If you will glance through the American Jewish yearbook [of] 1912–1913, you will note that most of the energy of organized Jewry was devoted to fighting the bills proposed in Congress, to further restrict immigration. And how far responsible the congestion evil is for the attempt to restrict immigration, you well know. The work of relieving congestion becomes therefore, of national scope (IRO Records. November 9, 1912. Letter from General Manager to Isaac Baer).

The massive movement of newcomers from Eastern, Central, and Southern Europe in the decades between the 1880s and the restrictive legislation of four decades later added to the ferment and social upheaval of an America reshaping itself into an industrial, urban society. It is thus hardly a coincidence that modern Jewish communal and welfare organizations, including the IRO, formed during this period, when progressive interests addressed the problems of crime, juvenile delinquency, exploitation in sweat shops, and similar concerns born of rapidly developing but troubled cities. The latter, made up of a congeries of immigrant groups, provided the seedbed for the extraordinary growth in reformist activity closely related to the commitment of Jewish groups to alleviate the plight of impoverished newcomers. The immigration issue thus represents only a part of the larger process of urbanization and industrialization which transformed the United States from a rural agricultural nation to a modern industrial state. Many individuals including political leaders in Congress and some professional social scientists, such as E. A. Ross, found more threat than promise in this transformation and argued passionately for immigration restriction. Ross's views represented a convergence of an older populist, agrarian attitude and a deeply flawed strain of early twentieth century sociological thought.

Associated with the populist tradition of the Midwest and the progressivism centered at the University of Wisconsin in the early decades of the century, Ross criticized the immigrants as much as national immigration policy. Fundamentally, Ross's populism and nativism, nurtured in his early agrarian midwestern experience, lay at odds with the major changes sweeping American society in the early twentieth century—changes associated with urbanization, industrialization, and massive immigration from areas of Europe considered inferior. Ross, like many other immigration restrictionists, sought "to discipline and constrain the force of industrialism and urbanism which were changing the configuration of American life and to retain a society in which earlier values would still be valid" (Weinberg 1972:176). In his book, *The Old World in the New: The Significance of Past and Present Immigration to the American People* (1914), he combines ethnic stereotypes, anti-Semitic quips, nativist prejudice, and crude biological arguments to support immigration restriction. Otherwise, American society would face, in Ross's view, debilitating social ills including prostitution, political corruption, crime, urban crowding, and an eventual decline in the intelligence level of the populace owing to the immigration of Eastern and Southern Europeans of below average intelligence. As a prolific writer, president of the American Sociological Society (forerunner of the American Sociological Association), friend of Woodrow Wilson, his former teacher, and activist in the Immigration Restriction League, Ross's intellectual standing during the height of the immigration debate was considerable (Weinberg 1972:161–162). As a respected sociologist, moreover, Ross's arguments, however defective, and his unabashed nativism inevitably assumed a certain "scientific" aura, thus lending them an added authority.

Such restrictionist arguments raging from the end of the nineteenth century until the mid-1920s were thus formidable. Before restrictionism realized its ultimate goal through the Immigration Act of 1924, the battle was joined by an energetic and resourceful American Jewish leadership seeking, through such means as IRO-sponsored secondary migration, to influence national policy while trying to protect recent and would-be immigrants and the wider community of American Jews.

## Conclusion

Secondary migration under the sponsorship of the IRO represented part of a wider current of social change sweeping across Jewish immigrant communities. Eager to enter the economic mainstream, immigrant Jews from Eastern Europe had before them Reform Jewish models of success. The immigrants quickly perceived a relationship between economic mobility and the assimilationist values of the established liberal Jewish community. If the Eastern European Jews at the same time remained critical of those who spurned important symbols of Jewishness, both in its ethnic and religious dimensions, they nonetheless recognized that economic mobility and the success of their children, increasingly acculturated through the public school and other civic institutions, would likely incur considerable cultural costs and generational discontinuities.

The relationship between the descendants of German-speaking Jewish immigrants—people who constituted the established American Jewish leadership in the years between 1880 and 1924—and the subsequent but much larger group of Eastern European Jewish immigrants does not represent a unique case. It parallels in many respects the experience of other ethnic and racial groups internally segmented by the period and circumstance of their immigration. Lieberson, for example, has systematically analyzed the differential achievement and position in American society of blacks, on the one hand, and Southern, Central, and Eastern European immigrants, and on the other. A critical difference between the European ethnics and blacks concerns the continuous, uninterrupted migration of the latter to northern cities and the dramatic cessation of European immigration in the mid-1920s. In his comparison, Lieberson notes the "harmful effect" newcomers can visit on the earlier immigrants:

> Sizable numbers of newcomers raise the level of ethnic and/or racial consciousness on the part of others in the city; moreover, if these newcomers are less able to compete for more desirable positions than are the longer-standing residents, they will tend to undercut the position of other members of the group. This is because the older residents and those of higher socioeconomic status cannot totally avoid the newcomers, although they work at it through subgroup residential isolation . . . Beyond this, from the point of view of the dominant outsiders, the newcomers may reinforce stereotypes and negative dispositions that affect all members of the group (1980:380).

In this view cessation of the European immigration at a time when the internal migration of blacks progressed unabated may have eased the plight of the Europeans in regard to ethnic and religious bias, for "it is more difficult to overcome the negative consequences of discrimination through special niches when the group is growing rapidly and/or is a large segment of the total population" (1980:380).

When settled American Jews began to perceive that their status and long-term political and economic interests were bound up with the fate of the newer wave of European Jewish immigrants, they worked assiduously to assist the latter. Established American Jews were tireless advocates for liberal immigration, which they argued before various bodies such as the influential Immigration Commission of 1907. Related to the work of the IRO, an equally ambitious and imaginative project diverted immigrants from New York and other eastern cities altogether. Known as the Galveston Plan, this undertaking encouraged Russian Jews to book passage directly to Galveston, thus completely avoiding the East Coast where the "removal" effort might prove insufficient in countering the restrictionists' arguments (Marinbach 1983:4). From Galveston, the immigrants might resettle themselves throughout the American West.

Although they perceived in the immigration issue a potential threat to their own position in American society, American Jews through their leadership continued their immigration advocacy. Ross's scathing indictment of the newcomers and the national policy making possible their immigration did not augur well for the immigrants or their supporters. That Ross chose to distinguish "vulgar upstart parvenus" from socialists (to whom he was disposed) among the Eastern European Jews and to differentiate this entire group from the assimilated Jews of earlier migrations (1916:165, 167) only indicates that such fine distinctions would mean little to less subtle and articulate xenophobes. It would be difficult to measure how extensively the end of mass immigration reduced the threat to those who had already arrived, for nativism and anti-ethnic sentiment remained potent forces in domestic politics during the ensuing years. Nonetheless, the brief history of the IRO points up how the political and social currents of American society stimulated an organized secondary migration to diminish the more portentous shadows lurking within the changing ethnic landscape.

## Acknowledgments

Research on the Industrial Removal Office has been made possible by a grant from Oberlin College, and I gratefully acknowledge that generous support. Thanks are also due the staff of the American Jewish Historical Society of Waltham, Massachusetts for their kind assistance in making available to me the records of the IRO. I thank Woody Watson of Harvard University, who offered useful criticism on an early version of this paper. The concept of secondary migration emerged from our several discussions.

## References Cited

Bogen, Boris.
    1917    Jewish Philanthropy. New York: Macmillan.
Bressler, David M.
    1910    The Removal Work, Including Galveston. Paper presented at the National
            Conference of Jewish Charities, May 17. St. Louis

Brandes, Joseph.
1971    Immigrants to Freedom. Philadelphia: University of Pennsylvania Press.
Brokensha, David.
1966    Social Change at Larteh, Ghana. Oxford: Clarendon Press.
Brown, Alan A. and Neuberger, Egon, eds.
1977    Internal Migration: A Comparative View. New York: Academic Press.
Higham, John.
1955    Strangers in the Land. New Brunswick: Rutgers University Press.
Industrial Removal Office Records.
1912    Letter from New York Office to Arthur Zinkin and Isaac Baer. October 15.
        I-91, Box 38. Waltham: American Jewish Historical Society.
1912    Letter from New York Office to Isaac Baer, November 9. I-91, Box 38.
        Waltham: American Jewish Historical Society.
Glazier, Jack.
1988    Stigma, Identity and Sephardic-Ashkenazic Relations Indianapolis. *In* Persistence and Flexibility, Anthropological Perspectives on the American Jewish Experience. Walter P. Zenner, ed. Albany: State University of New York Press.
Jewish Charities in the United States (JCUS).
1902    Second Conference, May 26–28, 1902, Detroit. Cincinnati: Press of C. J. Krehbiel and Co.
1904    Third Biennial Conference, May 24–27, 1904, New York. New York: Press of Philip Cowen.
Lieberson, Stanley.
1980    A Piece of the Pie: Blacks and White Immigrants Since 1880. Berkeley: University of California Press.
Marinbach, Bernard.
1983    Galveston: Ellis Island of the West. Albany: State University of New York Press.
Rabinoff, George.
1928    Annual Report of the Jewish Federation of Indianapolis.
Richmond, Anthony H. and Kubat, Daniel.
1976    Internal Migration: The New World and the Third World. London: Sage.
Ross, Edward A.
1914    The Old World in the New. New York: The Century Co.
Weinberg, Julius.
1972    Edward Alsworth Ross and the Sociology of Progressivism. Madison: The State Historical Society of Wisconsin.
Wirth, Louis.
1928    The Ghetto. Chicago: University of Chicago Press.

# 9

## The Gardens of San Jose:
## The Survival of Family Farming
## in a Developing Philippine Community

*James F. Eder*

The interactions over time of population growth and agricultural development and intensification pose many research problems of broad social scientific (and practical) interest. What sorts of social transformations in rural households, communities, and whole societies occur as agricultural land grows scarce and economic decisions are guided increasingly by market demand rather than by local needs? What are the consequences of such transformations for individual well-being? With such issues in mind, I undertook, during January to July, 1988, a restudy of San Jose, an upland Philippine farming community I first studied during 1970 to 1972. This paper concerns one aspect of this restudy and addresses the conditions under which small family farmers can survive in a developing capitalist economy without obliging themselves (or their neighbors) to become agricultural wage workers.[1]

### Background

San Jose is located eight kilometers from Puerto Princesa City, the capital of Palawan Province. Like numerous other farming communities up and down Palawan Island in this century, San Jose was established by spontaneous migration of land-seeking shifting cultivators, many from Cuyo Island, 300 kilometers distant. San Jose itself was settled beginning in the 1930s. By the time of my first research, San Jose's population had reached 112 households. Reflecting local response to economic changes in the wider region, its subsistence-oriented, upland-rice based economy had given way to a diversified market-oriented economy in which business and trade, off-farm employment, and production and sale of vegetables, tree crops, and livestock were the major income sources. Over the same interval, and because individual responses to the new market opportunities were not uniform, differences between residents in wealth, status, and political power grew apace. These circumstances provided, during 1970–1972, a strategic opportunity to examine the growth of social inequality under conditions of spontaneous resettlement and capitalist agricultural development (see Eder 1982).

After leaving San Jose in 1972, I turned my attention, during subsequent field visits to the Philippines, to an unrelated research project elsewhere on Palawan Island. During these visits, however, I maintained contact with San Jose residents and monitored changes in the community. When I returned in 1981, for example, the community had been electrified, a new high school had been constructed, the highway connecting San Jose with Puerto Princesa City had been improved, and new investment in the community was visible in business, in public transportation, and in tracts of previously fallow land now planted to tree crops. By the time I visited again, in 1987, much farm land had been subdivided for sale as residential lots and the community had grown to almost 300 households, in part due to domestic cycling, and in part due to an influx of new arrivals. Many of the latter were farmers, the sorts of people who have settled in San Jose all along, but many too were townspeople from Puerto Princesa City seeking living space in nearby farming communities. Despite the arrival of numerous urban wage-workers, however, San Jose's farming sector remained strong, although processes of socioeconomic differentiation were clearly at work, most visibly with respect to the growing variety and importance of secondary, off-farm income sources in households still primarily dependent on farming.

These and other local changes occurred within the wider context of the incorporation of Puerto Princesa as a chartered city; President Marcos's 1972 declaration of martial law and its aftermath; the increased visibility of the Philippine Army in Palawan; the penetration of Palawan by multi-national corporations; continued, large-scale immigration to Palawan by land-seeking settlers from throughout the Philippines, but particularly from areas affected by poverty, insurgency, or political unrest; a serious, nationwide pattern of inflation and economic stagnation, culminating in the national economic crises of 1984–85; the initiation of the Palawan Integrated Area Development Project; the February 1986 transition from the Marcos administration to the Aquino administration; and so forth.

Given these changes, I returned to San Jose in 1988 with three broad questions in mind. Ethnographically, I was curious to discover how the residents of one particular Philippine village had survived seventeen additional years of growth and "development" under the conditions just described. Theoretically, I intended to examine the conditions under which increasing social, economic, and political differentiation, rather than polarization, is the outcome of capitalist development in Asian peasant communities (Hayami and Kikuchi 1981). Methodologically, I hoped that an explicit concern with the impact over time of extra-local processes of change on a particular local social system would help resolve certain dilemmas associated with the study of such systems in analytical separation from the larger systems in which they are embedded (Cancian 1981). Underlying all three questions was a particular interest in how poorer farmers had fared during the study interval and with whether, how, and why their well-being had changed in the face of various local and extra-local demographic, economic, and social changes. This paper is a report on one aspect of this restudy project. It concerns the role that one particular agricultural activity, intensive vegetable gardening, has played in the socioeconomic changes that San Jose residents experienced between 1971 and 1988. In the first part of the paper, I briefly describe the changes that took place in San Jose economy and society between 1971 and 1988. I show that San Jose's own experience with agrarian change has been *relatively* favorable: a large and prosperous group of "middle" farmers remains the central feature of the community's socioeconomic order, and there is little evidence of either polarization in the community as a whole or deterioration in the circumstances of its poorer residents.

In the second part of the paper, I briefly describe technology, land and labor use, and economic returns in vegetable gardening, showing how these things, too, changed between 1971 and 1988. Examining the demographic and socioeconomic characteristics of those households that pursue gardening as a primary income source, I argue that gardening's basic characteristics (it is labor-intensive but remunerative, and it economizes on land) make it an attractive economic choice for land-poor, labor-rich households—the sorts of households normally most vulnerable to impoverishment and eventual proletarianization as agricultural development proceeds. I will also argue that, equally important, gardening is an *unattractive* choice for would-be capitalist farmers (some of whom have already begun to penetrate *other* agricultural activities), ensuring that, for the moment, it remains the domain of small family farmers relying primarily on their own household labor resources. In the final part of the paper, and with an eye toward San Jose's prospects for the future, I briefly locate vegetable gardening in the context of two wider socioeconomic processes promoting the survival of family farming.

Before proceeding with this enterprise, I want to make explicit several biases in my own perspective on agrarian change in capitalist peasant societies. The first, which I owe directly to David Brokensha, is my belief that there is no substitute for careful and dispassionate analysis in the study of social change in general (e.g., Brokensha 1966). Second, and as Brokensha has shown (e.g., Castro, Hakansson, and Brokensha 1981), socioeconomic inequality (even extensive socioeconomic inequality) will be a major feature of most rural countrysides for the foreseeable future. In this circumstance, I believe that *differentiation*, rather than *polarization*, is a more desirable outcome of developmental change—and that development strategies should work to encourage the former and discourage the latter. Third, and unlike, for example, Scott (1985), I see nothing inherently pathological about a family farmer selling cash crops, relying (in part) on non-agricultural employment opportunities, or otherwise participating in the "market economy"; the real issue is the *consequences* of such participation for household and individual well-being, which I believe are immensely variable.

## San Jose Socioeconomic Structure, 1971–1988

The most striking demographic feature of San Jose during the study period was its *openness*. That the community grew to 290 households by 1988, even as 47 households of the original 112 households present in 1971 became extinct or departed for other locales, testifies to the extreme mobility of persons and households in this part of the Philippines. Mobility of this order is also a sobering reminder of the artificial nature of community boundaries— and hence of the limitations of community-based studies. On the other hand, there *were* some important continuities; 65 households of the 1971 total were still present in 1988, and they had given rise in the interim, through domestic cycling, to 96 additional households whose experiences over time are also relevant to assessing the nature of change in the community. (The balance of the 1988 household total consists of post-1971 "new arrivals".) Future analysis will be more concerned with the separate circumstances and experiences of these different categories of households—and with taking account, as well, of those households and out-marrying children who *left* San Jose between 1971 and 1988. Meanwhile, however, even the aggregate community data employed here provide a valuable window to the direction of agrarian change.

What sorts of changes, then, in occupation, land ownership, living standards, and the like occurred in San Jose during 1971–1988? While some of the generalizations made below may be revised as additional data are tabulated and analyzed, certain broad patterns seem clear. These patterns should be understood against the broader background of a lack of anything resembling "class crystallization" in San Jose and the consequent difficulty of attempting to represent community socioeconomic structure in terms of, for example, the amount of land each household owns or controls. Such representations would not illuminate community socioeconomic structure at a particular point in time, and they would certainly not illuminate changes in that structure over time, because they do not illuminate individual economic behavior.

First, many San Jose households derive most of their income from off-farm sources. For some (but not all) of these latter households, agriculture is a significant secondary income source, and there are still many households whose primary income source remains farming. But for the community as a whole, the importance of land ownership to economic well-being ranges from very important to irrelevant. Second, even those households which derive significant incomes for farming—and hence for whom land ownership is important—may not easily be disaggregated in "land-based"categories.

For one thing, it is hard to capture in simple categories important gradations in land *security*. To "own" land in the narrowest sense is to possess *titled* land, but some San Jose farmers, who consider themselves "owners", still do not possess clear titles to land they long ago cleared and occupied under homestead laws and for which they pay real estate taxes annually. Other, younger residents are "inheritors", technically landless but with the expectation (although not the certainty) of receiving some portion of a parental estate. Still others rent land for their agricultural production activities; others "squat", rent free, on the land of friends or kin. (That vegetable gardeners in 1988 pay rents on the order of only 500 pesos per half-hectare per year further suggests that "land ownership" is a less crucial variable here than elsewhere.)[2] For another thing, land *use* is as important as land ownership. Some relatively prosperous vegetable gardeners, with little or no land of their own, employ one or two monthly laborers on their rented garden land. They are technically "landless", and yet they are closer to "rural capitalists" in their economic behavior than are their poorer, landed-counterparts who pursue more traditional, land-extensive production activities.

To this setting must be added complexities in *labor* use; the multiplicity of economic activities, even within single households, makes it difficult to operationalize even such seemingly basic concepts as "occupation" and "primary source of income". In one household, for example, not unusual, the wife attends market daily, both to sell her own produce and to engage in the buy-and-sell trade. The husband farms their three hectares of tree crops; he occasionally hires unskilled labor (to assist in the more onerous farm chores) or hires himself out as a skilled laborer (he knows some carpentry); and he engages in some petty entrepreneurship (he sprays mango trees to promote flowering, in return for a share of the harvest). Numerous other examples, involving different production activities, could be cited; the point is simply that many San Jose residents enter into different relations with the means of production at the same time, rendering impossible the demarcation and juxtaposition of clearcut collectivities of households standing in common relationships to those means (van Schendel 1981:37n, 293).

These things said, Tables 9.1–9.3 present data on changes in the distributions of landholdings, principal household income source, and occupations respectively, between 1971 and 1988. Table 9.1 shows that while the percentage of landless households in the community has remained about the same, there has been a marked decrease in the size of most households' landholdings. Indeed, mean landownership per household has declined from 3.26 hectares per household in 1971 to 1.22 hectares per household in 1988. This decline reflects the marked increase in community population during the study interval and, secondarily, a small decrease, from 365.4 hectares to 313.3 hectares, in the total stock of land owned by San Jose residents (the balance of San Jose's 792 hectares is public land or is owned by outsiders). Had other factors—income-producing activities, agricultural technology, etc.—remained constant during this interval, the consequences, for individual well-being, of this decline in per-household landholdings would likely have been very severe indeed.

Other factors were not constant, however. Table 9.2 shows that the percentage of San Jose residents relying entirely on off-farm income sources has more than doubled during the study interval. To be sure, among the 117 households receiving only non-agricultural income during 1988 (house-

Table 9.1 - Land Ownership in San Jose, 1971-1988

| Households with: | 1971 Households # | 1971 Households % | 1988 Households # | 1988 Households % |
|---|---|---|---|---|
| 0 (landless) | 31 | 27.67 | 76 | 29.57 |
| 0.01 - 0.1 ha. | 3 | 2.68 | 30 | 11.67 |
| 0.11 - 0.5 ha. | 4 | 3.57 | 52 | 20.23 |
| 0.51 - 1.0 ha. | 14 | 12.50 | 38 | 14.79 |
| 1.01 - 2.0 ha. | 10 | 8.93 | 15 | 5.84 |
| 2.01 - 3.0 ha. | 11 | 9.82 | 21 | 8.17 |
| 3.01 - 4.0 ha. | 7 | 6.25 | 3 | 1.17 |
| 4.01 - 5.0 ha. | 7 | 6.25 | 9 | 3.50 |
| 5.01 - 10.0 ha. | 17 | 15.18 | 9 | 3.50 |
| 10.01 - 15.0 ha. | 5 | 4.46 | 1 | 0.39 |
| 15.01 - 20.0 ha. | 2 | 1.79 | 2 | 0.78 |
| 20.01 and more ha. | 1 | 0.89 | 1 | 0.39 |
| Totals | 112 | 100.00 | 257* | 100.00 |

San Jose landholdings only, combining land owned and to be
   inherited.
* Land ownership data is lacking for thirty-three of the
   290 households present in 1988.

Table 9.2 - Principal Household Income Source, 1971 and 1988

| Income Source | 1971 Households # | 1971 Households % | 1988 Households # | 1988 Households % |
|---|---|---|---|---|
| Agricultural income only | 25 | 22.32 | 59 | 22.52 |
| Both agricultural and non-agricultural income | 64 | 57.14 | 86 | 32.82 |
| Non-agricultural income only | 23 | 20.54 | 117 | 44.66 |
| Total | 112 | 100.00 | 262* | 100.00 |

* Data on income sources is lacking for twenty-eight of the
   290 households present in 1988.

holds which, as a group, own little or no land) were 25 households relying
upon unskilled day labor opportunities on the farms of others as their
primary income source. At least some of these households presumably would
have devoted some effort to agricultural production—and perhaps been better
off than they were—had they had more land. Most of the other non-
agricultural households, however, were supported by urban wage-workers
who happened to reside in San Jose.

Table 9.3 - Primary Occupations of Husband and Wife, 1971-1988

| Primary occupation (a) | 1971 Husband | Wife | 1988 Husband | Wife |
|---|---|---|---|---|
| **Farmer** | 39 | 53 | 95 | 109 |
| **Self-employed** | 7 | 35 | 45 | 60 |
| charcoal maker | | | 4 | 4 |
| fisherman | 2 | 1 | 19 | 6 |
| storeowner | 1 | 3 | 1 | 18 |
| market vendor | | 23 | 3 | 23 |
| laundress | | | | 5 |
| tricycle driver/operator | 1 | | 16 | 1 |
| hilot/midwife | | 3 | 1 | 2 |
| matweaver | | 2 | | |
| rice mill operator | | 2 | | |
| dressmaker | | 1 | | 1 |
| mason | | | 1 | |
| fishpond operator | 1 | | | |
| cattle trader | 2 | | | |
| **Wage worker** | 49 | 5 | 96 | 35 |
| unskilled laborer | 16 | 2 | 27 | 2 |
| skilled laborer | 4 | | 8 | |
| private employee | 14 | 1 | 19 | 5 |
| government employee | 13 | 2 | 34 | 24 |
| salaried tenant | 2 | | 2 | 2 |
| overseas worker | | | 2 | 2 |
| pensioner | | | 4 | |
| **Grand Total** | 95(b) | 93 | 236(c) | 204 |

a. Excluding women not working outside the home in households
   receiving only non-agricultural income.
b. Seventeen of the 112 households present in 1971 were headed
   by women.
c. Data on occupation is lacking for thirty of the 290 households
   present in 1988. Of the remainder twenty-four were
   headed by women.

Table 9.3 displays the various occupations by which married San Jose men and women earn their farm and off-farm incomes. It shows that the number of men pursuing unskilled day labor opportunities as their primary income source has increased, but by less than community population as a whole. Table 9.3 also shows a marked increase, between 1971 and 1988, in the proportion of married women working in the wage sector. Many of these women belonged to the sorts of non-farming households discussed above, but many others were married to farmers. Table 9.3 shows that the proportions of men and women having farming as a primary income source remained roughly the same between 1971 and 1988. But production emphases and the returns to agricultural labor changed greatly during this interval (a subject to which I return below), rendering, again, uncertain the possible implications for well-being of declining landholdings, even within those households relying entirely on farming as a way of life.

In view of the earlier noted difficulties with the applicability of class-based analytical categories, the perceptions that San Jose residents themselves have of economic inequality provide especially valuable insights about the community's socioeconomic structure—and about the nature of social differentiation over time. To anchor my initial (1971) analysis of the economic and social characteristics of San Jose households, I in fact constructed a model of the status order as perceived by community residents themselves, using a standard sociometric procedure, a rating panel. In separate interviews, I asked nine "status raters", representing a variety of socioeconomic circumstances, to divide a stack of cards, each bearing the name of one of San Jose's 112 household heads, into groups to illustrate the local status order. This procedure generated nine separate sets of status placements for San Jose's households. Since different raters used different numbers of groups, I integrated their separate ratings on a single objective scale by first converting all raw scores to percentile scores, and then averaging the nine percentile scores for each household.[3]

During these interviews, I introduced the general notion of higher and lower "standing" in the community, but I otherwise took great care to avoid suggesting the particular ranking criteria to be employed. Most raters, however, said that their primary or sole ranking criterion was *pagcabetang*, a Cuyonon word meaning "level" or "standard of living", making the composite scale that resulted a good, usable index of each household's overall socioeconomic position in the community. So useful did I find this procedure in 1971 that in 1988 I replicated it, now using only six raters but otherwise generating a second set of status scores that was immediately comparable to the first set.

Raters in 1988 tended to use more, rather than fewer, status groups to make their status classifications. Five of the 1971 status raters used three groups, three used four groups, and one used five groups; only one of the 1988 raters used three groups, while two used four groups, two used five groups, and one used six groups. Table 9.4 compares the 1971 and 1988 composite scales with respect to the percent of households falling into each decile.[4] Taken together, these data show no apparent trend toward simplification or polarization of the status order; on the contrary, between 1971 and 1988 there appears to have been a *proliferation* of status levels and a clear *persistence* of households in the middle reaches.

Other data of a subjective sort also support this view, of a relatively benign process of social differentiation. There is no evidence that "class relations" are somehow "heating up"; such gossiping, arguing, and fighting as occurs in the community still takes place between spouses, friends, and neighbors—rather than, say, across class or status lines. Further, the overall ambience of the community remains one of general prosperity; residents at all socioeconomic levels speak of San Jose as a place where the "opportunities to be enterprising" remain broadly accessible and where individual initiative, entrepreneurship, and hard work can still be rewarded by economic advancement. (Both for them and for myself, such Arcadian attributes are only

Table 9.4 - Comparison of the 1971 and 1988 Composite Status Scales

| | 1971 Households | | 1988 Households | |
|---|---|---|---|---|
| Status scores | No. | % | No. | % |
| 0    - 0.10 | 0 | 0.00 | 0 | 0.00 |
| 0.11 - 0.20 | 0 | 0.00 | 0 | 0.00 |
| 0.21 - 0.30 | 10 | 8.92 | 9 | 3.38 |
| 0.31 - 0.40 | 9 | 8.04 | 22 | 8.27 |
| 0.41 - 0.50 | 5 | 4.47 | 45 | 16.92 |
| 0.51 - 0.60 | 12 | 10.71 | 40 | 15.03 |
| 0.61 - 0.70 | 24 | 21.43 | 32 | 12.03 |
| 0.71 - 0.80 | 14 | 12.50 | 35 | 13.16 |
| 0.81 - 0.90 | 23 | 20.53 | 45 | 16.91 |
| 0.91 - 1.00 | 15 | 13.04 | 38 | 14.29 |
| Total | 112 | | 266* | |

\* Twenty-four of the 290 households present in 1988 were not known
to any of the six status raters.

by way of implicit comparison with other rural Philippine communities in
less promising circumstances.) Finally, I suspect (pending analysis of the
relevant data) that even those households falling in the bottom 20–30 percent
of the community socioeconomic order have experienced at least some marginal
*improvement* in their actual socioeconomic well-being between 1971 and 1988
(while those nearer the top of the order have experienced much greater
improvements indeed).

More could be said, of course, about all of these issues, but I would like
to turn now to the role that one particular economic activity, vegetable
gardening, plays in *explaining* these relatively favorable socioeconomic circumstances.

## Vegetable Gardening, 1971–1988

San Jose is best known in Puerto Princesa City as a major supplier of
fresh vegetables to the town marketplace. Gardening there may be viewed
as a descendant of the traditional system of shifting cultivation. Gardens are
cleared by the same slash-and-burn techniques once used for rice fields, and
many of the major garden vegetables were traditionally grown in rice fields
as catch crops. Others were once grown more casually in houseyards or
kitchen gardens. The most common garden vegetables in San Jose are eggplant,
yardlong beans, bitter melon, Chinese cabbage, okra, yellow squash, and
bottle gourd. Those who grow vegetables also consume them in the home,
but the vast majority of garden output is destined for sale in the Puerto
Princesa City public market. Vegetables are typically picked three days a
week, in the afternoon, and brought to the market early the next morning.
In some gardening households, one member (usually the wife) is a regular
vendor in the marketplace and remains there to retail most of the output
herself. In other households, however, a member wholesales the output to
four or five such retail vendors and then returns home.

Despite certain similarities with shifting cultivation, however, gardening involves a variety of technological inputs and cultural practices unlike any employed in traditional agriculture. Gardens are plowed before planting, or individual plots are dug up by hand. Both seedlings and established plants are hand watered during the dry season, and hand cultivated. Chemical fertilizers and pesticides are used by all growers. Trellises must be built for yardlong beans, bitter melon, and the various gourds, and large labor inputs are also needed for weeding, harvesting, bundling, and marketing. In short, vegetable gardening is an intensive agricultural regime needing only small amounts of land (see below) but considerable application of labor.

At the time of my first study, in 1971, gardening was an important secondary income source in many agricultural households whose primary incomes derived from shifting cultivation of rice or from tree crops—two relatively extensive forms of agriculture. Only for a handful of gardeners was gardening a primary source of livelihood, and no household made it their sole source of livelihood. The largest gardens were on the order of 0.20 or 0.25 hectare.

By the time of my return in 1988, the gardening sector of San Jose economy was considerably more robust: 53 farming households made it a major or even a sole source of livelihood, and gardening itself had changed accordingly. The largest gardens were now on the order of 0.50 to 0.75 hectare. Compared to 1971, gardeners in 1988 were more likely to specialize in only two or three kinds of vegetables, they were more likely to wholesale than to retail their output, and they were more likely to keep gardens in continuous, year-round production, rather than letting output wax and wane as other economic activities demanded attention. There had also been some important technological changes: some farmers were using liquid (foliar) fertilizer, instead of the older, granular kind, and a few were operating small gasoline pumps to facilitate watering. Further, a number of gardeners now supplemented or replaced household labor resources by employing daily or monthly laborers to assist them with the more onerous garden chores.

Finally, and most dramatically, labor productivity (the per hour returns to gardening labor expended in the field and in marketing, net of all cash costs) *increased* during the study period. Whereas, in 1971, I had found the returns to gardening labor to be on the order of seven pesos per seven-hour man-day (Eder 1977), such returns in 1988 (and in 1988 prices) were on the order of 85 pesos per man-day. Depending on what measure is used to deflate, for comparative purposes, this latter figure to 1971 prices (e.g., the increase in the Consumer Price Index, the increasing cost of one kilogram of hulled rice), effective 1988 returns are at least 10 and possibly as much as 16 deflated pesos per man-day—significantly above the actual level of return in 1971. This increase occurred despite the fact that land had grown more scarce and more people were gardening, and gardening more intensively, than ever before—the very conditions under which declining returns to labor might be expected to appear. But, at least for the moment, returns to labor have *not* declined, because growing population and growing incomes in

Puerto Princesa City have insured that demand has grown even more rapidly than supply.

A closer look at the demographic and socioeconomic characteristics of those households that pursue vegetable gardening as a primary or secondary income source helps clarify gardening's contribution to maintaining San Jose's relatively favorable socioeconomic circumstances. Gardening is a classic example of an agricultural innovation that increases labor productivity while economizing on land (Eder 1977), and gardening households in fact own little or no agricultural land. The 53 households that made gardening a primary or secondary source of income owned, on the average, only 0.57 hectare of land, less than half the average for San Jose households in general. These households were distributed at all socioeconomic levels, but their mean status score (see above and Table 9.4) was 0.661, nearly identical to that for community households in general (0.663). Even the 14 households whose *sole* income source was gardening, and which averaged 0.43 ha. in landholdings, enjoyed a mean status score of 0.702—only slightly lower. An instructive comparison is with the 46 households that do *not* garden but which otherwise receive only agricultural incomes. Most are long-time San Jose residents; their average landholdings, 4.11 hectares per household, are far greater than those of gardening households, but their mean status score, 0.596, is only moderately higher. A second instructive comparison is with the 35 households for which unskilled day labor is a primary or secondary income source. In comparison to the 53 gardening households, these households have only slightly less land (0.318 hectare per household), but their mean status score, 0.874, places them near the bottom of San Jose's socioeconomic order.

In short, gardening households appear to be drawn from the very sorts of households otherwise most vulnerable to marginalization. Although I am still gathering data on the matter, the cost to these households, for successfully resisting marginalization in this fashion, may be somewhat longer work hours. Gardeners appear to work longer hours than wealthier farmers (with their relatively greater land resources) need to work, or that poorer residents (who typically pursue day-labor opportunities or low-paying government jobs) are willing or able to work.

## Discussion

Based on the research I did during 1970–1972, and because "honeymoons" with cash cropping have come to an end often enough elsewhere, I speculated previously (Eder 1977:19) that San Jose's own honeymoon with vegetable gardening was likely to end soon as well. The material presented here suggests that this prediction was unduly pessimistic; gardening is more common and more, productive than ever, and it remains fully accessible to small farmers with little or no land or capital. With an eye toward the future direction of socioeconomic change in San Jose, these attributes of gardening can profitably be placed in the wider context of two major processes which, at least in this particular community, have militated against polarization of wealth and income and attendant proletarianization of formerly self-sufficient farmers.

The first is the general resilience of the household structure by which many peasants survive as petty commodity producers (Hopkins 1987:167). For our purposes here, this resilience may be traced to the Chayanovian calculus employed by the household firm, which in principle allows it to produce commodities at a price that no capitalist farm could match and still make a profit (Maclachlan 1987:16). Theoretically, much of the debate between the "peasantization" and "proletarianization" schools, about the outcome of capitalist development in agriculture, concerns whether the farm-family's capacity for self-exploitation of labor is, in the long run, sufficient to offset the productivity and other advantages of large, capitalist farms (de Janvry and Vandeman 1987:28–30). Empirically, much fruitful research has been devoted to the particular sociopolitical circumstances and economic activities which confer maximum competitive advantage on peasant farming households (and their Chayanovian calculus), and which are hence likely to stimulate small-scale entrepreneurship and socioeconomic differentiation (rather than simple polarization) in the countryside (Goodman and Redclift 1982:109–112).

Vegetable gardening in San Jose (thanks, in turn, to the community's own wider sociopolitical circumstances) appears to do just this: to allow the small farmer to flourish. At the same time, these wider circumstances, and the nature of gardening itself, do not allow larger farmers to drive out the smaller ones. During my 1988 research, I met several wealthy townspeople with landholdings in San Jose they were seeking to develop along capitalist agricultural lines. Lured by stories of high productivity, all had recently attempted to "break in" to gardening. Each had encountered the same difficulties, and each had given up in frustration. The basic problem was the Chayanovian one, that after meeting all expenses these would-be gardeners were not able to pay themselves an adequate wage. But this problem in turn arose because gardening demanded such long hours of *them*: despite their willingness to "pay", as it were, the incessant, day-to-day tasks of *management* and of *marketing* could not be farmed out to unskilled labor and hence placed intolerable demands to the owner's own time. As one of these men wryly observed, in order to be a successful gardener, you either had to be a peasant yourself, or be married to one.

The second general process militating against polarization and proletarianization in San Jose has been penetration of a wide variety of off-farm activities and incomes, particularly among women. The resulting "rural transformation" (Koppel 1986) in local socioeconomic structure has brought San Jose toward greater integration with the national class structure while somewhat preempting local-level processes of polarization (Hopkins 1987:167). Vegetable gardening is an important element in this process as well, because it combines so readily with off-farm economic activities. From the standpoint of the occupational structure of the community, in many households the husband is a full-time gardener while the wife is a teacher, a store-owner, or is otherwise working fulltime off the farm. Bhaduri, Rahman, and Arn (1986) have recently examined a similar phenomenon in Bangladesh, in which whatever dynamic toward polarization is present has been effectively counteracted by the growth of supplementary income opportunities—and the consequent persistence of large numbers of small-owner farms.

For San Jose, then, gardening has articulated with wider processes of change in a way that (at least by the dismal comparative standards of the lowland Philippines) has prolonged its honeymoon with agricultural development and intensification. True, the community enjoys some unique advantages—strategic market location, for example—but these same "advantages" have also subjected the community to some marked pressures; consider only the tremendous population increase between 1971 and 1988. That San Jose, and its residents, have survived this and other traumas of recent decades provides, in my opinion, substantial case for optimism about the prospects for further agricultural development in this part of the world.

## Acknowledgments

A National Institutes of Mental Health Pre-Doctoral Research Fellowship supported my fieldwork in San Jose during 1970–72. A sabbatical leave from Arizona State University and a grant from the Social Science Research Council supported my fieldwork there during January to July, 1988; a grant from the National Science Foundation is supporting analysis and preparation for publication of the resulting data. I would like to thank Julieta Buaya and Evelyn Martinez, for their assistance in gathering data during 1988, and Janet Fernandez, for her assistance in analyzing data from both periods.

## Notes

1. This formulation of the problem owes to a series of papers in Maclachlan, ed., 1987, and particularly to Maclachlan (1987:16).

2. In 1971, the peso was worth about U.S. $0.13; in 1988, it was worth U.S. $0.05.

3. To convert raw scores to decimal scores, I divided the level a household was placed in by a rater by the total number of levels that particular rater employed. (This procedure assumes that all intervals had equal significance for the raters who made them.) In a three-level status classification, a placement in the first group was scored as 0.33, in the second group as 0.67, and in the bottom group as 1.00. Decimal scores in a ranking system employing four strata were 0.25, 0.50, 0.75, 1.00, and so forth. A household consistently placed in the top group of each of the nine status classifications in 1971 had a mean score of 0.287; households consistently placed in all bottom groups had a mean score of 1.0.

4. There is a slight difference in length between the two scales; the 1988 scale runs from 0.233 (rather than from 0.287) to 1.00 because the 1988 raters tended to use more groups to make their ratings than did the 1971 raters.

# References Cited

Bhaduri, Amit, Hussain Zillur Rahman, and Ann-Lisbet Arn.
1986 Persistence and Polarization: A Study in the Dynamics of Agrarian Contradiction. Journal of Peasant Studies 13(3):82–89.

Brokensha, David.
1966 Social Change at Larteh, Ghana. Oxford: Clarendon Press.

Cancian, Frank.
1981 The Boundaries of Social Stratification Systems. Paper presented at the annual meeting of the American Anthropological Association, December 1981.

Castro, Alfonso Peter, N. Thomas Hakansson, and David Brokensha.
1981 Indicators of Rural Inequality. World Development 9(5):401–427.

de Janvry, Alain and Ann Vandeman.
1987 Patterns of Proletarianization in Agriculture: An International Comparison. *In* Households Economies and their Transformations. Monographs in Economic Anthropology No. 3. Morgan D. Maclachlan, ed. Pp. 28–73. Society for Economic Anthropology and University Press of America.

Eder, James F.
1977 Agricultural Intensification and Returns to Labour in the Philippine Swidden System. Pacific Viewpoint 18:1–21.

1982 Who Shall Succeed? Agricultural Development and Social Inequality on a Philippine Frontier. New York: Cambridge University Press.

Goodman, David, and Michael Redclift.
1982 From Peasant to Proletarian: Capitalist Development and Agrarian Transitions. New York: St. Martin's Press.

Hayami, Yujiro, and Masao Kikuchi.
1981 Asian Village Economy at the Crossroads: An Economic Approach to Institutional Change. Tokyo: University of Tokyo Press.

Hopkins, Nicholas.
1987 The Agrarian Tradition and the Household in Rural Egypt. *In* Household Economies and their Transformations. Monographs in Economic Anthropology No. 3. Morgan D. Maclachlan, ed. Pp. 155–172. Society for Economic Anthropology and University Press of America.

Koppel, Bruce M.
1986 Agrarian Problems and Agrarian Reform: Opportunity or Irony? *In* Rebuilding a Nation: Philippine Challenges and American Policy. Carl H. Lande, ed. Pp. 157–187. Washington, D.C.: The Washington Institute Press.

Maclachlan, Morgan D.
1987 From Intensification to Proletarianization. *In* Household Economies and their Transformations. Monographs in Economic Anthropology No. 3. Morgan D. Maclachlan, ed. Pp. 1–27. Society for Economic Anthropology and University Press of America.

Scott, James C.
1985 Weapons of the Weak: Everyday Forms of Peasant Resistance. New Haven: Yale University Press.

van Schendel, Willem.
1981 Peasant Mobility: The Odds of Life in Rural Bangladesh. Assen, the Netherlands: Van Gorcum.

# 10

## Ethnicity, Economic Choice, and Inequality in a Philippine Frontier Community

*W. Thomas Conelly*

The importance of studying socioeconomic inequality[1] in order to better understand the process of development has been a significant contribution of David Brokensha's perceptive research in Africa over the past three decades (Brokensha 1966; 1987; Castro, Hakansson, and Brokensha 1981; Riley and Brokensha 1988:314–318). In conjunction with Thayer Scudder and the Institute for Development Anthropology, Brokensha has also had a long-term interest in the analysis of resettlement and its impact on the welfare of people (Brokensha 1963; Brokensha and Scudder 1968). These two themes in Brokensha's work, along with his concern for understanding the process of agricultural change, strongly influenced my own research in the Philippines which examined variation in economic choice and resource utilization among migrant farmers in a frontier resettlement community on the island of Palawan.

Frontier communities settled by voluntary migrants often provide an ideal environment for observing and understanding the process of growing socioeconomic inequality (Barlett 1982; Eder 1982; Fernandez 1972; Margolis 1977; Stone, Johnson-Stone, Netting 1984). In the first years of settlement, frontier communities are typically egalitarian, as access to land is open to all, and settlers usually arrive with only a minimum of possessions and equipment necessary for survival. Within one or two generations, however, as population increases and access to land becomes limited, and as individual households pursue a variety of alternate subsistence and commercial enterprises, socioeconomic inequality in frontier communities begins to develop.

This paper focuses on the process of increasing inequality in the frontier settlement of Napsaan on the west coast of Palawan Island in the southern Philippines. In particular, it seeks to explain the initial development of economic differentiation in the context of ethnic diversity and the alternate economic strategies pursued by members of the two main ethnic groups that settled in the community—indigenous ethnic minority Tagbanua who migrated from the east coast of Palawan, and lowland Christian settlers originally from the Visayan Islands in the central Philippines (see Figure 10.1).

The ethnic distinction between "tribal" minority groups such as the Tagbanua and "lowland" Christians is widely recognized in the Philippines. Ethnic minority groups have historically occupied upland forested environments where they have subsisted by a combination of swidden agriculture and hunting and gathering. Until recently, most of the ethnic minority groups resisted the adoption of Christianity and have been only marginally integrated into the wider Philippine society. On Palawan, the ethnic minority groups include the Tagbanua and the Pala'wan who are principally shifting cultivators as well as the Batak, a "Negrito" people who are primarily hunter-gatherers living in the north-central region of the island.

In contrast, the lowland areas of the Philippines have for centuries been occupied by Christian Filipinos who, though they speak different languages and recognize regional distinctions, share important cultural similarities. Virtually all of these people identify themselves as Catholics, are conversant in the national language (Tagalog or Pilipino), participate in and dominate national politics, and engage in "lowland" subsistence practices including irrigated rice production, tree crop farming, and ocean fishing. Lowland Christians recognize these similarities and consciously contrast their own lifestyle with that of upland ethnic minority groups.

## Settlement History

Well into the 20th century, Palawan remained a sparsely populated frontier area outside the mainstream of Philippine political and economic development, occupied primarily by ethnic minority groups. In the 1930s, however, in response to increasing population pressure and land scarcity, a wave of migrant Christian farmers from Cuyo Island and the Visayas in the central Philippines began to settle on the east coast of Palawan (see Figure 10.2). By the 1950s, as the east coast of the island became fully occupied, these lowland settlers started to spill over the central mountain chain in search of land to homestead on the west coast of the island. There the lowlanders found an area that was only sparsely populated by scattered communities of Tagbanua (Conelly 1983).

Though there were Tagbanua communities approximately five kilometers to the north and south, the Napsaan area was largely uninhabited in 1950. The first settlers to arrive in Napsaan in 1954 were a number of Tagbanua families who originally lived in Irawan near the provincial capital of Puerto Princesa on the east coast of the island. These migrant Tagbanua had abandoned their homes and moved to the west coast in response to the intrusion of Christian lowland settlers into the Irawan area in the previous decades. Many east coast Tagbanua lost or sold their land to lowlanders during this period. The Tagbanua were unfamiliar with the formal land registration process and, in some cases, the lowlanders simply occupied parcels of unimproved secondary

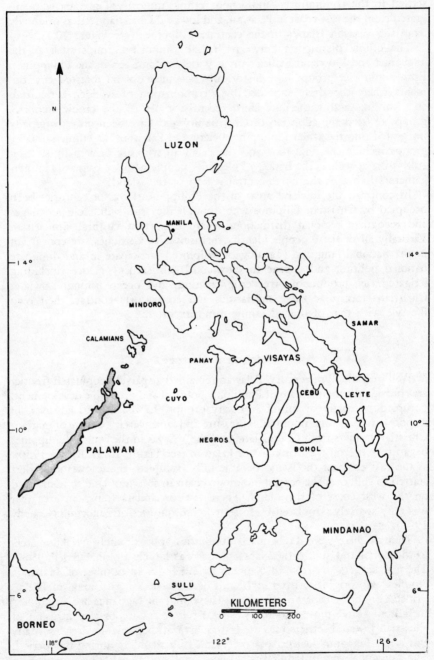

Figure 10.1 - The Philippines

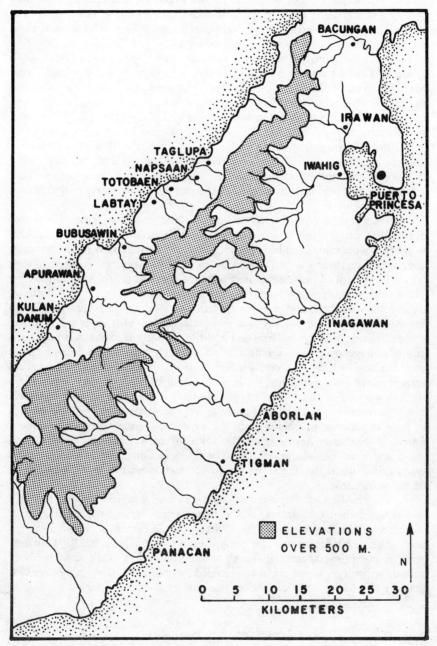

BACUNGAN

IRAWAN

TAGLUPA
NAPSAAN
TOTOBAEN
LABTAY

IWAHIG

PUERTO
PRINCESA

BUBUSAWIN

APURAWAN

KULAN-
DANUM

INAGAWAN

ABORLAN

TIGMAN

ELEVATIONS
OVER 500 M.

N

PANACAN

0    5    10   15   20   25   30
KILOMETERS

Figure 10.2 – Central Palawan ca. 1950

growth not actively being cultivated by the Tagbanua and claimed it as their own. In other cases, in need of immediate cash to repay debts or to pay medical expenses, Tagbanua sold their land to lowlanders who were anxious to own property close to the capital city.[2]

Only a year after the arrival of the east coast Tagbanua in Napsaan, a group of lowland settlers from the Visayas arrived to homestead land across the river from the Tagbanua settlement. This time the Tagbanua chose not to retreat away from the Christian settlers but to remain in Napsaan and maintain their claims over the land they had homesteaded. In subsequent years, many of the Tagbanua families in Napsaan allowed their children to marry the offspring of lowland settlers and most of the Tagbanua eventually adopted Catholicism, the dominant religion of the lowland majority in the Philippines. At the same time, a few Tagbanua began to adopt lowland subsistence techniques, including irrigated rice production, tree crop farming, and ocean fishing.[3]

Interviews with both Tagbanua and lowland migrants about their lives during the early years of settlement indicate that differences in economic well-being were initially of little consequence. All early settlers report arriving, after a two or three day walk over the mountains from the east coast, with only a minimum of possessions necessary for survival on an isolated frontier. Their belongings typically included only a few household items and clothing, basic tools (machete and axe for clearing swiddens), and enough rice to survive until the first harvest was complete. A few also reported bringing some medicine (e.g. for malaria) and a "little" money. If lowlanders possessed any advantage over the Tagbanua at the time it was not in wealth (most were landless or land poor on their home islands) or education (the education system in the Philippines had broken down during the war years when these settlers were children), but in experience they had in dealing with outsiders and government officials. The Tagbanua, on the other hand, had the benefit of long experience in coping with the type of tropical forest environment found in Napsaan. Recognizing the value of their hunting and gathering skills and their knowledge of forest swidden farming, the lowland settlers often called upon the Tagbanua for advice and assistance in the early years of the settlement.

As the children of the original Tagbanua and lowland settlers matured and claimed their own farms, and as new settlers arrived the population of Napsaan gradually increased. In 1980, after 25 years of settlement, the community had grown to 350 people living in 68 households. Tagbanua families comprised about one-fourth of the population, while households of mixed ethnicity (Tagbanua inter-married with lowlanders) accounted for another one-fourth and lowlanders one-half of the community.

## Socioeconomic Inequality

By 1980, 25 years after initial settlement, a significant degree of socioeconomic inequality had developed in Napsaan. Anthropologists often measure such inequality with surveys of household income or size of landholding, but neither method is appropriate for Napsaan. Though cash income is important for some households, others are primarily subsistence-oriented and the irregular cash income they receive would be difficult to estimate accurately. Likewise, size of landholding, which roughly ranges from 3 to 10 hectares, is an inappropriate indicator in Napsaan. Many of the homesteads have not yet been titled or surveyed and in many cases neither the farmers nor I were able to accurately estimate the size of the parcels. In any case, though differences in farm size exist, they are only now becoming significant because until the mid-1970s, when the government restricted further clearing of the forest for swidden agriculture, unoccupied forest land was freely available to all settlers.

As an alternate method to measure socioeconomic inequality in Napsaan, a household survey assessing the type of each family's house as well as the household items and productive equipment they own was used to measure the differences in economic status within the community (Castro, Hakansson, and Brokensha 1981; Fleuret 1978). Each household possession (e.g. farm equipment, radio, lantern) as well as the types of materials used in constructing the house were assigned a point score based on relative value. The individual points were totaled to arrive at an overall score that indicates the socioeconomic status of each household in the community. Based on this method, 15 percent of the households are in the upper group while middle and lower group families account for 37 and 48 percent of the community.[4]

Explaining the variation in economic success in Napsaan is a complex problem involving a number of variables. Both Eder (1982) and Fernandez (1972), who discuss resettled communities on the east coast of Palawan, emphasize the importance of variation in individual competence and life experience as well as fortuitous events and differences in opportunity in explaining why certain settlers are more successful than others in adjusting to frontier life. These personal characteristics and individual events are also certainly relevant in an explanation of success and failure in Napsaan. In addition, however, extrinsic factors, such as differences in the date of arrival and stage of the domestic cycle, also influence the socioeconomic status of particular households in the community (Conelly 1983:126–129).

In this paper I focus on ethnicity and choice of economic strategy, which are the two household characteristics most strongly associated with the initial development of inequality in Napsaan. Though a number of Tagbanua have achieved upper group status through a judicious combination of traditional upland subsistence activities with intensive agricultural techniques borrowed from the lowlanders, many others have failed to emulate their success. In addition, unlike the lowlanders, upper group Tagbanua do not seem to be passing their success on to their married children who all occupy the lower economic strata and who, with few exceptions, appear to have no prospects for improvement in the years ahead. (Table 10.1 illustrates the relationship between ethnicity and socioeconomic status.)

Lowland settlers in Napsaan often comment on the poverty of the Tagbanua and attribute this to what they see as the laziness and poor planning typical

Table 10.1   - Household Socioeconomic Status by Ethnicity*

| Status | TAGBANUA | | LOWLAND | |
|--------|:--------:|:--:|:-------:|:--:|
|        | #        | %  | #       | %  |
| Upper  | 5        | 14.3 | 6     | 16.7 |
| Middle | 5        | 14.3 | 21    | 58.3 |
| Lower  | 25       | 71.4 | 9     | 25.0 |
| Total  | 35       | 100.0 | 36   | 100.0 |

* Household counted as "Tagbanua" if either spouse is Tagbanua

of tribal minorities. In contrast, they see themselves as being highly industrious and competent managers of both their farm operations and business enterprises. This ethnic stereotype, widespread among lowlanders throughout Palawan, does not hold up well under scrutiny. First, as seen in Table 10.1, there *are* successful Tagbanua families in Napsaan who, at least by local standards, have achieved economic success. Napsaan lowlanders recognize this achievement, if somewhat reluctantly, and explain it by admitting that a few exceptional Tagbanua have assimilated their values of hard work and careful planning.

Second, the notion that the Tagbanua are poor because they are unwilling to work as hard as lowlanders is not supported by data collected on household time allocation. A year-long time use survey based on random observations of the daytime activities of adults in Napsaan[5] found no significant difference between Tagbanua and lowlanders in the overall amount of time allocated to economic tasks over the year. As shown in Table 10.2, Tagbanua women engage in economic activities to the same extent as lowland women while Tagbanua men are only slightly less active than their lowland counterparts (see Conelly 1983 for details).

Though the *amount* of labor expended is roughly equal, the time allocation data do indicate important differences in the *type* of economic activities that the Tagbanua and lowlanders choose to pursue. For both ethnic groups, swidden rice production remains the dominant subsistence activity. But rapid population growth and a government ban on clearing swiddens from forest land above the village have resulted in fallow periods that now average only two or three years. As a result, the returns to swidden rice production in Napsaan are now precariously low, averaging only about 700 kilograms per hectare. This figure is less than one-half of the yield achieved in earlier years when fallow periods were typically ten years or more, and it is one of the lowest rice yields reported for a swidden system in all of Southeast Asia (Conelly 1983). In response to these declining returns, in recent years many Tagbanua men have intensified their collecting of rattan and copal in the forest for sale on the market. In contrast, lowlanders have increasingly focused their efforts on wage labor, irrigated rice production, tree crop production (e.g. cashew), and ocean fishing.[6]

Table 10.2 - Adult Daylight Time Allocation to Economic Activities
by Ethnicity

| | TAGBANUA | | LOWLAND | |
|---|---|---|---|---|
| TASK | Females (n=640) | Males (n=728) | Females (n=425) | Males (n=631) |
| | | Percent of daylight time | | |
| **Agriculture** | | | | |
| Swidden | 10.2 | 8.9 | 8.9 | 10.1 |
| Irrigated/Plow | 0.9 | 2.3 | 3.3 | 3.7 |
| Tree crops | 0.6 | 1.8 | 1.0 | 1.6 |
| House gardens | 1.1 | 0.0 | 0.7 | 0.2 |
| Livestock care | 0.3 | 1.9 | 1.2 | 1.4 |
| Share/debt/wage | 5.2 | 4.5 | 8.2 | 9.4 |
| **ALL AGRICULTURE** | **18.3** | **19.4** | **23.3** | **26.4** |
| Fishing (ocean) | 0.6 | 2.6 | 1.2 | 4.1 |
| **Forest** | | | | |
| Collecting | 0.2 | 10.4 | 0.0 | 0.3 |
| Hunting | 0.0 | 1.7 | 0.0 | 0.0 |
| Wage labor (non-farm) | 2.0 | 4.2 | 1.2 | 10.6(a) |
| Business | 2.3 | 0.4 | 0.5 | 0.8 |
| Other(b) | 9.1 | 7.6 | 6.1 | 9.1 |
| **ALL ECONOMIC ACTIVITY** | **32.5** | **46.3** | **32.3** | **51.3** |

a. Wage labor for lowland males primarily work for logging company.
b. Other includes travel time (primarily business or work related),
   seasonal labor outside the community (e.g. harvesting coffee
   for wage), and equipment manufacture and repair.

Table 10.3 - Household Socioeconomic Status by Subsistence Type

| | FOREST | | FISHING | | IRRIGATION | |
|---|---|---|---|---|---|---|
| STATUS | # | % | # | % | # | % |
| Upper | 0 | 0.0 | 0 | 0.0 | 8 | 61.5 |
| Middle | 1 | 7.1 | 10 | 55.6 | 5 | 38.5 |
| Lower | 13 | 92.9 | 8 | 44.4 | 0 | 0.0 |
| TOTAL | 14 | 100.0 | 18 | 100.0 | 13 | 100.0 |

   This contrast in the choice of productive activities is, I believe, a major
determinant of the socioeconomic inequality found in Napsaan between the
Tagbanua and lowland settlers.[7] Table 10.3 shows the relation between the
primary economic orientation of a household and socioeconomic status.
Households are divided between those that focus on forest collecting and
those that emphasize ocean fishing or irrigated rice production. While the
large majority of forest collecting households are in the lower socioeconomic
group, ocean fishing and irrigated rice production are associated mainly with
middle and upper group status.

## Economic Choice and Inequality

A comparison of households that emphasize forest collecting with others in the community that focus on ocean fishing will help demonstrate the relationship between choice of economic strategy and inequality in Napsaan.

The Tagbanua participated for centuries in a regional trade network in which they exchanged minor forest products for manufactured goods such as cloth, metal, and ceremonial brass gongs obtained from Chinese and Muslim merchants (Conelly 1983; Warren 1985). In recent decades, many Tagbanua have continued to collect forest products but now do so from government regulated concessions located in the central mountains of the island that have been awarded to Chinese and lowland Christian merchants in Puerto Princesa City. Their efforts focus the sale of rattan (primarily *Calamus caesius*) and Manila copal—a resin produced by the tree *Agathis dammara* that is used in the manufacture of varnish and other industrial products. Though there is evidence that sources of rattan and copal are in danger of depletion and that the efficiency of collecting is declining, many Napsaan Tagbanua continue this forest activity as their main source of income (Conelly 1985). In contrast, the hunting of forest animals, primarily wild pig, is today much less important than in the past. In addition, women now rarely visit the forest and the gathering of wild plant foods has all but disappeared in the community.

An alternate subsistence strategy pursued by many of the lowland households in Napsaan is ocean fishing in small double outrigger boats. Several methods of fishing are employed by the settlers, the most common of which is the use of a baited hook on a nylon fishing line attached to a small wooden spool. During the day the line is simply thrown overboard and allowed to drift behind the boat. Successful nighttime handline fishing requires the use of a flashlight or, preferably, a kerosene pressure lantern on cloudy or moonless nights. In the absence of competing light from the moon, the lantern attracts the fish to the vicinity of the boat where they can be more easily caught. In addition to handline fishing, a few lowland men also use nets to catch fish from their boats. Finally, both (a few) Tagbanua and lowland men use homemade spear guns to capture fish and other marine animals such as lobster and squid in shallow waters near the edge of the reef. Roughly one-third of the fish catch is sold, usually to local buyers, but it is occasionally transported by vehicle to Puerto Princesa City.

Measurement of the returns to forest collecting and ocean fishing, in terms of the cash value of the products collected, indicates that the two activities are equally remunerative. Both enterprises produce a return that averages in the range of 15–18 Pesos/day (Table 10.4).[8] Though both forest collecting and ocean fishing provide similar cash returns to labor, there are important differences in the overall consequences of the two activities. First, forest collecting results in a greater conflict in the scheduling of labor than is the case for fishing. While fishing generally takes place just off-shore from Napsaan, forest collecting sites are located two to five hours walk away from

Table 10.4 - Estimated Returns to Forest Collecting & Fishing

|                              | RATTAN    | COPAL     | FISHING    |
| ---------------------------- | --------- | --------- | ---------- |
| # trips observed             | 20        | 43        | 20         |
| Total person hours labor     | 227       | 1146      | 396        |
| Total kg.                    | n/a       | 3296      | 251        |
| Peso value per kilo          | n/a       | 1.00      | 3.50       |
| Ave. peso earned/ day (8 hr.)| 15.40     | 18.40     | 16.90      |
| Range peso earned/day        | 5.6-38.7  | 0.0-50.0  | 4.2-63.0   |

Note: in 1981 U.S. $1.00 equaled 8 Philippine pesos

the village, typically requiring an overnight stay in the forest. Though collectors actually work only about an eight hour day, overnight trips require that they be away from their farms and other work demands a full 24 hours. In effect, a "work day" in the forest is longer than a comparable work day fishing because it monopolizes a collector's entire day and prevents him from working on other tasks that compete for his time.

As a result, forest collecting trips, typically two to three days in duration, at times conflict with the essential labor requirements of swidden agriculture. In the months February through April 1981, for example, when rainfall was low and travel easy, forest collecting accounted for an average of 15.4 percent (or about 14 days) of Tagbanua men's daylight time. This high proportion of time allocated to collecting might have been better spent working harder on the clearing of rice swiddens, a task that must be completed before the rainy season begins in May. With the very low yields now achieved in Napsaan swiddens, the preparation of large fields is necessary to assure an adequate supply of rice for household consumption throughout the year.

Rice swiddens cleared by the households of men who regularly collect copal and/or rattan (N=12) were quite small by Napsaan standards, averaging only .74 hectares in 1981. In contrast, though there is greater variability, swiddens cleared by households of men who regularly fished (N=11) averaged 1.24 hectares in size. For the community as a whole, the mean swidden size of a representative sample of 35 households was 1.08 hectares. The differences in swidden size cannot be accounted for simply by variability in household size or composition. The households of the fishermen are only slightly larger, on the average, than the households of the forest collectors and both groups consist almost entirely of households headed by young couples in their twenties or thirties with children under 15 years of age.

In addition to clearing smaller swiddens, the families of forest collectors also achieved lower rice yields in 1981. While the swiddens of fishermen averaged 610 kilograms of rice per hectare, those of forest oriented households

Table 10.5 - Swidden Size and Productivity by Subsistence Type

| | FOREST COLLECTORS (N=12) | FISHERMEN (N=11) |
|---|---|---|
| Average swidden size (ha.) | 0.74 | 1.24 |
| Range swidden size (ha.) | .36-1.14 | .28-2.33 |
| Average yield per ha. (kg.)* | 515 | 610 |
| Average household size | 5.0 | 5.8 |
| Average kg. rice per member/year | 76 | 130 |

**\* Kilograms of unmilled rice. Sample size for yields is seven for forest collectors and eleven for fishermen.**

averaged only 515 kilograms, a reduction of about 15 percent. As a result of these differences in swidden size and yield, forest collecting households produced an average of only 76 kilograms of rice per member in 1981, as compared to approximately 130 kilograms per person for the households of fishermen. As a consequence, forest collectors find themselves more vulnerable to shortages of rice during the "hunger" season in the months before the harvest in September. Table 10.5 summarizes differences in swidden size and productivity for the two groups.

## Food Security and Socioeconomic Inequality

Fishing, by virtue of its proximity to the village, results in less of a scheduling conflict than does forest collecting. This permits fishermen to devote more time to other pursuits, including swidden labor, than is possible for forest collectors (see Table 10.5). Another advantage of fishing is that it provides both a source of cash income *and* a source of high quality protein. Forest collecting of copal and rattan provides few nutritional inputs for the families of collectors and the cash earnings that they receive are not always spent on food. Though collectors are sometimes paid with a sack of rice as an advance, these advances are provided at unfavorable rates of interest and contribute to their chronic indebtedness (see below). Cash payment for forest products is often irregular and made in lump sums. This encourages the diversion of forest income to non-subsistence ends, such as debt repayment or purchases of consumer goods and other non-food items.

Both of these factors—a shortfall in swidden rice production and limited access to fish as a source of protein—would be expected to result in a lower quality diet for the families of forest collectors. This expectation is in fact supported by food consumption diaries, completed at intervals over an eight month period by a representative sample of households, and by an anthropometric assessment of preschool age children.[9]

Table 10.6 - Napsaan Dietary Intake by Subsistence Type

| FOOD ITEM | FOREST (N=147 meals) | FISHING (N=204 meals) | ALL (N=906 meals) |
|---|---|---|---|
| | Percent of meals food consumed | | |
| Rice | 77.5 | 100.0 | 93.7 |
| Fish | 27.2 | 58.8 | 50.0 |
| Meat | 4.1 | 2.4 | 6.8 |
| Other Protein | 4.7 | 12.7 | 9.3 |

Note: The morning and afternoon snack ("merienda"), if consumed, was counted as part of the breakfast or evening meal.

The results of the dietary survey show that the families of forest collectors consume significantly less rice and fish, the two staples of the Napsaan diet, than the families of fishermen. In contrast, the households of men who regularly fish were found to have a diet superior to that of the population as a whole. In terms of carbohydrate consumption, the fishing families reported eating rice at 100 percent of their meals while the families of forest collectors ate rice at only 77.5 percent of their meals. Rice is perceived as an essential part of all meals (including breakfast) and to be forced to do without is considered a real hardship. Fishing households also report a higher consumption of alternate carbohydrate sources, such as cassava and sweet potato. Likewise, the families of fishermen reported eating fish at 58.8 percent of their meals while fish was consumed less than half as often in forest collecting households. The overall consumption of other less common sources of protein, such as eggs, legumes, and shellfish, was also higher for the families of fishermen. Forest collecting families consumed slightly more meat than fishing families—reflecting the returns from forest hunting of a few Tagbanua males. Table 10.6 summarizes the results of the dietary survey for both fishing and forest collecting households.

Two anthropometric surveys conducted during January and July in 1981 provide evidence that the children of men who regularly collect forest products have a markedly lower nutritional status than children of men who specialize in fishing. As shown in Table 10.7, the proportion of children with a normal weight for age is lower for the offspring of forest collectors while the degree of moderate or severe malnutrition among their children is high, especially in the month of July near the end of the preharvest "hunger" season.

## Discussion

The association between ethnicity and inequality in Napsaan is misleading. The popular stereotype among lowlanders that Tagbanua are poor simply because they are a tribal minority who by nature are lazy and less ambitious than lowlanders is contradicted by data showing that they expend an equivalent amount of time on economic activities. Nor are they poor because their forest collecting strategy is irrational or inefficient using the conventional

Table 10.7 - Gomez classification of Weight-for-age for Napsaan
Children by Household Subsistence Type

| | JANUARY | | JULY | |
|---|---|---|---|---|
| DEGREE OF | Forest | Fishing | Forest | Fishing |
| MALNUTRITION* | (N=25) | (N=27) | (N=21) | (N=26) |
| Normal | 24.0 % | 33.3 % | 14.2 % | 19.2 % |
| Mild | 44.0 | 40.7 | 38.1 | 61.5 |
| Moderate | 32.0 | 25.9 | 42.9 | 19.2 |
| Severe | 0.0 | 0.0 | 4.8 | 0.0 |
| TOTAL | 100.0 | 100.0 | 100.0 | 100.0 |

* In the Gomez classification, normal is defined as greater
than 90% of "ideal" weight. Mild malnutrition is 90-75% of
ideal weight, moderate malnutrition is 74-60%, and severe is
defined as less than 60% of ideal weight. Weight for age score
for any child is actual weight divided by ideal weight, times
100. Ideal weight is the 50th percentile value of normal
children the same age as the index child (Martorell 1982:15).

measure of returns to labor. The cash received for rattan and copal collecting
is equivalent to that of ocean fishing, and considerably higher than the typical
agricultural wage labor rate of 10 pesos/day. Rather, I argue, many Tagbanua
are poor because of the indirect costs of their subsistence strategy. Forest
collecting creates scheduling conflicts with essential agricultural tasks and,
as a "cash crop" enterprise, it fails to provide protein in the diet. As a
result, the diet of Tagbanua forest collecting households is deficient in rice
and protein compared to others in the community, and a disproportionate
number of their children are malnourished as evidenced by anthropometric
measurements.

In contrast, other Tagbanua have pursued alternate economic strategies
and, by local standards are prospering. All five of the Tagbanua in the upper
socioeconomic category (Table 10.1), for instance, grow irrigated rice to
supplement their swidden production. With its increased reliability and
potential for double-cropping, irrigation provides a dependable source of rice
throughout the year. These Tagbanua households have good diets and the
large majority of their children were found to have a normal weight for age
in the anthropometric survey (Conelly 1983:268–282).

Household economic security in Napsaan requires food self-sufficiency.
Families that fail to produce sufficient rice and protein must do without or
borrow from relatives, neighbors, storeowners, or the agents who purchase
forest products in the village. Though loans of rice from a close relative
may have no explicit interest charge, other loans are made with the understanding that they will be repaid in labor or cash with interest. A common
form of loan is the *timpuan* in which the borrower is required to repay the
loan with a portion of the next harvest. Typically, a loan of one *cavan* of
rice (44 kilogram) during the hunger season is repaid with two *cavan* at
harvest time—an interest rate of 100 percent over a period of two to five

months. As would be expected given their smaller field size and lower yields, the households of forest collectors borrow rice more frequently and lose a larger share of their harvest in debt repayments. In 1981, for example, forest collecting households for which I have yield data (N=7) turned over 22 percent of their rice harvest to their creditors. In contrast, fishing households (N=11) lost only 7 percent of their newly harvested rice to debt repayments.

Another form of indebtedness associated with forest collecting is the practice by purchasing agents of sometimes paying the collectors in advance with rice, cigarettes, or tobacco. These loans must be repaid, with interest, by forest products. The two types of debt—advances from the agents and loans of rice during the hunger season—lead many collectors into a vicious circle of continuing indebtedness as their obligations carry over and accumulate from one year to the next. This type of indebtedness is a problem for other households in the community as well, but forest collectors, because of their low rice yields, are especially vulnerable. Unable to accumulate capital for investment in economic enterprises, forest collectors remain at the bottom of the socioeconomic scale, poorly nourished, and unable to improve their level of living.

## Conclusion

Economic choices made by individual settlers and the consequences of pursuing different subsistence strategies were important elements in the initial development of inequality in Napsaan. By the 1980s, however, new social and economic forces were beginning to influence the ability of households to achieve prosperity. Land scarcity, brought about by continued immigration and the closing of the frontier by government regulations banning forest swiddens, had become a factor in a family's success or failure. In particular, access to the limited irrigable land in Napsaan, on which double-cropping of rice is possible, is now one important way to assure an adequate supply of rice. The continuing construction of irrigated fields, the emergence of a small number of poorer farmers who rent irrigated land, and active maneuvering to purchase irrigable land, sometimes from debt-ridden families, are all signs of this trend. At the same time, the ability to provide children with a higher education has become increasingly important. Because of economic choices made during the early years of settlement, some families are in a better position than others to take advantage of these new circumstances. Napsaan, in other words, is becoming an established lowland Philippine community in which individual initiative and wise use of resources, while still important, will no longer be sufficient to achieve prosperity. Unequal control over land and differences in access to education and wage employment will in the future play an increasingly important role in economic success.

## Notes

1. By socioeconomic inequality I refer to differences in wealth, income, possessions, and access to natural resources, services, and power (Brokensha 1987:1). The phrase

*economic differentiation* will also be used to describe the process of growing socio-economic inequality and *socioeconomic status* will be used to refer to groups of households that share a similar level of economic well-being as measured by a survey of household possessions (see below).

2. Compare Brown 1988, Eder 1987, Lopez 1987, Warner 1979 for discussion of similar loss of land among other indigenous groups on the island of Palawan.

3. This conscious effort at assimilation into lowland society by the Napsaan Tagbanua contrasts with the strategy of other ethnic minority populations in Palawan that have attempted to withdraw from contact with lowlanders and maintain a separate ethnic identity. See Brown 1988, Lopez 1987, Eder 1987, Warner 1979.

4. Households in Napsaan are typically two generation nuclear families, though a few are comprised only of single males (either unmarried or new arrivals waiting to send for their families) or three generation families in which a widowed parent lives with an adult child and his/her offspring. The total household scores ranged from just 9 points for the poorest household to 77 for the wealthiest family in the community. Upper group families are classified as those with 40 or more points, middle group households scored 20–39 points, and lower group households are those with less than 20 points. Note that 71 households are included in the discussion of inequality while only 68 households were listed in the community census discussed in the text. The discrepancy is due to the arrival of several new families in the community after the census was completed in November 1980.

5. In the random time allocation method, households in the community were divided into neighborhood clusters of 2–5 households. Each cluster was visited at randomly chosen hours of the day several times each month over a one year period. At the selected time I would approach the houses in the cluster and record the activities of all adults in each household before they were able to react to my presence. If I was unable to determine with confidence a person's activity or the person could not be located the observation was discarded (less than 8 percent of total observations over the year). If an individual was not present (e.g. collecting in the forest) I would accept reports only from reliable members of the household and attempted to confirm the report whenever possible. Because of the scattered settlement pattern of the community and the time constraints of other research, I was able to visit only one cluster per day, resulting in about 200 observations of individuals per month and a total of 2424 observations over the year. See Johnson 1975 and Conelly 1983 for details.

6. The importance of ocean fishing as an economic activity is underestimated by the random time allocation technique because much fishing takes place by lantern at night when the spot-check visits were not possible. I estimate that the actual importance of fishing is at least double that indicated by the survey of daytime activities shown in Table 10.2.

7. This argument about the origins of inequality is directly relevant only to the Napsaan Tagbanua who, like the lowlanders, are recent *migrants* and who have chosen to assimilate into lowland society. I agree with the evidence that elsewhere in Palawan inequality is largely the result of loss of land and resources by ethnic minority groups as a result of encroachment and exploitation by lowland settlers onto lands traditionally belonging to indigenous groups (see Brown 1988; Lopez 1987; Eder 1987; 1988; Warner 1979). Indeed, it is just this process that initially led the Napsaan Tagbanua to leave their original home area on the east coast of Palawan. Other Tagbanua in the west coast area have, with more or less success, attempted to resist assimilation by retreating away from the coastal settlements of the lowland Christians.

8. In most cases, my data on returns to forest collecting in Napsaan are based on brief interviews with collectors upon their return from a forest trip. However, I

also accompanied the Tagbanua to their forest camps and/or collecting sites on three occasions totaling five days in length. In eight cases I actually witnessed the weighing of the copal, in the remainder the collectors were asked to estimate the weight of their load or the number of pieces of rattan. From experience I can say that they are able to estimate weights quite accurately as this is the measure by which copal payments are made. It should also be noted that the data do not cover all forest trips during the year. Rather, they are drawn only from those trips that I became aware of in advance, usually during my daily random time allocation visits. Because of the generally random way in which the trips were selected for measurement, I do not feel that the sample is biased in favor of the more successful trips.

Returns to fishing were measured by weighing the catch with a hanging scale at the beach as the fishermen landed their boats. Time estimates for fishing were based on observation in some cases, but more often by interviewing the fishermen as they returned in the morning about the time of their departure, which was typically determined by reference to time of sunset (when many boats departed) or the height of the moon at departure. Measurements of fish yield were made only during the period May-August which corresponds with the end of the dry season and beginning of the rainy season.

9. For the dietary diaries, female heads of household who were literate (or with assistance of a literate household member) were asked to record the foods prepared for family members each day for a week. The survey was repeated with a representative sample of households several times over an eight month period. Considerable care was taken to assure that the diaries were as accurate as possible. The purpose of the diaries was carefully explained and several examples were discussed with each participant. When collecting the diaries, we discussed the responses with the informant to clarify any information that was unclear. The technique does not provide data on the amount of food consumed nor does it capture all types of food eaten (e.g. casual foods taken away from the household) but does provide data on the frequency with which each household consumes the most important staple foods such as rice, fish, and meat.

Anthropometric measurements of virtually all preschool age children in the community were taken in January and July. My colleague M. Chaiken and I weighed all of the children ourselves to assure the highest degree of accuracy. A hanging scale with spring mechanism was used to weigh the smaller children while older children were weighed on a standing scale that had been tested for accuracy by comparing it to a balance scale at the City Nutritionist's Office in Puerto Princesa. See Conelly 1983, for details of dietary and anthropometric survey methodology.

## References Cited

Barlett, Peggy F.
    1982    Agricultural Choice and Change: Decision Making in a Costa Rican Community. New Brunswick, N.J.: Rutgers University Press.
Brokensha, David W.
    1963    Volta Resettlement and Anthropological Research. Human Organization 22(4):286–290.
    1966    Social Change at Larteh, Ghana. Oxford: Clarendon Press.
    1987    Inequality in Rural Africa: Fallers Reconsidered. Manchester Papers on Development 3(2):1–21.

Brokensha, David and Thayer Scudder.
    1968    Resettlement. *In* Dams in Africa. N. Rubin and W.M. Warren, eds. Pp. 20–62. London: Frank Cass.
Brown, Elaine C.
    1988    Land for Tribal Filipinos: the Dynamics of Social Differentiation and Agrarian Reform. Paper Presented at the Annual Meeting of the American Anthropological Association, Phoenix.
Castro, Alfonso Peter, N. T. Hakansson, and David W. Brokensha.
    1981    Indicators of Rural Inequality. World Development 9(5):401–427.
Conelly, W. Thomas.
    1983    Upland Development in the Tropics: Alternative Economic Strategies in a Philippine Frontier Community. unpublished PhD. dissertation. Dept. of Anthropology. University of California, Santa Barbara.
    1985    Copal and Rattan Collecting in the Philippines. Economic Botany 39(1):39–46.
Eder, James F.
    1982    Who Shall Succeed? Agricultural Development and Social Inequality on a Philippine Frontier. Cambridge: Cambridge University Press.
    1987    On the Road to Tribal Extinction: Depopulation, Deculturation, and Adaptive Well-Being Among the Batak of the Philippines. Berkeley: University of California Press.
    1988    Hunter-Gatherer/Farmer Exchange in the Philippines: Some Implications for Ethnic Identity and Adaptive Well-Being. *In* Ethnic Identity and the Control of Natural Resources in Southeast Asia. A. Terry Rambo, Kathy Gillogy, and Karl Hutterer, eds. Pp. 37–57. Center for South and SE Asian Studies. University of Michigan.
Fernandez, Carlos.
    1972    Blueprints, Realities, and Success in a Frontier Resettlement Community. Philippine Sociological Review 20:176–273.
Fleuret, Patrick.
    1978    Farm and Market: A Study of Society and Agriculture in Tanzania. unpublished PhD. dissertation. Dept. of Anthropology. University of California, Santa Barbara.
Johnson, Allen.
    1975    Time Allocation in a Machiguenga Community. Ethnology 14:301–310.
Lopez, Maria Elena.
    1987    The Politics of Lands at Risk in a Philippine Frontier. *In* Lands at Risk in the Third World. Peter D. Little and Michael M Horowitz, eds. Pp.230–248. Boulder: Westview Press.
Margolis, Maxine.
    1977    Historical Perspectives on Frontier Agriculture as an Adaptive Strategy. American Ethnologist 4:42–64.
Martorell, Reynaldo.
    1982    Nutrition and Health Status Indicators: Suggestions for Surveys of the Standard of Living in Developing Countries. Living Standards Measurement Study. Working Paper No. 13. Washington, D.C.: The World Bank.
Riley, Bernard W. and David Brokensha.
    1988    The Mbeere in Kenya. Vol I: Changing Rural Economy. Lanham, MD: University Press of America.

Stone, Glenn D., M. Priscilla Johnson-Stone, and Robert M. Netting.
1984    Household Variability and Inequality in Kofyar Subsistence and Cash-Cropping Economies. Journal of Anthropological Research 40:90–108.
Warner, Katherine.
1979    Walking on Two Feet: Tagbanwa Adaptation to Philippine Society. unpublished PhD dissertation. Dept. of Anthropology. University of Hawaii.
Warren, James F.
1985    The Sulu Zone, 1768–1898. Singapore: University Press, Singapore.

# 11

## Socioeconomic Stratification and Marriage Payments: Elite Marriage and Bridewealth Among the Gusii of Kenya

*Thomas Hakansson*

Socioeconomic differentiation in eastern Africa is increasing and a stratum of wealthy elites is forming. Such elites command substantial economic and political resources and have a lifestyle which culturally and socially separates them from the poor farming population. The elite form a self perpetuating class which protects its control over scarce resources and a privileged lifestyle (cf. Brokensha 1987; Cohen 1981). In East Africa, as in other parts of the world, marriage is part of elite strategies for establishing social networks and alliances (cf. Cohen 1981; Staudt 1987; Obbo 1987).

Cohen (1981) points out that elite members consciously strive to form corporate organizations or socioeconomic networks which serve a number of purposes; as channels for mutual support, as a means of excluding others from privilege, and to promote the perpetuation of their high socioeconomic status for their children. I suggest that it is in this context that bridewealth has attained new significance. First, bridewealth serves as a means of establishing social and economic networks based on class rather than descent groups. Second, it is used by women and parents to arrange marriage to financially able men, thereby maintaining social and economic status of the women and their future children. The establishment of marriage in eastern Africa is dependent on payment of bridewealth which, rather than disappearing, is retaining its importance as an institution of central social and economic significance (cf. Ferraro 1976; Hakansson 1988; Parkin & Nyamwaya 1987; Parkin 1978; Schuster 1978).

There are few studies (cf. Hakansson 1988; LaFontaine 1962; Weinreich 1983) which pay attention to how the institution of bridewealth has changed in relation to increased social and economic stratification, and how it is used by the new elites. This paper presents a brief outline of how the elite of the Gusii people in western Kenya manage marriages aiming at establishing favorable social connections and how the bridewealth system contributes to the perpetuation of socioeconomic status through generations.[1]

## Stratification and Marriage Payments

The most influential theoretical framework relating marriage payments to socioeconomic stratification and property control was formulated by Goody (1973) and modified by Schlegel and Eloul (1988). Their approach may be summarized as follows: bridewealth in African societies is causally connected to relative economic equality and the absence of socioeconomic stratification based on unequal access to the means of production. Most African societies are patrilineal. Bridewealth secures the affiliation of children to their father's lineage and gives the husbands rights in their wives' productive power. In sub-Saharan Africa, where land is plentiful and labor scarce, women carry out the majority of labor. Acquisition of many wives enhances agricultural production and the family's wealth. Wives also produce sons for the perpetuation of the patrilineage.

A potential husband's economic position is therefore not an important factor in choosing a spouse for a daughter. The future position of the women and her children is dependent on the labor input of their family. Inheritance of wealth is usually only passed on to men, and concern livestock rather than land. Women obtain land and access to property through their husbands or brothers.

An important aspect of bridewealth, according to these authors, is that wealth (i.e. livestock in East Africa) is dispersed between families through marriage payments consuming most of the available herd (Goody 1973). A rich man has many wives and sons, hence his wealth has to be divided between many inheritors. This precludes his wealth from being passed on intact to the descending generation. The importance of bridewealth is to accumulate people and labor, while dispersing livestock between families (see also Turton 1980).

According to Goody (1973), dowry is directly related to bilateral descent systems since property is passed on to both sexes, as inheritance, after the parents' death to sons, and as a dowry to daughters. In societies where land is scarce and held by an elite, it is important to limit the number of heirs and to ensure that the children retain their social and economic status. Dowry occurs in societies where containment of wealth within the nuclear family is essential to its maintenance of power and status (Schlegel and Eloul 1988:294). It becomes important to insure that children marry spouses of equal or superior position. Women therefore have to be endowed with property in order to attract men of similar status (Goody 1973:25; 1976:109).

In agricultural societies where land is scarce and the plow is used, agricultural labor is mostly performed by men. Among the property owning class, wealth is produced through extraction of rents and business profits. Women's labor is peripheral to economic achievement.

The existence of status differences based on property control has two effects; first, women inherit property as dowry which they bring into marriage in order to balance the economic claim they make on the husband's household. Second, dowry can also be used to establish marriages by families of lower status to higher status families by endowing their daughters with substantial wealth.

According to this theory the presence of dowry in a society is ultimately dependent on the existence of the socioeconomic stratification based on land scarcity. It may thus be predicted that when socioeconomic conditions change from stratification based on age and sex to stratification based on socioeconomic classes with unequal access to productive resources, marriage payments should shift from bridewealth to dowry. As I will show, such a prediction is not borne out in the case of the Gusii.

A number of assumptions contained in the model diminish its applicability to current bridewealth patterns and their relation to stratification. First, it assumes that women as brides have little independent influence on the marriage system. Rights in women are primarily exchanged between men. Second, it views dowry and bridewealth as functionally similar institutions regulating marriage and transferring women between men. The model thereby overlooks a crucial difference; bridewealth in eastern Africa establishes paternal affiliation of children while dowry does not in itself, affect affiliation. Third, the model also contains several functional arguments, which stress the leveling function of bridewealth and the concentrating effect of dowry. It is not clear whether bridewealth exists because of its leveling effect or if that effect is really caused by some other mechanism.

### Bridewealth and Stratification in Eastern Africa

The current socioeconomic inequality found in Eastern Africa correspond to Schlegel's and Goody's defining criteria for economic stratification in dowry paying societies. The modern elite among the Gusii, as well as in other eastern African societies, is of recent origin, and social status and prestige is achieved through education, business activities and political involvement. The elite class is still relatively open to social mobility, but possess substantial wealth in land, buildings, investments and access to large amounts of cash. In addition they are occupationally, educationally, and culturally differentiated from the farming population.

According to Goody and Schlegel, dowry rather than bridewealth is connected with the preservation of status and marriage among wealthy elites, however the available information suggests that elites in eastern Africa combine bridewealth with status marriages and elite endogamy.[2] A number of studies of urban elites have noted that wealth and social class strongly affects partner choice in urban situations (Gutkind 1974; Staudt 1986; Stichter 1988). Elite marriage is often accompanied by conspicuous weddings and the display of wealth (cf. Little 1974; Parkin 1978; Weinreich 1982).

Marriage choice within elites depends not only upon economic standing and educational achievement, but also symbolic characteristics. In his study of the Creole elite in Sierra Leone, Cohen (1981) points out that it is not just political power, education and wealth which constitute the elite as a group, but also a number of symbolic markers such as dress, marriage rules, and rituals. The Creole elite is a self-conscious group with roots in the 19th century and has evolved a number of specific cultural characteristics outside education that are used as symbolic barriers to intermarriage.

Modern African elites are not interested in establishing kinship relationships with the poor, but strive to accumulate and preserve property and status (cf. LaFontaine 1962). Economic and political benefits are not developed through local level patron-client relationships, as much as by obtainment of positions in the national level hierarchy, ownership of shares in capitalist enterprises, and employment and connections with persons of similar socio-economic status (cf. Staudt 1986).

A new system of marriage combining bridewealth with socioeconomic stratification and status endogamy is emerging in many parts of Africa. I will attempt to explain how bridewealth is compatible with elite marriage among the Gusii. The conclusions arrived at must at this stage of research remain tentative, and I do not make any claim of statistical validity for the numerical material, however I hope that it will contribute to the sparse information on elite formation in East Africa in which bridewealth continues as part of the wealthy groups' status management.

## Gusii Society

### Social Organization

The Gusii are Bantu speakers inhabiting a hilly highland area in western Kenya, 50 kilometers east of Lake Victoria. Their territory comprises present day Kisii District which is one of the most productive cash crop areas in Kenya due to the abundant rainfall and very fertile soils.

The population density was 395 persons per square kilometer in 1979 (Republic of Kenya 1979). The population size is increasing by three to four percent per year and is currently over one million. The extreme population density has forced the Gusii to utilize every available piece of land for agriculture, and many families are unable to produce enough food for subsistence needs. Thus many Gusii engage in non-agricultural employment or business, either in locally or in the large urban centers.

Traditionally land was held by corporate clan groups comprised of patrilineally related extended, polygynous households. During the 1940s, population increase and cash cropping contributed to the establishment of enclosure, and private ownership of land formerly held by polygynous extended families. Land was in turn distributed by a husband to each wife, who gained exclusive rights of use to it in relation to other wives. Each such parcel became the inheritance of the sons of that particular wife. Women could not inherit any property in their own right.

## Socioeconomic Stratification

The profound economic and social changes of the last 50 years have led to the emergence of socioeconomic stratification as a framework for social interaction that cross-cuts lineage ties. It is possible to discern the formation of different social groups based on economic and sociocultural characteristics.[3]

For the purpose of this study, I have made a tentative division of Gusii society into five broad socioeconomic strata, based upon unequal ownership of land and capital goods, and income differentiation, as well as differences in education, employment status, and cultural values. These stratified classes have emerged within the last generation. It must be stressed that these do not form discrete categories, e.g., it is not uncommon to find farming families with one or two children who have skilled employment.

These strata are; a small elite of very wealthy, politically influential individuals and families; a group of wealthy farmers with long experience in off-farm employment; young employed men and women with a high level of education and well-paying jobs; farmers with little education and access only to unskilled employment; and single mothers living on rented land and housing who subsist on casual work and beer brewing. The last two comprise the majority of the Gusii population.

The analysis of stratification must take into account sex as well as class. It is grossly misleading to assume that women are included as dependents of their husbands and therefore share the latters' status (Bujra 1986; Oboler 1985; Robertson and Berger 1986). Women of all social strata usually form a lower status category than men with little independent access to property. With the exception of women who have skilled employment, i.e., requiring at least high school education, it is only men who control resources in their own right. Thus, among the Gusii and other East African societies the poorest stratum consists of women (cf. Robertson and Berger 1986; Hakansson 1988; Swantz 1985, Udvardy 1988). Men also have a higher level of education and knowledge of how to act in modern Western institutions. The emerging middle class and elite include men have direct control over resources, women have indirect access to these resources in their roles as wives.

This paper is concerned with the elite and the wealthy farmers. I will therefore focus my description of stratification on the characterization of these strata including young men and women with skilled employment.

## Wealthy Farmers

The patriarchs of the wealthy farmer strata are fifty to sixty year old men who often are employed, or have in the past been employed as teachers, agricultural officers, or clerks. This enabled them to buy land, to invest in businesses and to finance in their childrens' education. This category includes both families with rather modest economic resources and families whose members approach elite status (cf. Kitching 1980:310–11).

Moderately wealthy families have four to five hectares of land, and a good deal of income derived from off-farm sources. They own a cement plastered mud house with a corrugated metal roof, have a secondary school education, and may also have one or two children at university. The children who have completed high school work as teachers or nurses, and, in turn assist their siblings with school fees, clothes, and other expenditures.

The wealthier families have cement houses. They often own an old car and manage a small business. Land ownership may approach ten hectares and the male heads of households have salaried employment such as, low-level civil servants. Their wives may also have low paying employment, such as cooks, cleaners at hospitals, and shop keepers. These families aspire to give their children university education and to establish relationships with other wealthy families. Their economic standard approaches the elite, and many of their children have become part of the "middle class" as civil servants and business employees in urban areas.

## The Elite

Today, the young adult members of the elite have high levels of education, skilled and often highly-paid employment. Their fathers, and possibly grand-fathers, received school educations, and were early Christian converts. They worked as clerks, teachers, and pastors during the colonial era. Many of the chiefs of the 1920s and 1930s followed the traditional pattern of big men and acquired many wives. In contrast, the current elite had only one or two wives. They obtained land, financed their sons' educations and invested in businesses.

The majority of the elite live in the Borabu settlement scheme in the eastern part of the district (see Figure 11.1), apart from their natal clans, and the rest of the Gusii population. I define a family as elite if they own a stone or cement house, at least one car, more than ten hectares of land (or if a polygynous household, at least ten hectares per wife), and where the father fulfills at least one of the following characteristics; ownership of a hotel, shop, or transport company, or owning shares in a nation-wide business. In addition, male elite members occupy positions on the boards of cooperatives and parastatal enterprises, and some are also involved in national and local politics.

Elite families invest in daughters' as well as in sons' education. University education is common among younger women within this stratum. Parents consider education as necessary in order to give their daughters a means of supporting themselves and their children. Furthermore, parents also expect that their daughters, with well paid employment, will attract men from the elite as husbands.

## Changing Bridewealth and Marriage and Persisting Norms

During the 1940s, bridewealth payments consisted of between eight and twelve cows, which were transferred to the bride's father before the performance of the wedding ceremony. The parents wanted their daughter to get married as young as possible, and to receive as much bridewealth as possible, in order to enable either her father or one of her brothers to get married by

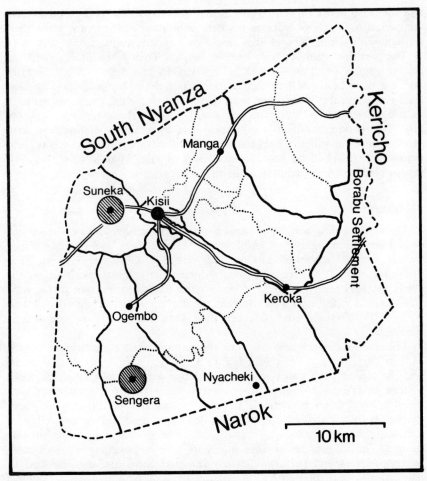

Figure 11.1 - Location of Research Sites, Kisii, Kenya

in turn using her bridewealth. There was no culturally prescribed alternative adult status open for a women other than to be a wife.

Jural norms which determine women's access to resources and the definition of their social status have remained largely intact since the colonial period, when elopement unions were uncommon. As long as bridewealth is not paid a woman has no rights in her partner's land and can be expelled at any time without any recourse to adjudication or support from relatives.

Forty years ago, the husband gained rights in a wife which were also part of his status as a husband. These were sexual rights, rights to a wife's labor capacity, and rights in children. Through bridewealth, the wife gained managerial and use rights in land, the right of maintenance of herself and her children, and the right for her sons to become legal heirs to the land

Table 11.1 - Value of Bridewealth and Women's Employment(a)

| Employment Status | Average Bride-wealth (Kshs.) | Period | N | Income per month (Kshs.) |
|---|---|---|---|---|
| Employed with academic training(b) | 36,000 | 1980-83 | 4 | >6,000. |
| Employed with high school & vocational training(c) | 12,000 | 1982-83 | 10 | 1-2,000. |
| Non-employed(d) | 2,400 | 1982-83 | 12 | ca. 400. |

a. Source: Surveys of employed and non-employed women. The data on non-employed women derive from two study areas; Suneka near Kisii town, and Sengera in southern Gusii-land. The information on employed women is compiled from a special survey of employed women, and from informants among the elite. See Hakansson 1988 for details.
b. These women are employed as accountants, physicians, auditors, and insurance managers.
c. Nurses, teachers, secretaries.
d. It is very difficult to estimate the monetary income that a man may derive from a wife who works on the farm. According to Bager (1980) the average annual income from farm products in his study area in 1978 was about Kshs. 4,627. This is a "guesstimate" which agrees with my own limited information indicating that average farm income was around Kshs. 6,000 per year in 1982-83. Assuming that a wife contributes 75% of that income yields an estimated income of Kshs. 400 per month. This estimate does not include the value of subsistence production. The cost of subsistence does not affect employed women to a great degree since many have free staff housing and food at their place of work. In addition, employed men and women often get food from their families' farms.

allocated to her. Selection of a wife was guided by criteria such as presence of witchcraft in certain families and the prospective bride's labor capacity. At this time stratification was ephemeral and wealth was achieved by men through control over female labor and by engaging in trade.

*Marriages Among Wealthy Farmers*

In contrast, in the modern bridewealth system, women are evaluated according to earning capacity and parents' socioeconomic status. The bridewealth paid for women with qualified employment, e.g., teachers, secretaries, and nurses, is much higher than for non-employed women (see Table 11.1). In addition, fewer of the former elope, and the time between cohabitation and payment is shorter.

Beginning in the late 1960s elopements started to increase in number, and the period between the initiation of cohabitation and the payment of bridewealth has become progressively longer. In a survey of marital status (Hakansson 1988), 28 percent of peasant women who entered into unions with men during the six year period 1962–68 had eloped. Bridewealth payments followed all of these unions within four years. Thus 72 percent of all unions during this period were preceded or accompanied by bridewealth payment. By the period 1981–1983 only 14 percent of peasant women entered into "regular" marriages, i.e. unions preceded or accompanied by bridewealth payment, and 86 percent of couples eloped. After two years, only 28 percent of these had been paid.

A major reason for the increase in elopement is land scarcity which has caused a decline in demand for wives and competition within the family over scarce resources. Sisters experience conflict with brothers' wives and partners in the competition for family resources. Since adult daughters have no recognized rights to subsist on their natal family's resources they receive very little of the family income, and they occupy the lowest status in the family.

Elopement and consensual unions are the common way for young men and women to establish households. The prevalence of elopement and subsequent estrangement is placing more and more Gusii women outside the system for resource distribution and accepted social statuses, making them socially and economically marginalized as single mothers.

The situation for employed women is radically different. The bridewealth paid for both employed and non-employed women was similar in 1965, but since that time the value of payments involving employed women has increased while there has been a drastic decline in the value of bridewealth paid for the non-employed. The average bridewealth paid for employed women in 1982 and 1983 was equivalent to the value of 15 cows, or 12,000 Kenya shillings (Kshs.),[4] while the value of payments for non-employed women was three cows, or 2,400 Kenya shillings.

These differences in bridewealth payments reflect changes in the social and economic goals of wife-givers and wife-takers, as well as in women's status, and the latter's control over resources. First, bridewealth today is seen by wife-givers as compensation for the loss of the daughter's current and future earning capacity and for their expenditure on her education. Second, the employed non-elite women are unwilling to elope and have means to put pressure on their husbands to pay. Payment is necessary also for employed women to obtain rights in the husband's estate, as a means of maintaining a good relationship with their parents and brothers, and to become recognized as proper women. Third, employed women are in high demand by employed men, who are willing to pay a higher bridewealth, and to pay sooner, in order to secure their uxorial rights, as well as to please their partners.

*Marriages Among Elites*

Most elite children are educated in expensive boarding schools in Nairobi and other cities. They attend universities where they often meet partners from their own socioeconomic background. Economic standing and cultural norms make it probable that they will marry within the same stratum.

Although often denied by members of the elite class, others report that elites "arrange" their marriages. Informants maintain that mothers are particularly active in managing their children's marriage choices. They act as match-makers suggesting choices and trying to discourage their children from marrying spouses from less wealthy families. Parents may also charge exorbitant bridewealth for daughters or force sons to relinquish girl friends and arrange agreements with other suitable families.

Marriage is legitimized by a wedding in a church or at the District Commissioner's Office. The official proclamation takes place through expensive receptions and feasts with hundreds of guests in attendance. At one wedding reception for the children of two very wealthy families I counted approximately 400 people. The wedding itself is an opportunity to reinforce the customary role of rich families as being generous with food. For the groom's parents who pay for the celebration it is an occasion for display of wealth and to demonstrate connections with wealthy and powerful persons. For example, the number and style of guests' cars are very important since these show the guests' economic standing. Members of parliament, ministers, and high ranking civil servants are desired guests who, together with the couple's parents, are seated at a special place in the reception hall.

The Christian wedding is accompanied by certain traditional components, such as gifts of goat meat and millet porridge to the female relatives of the bride. A generation ago slaughter of livestock at traditional weddings was characterized by reciprocal responsibility between the two families. While the bride's family provided the food and beer during the wedding ceremony itself, the groom's family made the most valuable contributions to the wedding celebrations, providing most of the livestock for slaughter (Mayer 1950). The practice among the elite is a divergence from "custom" in that the element of reciprocity has disappeared.

Bridewealth, although large, is usually not the subject of public display but, as an elite informant said, "The in-laws talk privately with each other. With animals you can tell people to view the animals, *okomana chi'ombe*, but it is more private with money." Another informant said that, "when deciding about the bridewealth you want privacy. Gossip will otherwise be involved if many people are present. And if you bring all these people they may offend you with bad language."

The private nature of the agreement is a direct negation of the traditional, common way of negotiating and transferring the bridewealth. Bridewealth negotiation was attended by many male elders and its transfer was a public occasion among all Gusii thirty years ago, as it still is today among non-elites. Negotiations involve lengthy bargaining between the elders of both sides, i.e., fathers and their brothers, other close patrilineal male relatives, and the mother's brother of the bride and the groom. When the bridewealth has been agreed upon, the cattle are publicly transferred on hoof to the bride's natal home.

Although the father's role in elite marriage is mandatory, the form of negotiation practiced by many elite families denies the common interest of the patrilineage in the marriage and emphasizes the mutual and dyadic agreement between two nuclear families.

Bridewealth for daughters from the elite is much higher than the average paid for employed women. The average bridewealth paid in an elite marriage is around Kshs. 36,000, compared to Kshs. 12,000 in 1982–1983 for employed women in general. Most payments included a large proportion of exotic cattle and few or none of the local Zebu cows. The highest payment I recorded was valued at Kshs. 50,000, paid by a young civil servant's family in 1983, for his wife who is a medical doctor and the daughter of a former Cabinet Minister.

An examination of elite womens' educational levels and types of employment reveal that they usually have a higher level of education, and have more remunerative employment than non-elite women. The latter are often teachers, nurses or secretaries while the former have higher paying jobs as accountants, auditors, and principals at girls' schools. Such employment demands college or university education, and the high bridewealth may be seen as a result of their higher earning capacities.

Figure 11.2 shows the difference in the value of bridewealth between elite and non-elite employed women. Of eight elite women in the diagram, three lack university education (indicated by an asterisk). One is employed as a stenographer, and two as primary school teachers.

As shown in the diagram, the payments for non-elite employed women are consistently lower than for elite women, reflecting the lower earning capacity of the former. Their lower salaries are in turn the result of lower educational attainment. Most non-elite families cannot afford to give their children the same level of education as the elite. Less wealthy farmers hope that their daughters will obtain employment immediately after completing secondary school and subsequent training, in order to assist in paying school fees for other siblings.

## The Effect of High Bridewealth on Socioeconomic Differentiation

The effect of this graded system of payments is to exclude men of lower economic and social standing from marrying into elite families. An employed man, for example a teacher or lower level civil servant, earns approximately 2,000–4,000 Kenya shillings per month, or Kshs. 24,000–48,000 per year. If he comes from a poor or moderately wealthy family, he will have to spend much of his salary supporting his siblings with school fees, and his parents and other relatives with money. Hence, he will not be able to pay the high bridewealth of Kshs. 30,000–40,000 demanded for a university educated elite woman. Even among those few non-elite men with a university education, and therefore a higher salary, the financial demands placed upon him by his extended family preclude marriage to elite, educated women.

Many men settle for a wife with a lower bridewealth and a lower paying job, rather than going into debt in order to obtain enough money to pay bridewealth for a university educated woman with a high salary.

## Management of Marriage

The maintenance of the bridewealth system is directly dependent on the women's desire for bridewealth to be paid. Both elite and non-elite employed

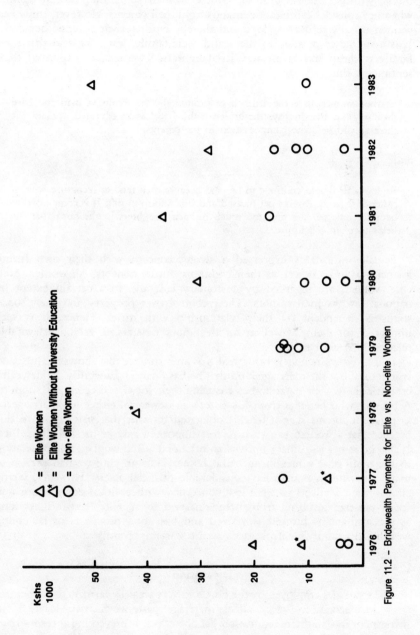

Figure 11.2 – Bridewealth Payments for Elite vs. Non-elite Women

women indirectly influence the level of bridewealth by refusing to elope or marry without bridewealth. Of course women sometimes protest against what they consider exorbitant demands from their parents. However, employed women usually refuse to elope and thereby enforce their parents' demands. It is a source of prestige to them and their family, lest it be said that their family is cheap and gives away its daughters. Two women expressed their sentiments thus:

> Learned women have the acumen or ground for threatening a man and have their way [i.e. that he pays the bridewealth]. I feel as an educated woman that there should be some compensation to the parents.

and

> Bridewealth should continue to be paid because men tend to recognize women [when it is paid]. Parents get pleased and it is a form of gift. It is compensation because some parents give too much to their daughters in the hope that she helps them in the future.

Female informants expressed a strong concern with their own future financial security as well as their childrens' future benefits. All women, even elite women, are regarded by customary law, and to a certain extent by national law, as jural minors. Their control over property and their social status is dependent on their relationship with males. Hence, it is very important for them, as well as for their poorer sisters, to establish favorable relationships with males.

Employed women view bridewealth as an insurance that shows the husband is serious about the marriage, and that he has financial capability. Bridewealth creates a tie to their natal homes ensuring their social and economic support. A brother who benefits from his sister's bridewealth, either for marriage or as payment for his school fees, is obligated towards that sister. It is to this brother that a woman can turn to for support in case of marital difficulties. It also gives her legitimacy both as an urban educated woman, and in relation to the traditional values in her rural home. Thus an elite woman prefers to marry an elite man who has considerable financial assets. However, young elite women I talked to were less concerned with political connections and social prestige resulting from being married to an elite husband. As long as the husband is himself employed and has good prospects of becoming wealthy, his family's elite status may be less important.

## Discussion

The strategies employed by the elite and very wealthy farmers to perpetuate their socioeconomic status affect marriage patterns in two ways. First, investment in daughters' education has the effect of preventing intermarriage with men from non-elite and less wealthy families. Second, elite members use marriage and bridewealth as a means for reaching social and economic goals, resulting in a high degree of endogamy within the wealthiest strata of society.

The formation of the Gusii elite is too recent to have achieved symbolic exclusiveness. Access to elite status is still comparatively open through education, employment, and involvement in political activities. In the absence of such symbolic controls as Cohen (1981) found among Creoles, bridewealth becomes an important means through which parents can manage their children's marriages, and a way for women to assess prospective husbands' ability and willingness to contribute to their children's future.

Although the elites stand out as a socioeconomic group, all its members are not of identical economic status. The elites overlap with the upper level wealthy farmers who are aspiring to become even wealthier, and to give their children university education. The elite class is small, therefore marriage with partners from families of lower economic status must occasionally occur. Such marriages tend to be confined within the upper level wealthy farmers.

The tendency for endogamy within the wealthiest strata is not only a reflection of the members' common education and employment. The economic status of parents is also becoming important, diminishing the role of personally achieved status through education and employment alone. Hence, the bridewealth system lends itself to perpetuation of status over generations.

The search for a pattern should not overshadow the fact that a number of men and women attempt to marry partners from other socioeconomic backgrounds. Such attempts are sometimes successful, and sometimes result in tragedy. In one case, independently verified by two sources, I was told about a very wealthy and politically important man's daughter who became pregnant by the son of a wealthy but non-elite family. Her father disapproved of their marriage plans and forced her to abort the pregnancy. She was later married to a son from an elite family of her parents' choosing.

## Conclusion

It is apparent from this brief account that bridewealth among the Gusii elite is indeed compatible with the maintenance of status marriages and class endogamy. The general models espoused by Goody and Schlegel and Eloul do not account for this.

First, according to Goody (1973, 1976), dowry is related to resource scarcity and unequal ownership of land and other means of production. In a situation of land scarcity it is important to ensure that daughters marry within the same status group to preserve their future status and that of their children. But bridewealth can also serve this purpose. By demanding a high bridewealth one is ensured that the groom is financially able. Therefore, dowry may not emerge as a necessary concomitant to property concentration.

Second, the model assumes that the woman's contribution to the estate has low value and therefore the groom has to be compensated by dowry (Goody 1973; Schlegel and Eloul 1988; Spiro 1975). However, many elite women in Africa have salaried occupations and thus contribute to most of their own and their childrens' living expenses (cf. Bujra 1986; Stichter 1988). The assumption that women are chattels in male status games denies women as brides any influence on the system of marriage payments. Women's strategies in relation to such payments must be taken into account (Bossen 1988; Hakansson 1988). Women's desire for high bridewealth is related to their own interests in creating stronger relationships with their natal families, and to obtain prestige in their natal community.

Third, bridewealth is assumed to disperse property and is thus antithetical to the need to conserve property. This overlooks the fact that, among the elite, high bridewealth is actually not very high in relation to their income and assets. It is only high in relation to the assets of non-elite men. Thus, its effect is to discourage men of non-elite families from marrying the daughters of the elite, and for women to ensure marriage to financially able men. Furthermore, by allowing bridewealth to circulate among siblings, no direct costs are incurred by the parents.

Parents use high bridewealth as a means of controlling marriages by allowing payments for daughters to be used for arranging the marriages of sons, or by paying it from the family income. In this way, high bridewealth can be used to hinder undesirable men from marrying their daughters, and by threatening to withhold bridewealth to discourage sons from marrying undesirable women. Thus the changing economic conditions of recent decades has not resulted in the decline of the traditional institution of bridewealth, but an alteration of the practice which serves to solidify the growing socioeconomic stratification in Gusii society.

## Acknowledgments

I would like to thank Monica Udvardy, University of Uppsala, for constructive criticism and Miriam Chaiken, Indiana University of Pennsylvania, for editing and commenting on the manuscript.

## Notes

1. The essay is based on 12 months fieldwork conducted in Kisii District, Kenya, 1982–83 and 1985. Information about elite marriage was obtained form both elite and non-elite informants. It was not possible to make any random selection of elite families for investigation.

2. LaFontaine (1962) describes how high bridewealth among the Gisu of Uganda was used by the local elite to establish marriages within their own stratum and to exclude poorer men from marrying their daughters. Whether high bridewealth in itself is used by the Gusii for similar purposes could be investigated by comparing bridewealth payments for elite and non-elite women while holding education and employment status constant. Informants support my preliminary interpretation by stressing that it is the woman's earning capacity which determines the value of bridewealth.

3. Bager (1980) and Lanting (1977) have shown, with the exception of the settlement schemes, land is not concentrated in the hands of a few; it is fairly equally

distributed among men and access to non-farm income is the basis for economic differentiation.

4. In 1983 one US dollar was about 14 Kenya shillings (Kshs).

# References Cited

Bager, Torben.
1980 Marketing Cooperatives and Peasants in Kenya. Uppsala: Scandinavian Institute of African Studies.

Bossen, Laurel.
1988 Toward a Theory of Marriage: The Economic Anthropology of Marriage Transactions. Ethnology 27:127-144.

Brokensha, David W.
1987 Inequality in Rural Africa: Fallers Reconsidered. Manchester Papers on Development 3:1-21.

Bujra, Janet.
1986 "Urging Women to Redouble Their Efforts . . .": Class, Gender, and Capitalist Transformation in Africa. *In* Women and Class in Africa. C. Robertson and I. Berger, eds. Pp. 117-140. New York: Africana Publishing Company.

Cohen, Abner.
1981 The Politics of Elite Culture: Explorations in the Dramaturgy of Power in a Modern African Society. Berkeley: University of California Press.

Ferraro, Gary.
1976 Changing Patterns of Bridewealth Among the Kikuyu of East Africa. *In* A Century of Change in Eastern Africa. W. Arens, ed. Pp.101-114. The Hague: Mouton.

Goody, Jack.
1973 Bridewealth and Dowry in Africa and Eurasia. *In* Bridewealth and Dowry. J. Goody and S.J. Tambiah, eds. Pp.1-58. Cambridge University Press.
1976 Production and Reproduction. Cambridge: Cambridge University Press.

Gutkind, Peter C.W.
1974 Urban Anthropology. Assen, the Netherlands: van Gorcum

Hakansson, N. Thomas.
1988 Bridewealth, Women and Land. Social Change among the Gusii of Kenya. Uppsala Studies in Anthropology 10. Stockholm: Almqvist and Wiksell International.

Kitching, Gavin.
1980 Class and Economic Change in Kenya. London: Yale University Press.

Kuper, Adam.
1982 Wives for Cattle. London: Routledge and Kegan Paul.

LaFontaine, Jean.
1962 Gisu Marriage and Affinal Relationships. *In* Marriage in Tribal Societies. M. Fortes, ed. Pp. 88-120. Cambridge: Cambridge University Press.

Lanting, H.
1977 Land Utilization Types in the Kisii District, a Preliminary Study. Preliminary Report 15. Wageningen, the Netherlands: Agricultural University.

Little, Kenneth.
1974 Urbanization as a Social Process. London: Routledge and Kegan Paul.

Mayer, Phillip.
    1950    Gusii Bridewealth Law and Custom. The Rhodes Livingstone Papers 18.
            London: Oxford University Press.

Obbo, Christine.
    1987    The Old and the New in East African Elite Marriages. *In* Transformations
            of African Marriage. David Parkin and David Nyamwaya, eds. Pp. 263–
            280. Manchester: Manchester University Press.

Oboler, Regina Smith
    1985    Women, Power, and Economic Change. The Nandi of Kenya. Stanford:
            Stanford University Press.

Parkin, David and David Nyamwaya.
    1987    Introduction: Transformation of African Marriage: Change or Choice. *In*
            Transformation of African Marriage. D. Parkin and D. Nyamwaya. eds. Pp.
            1–36. Manchester: Manchester University Press.

Parkin, David.
    1978    The Cultural Definition of Political Response. London: Academic Press.

Republic of Kenya.
    1981    Kenya Population Census 1979. Nairobi: Central Bureau of Statistics.

Robertson Claire, and Iris Berger.
    1986    Introduction: Analyzing Class and Gender-African Perspectives. *In* Women
            and Class in Africa. C. Robertson and I. Berger, eds. Pp. 3–26. New York:
            Africana Publishing Company.

Schlegel, Alice and Robert Eloul.
    1988    Marriage Transactions: Labor, Property, Status. American Anthropologist
            90:291–309.

Schuster, Ilsa M. Glazer.
    1979    New Women of Lusaka. Palo Alto, CA.: Mayfield.

Spiro, Melford.
    1975    Marriage Payments: A Paradigm from the Burmese Perspective. Journal of
            Anthropological Research 31:89–115.

Stichter, Sharon B.
    1988    The Middle-Class Family in Kenya: Changes in Gender Relations. *In*
            Patriarchy and Class. S.B. Stichter and J.L. Parpart, eds. Boulder: Westview
            Press.

Staudt, Kathleen.
    1986    Stratification: Implications for Women's Politics. *In* Women and Class in
            Africa. C. Robertson and I. Berger, eds. Pp. 197–215. New York: Africana
            Publishing Company.

Swantz, Marja-Liisa.
    1985    Women in Development: A Creative Role Denied. London: Hurst.

Turton, David.
    1980    The Economics of Mursi Bridewealth: A Comparative Prospective. *In* The
            Meaning of Marriage Payments. J. Comaroff, ed. Pp. 67–92. New York:
            Academic Press.

Udvardy, Monica.
1988 Women's Groups Near the Kenyan Coast: Patron-Clientship in the Development Arena. *In* The Anthropology of Development and Change in Eastern Africa. D.W. Brokensha and P.D. Little, eds. Pp. 217–236. Boulder: Westview Press.
Weinreich, A.K.H.
1982 African Marriage in Zimbabwe. Harare: Mambo Press.

# 12

## "Bringing Home Development": The Impetus of Ideology for Women's Groups Near the Kenyan Coast

*Monica Udvardy*

Voluntary, grass-roots women's groups proliferate locally throughout Kenya. They are acknowledged by administrators, from local levels to the President, as crucial to the achievement of national development goals, but unlike women's organizations in the First World, the primary aim of those in Kenya is pragmatic, rather than political. Their goals are to develop local infrastructure, generate income, and to improve the quality of life of members' families.

This chapter explores the motivation of women's groups' members among the northern Mijikenda in Kaloleni Division, Kilifi District, Coast Province. Women say they participate in groups because they want to "bring development" to the local community. Yet few groups achieve these formal, long-term objectives. Why do women take time from their full home work schedule to voluntarily organize groups and contribute labor each week, despite the demonstrably few achievements of their own or neighboring groups?

A now considerable literature on voluntary, Kenyan women's associations confirms that achieving community, infrastructural development or income-generating goals is problematic everywhere in the country (e.g., Muzaale and Leonard 1982; Business & Economic Research Co. 1984). Many studies address the constraints within which groups operate (e.g., Pala et al. 1975; Musyoki & Gatara 1985; McCormack et al. 1986), or discuss the limitations or possibilities of groups for helping women alter gender-based inequality (e.g., Komma 1984:182–184; Wipper 1984; Stamp 1986; Staudt 1986; Ahlberg 1988:214). Yet seldom do studies address why women persist in group activities when they rarely receive any tangible return for their efforts.

This analysis proposes that Kenya's unusual development ideology provides the medium for the establishment of groups, but not the means for achievement of their success.[1] Following Brokensha's emphasis upon indigenous responses to planned development efforts (cf., e.g., Brokensha and Glazier 1973), it presents data which suggest that while women's groups strive for the ideological goals of development, it is the unintended benefits to members which sustain their viability. Groups may persist because they constitute unorthodox fora where women acquire knowledge and engage in activities unavailable within indigenous gender stratification and social organization.

## Development as Ideology in Kenya

In their analysis of the meaning and message of "development", Dahl and Hjort (1984) observe that its abstract ideology will be interpreted differently by each party involved in its processes. In Kenya, a strong ideology of development (Swahili: *maendeleo*, progress) at the national level is inextricably linked and constantly reiterated with pronouncements of the nationhood of Kenya, and both concepts are reinforced by administrators at all levels. These words from a song sung by a women's group performing in Kaloleni in 1985 at a national holiday celebration are illustrative:

> We, the children of *nyayo* [footsteps], we are proud,
> We, the children of Kenya, we are proud.
>
> We see the president of Kenya with his stick.
> It's the symbol of *maendeleo*.
> Our president obeys God. Every Sunday he goes to church.
>
> Truly, our Kenya will be blessed.
> Moi, our driver, the car is going smoothly.
> Moi, you discovered the car was in danger.
>
> You knew and then you stopped the smuggling.
> The passengers are the people. A bad passenger, leave him behind . . .
>
> We, the children of *nyayo*, we are proud.
> We, the children of Kenya, we are proud.

Through explicit reference to his elder's stick as a symbol of development, and by referring to Kenya's current political leader, President Moi, as the nation's "driver", this example of official ideology neatly intertwines the notions of development and nationhood in the symbolically loaded personage of Kenya's president. Both the narrative and its presentation as song also arouse joy, danger, and relief, but simultaneously conspicuously lack specific directives for the achievement of "development".

Building on Bailey's (1969) analysis of political rhetoric, Parkin (1975) likens the nature of ideological statements to that of symbols (Turner 1967). Both (1) evoke emotion and thereby draw attention, (2) are polyvalent in the message being conveyed, and (3) offer scope for creativity and for a wide range of interpretability. Like the above example, statements of ideology reach out to the widest possible audience at the expense of depth or specificity of the message being conveyed.

Bailey and Parkin view statements of political rhetoric as falling on a three-part continuum from general, such as ideological pronouncements; to programs and specific plans of action. In 1985, Kaloleni Division politicians and community leaders encouraged women's groups through verbal rhetoric corresponding to all three categories. Examples of speeches that fall in the middle category promoted women's groups by linking their work to such national political slogans as *harambee* and *nyayo*. Such statements were common because they easily convey the method and spirit in which "development" should take place.

> You women have been asleep. You must wake up! You must contribute to the future. No one would wish to be left behind. You must make a good foundation for your own children. It's a *nyayo* year!

*Nyayo* (Swahili: "footsteps") is the current president's own choice of a verbal symbol to provide continuity to an ideology of development through voluntary and cooperative self-help created by Kenya's late President Jomo Kenyatta, and conveyed through the slogan *harambee* (Swahili: "pull together"; Mbithi and Rasmusson 1977; Thomas 1985). These terms may be seen as "programs of action" because they continue to evoke the emotional and ideological content of development, while indicating the general form in which it should take place. Women learn that they can appropriately contribute to community development through voluntary, collective participation.

Other programmatic political rhetoric simultaneously introduces, promotes and sanctions the new qualifications needed to implement community development goals, as in this speech by the local Member of Parliament:

> There are various leaders. The M.P. [Member of Parliament] is a leader. Mr. D.O. [District Officer] is a leader. Teachers are leaders, chairpersons [of women's groups] are leaders, councilors are leaders. But what is leadership and who is a leader? . . . The leader must be in the front line of all those he or she is leading in order to bring development to the people. Development means to raise the people's standard to become better when compared to yesterday. You should always elect a leader who will understand his or her people and who will always stand where the people wish him or her to stand, forever and ever, Amen!

Women's groups chairpersons are here both defined and condoned as among those who are "development" leaders. These special leadership qualities are remarkable in their diametric opposition to those appropriate to a traditional Mijikenda leader. The latter should ideally be an elderly man who both symbolically and intellectually embodies the unchanging customs of the people.

Finally, public statements that espoused more specific directives concerning the content of group activities, confirm Dahl and Hjort's suggestion for how affected parties may initially respond to the introduction of an ideology of development.

. . . [W]e would suggest that the linking of development with technological innovation on the one hand, and with a prestige-ranking system on the other are particularly effective, so that, at the receiving end, these are the elements that first permeate local ideas of what development entails (1984:178).

Indeed, local administrators' speeches underscoring the need for "development" repeatedly promoted the building of community infrastructure. Women's groups were encouraged to strive for the installation of sorely-lacking water pipelines, and were prodded to work hard through frequent reference to the relative "backwardness" Coast Province inhabitants, compared to the "progress" of peoples inhabiting the fertile Kenyan Highlands.

But conspicuously absent from all political speeches addressing women's groups are systematic descriptions of the real criteria needed to achieve their goals. Groups are told by politicians and community leaders alike that they will succeed if they work hard, contribute money and save it in a bank. They are told that when they have demonstrated the energy and ability to organize for development, and when their savings have reached a certain amount, they will be eligible for government assistance that will facilitate the implementation of their projects.

However, this agenda for group success leaves out the most crucial factor of all, i.e., the group leaders' literacy and business skills; and knowledge of and access to non-indigenous resources. More than any other, these skills influence a group's ability to identify viable projects and to solicit funding or skills training from governmental or non-governmental donor agencies.[2] While the energy, effort and enthusiasm of group members are impressive and important, their leaders' ability to guide the group, and to tap outside agencies' sources of aid are more crucial variables to achievement of formal group objectives (McCormack et al. 1986; Mwaniki 1986; Levy 1988).

## Women's Groups Near the Kenyan Coast

### The Mijikenda and Gender Relations

Five groups were selected for intensive study from a representative sample of 12 coastal hinterland groups (c.f. McCormack et al. 1986).[3] All are located near Kaloleni town, situated approximately 30 kilometers east of the Indian Ocean in the warm and humid, palm-clad coastal ridges (elevation 200–300 meters). Annual precipitation is abundant (1,000 mm. mean per annum), but its distribution is unreliable, and soil conditions make water catchment problematic without technical innovations.

Kaloleni Division encompasses eight of the nine culturally and historically related Mijikenda peoples,[4] who had a total population of 732,820 in 1979. The palmbelt Mijikenda are horticulturalists, cultivating maize, wet-season rice, varieties of legumes and greens for subsistence. The coconut palm is the most important cash crop, providing income to men from copra and illicit palm wine sales, and to women, who manufacture palm-thatched roof tiles, called *makuti*, for sale and home use. While small relative to men's palm-based incomes, *makuti* sales are the most important income-generating activity for individual women and women's groups. The northernmost Mijikenda peoples have non-corporate, dispersed patriclans and lineages. Gender is an important principle of social stratification in that it defines access to power, authority, prestige and resources. Similar to a widening social inequality documented for various social institutions in East African societies (e.g., Brokensha 1987; Hakansson 1988), continuing colonial and post-colonial processes have undermined earlier more interdependent, albeit male-dominated gender roles. Women are jural minors according to customary law, and although they have usufructory rights to the products and cash income of some tree crops, land and other important economic resources are either individually or corporately owned by men.

By gender ascription, homestead heads are always men, and while they generally have seniority over household women, age interacts to modify this principle. From the time she marries, the life career of a women may be characterized as one of gradually increasing authority, expanding spatial mobility, and growing personal autonomy. For example, a younger woman's daily movements are restricted, and her attendance at social gatherings limited. These constraints hinder her participation in such voluntary activities as women's groups, and are reflected in the higher average of group members, relative to the age distribution of the overall population.

## The Composition and Activities of Women's Groups in Kaloleni Division

The history of contemporary Kenyan women's groups is well-documented elsewhere (e.g., Monsted 1978; Riria-Ouko 1985; Wipper 1975). The remarkable expansion in numbers of women's groups that occurred in the highlands in the late 1970s, took place somewhat later in Coast Province, and a real growth in their numbers was still occurring through 1985, when this study ended.[5] The five groups presented here ranged in size from 30–40 women, typically drawing members from the same neighborhood and sometimes from the same compound, but rarely including women with multiple membership in various groups. Located in the vicinity of one another, two groups were three and five years old respectively, while the other three were just under a year old at the time of study.

All but one group had local water development as a long-term objective, and of these, the oldest group had succeeded in developing water infrastructure through an extraordinary ability to tap donor agency funds and foreign voluntary expertise. The remaining group's objective was livestock-keeping, because it was located near the successful group's water pipelines and was soon to receive permission to use them.

Typical to the developmental cycle to Kenyan women's groups, these five groups undertook a number of short term projects, in order to generate savings for their long-term goals. Smaller projects closely reflect women's work tasks in the indigenous economy, including farming on a collective borrowed or purchased plot, and *makuti* roof-tile making. The latter is either a collective activity carried out while chatting amiably at weekly meetings, or else the *makuti* are delivered weekly by individual members. When asked what they would normally be doing at home during the group meeting time, most respondents replied that they would be carrying out the very same activities as those conducted during group meetings.

Significantly, all but one group had provided little return to members for their efforts. All groups receive routine visits and lectures from local family planning and agricultural extension officers. One group had distributed maize cobs for use as seeds to each member after harvest of the group plot, and another had paid a dividend of 30 Kenya Shillings (about US$ 2.00) to each member before Christmas. In contrast, the array of benefits achieved by the single, successful group was impressive, including free homestead water taps and water, free group uniforms and tailoring training, distribution of group harvests and vegetable seeds, and school scholarships for the needy members' children. The other groups were well aware of these achievements, and spoke of them with no small amount of envy.

The factors contributing to the success or failure of these groups are similar to those that have been identified in other parts of Kenya. Although demonstrating members' motivation and ability to organize, earnings from short-term projects contribute only a minor portion of the capital necessary for successful implementation of long-term projects (Business and Economic Research 1984). The extraordinary achievements of the single successful group depended upon its leader's education, energy, and knowledge of the outside world, and upon her early ability to tap donor agency funds and expertise.[6] Neighboring groups knew little about the necessity of a leader's influence as strategic to group success.

## Individual Motivations to Group Participation

Selected from the five groups, 79 members were interviewed with both open and closed-ended questions. Their socioeconomic backgrounds are representative of rural hinterland homesteads in their subsistence-farming orientation, limited presence of material goods and lack of cash surplus (Table 12.1). Homes are typically mud walled, with *makuti*-thatched roofs. Few of the respondents owned any such larger cash-purchase items as a kerosene stove, wristwatch, radio or sewing machine. Although most own flocks or chickens or ducks, only one-fifth own any livestock, and more than one-third owned no poultry or livestock at all. Only a few members receive any monetary or material assistance from grown children, but most have at least one child in school, requiring cash outlays for tuition or other fees.

Most group members are illiterate, or have only a few years of primary school education. They are married either monogamously (47 percent) or polygynously (33 percent), but relative to the general population, a disproportionately high number are widowed. Their marital status reflects the relatively older age of group members, more than half being between 30–54 years old, and an additional 14 percent being 55 years or older. Almost

Table 12.1 - Social and Economic Profile of Sampled Women's Group
Members in Kaloleni Division, 1985-86 (a)

| ECONOMIC INDICATORS | # | % | SOCIAL INDICATORS | # | % |
|---|---|---|---|---|---|
| **Members' Occupations** | | | **Approximate Age** | | |
| Farmer/retired farmer | 77 | 97 | 17-29 | 21 | 27 |
| Other (tailor, teacher) | 2 | 3 | 30-55 | 47 | 59 |
| | | | 56+ | 11 | 14 |
| **Husbands' Occupations (75)** | | | | | |
| Farmer/retired farmer | 34 | 45 | **Formal Education** | | |
| Temp. wage/self employ. | 21 | 28 | None | 57 | 72 |
| Semi-skilled/salaried | 11 | 15 | Primary | 20 | 25 |
| Other | 9 | 12 | Secondary | 2 | 3 |
| **Members' House Construction** | | | **Marital Status (77)** | | |
| Mud walls/palm thatch | 73 | 92 | Married | 62 | 80 |
| Improved (b) | 6 | 8 | Widowed | 11 | 14 |
| | | | Divorced | 2 | 3 |
| **Livestock Ownership (77)** | | | Never married | 2 | 3 |
| Poultry only | 35 | 45 | | | |
| None | 29 | 37 | **Religion** | | |
| Goats and poultry | 12 | 16 | Traditional | 37 | 47 |
| Cattle | 1 | 1 | Christian | 29 | 37 |
| | | | Muslim | 13 | 16 |
| **Household Ownership of Major Consumer Durables (c)** | | | | | |
| None | 64 | 81 | | | |
| One or more | 15 | 19 | | | |
| **Receiving Monetary/Material Assistance from Children:** | | | | | |
| No | 63 | 80 | | | |
| Yes | 16 | 20 | | | |

a. **N=79 unless otherwise indicated in parentheses.**
b. **Plaster or cement walls, cement floors, and/or iron roofs.**
c. **I.e. kerosene stove, wristwatch, radio, sewing machine. Sample
   method based on Castro, Hakansson, and Brokensha (1981).**

half hold indigenous religious beliefs; the remaining being Christians or
Muslims.

Table 12.2 summarizes members' recollections of their reasons for joining
a women's group. A small number cited the role model effect of the
neighboring, successful group as one reason for their own recruitment. "I
was impressed by [the] group, how they've succeeded and how they take
care of their members." The high visibility of its achievements were apparent
in women's statements that if that group could be successful, so could their
own. Alternatively, respondents cited as motivation seeing their own friends
and neighbors join groups. Yet personal reasons comprise almost half the
answers to this question. Almost all of these responses reflect the hope of
a personal loan or assistance to help women with their daily problems:

I have problems. I thought if I join the group, it will help me. I don't have
any income and my husband is jobless . . . [I]f they divide some money, I

Table 12.2 - Categorized Responses to the Query, "How is it that you decided to join a Women's Group?" (N=66)

| RESPONSE | # | % |
|---|---|---|
| To get a loan or other assistance | 32 | 48 |
| Due to the role model effect of other Women's Groups or other women | 16 | 24 |
| To solve the community water problem | 15 | 23 |
| To learn new skills | 3 | 5 |

shall [get a cow, which will] change all my life. I will get milk for my children and sell some for cash. It will help me in getting fees for my children.

Surprisingly, those reasons propounded by community leaders for the formation of groups, i.e., solving community-wide infrastructural development problems, account for less than a fourth of all reasons cited by members for joining groups.

Later, respondents were asked to describe what they *currently* enjoy most about their group participation, and then to rank a number of fixed alternative responses that other women had given. These motivations are summarized in Figure 12.1. Politicians' and community leaders' political rhetoric was referred to as the most important reason for continued group participation almost as frequently as the future personal benefits that women hope to gain.[7] While a minority cited a desire to see the group's long-term project through to completion, most responses in this category were almost word for word renderings of political speeches concerning the ability of women's groups to "bring development", for example, "all Kenyans [have been] asked to awaken and develop the area. Nobody would wish to refuse development."

But almost as important to their continued group participation is the persistent hope for personal benefit in the future. As in their motivations for joining groups, what they continue to hope for is a small, monetary loan to help ease the burden of such domestic outlays as school fees, the purchase of hybrid seeds, and medical costs. Women also cite learning new skills as a valuable, current benefit to their membership. They enjoyed learning new agricultural techniques and cooking skills, taking literacy classes, or gaining new knowledge about improved seeds and poultry, family planning, or hygiene.

Finally, a smaller, but still important number of women responded that what they enjoyed most was the opportunity to be together with community women who they would not otherwise encounter; and/or the opportunity to get away from home, where there were conflicts with husbands or other homestead members; or for widowed or divorced women to escape loneliness:

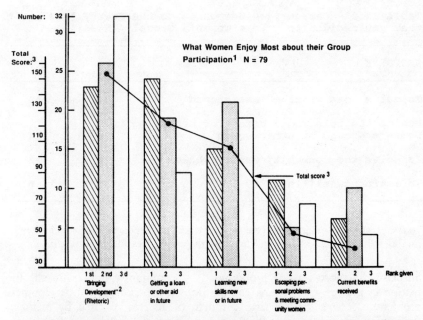

Figure 12.1 - Women's Group Participation

1. Respondents were asked two questions in order to elicit their spontaneous reflections on their group activities: 1) "What do you enjoy most about the Women's Group? and 2) "I am going to name for you some of the things that women have said they enjoy about women's groups. After you've heard the list, could you name for which you enjoy most, then the second most enjoyable and the third." For the latter, respondents were asked to rank any 3 of 7 fixed, alternative answers. Motivations for rankings were carefully noted. During analysis, consistency between answers to the two queries was compared. Examination of motivations to the 7 ranked alternatives allowed collapsing to 5 categories instead.

2. Choosing this alternative could conceivably include interviewer bias, since rural residents perceive of Europeans as representing potential material aid . However, the author was careful to address this issue in the introductory group meeting that preceded individual interviews, and during which the scope and limitations of her work were described.

3. I. e. , the sum of all 3 ranks for each category, where Rank 1 = 3 points ; Rank 2 = 2 points ; and Rank 3 = 1 point.

I will rest from watching and caring for children [who are] fighting now and then. Also, courage. I always get courage to work and be independent. As when we meet together we always advise one another on such a basis. I like to be together with other women. I like that when I feel annoyed, I can go to the group and feel happy. I like to contribute to the future and to be woken up!

At home I feel very lonely and have many thoughts about how I stay alone. At the group, we discuss ideas, and it makes me forget.

Table 12.3 summarizes the future group activities that respondents would like. Half named such income-generating projects as small, local service enterprises, livestock-keeping, or collective farm ownership. The desire to learn new skills was again mentioned frequently. Surprisingly, community development projects, from which both group members and other area residents could benefit, received only 12 percent of responses, and despite

Table 12.3 - Responses to the Query, "What things (projects, courses, programs) would you like to see the Women's Group doing in the future?" (N=94)(a)

| RESPONSE | # | % |
|---|---|---|
| Own Women's Group business (b) | 47 | 50 |
| Learning new skills | 24 | 26 |
| Community development (c) | 11 | 12 |
| Generate loans for members | 7 | 7 |
| Other | 5 | 5 |

a. Of the 79 respondents, some mentioned more than one desired, future activity.
b. I.e. income-generating activities.
c. E.g. water, electricity development.

earlier explications of their need for loans, only a few women repeated the hope for individual loans as a future group endeavor.

## Discussion

In light of the subsistence orientation of members' households, and members' limited access to cash, savings, or credit, it is not surprising that the hope of a loan is a primary motivation for joining women's groups. This motive is only remarkable in light of the long-term objectives of groups; none serve as rotating savings or credit associations, nor do any aim for the future distribution of loans. Even the most successful group does not favor giving personal loans, and has done so only in exceptional circumstances.

Yet in other parts of Kenya, groups commonly serve as peasant women's savings associations, usually distributing accumulated capital to individual members in turn (e.g., Thomas 1985, Mwaniki 1986, Thomas 1988). In contrast, goals of Kaloleni Division groups reflect political and administrative leaders' notions of appropriate community development projects. Why do women join groups and persist as members in the hope of future loans, when this need is not on any group agenda? Or, put another way, why do group goals reflect community development objectives, and fail to accommodate this urgent need of peasant Mijikenda women?

The responses presented here indicate that Mijikenda women and men have absorbed the message of development through community participation and interpret it positively. Asked about husbands' reactions toward their group participation, 71 percent said his attitude was positive, either because he viewed "development" favorably, or for possible indirect benefits to himself.[8]

As the subordinate gender, it is possible that women tacitly understand that their ability to form groups and to participate in them depends on the approval of men and community leaders. Any community developments achieved by women's groups would reflect favorably upon those whose responsibility it is to enact and encourage local development. Group goals that conform to community-wide notions of "development" are most likely to be accepted by those in authority. Personal loans might not receive approval because they do not provide equally widespread benefits to the neighborhood.

Yet, if this explanation accounts for the nature of the official objectives, why do women continue to participate in groups when they rarely achieve the stated goals, and do not provide the material assistance that is the real motivation for joining groups? As shown by the data in Table 12.2, the demonstration or role model effect of a highly successful group clearly serves as motivation for group formation and for initial recruitment of its membership. Envious of the highly visible rewards achieved by a few groups, other women reason that they can gain similar benefits through group effort. However, neither new group leaders, nor regular members know the real skills and wider network needed for success, and the information they receive from community leaders is incomplete at best.

Based on these data, I suggest that women persist in group activities for small, and mainly non-material rewards, and for the continued hope of future benefits, because the opportunity cost to women of group participation is low. Women say that they would be carrying out the same activities at home as they conduct collectively at women's group meetings. Some go further to state that they would be "carrying out duties [at home in order] for other people to get money". Older women are freer than younger women from the burden of farmwork and food processing, and because their children are grown, they are freer to engage in extra-domestic activities. Others say that meetings coincide with times of rest. The few young members say that other compound women watch their children during group meetings, which they can repay with little inconvenience. Thus the value of the activity alternative to group participation is low. But although they have little to loose by participating, do the current activities named by women as most enjoyable adequately account for the persistence of groups?

With the exception of members of the successful group, the data in Figure 12.1 indicate that members of all other groups recalled non-material, personal benefits as the most rewarding aspects of group participation. Gaining new agricultural skills or listening to talks by extension officers and other visitors are kinds of knowledge that women have little access to within the terms of existing gender stratification. Yet these data indicate that women are eager for such knowledge. Even older women, whom we might expect to act conservatively when confronted with new ideas, participate enthusiastically when knowledge is presented to them within this unconventional forum. Women's interest in learning is confirmed by the kinds of projects they hope to undertake in the future. Skills training is named second only to income-generating activities.

Finally, women's groups are an opportunity to meet community women not otherwise encountered in the daily rhythm of domestic affairs. Women say that they appreciate the possibility of escaping or receiving advice on domestic problems as they participate in group activities. Thus, it appears that learning new skills, being together with other women, and exchanging ideas, are opportunities uniquely available in the fora of women's groups. Coupled with a low opportunity cost of group activities, these non-material benefits, and the continuing hope of future material gain, are valuable enough to stimulate women to continued group participation.

## Conclusions

A national ideology of development through community participation, including the mobilization of women's groups, is constantly reaffirmed by local politicians and administrators in Kaloleni Division in the coastal hinterland of Kenya. Although they constitute a new social institution with potential to alter existing gender relations, women's groups are perceived positively and have attached community-wide acceptance by women and men, development and indigenous leaders alike. Group projects in the area heavily reflect this development ideology, yet few groups ever achieve their long-term objectives. Furthermore, women's responses to questions concerning their motivation for joining and for persisting in groups reflect personal needs rather than community development objectives.

This chapter suggests that the very lack of clear directives inherent in the ideological rhetoric of development may enable this new women's forum to emerge in an indigenous setting of gender inequality, where women form the subordinate stratum. Promoted as part of a positively valued development program, women's groups are perceived as idioms of the national ideology. But lacking specific agenda for achievement of their community-approved goals, most groups fail as vehicles for the implementation of nationally-defined development.

Nevertheless, the groups fulfill other, important, needs of members, which cannot be satisfied within the matrix of indigenous institutions. Coupled with a low opportunity cost of participation, these non-material rewards account for the persistence of groups and the continued enthusiasm of members. It may be that these unconventional, and unintended benefits of women's groups are serving as precursors to structural changes in gender relations of a more fundamental nature than any envisioned within the national rhetoric of development.

## Acknowledgments

The author gratefully acknowledges the sponsorship of the Swedish Research Council in the Humanities and Social Sciences (H.S.F.R.); the Swedish Institute; and the African Studies Program, Department of Cultural Anthropology, University of Uppsala, Sweden. Warm thanks are due to Mijikenda women's group members for their enthusiastic reception; to Alvina Kazungu, women's leader, research assistant, and friend; Mohamed Salim Baya and Mohamed Mashin. I am also grateful to N. Thomas Hakansson and Enid Nelson for their comments and support.

## Notes

1. For inspiring a critical examination of the concept of "development", the author wishes to thank Dr. Gudrun Dahl and participants in her seminar, *Development as Ideology*, Department of Social Anthropology, University of Stockholm. An early draft of this chapter was presented to that seminar in May, 1987.

2. The importance of strong leadership was stressed by Tototo Home Industry representatives during interviews conducted with them in September and October, 1985. In 1984, governmental and non-governmental funds to women's groups in Kilifi District constituted a sum larger than that available to all other self-help groups together (Udvardy 1988:221). The Ministry of Culture and Social Services had KShs. 75,000 (US$ 5,000) to distribute to all types of self-help groups, and KShs. 100,000 (US$ 6,700) to distribute to women's groups alone.

3. Fieldwork was conducted in Kaloleni Division for a total of 12 months during 1985 and 1986. Research on women's groups was part of dissertation field research on the elderly in Giriama society. In addition to interviews of the intensive study sample, the main methods used in the women's groups study was participant observation in 12 representative groups; attendance at all divisional women's group and development committee meetings; and open-ended interviewing of group leaders, representatives, and administrative heads.

4. The northern Mijikenda include the Giriama, Kauma, Jibana, Chonyi, Kambe, Ribe, Rabai, and Duruma.

5. The numbers, composition and ultimate project objectives of women's groups in Kilifi District has been summarized in Udvardy, 1988.

6. See Chapter 6 of McCormack et al. 1986. The findings of that research group are largely corroborated by my own interviews with the group's committee members, and by monitoring the group's activities during the course of fieldwork.

7. Concerning possible interviewer bias, see Note 2, Figure 12.1.

8. Of the remaining answers to this question, 29 percent said their husbands were neutral, and only 2 respondents said their husbands had at first refused to give them permission to participate, but had later been convinced by others that their wives should be allowed to join.

## References Cited

Ahlberg, Beth Maina.
    1988    Women's Collective Participation in Development. Ph.D. Dissertation. So-
            ciology Department, Uppsala University.
Bailey, F.G.
    1969    Political Statements. Contributions to Indian Sociology. N.S. 3:1–16.
Brokensha, David.
    1987    Inequality in Rural Africa: Fallers Reconsidered. Manchester Papers on
            Development 3(9):1–21.
Brokensha, David and Jack Glazier.
    1973    Land Reform among the Mbeere of Central Kenya. Africa 43(3):182–206.

Business & Economic Research Company, Ltd.
1984    Study on the Production and Marketing of Women's Groups Products in Kenya. Draft. Submitted to S.I.D.A. Vol. 1. Main Report. Nairobi: Business and Economic Research Co., Ltd.

Dahl, Gudrun and Anders Hjort.
1984    Development as Message and Meaning. Ethnos (Special Issue on Notions of Development) 49:165–185.

Hakansson, Thomas.
1988    Bridewealth, Women and Land. Social Change among the Gusii of Kenya. Uppsala Studies in Cultural Anthropology 10. Stockholm: Almqvist and Wiksell International.

Komma, Toru.
1984    The Women's Self-help Association Movement among the Kipsigis of Kenya. Senri Ethnological Studies 15:145–186.

Levy, Marion F.
1988    Each in Her Own Way. Five Women Leaders of the Developing World. Boulder: Lynne Rienner Publishing.

Mbithi, Philip M. & Rasmus Rasmusson.
1977    Self Reliance in Kenya. The Case of Harambee. Uppsala: Scandinavian Institute of African Studies.

McCormack, Jeanne, Martin Walsh and Candace Nelson.
1986    Women's Group Enterprises. A Study of the Structure of Opportunity on the Kenya Coast. Boston, MA: World Education, Inc.

Monsted, Mette.
1978    Women's Groups in Rural Kenya and Their Role in Development. CDR Paper A.78.2. Copenhagen: Centre for Development Research.

Musyoki, Rachel N. and Timothy H. Gatara.
1985    Women [sic] Group Activities in Kenya: An Evaluation. Unpublished Report for the Women's Bureau, Ministry of Culture and Social Services, Government of Kenya.

Muzaale, Patrick J. and David Leonard.
1982    Women's Groups and Extension in Kenya: Their Impact on Food Production and Malnutrition in Baringo, Busia, and Taita-Taveta. mimeo. Berkeley: Project on Managing Decentralization, University of California.

Mwaniki, Nyaga.
1986    Against Many Odds: The Dilemmas of Women's Self-Help Groups in Mbeere, Kenya. Africa 56(2):210–228.

Pala, Achola O., J.E. Reynolds, M.A.H. Wallis & D.L. Brown.
1975    The Women's Group Programme in the S.R.D.P. Occasional Paper No. 13. Institute of Development Studies. University of Nairobi.

Parkin, David.
1975    The Rhetoric of Responsibility: Bureaucratic Communications in a Kenya Farming Area. *In* Political Language and Oratory in Traditional Society. Maurice Bloch, ed. Pp. 113–139. Orlando, FL: Academic Press.

Riria-Ouko, J.V.N.
1985    Women's Organizations in Kenya. Journal of Eastern African Research and Development 15:188–197.

Stamp, Patricia.
  1986    Kikuyu Women's Self-Help Groups. Toward an Understanding of the Relation
          Between Sex-Gender System and Mode of Production in Africa. *In* Women
          and Class in Africa. Claire Robertson and Iris Berger, eds. Pp. 27–46.
          New York: Africana Publishing Co.
Staudt, Kathleen.
  1986    Stratification. Implications for Women's Politics. *In* Women and Class in
          Africa. Claire Robertson and Iris Berger, eds. Pp. 197–215. New York:
          Africana Publishing Co.
Thomas, Barbara P.
  1985    Politics, Participation and Poverty. Development Through Self-Help in
          Kenya. Boulder, CO: Westview.
  1988    Household Strategies for Adaptation and Change: Participation in Kenyan
          Rural Women's Associations. Africa 58(4):401–422.
Turner, Victor.
  1967    The Forest of Symbols. Ithaca, NY: Cornell University Press.
Udvardy, Monica.
  1988    Women's Groups Near the Kenyan Coast: Patron-Clientship in the Devel-
          opment Arena. *In* Anthropology of Development and Change in East Africa.
          David Brokensha and Peter Little, eds. Pp. 217–235 Boulder, CO: Westview
          Press.
Wipper, Audrey.
  1975    The Maendeleo ya Wanawake Movement in the Colonial Period: The
          Canadian Connection, Mau Mau, Embroidery and Agriculture. *In* Rural
          Women: Development or Under-development? Rural Africana 29. Audrey
          Wipper, ed. Pp. 195–214. East Lansing, MI: African Studies Center,
          Michigan State University.
  1984    Women's Voluntary Associations. *In* African Women South of the Sahara.
          Margaret J. Hay and Sharon Stichter, eds. Pp. 69–86. New York: Longman.

# 13

## Migratory Wage Labor and Rural Inequality in Taita/Taveta District, Kenya

*Anne K. Fleuret*

Rural inequality has been a consistent theme in the work of David Brokensha (cf. Brokensha 1966; 1987; Castro, Hakansson, and Brokensha 1981). The 1981 paper is a detailed discussion of variables which can be examined to assess the extent of economic inequality in rural communities. Income is one of these variables. Rather than depending on just one source of income, rural-dwellers in Africa generally try to maintain access to several different income streams. These may include agricultural production for own consumption, sales of agricultural, livestock, or collected produce, sales of locally-manufactured items, and/or sales of labor or specialized services.

As off-farm employment opportunities are often limited in rural areas, many job-seekers must look for income-generating opportunities away from home. Such migratory wage labor affects both those who migrate and those household members who remain at home, but whose social and economic well-being is linked to migrant activity. However, while the importance of migrant labor is acknowledged, there is no consensus on the nature of its impact, and in particular on its contribution to social and economic inequality in rural areas.

Some of the disagreement on the impacts of migratory wage labor may emanate from a lack of precision in discussing this institution, which in turn arises at least in part from the highly variable nature of labor migration. Migrants may be absent intermittently for short periods, routinely on a seasonal basis, or continuously for months or years. Migration may be rural-rural, rural-urban, or even international, and the migrant may be found near to or quite distant from the sending community. A common feature, however, is that the migration is intended to be temporary rather than permanent, and sooner or later most migrants return to a rural place of origin.

In this paper I will advance a definition of migratory wage labor, and summarize the existing arguments on the relationships between the migrant

*197*

institution and household well-being. I will also present evidence from the Taita Hills of Kenya which suggests that the income obtained from migratory wage employment is a major contributor to, although not the sole determinant of, the economic inequality which so visibly exists in contemporary Taita communities.

## Labor Migration

Migratory wage labor as the term is employed in this paper refers to the widespread practice in Eastern and Southern Africa of largely male participation in salaried employment, principally, although not exclusively, in urban localities physically distant from the home or birthplace (cf. Stichter 1982). Parents, spouses, and/or children almost always remain in the rural areas of origin and are employed primarily in agriculture. These non-migratory family and household members make occasional visits to the urban workplace and some may remain there to seek education or employment in their turn.

Workers ordinarily visit their rural homes at irregular intervals; in fact this sort of movement has often been referred to as oscillating or circulatory migration (cf. Mitchell 1959; Mayer 1960) because of the tendency to circulate between a rural home base and urban workplace(s). The workers are expected to bring gifts with them when they return home, and more importantly to provide financial support in the form of cash remittances at regular intervals throughout their work careers.

On retirement from wage employment the migrants return to their rural area of origin, often to a farm that has been maintained by the efforts of other household members during their absence. Such employment is not seasonal, but rather may have a continuous duration of years or even decades. It is particularly prevalent in densely-populated areas where farm sizes and per capita land availability are declining, and in arid or semi-arid areas where returns to agriculture are low. In parts of Zambia, Botswana, Malawi, and Kenya, 40 to 60 percent of adult married men are absent at any given time, and many of the remainder either will go in search of such employment in the future, or have retired from it (Brown 1983; Stichter 1982; Watson 1958).

The development implications of the migratory wage system, in terms of whether it delivers meaningful social and economic benefits to those involved in it, are a matter of some dispute. One view is that labor migration is an essentially extractive system that impoverishes rural areas and forces them to subsidize under-compensated urban workers. Tostensen (1986) argues, for example, that urban salaries paid to lower-income workers in Kenya are as a matter of policy too small to permit the entire household to join the migrant at his workplace; the labor of those who remain in the rural areas is critical to the ability of one member to engage in salaried work, and the migrant, in effect, has two sources of income, urban wage employment and rural agriculture. "[P]art of the reproduction cost of the labourer and his family is borne by non-capitalist agriculture which in actual fact thus subsidizes heavily industrial wages" (Tostensen 1986:1).

Gugler and Flanagan contend of migrants that ". . . their contribution to the economy will frequently be less than it would have been had they continued to work in the rural sector" (1978:61) and that migrant income is depressed while the costs of migrant life are high. Brown (1983) maintains that male labor migration from Botswana discourages local development, creates manpower shortages, contributes to stagnant or declining productivity, and does not permit the accumulation of capital.

Negative impacts on patterns of labor allocation in rural households as a consequence of labor migration have been noted by a number of authors. In particular, adult women who remain on the farm are said to incur substantial increases in their work burdens, as they attempt to compensate for the labor of those absent (cf. Moore and Vaughan 1987). Greater poverty in those households from which male wage-earners are absent has been noted, and several authors have argued that higher rates of undernutrition occur among the rural-dwelling children of migrants, in comparison with those in households where husbands and fathers are present (cf. Connell et al. 1976; Gugler 1976; Richards 1939).

Lack of direct male participation in family life and the absence of appropriate male role models in the household and community has been linked to disintegration of the family and undisciplined behavior of youth (Mitchell 1959; Akong'a 1989). Van Donge (1984) looks upon the continued migration of young men from the Eastern Province of Zambia as a response to insufficient rural employment opportunities and the lack of capital for establishing themselves as commercial farmers; but migration is a last resort, as it is among Dioula women who are unable to sustain rice production (Reboussin 1986). Lipton (1980) contends that rural inequality is both a source of and a function of rural to urban migration, and that rural productivity is not increased by migration.

On the other hand, a number of observers have pointed to positive features of the migratory wage labor system. Van Velsen, writing in 1960, regarded labor migration as a "positive factor" in the life of the Tonga of Malawi. Labor migrants ". . . generally maintain a stake in the social and political structure of Tongaland . . . they have a vested interest in its continued functioning" (1960:266). Despite their long-term absence, most migrants maintained both social and economic links with their villages of origin, and retired to them; remittances were "net income" to those who remained at home. More recently, in situations where farm sizes have become too small to permit all or even most household income to be obtained from agricultural activities, or where commodity prices are so low that the essential conversion of some part of agricultural production to cash for critical purchases cannot generate enough money to meet needs, non-farm employment is essential (cf. Chaiken 1988; Conelly and Chaiken 1987).

Because the rural employment sector is small and cannot accommodate all those who need employment, migratory wage labor is an essential component of the income-generating strategy of many rural households. By far the majority of migrants—over 90% in studies by Tostensen (1986),

Adepoju (1974), Lux (1972). and Knowles and Anker (1981)—make regular remittances that amount to from 7 to 30 percent of gross income. While on the receiving end remittance money is used principally to satisfy consumption needs, it also has important investment functions, especially in education, housing and livestock, and land purchases (A. Fleuret 1988b; O'Leary 1980; 1983; Rempel and Lobdell 1980).

The net flow of wealth is from urban to rural areas; for example, Knowles and Anker found that of 1166 cash transfers between urban and rural areas of Kenya, only 6.5 percent of the transfers, and 6.3 percent of the money, moved from a rural locality to an urban one. The circulation of labor migrants and the information, goods and other resources they bring with them also contributes to regular exchanges and interactions between rural and urban areas. Migrants' rural kin are often better housed, clothed, fed and/or educated than those of non-migrants (Graedon 1980; Were 1989).

Migration is also an important strategy for coping with drought, famine, and other forms of adversity. A number of writers, including A. Fleuret (1986), O'Leary (1983), and Sperling (1986), have noted that rates of labor migration rise during times of stress, and that the cash generated by labor involvement both satisfies consumption needs and permits investment to occur when other income-generating opportunities, including food production, are limited or eliminated.

Finally, so far as impacts on the family are concerned, Stark and Lucas (1988) note that the decision to migrate is embedded in a household or family context. Rather than signaling the disintegration of a domestic unit, migration implies rather the efficiency, flexibility and mutual interdependence of the household and its members.

Although Third World cities are characterized by enormous inequality in access to income and standards of living, they also offer to the migrant a variety of opportunities that does not exist in the rural setting. Some of these opportunities may be dangerous or illegal, available housing is often poor, hygiene substandard or non-existent, and domestic energy, food, and transportation costly; but a disproportionate amount of national income is both earned and spent in urban areas,[1] and it is some share of this wealth that the migrant seeks to obtain.

Despite the abundance of literature, however, studies on both sides of this argument are inconclusive, because they do not present specific evidence which clearly links the migration variable to particular household outcomes or circumstances in the sending communities.


## Labor Migration: The Taita Case

Taita District, and more explicitly the Taita Hills portion of the District, is a "sending community" in Kenya with a long history of involvement in migratory wage labor. The hills are an island of medium to high potential agricultural land in a sea of uninhabited arid thorny scrub, and are located about 200 kilometers from Kenya's second-largest city, Mombasa. Declining availability of land for agricultural purposes, coupled with colonially-imposed taxes and the introduction of desirable and useful consumer goods which could only be acquired by paying cash, stimulated wage labor involvement before the turn of the century. In 1920 an estimated 15 percent of adult Taita men were engaged in salaried employment on sisal estates in the dry lowland areas of the district, and cash taxes in excess of 54,000 rupees were collected from the District in that year.[2] In the early 1950s about half the male population was estimated to have current or past wage labor experience outside the district. According to national census figures, in 1979 26.9 percent of all Taita lived outside of Taita/Taveta District (cf. Kapule 1986:22).

In the 1980s Taita participation in migratory wage labor remains high. In three farming communities which were studied between 1981 and 1985 the rate of male absence was affected by the viability of commercial agriculture, levels of education, and social network linkages with Mombasa and other labor markets. Male absence and ranged from a low of less than 20 percent in an area with lucrative commercial vegetable and dairy production on irrigated land, to over 40 percent in a physically isolated community without much commercial agricultural potential but with a long history of Mombasa connections. This latter village, called Msidunyi, will provide a case study.

Data were collected in two phases. In 1981 and 1982, a random sample of 65 households was selected from the total pool of 268 households which constituted Msidunyi. Many of these households did not contain any young children among their members. In 1984 and 1985, data were collected from a stratified random sample of 90 households, recruited equally from three structural categories: jointly managed, with both spouses present and no or a negligible history of labor migration; migrant, with the husband currently absent as an income earner; and households containing the child(ren) of one or more unmarried women. All of these households had among their members one or more children under the age of six years whose nutritional status was assessed. With the exception of the last structural category, the households are overwhelmingly two generation deep units consisting solely of parent(s) and child(ren) without any additional kinsfolk or dependents. A. and G. Harris (1964) have noted the jural and economic independence of the nuclear family household in Taita; in the early 1950s almost half of the households they studied were nuclear, and the proportion has increased over the intervening 35 years, as shown in Table 13.1.

Labor migration from Msidunyi remains a predominantly male activity. Most migrants seek employment in Mombasa where network contacts often ensure that they have job prospects before departing for the city. Current migrants have a mean duration of absence in employment of 13 years. Married women generally are not migrants independently of their husbands; while there are cases of married women living away from Taita with the rest of their nuclear family household and working in town, there are no instances of husbands remaining on the farm while their wives look for jobs elsewhere. Divorced and single women do seek migratory employment opportunities, however. In addition to the 40 percent of Msidunyi adult married men who

Table 13.1 - Household Structure and Linkages, Msidunyi Sample

|  | Joint | Migrant | Never-Married | Widow/Divorced | Total |
|---|---|---|---|---|---|
| Independent Nuclear | 51 | 46 | 5 | 14 | 116 |
| Patrilateral Extended | 1 | 7 | 0 | 0 | 8 |
| Matrilateral Extended | 0 | 0 | 29 | 0 | 29 |
| TOTAL | 52 | 53 | 34 | 14 | 153 |

are absent, about a quarter of the unmarried women who have children have left the children with the maternal grandparents and are employed in town mainly as barmaids or housemaids.

All of the migrant wives living in Msidunyi report receiving remittances from their absent spouses. Some of these payments are irregular in amount and timing but most receive predictable amounts at regular intervals, ranging from 200 to 800 Kenya shillings (Kshs.) per month.[3] The money is usually sent as a money order to a specific payee through the post office. The system is fairly reliable, in that the intended recipient usually does collect.

When added to what wives and other household members earn from their agricultural and other economic activities, the income of migrant households is substantially above that of households dependent on local employment and food production. Hence these households have considerable consumption and investment capability.

## Migration and Economic Differentiation

The analysis of Taita households which follows considers only those units which are economically independent. The patterns of expenditure and investment are not distorted by the inclusion of resources obtained from a wider circle of kin, or because the household is part of an extended social and economic unit. The comparisons are made between independent joint and migrant households. Unless otherwise noted, data are drawn from the 1984 and 1985 surveys.

Taita householders can invest in land, agricultural inputs, their dwelling, consumer durables, livestock, and education for their children, and may also vary in their estimated monthly expenditures and in the sums of money they contribute to self-help (*harambee*) activities. It can be noted that the primary means for acquiring the capital to purchase land is cash income from wage labor. Good agricultural land has escalated in price to the point where a single hectare commands thousands of shillings. Most land purchasers

Table 13.2 - Housing in Msidunyi

| Household Type | Joint | Migrant |
|---|---|---|
| Mean Number of Rooms | 2.35 | 4.25 |
| Percent of houses with permanent roof | 56 | 93 |

have had migrant labor experience; but purchasers are not numerous (cf. P. Fleuret 1980; A. Fleuret 1988b).

Lucas (1986) found little investment in agricultural inputs (apart from hired labor) among migrant wives, since they are less dependent on agriculture as a source of food or cash income than are other women. In any case the annual expenditures even for the heaviest users of non-labor inputs are very low—less than Kshs. 100.

Education becomes costly at the secondary level and few children from the sample households are old enough for secondary education, so these expenditures are not a meaningful indicator of household variability. Hence we are left with housing, ownership of consumer durables, and livestock holdings as the three most significant variables for measuring differential household economic prosperity in the Msidunyi population.

Traditional Taita houses were single room, wattle and daub structures with thatched roofs. The main improvements undertaken when financial circumstances permit are increasing the number of rooms and replacing the thatch with corrugated iron. As Table 13.2 indicates, while independent joint houses have an average of 2.35 rooms each, migrant houses have 4.25 rooms. Forty-four percent of joint families have only thatched roofs on their houses, while only one of the 30 migrant dwellings is still thatched–all of the others have invested in improved roofing, indicating that migrants' families are significantly better-housed than joint household members.

The investment in consumer durables, such as radios, furniture, appliances and other articles, was arrived at by allocating points proportional to the purchase price when new to each item owned and totaling the points to create a consumer index. Table 13.3 presents the results for joint and migrant households, and illustrates the advantageous position of migrant families.

In their ability to invest in various sorts of household conveniences and status symbols, migrants again significantly surpass joint householders.

There is no difference in the ownership of livestock, as calculated in terms of cattle equivalents, between joint and migrant households. The data do not reflect the extent to which there may be differential ownership of improved or dairy animals as opposed to unimproved local breeds; cattle ownership is a traditional path to wealth and status, and herds are obtained, more than other valuables, from inheritance rather than purchase. Livestock are also a traditionally male domain.

Table 13.3 - Consumer Durable Point Scores, Msidunyi

| Household Type | Mean | Range | Percent of House-holds with <10 pts. |
|---|---|---|---|
| Joint | 97 | 0-636 | 42 |
| Migrant | 201 | 0-546 | 0 |

In Msidunyi, then, migrant households and their members enjoy a significantly better standard of living than do their non-migrant neighbors, as measured by the size and permanence of their homes and the value of consumer goods owned. Further, despite the absence of adult men from migrant households, livestock holdings, generally viewed as the prerogative of men, are equivalent in the two groups of households.

It has frequently been argued that the absence of male labor increases the work burden of migrant wives and compromises their ability to care adequately for their children. In order to examine the validity of this argument both time-allocation data and information on patterns of utilization of cash-compensated casual labor within the community were collected. Analysis of the time-allocation data shows that migrant wives do not have a pattern of labor-time expenditure significantly different from that of other women in the community, perhaps cultivating a bit less and socializing and traveling a bit more.

The wives of absent labor migrants, then, are not placed in the position of doing "double duty", that is, of carrying out both those tasks allocated to women and those which would otherwise be carried out by absent husbands. What makes this possible is their consistent pattern of the purchase of the labor of other members of the community, especially husbands in joint households and unmarried women who have established their own independent households. Five of the latter, in fact, are full-time domestics in migrant households. Those who employ workers on a casual basis hire them to cultivate, haul water and firewood, make bricks, herd animals, and look after their younger children. Hence the work burden has *not* shifted to the wives of men who are absent, but to other community members, both male and female, who desperately need cash and have no other way to get it. Thirteen out of 24 employers are migrants; 21 out of 23 workers are either joint or never-married household members.

Such patterns in the disposition of purchased labor are open to two interpretations. On the one hand, the wages paid to these workers help spread the benefits of migration beyond the boundaries of migrant households. Alternatively, the labor of the poor is, through this system, being appropriated by a small, wealthy minority. Regardless of which interpretation is employed, however, the fact remains that such employment gives the workers access to vital cash which they have no other means to acquire.

So far as lack of discipline and family disintegration are concerned, there is no indication that substantial or deleterious change has permanently occurred in Taita family or household structure as a consequence of labor migration. Almost all male migrants do return permanently to the farm when their employment careers are over, and regular interaction between fathers and their children does take place during visits and holidays. In any case, grandparents have traditionally had the most important role in the training and education of young people in Taita society, rather than parents. Grandparents are generally present in the community and continue to carry out these functions. Although they are not necessarily co-resident, male role models for youth do exist in the community. Further, rates both of divorce and of polygyny are low compared with other areas of Kenya. If anything, family dissolution, alcoholism, spouse abuse and domestic violence seem to be more prevalent among the most impoverished joint families.

## Summary and Conclusions

Castro, Hakansson, and Brokensha (1981) identify a number of other indicators apart those discussed above which separate rich from poor. Among these are diet and nutritional status, condition of health and utilization of health care services, type of fuel consumed, and ownership of goods that can be used to produce income. It has not been able to consider all of these variables in this paper, but the positive association between access to migrant labor income on the one hand, and both improved nutritional status, and fuel consumption, on the other, has been shown elsewhere (cf. A. Fleuret 1988a; P. Fleuret, this volume).

As suggested in the introduction, earnings from migratory wage labor are not the only basis for social and economic inequality in rural Taita. Membership in a "core" lineage, for example, is the primary determinant of unequal landholdings. As has been shown elsewhere, members of "core" lineages in Msidunyi have landholdings averaging twice the size of those who do not belong to these kinship groups (A. Fleuret 1988b; see also P. Fleuret 1980; Vincent 1973). In other Taita communities where high-potential agricultural land is available, differential participation in commercial agriculture has contributed importantly to increased inequality. Those fortunate enough to obtain salaried employment close to home, so that migration is not a element in obtaining wage labor, are also advantaged in comparison with those who depend on food production, local market vending, and unskilled or piecework employment to earn a living.

To a limited degree, the benefits of wage labor income go beyond the boundaries of the households of absent migrants. The practice of hiring community members on a full or part-time basis to replace the labor of adult men who are not present distributes cash to individuals who are part of the wider circle of the community.

The forgoing discussion should not be taken to mean that labor migration has unequivocal benefits to all individuals in all places. Rural-dwelling wives may be neglected or abandoned by migrant husbands; men may be employed in menial jobs which leave them little or nothing with which to return to their homes; priorities in the disposition of income from labor migration may contribute to stagnant or declining nutritional status among the children of migrants. Since much of the income that migrants return to the rural areas is used to satisfy consumption needs, investment in income-generating activity or capital equipment is often minimal.

Despite these caveats, it is evident from the data on Taita presented above that the income generated from migratory wage labor contributes substantially to economic inequality in Msidunyi. It is not the migrants and their families who are disadvantaged, but men, women and children who do not have access to distant employment and the material prosperity generated by it. In meaningful and easily-measurable indicators of differentiation, migrant householders are substantially better-off that those who have not had access to migrant labor income.

## Acknowledgments

Fieldwork was carried out in Taita from January 1981 to June 1982, June–August 1984, and May–August 1985. The research was supported by grants from the Social Science Research Council and the National Institutes of Health—National Institute of Child Health and Human Development. Authorization to conduct research was granted by the Office of the President; affiliation was with the Population Studies and Research Institute, University of Nairobi. I am grateful to all of these organizations for their assistance and support. Research assistants Griphin C. S. Msaga and Catherine Mjomba contributed substantially to this paper; thanks are also due to Lucy Mwandoe, Joyce Mzenge, and other residents of Msidunyi. A somewhat different version of this paper was presented at the 1988 annual meeting of the American Anthropological Association, Phoenix, Arizona.

## Notes

1. For example, the International Labour Organization estimates (cf. P. Fleuret and Greeley 1982) that 42 percent of Kenyan national income is earned in Nairobi; yet Nairobi contains less than ten percent of Kenya's population.

2. The information on absenteeism and tax collections was obtained from District Annual Reports lodged in the Kenya National Archives, Nairobi. 54,000 rupees was equivalent in value to about U.S.$20,000 in 1920.

3. In 1985 the exchange rate was approximately U.S.$1=Kshs. 16; presently (1989) the rate is U.S.$1=Kshs. 21.5.

## References Cited

Adepoju, A.
   1974    Migration and Socio-economic Links between Urban Migrants and their Home Communities in Nigeria. Africa. 44:383–392.

Akong'a, Joshua.
1989   Personal Communication. Institute of African Studies. University of Nairobi.

Brokensha, David W.
1966   Social Change at Larteh, Ghana. Oxford: Clarendon Press.
1987   Inequality in Rural Africa: Fallers Reconsidered. Manchester University Papers on Development III(2):1-21.

Brown, B.
1983   The impact of Male Labour Migration on Women in Botswana. African Affairs. 82:367-388.

Castro, Alphonso P., Thomas Hakansson and David Brokensha.
1981   Indicators of Rural Inequality. World Development. 9(5):401-427.

Chaiken, Miriam S.
1988   Household Resource Allocation and Food Security in Western Kenya. Paper presented at the annual meeting of the American Anthropological Association. Phoenix.

Conelly, W. Thomas, and Miriam S. Chaiken.
1987   Land, Labor, and Livestock: The Impact of Intense Population Pressure on Food Security in Western Kenya. Paper presented at the annual meeting of the American Anthropological Association. Chicago.

Connell, J., B. Das Gupta, R. Laishley and M. Lipton.
1976   Migration from Rural Areas: the Evidence from Village Studies. Delhi: Oxford University Press.

Fleuret, Anne.
1986   Indigenous Responses to Drought in sub-Saharan Africa. Disasters. 10(3):225-229.
1988a   Migratory Wage Labor and Nutritional Status in Taita, Kenya. Paper presented at the annual meeting of the American Anthropological Association. Phoenix.
1988b   Some Consequences of Tenure and Agrarian Reform in Taita, Kenya. *In* Land Concentration in Africa. R. Downs and S. Reyna, eds. Pp. 136-158. Hanover, NH: University Press of New England.

Fleuret, Patrick.
1980   Sources of Material Inequality in Lushoto District, Tanzania. African Studies Review. 23(3):69-87.

Fleuret, Patrick with Edward H. Greeley.
1982   Kenya Social and Institutional Profile. Nairobi: United States Agency for International Development.

Graedon, T.
1980   Nutritional Consequences of Rural-Urban Migration. unpublished paper prepared for USAID.

Gugler, J.
1976   Migrating to Urban Centers of Unemployment in Tropical Africa. *In* International Migration: the New and the Third World. A. Richmond and D. Kubat, eds. Pp. 184-204. Beverly Hills, CA: Sage.

Gugler, J. and W. Flanagan.
1978   Urbanization and Social Change in West Africa. Cambridge: Cambridge University Press.

Harris, A. and G. Harris.
1964    Property and the Cycle of Domestic Groups in Taita. *In* The Family Estate in Africa. R. Gray and P. Gulliver, eds. Pp. 117–153. Boston: Boston University Press.

Kapule, H.
1986    Demographic Profile. *In* Taita Taveta District Socio-cultural Profile. R. Soper, ed. Pp. 17–28. Nairobi: Ministry of Planning and National Development and Institute of African Studies.

Knowles, J. and R. Anker.
1981    An Analysis of Income Transfers in a Developing Country. Journal of Development Economics. 8:205–226.

Lipton, Michael.
1980    Migration from Rural Areas of Poor Countries: the Impact on Rural Productivity and Income Distribution. World Development. 8:1–24.

Lucas, K.
1986    The Adoption of Agricultural Innovations by Women Farmers in Taita. Unpublished MA thesis. Department of Anthropology. The American University.

Lux, A.
1972    Gift Exchange and Income Redistribution between Yombe Rural Wage Earners and their Kinsfolk in Western Zaire. Africa. 42:173–191.

Mayer, Phillip.
1960    Townsmen or Tribesmen. London: Oxford University Press.

Mitchell, J. C.
1959    The Causes of Labour Migration. Bulletin of the Inter-African Labour Institute. 6(1):12–46.

Moore, H. and Megan Vaughan.
1987    Cutting Down Trees: Women, Nutrition and Agricultural Change in the Northern Province of Zambia, 1920–1986. African Affairs. 86(345):523–540.

O'Leary, M.
1980    Responses to Drought in Kitui District, Kenya. Disasters. 4(3):315–327.
1983    Population, Economy and Domestic Groups: the Kitui Case. Africa. 53(1):64–76.

Reboussin, D.
1986    Social Organization and the Outmigration of Rural Diola Women. Paper presented at the Conference on Gender Issues in Farming Systems Research and Extension. Gainesville, Florida.

Rempel, H. and R. Lobdell.
1980    The role of Urban-to-rural Remittances in Rural Development. Journal of Development Studies. 14:324–341.

Richards, Audrey.
1939    Land, Labour and Diet in Northern Rhodesia: An Economic Study of the Bemba Tribe. Oxford: Oxford University Press.

Sperling, Louise.
1986    Food Acquisition by East African Herders during the Drought of 1983–1984. Paper presented at the annual meeting of the American Anthropological Association. Philadelphia.

Stark, Oded and Robert E.B. Lucas.
  1988    Migration, Remittances, and the Family. Economic Development and Cul-
          tural Change. 36(3):465–482.
Stichter, Sharon.
  1982    Migrant Labour in Kenya. Essex: Longman.
Tostensen, A.
  1986    Between Shamba and Factory: Preliminary Results from a study of Oscillatory
          Labour Migration in Kenya. Working Paper No. 423. Institute for Devel-
          opment Studies. University of Nairobi.
Van Donge, J.
  1984    Rural-urban Migration and the Rural Alternative in Mwase Lundazi, Eastern
          Province, Zambia. African Studies Review. 27:83–96.
Van Velsen, J.
  1960    Labor Migration as a Positive Factor in the Continuity of Tonga Tribal
          Society. Economic Development and Cultural Change. 8:265–278.
Vincent, Joan.
  1973    African Elite. New York: Columbia University Press.
Watson, W.
  1958    Tribal Cohesion in a Money Economy. Manchester: Manchester University
          Press.
Were, Gideon S.
  1989    Personal Communication. Institute of African Studies. University of Nairobi.

# PART FOUR

# Natural Resource Management

Anthropological approaches to understanding strategies of natural resource management have developed from a number of theoretical perspectives. The first of these, and the most important, was the field of ecological anthropology, particularly the early work of Julian Steward (1936; 1955). Steward argued that cultural adaptation to a particular environment could be understood through the interplay between resources, technology, and social organization. More recent work in ecological anthropology has stressed the flexibility and variability of human interaction with and exploitation of natural resources, including land, water, flora, and fauna (cf. Barth 1956; Netting 1968; Rappaport 1984 [1968]).

The subfield of cognitive anthropology has also contributed importantly to anthropological studies of resource management. Indigenous, "folk", or "native" taxonomies have provided the sort of discrete and bounded linguistic domain appropriate for componential analysis. Plants, animals, land, even firewood are among the categories of natural resources to have been examined from the cognitive perspective (Metzger and Williams 1966; Bulmer 1967; Berlin, Breedlove, and Raven 1974).

As early as 1954, Harold Conklin advocated joining cognitive with ecological interpretations of the environment. This "ethnoecological" approach involved examining environment and resources from both "etic" and "emic" perspectives, integrating the viewpoints both of scientific ecology and indigenous perception (cf. Conklin 1954; Frake 1962). The value of combining these perspectives has been shown by many subsequent studies (see, for example, A. Fleuret 1980; Brush et al. 1981).

The correlation that can exist between "folk" cognitive categories and actual behavioral outcomes has been demonstrated in Johnson's study of agricultural practices in Brazil (1974). Johnson found that the folk model of cropland types and local beliefs about the preferences of common food crops for these land categories were good predictors of actual planting behavior. His study demonstrated the practical applications of ethnoecological studies.

Ecological and cognitive approaches to questions of environmental perception and resource management have been an important theme in the work of David Brokensha, beginning with his work in Ghana and embracing such diverse resources as bees; agricultural, pastoral, and "bush" lands; fuelwood trees; and systems of vegetation (Brokensha 1966; Brokensha and Glazier 1973; Brokensha, Mwaniki, and Riley 1972; Brokensha and Riley 1978; 1980; Riley and Brokensha 1988). His concern with resource management questions became most explicitly linked with his interests in social change, inequality, and development anthropology in the 1980 collection, co-edited with Warren and Werner, entitled *Indigenous Knowledge Systems and Development*. With the appearance of this volume the issue of the relationships among environment, local knowledge, and development was first clearly addressed. The growing interest in the interactions of environment and development in the past decade is reflected in a number of publications following on the 1980 collection, including Little and Horowitz (1987), and Brokensha and Little (1988). The essays in this section build and expand upon this long-established and diverse theoretical and practical background.

In his contribution, Little discusses the impact of formal institutions on resource management in the Tana River Basin, Kenya. He argues that these institutions, including government ministries, parastatal organizations, co-operative societies, and international donors, have affected and altered local communities' access to and control over resources, particularly water. The goals of these institutions are frequently at odds with the needs of the people who live in the Basin, and who have often failed to obtain tangible benefits from development activities carried out there.

Michael Painter discusses, in more general terms, the impact of social and economic inequality on natural resource management in Latin America. Painter finds, as does Little, that formal institutions, particularly national and regional governments and large enterprises, have contributed both to environmental degradation and to increasingly unequal access to resources. Particularly disadvantaged are smallholder farmers, who bear a disproportionate burden of blame for environmental destruction at the same time that their access to agricultural land, water, and inputs, among other resources, is threatened by larger state and regional interests.

Baxter, in contrast, focuses on a single resource, mineral salts fed to their livestock by the Oromo and Arssi pastoralists of Kenya and Ethiopia. He emphasizes that apart from any nutritional importance that these salts might have for livestock, the relationships between animals and people that are created and sustained by their provision and consumption are crucial to the societies themselves. Baxter's work shows again the importance of considering both etic and emic views in questions of resource management.

The last two articles, by P. Fleuret and Castro, both concern themselves with aspects of the management and utilization of forest resources in different parts of rural Kenya. Fleuret addresses himself to domestic fuel sources, most importantly trees and woody shrubs, utilized in the Taita Hills. He makes the point that the types and quantities of fuels consumed vary with respect to local conditions of scarcity, ecological variability, socioeconomic disparities within communities, and household size, composition, and organization. Such variation in the use of resources is often overlooked in narrow, highly-focused analyses, but has important implications for development and applied anthropology. Castro directs his attention to sacred groves among the Kikuyu of Kirinyaga District. He shows that social change, particularly religious conversion, has led to the disappearance and destruction of many sacred groves. Places of worship, centers of public ritual, and symbols of unity in precolonial Kikuyu society, the groves have suffered as social, economic, and religious diversity have contributed to division and disunity in contemporary Kirinyaga.

The essays in this section are diverse, but nonetheless adhere to these common themes: the necessity of an integrated and wide-ranging approach to environmental and resource management issues; the crucial importance of increasing social and economic inequality in understanding questions of resource access and utilization; and the implications of differential patterns of perception and management of natural resources for social change and development.

# References Cited

Barth, Frederick.
1956    Ecologic Relationships of Ethnic Groups in Swat, North Pakistan. American Anthropologist. 58:1079–1089.

Berlin, B., D. Breedlove, and P. Raven.
1974    Principles of Tzeltzal Plant Classification: An Introduction to the Botanical Ethnography of a Mayan-Speaking People of Highland Chiapas. New York: Academic Press.

Brokensha, David W.
1966    Social Change at Larteh, Ghana. Oxford: Clarendon Press.

Brokensha, David W. and Jack Glazier.
1973    Land Reform among the Mbeere of Central Kenya. Africa. 43(3):182–206.

Brokensha, David W., and Peter D. Little, eds.
1988    Anthropology of Development and Change in East Africa. Boulder, CO: Westview Press.

Brokensha, D., H. Mwaniki and B. Riley.
1972    Bee-keeping in Embu District, Kenya. Bee World. 53(3):114–123.

Brokensha, David W., and Bernard Riley.
1978    Forests, Foraging, Fences and Fuel in a Marginal Area of Kenya. Paper prepared for USAID.

1980    Mbeere Knowledge of Vegetation and its Relevance for Development. *In* Indigenous Knowledge Systems and Development. David W. Brokensha, Dennis Warren and Oswalt Werner, eds. Pp. 113–130. Lanham, MD: University Press of America.

Brokensha, David., Dennis Warren and Oswald Werner, eds.
1980    Indigenous Knowledge Systems and Development. Lanham, MD: University Press of America.

Brush, S., H. Carney and Z. Huaman.
1981    Dynamics of Andean Potato Agriculture. Economic Botany. 35(1):70–88.

Bulmer, Ralph.
  1967    Why is the Cassowary not a Bird? A Problem of Zoological Taxonomy among the Karam of the New Guinea Highlands. Man. 2:5–25.
Conklin, Harold.
  1954    An Ethnoecological Approach to Shifting Agriculture. Transactions of the New York Academy of Sciences. 17(2):133–142.
Fleuret, Anne.
  1980    Nonfood Uses of Plants in Usambara. Economic Botany. 34:320–333.
Frake, Charles.
  1962    Cultural Ecology and Ethnography. American Anthropologist. 64(1):53–59.
Johnson, A.
  1974    Ethnoecology and Planting Practices in a Swidden Agricultural System. American Ethnologist. 1:87–101.
Little, Peter D. and Michael M Horowitz, eds.
  1987    Lands at Risk in the Third World. Boulder, CO: Westview.
Metzger, D., and G. Williams.
  1966    Some Procedures and Results in the Study of Native Categories: Tzeltzal "Firewood". American Anthropologist. 68:389–407.
Netting, Robert M.
  1968    Hill Farmers of Nigeria. Seattle: University of Washington Press.
Rappaport, Roy.
  1984    Pigs for the Ancestors. Revised Edition. New Haven: Yale University Press.
Riley, Bernard, and David W. Brokensha.
  1988    The Mbeere in Kenya. Vols. I and II. Lanham, MD: University Press of America.
Steward, Julian.
  1936    The Ecological and Social Basis of Primitive Bands. *In* Essays in Honor of A. L. Kroeber. Pp. 331–350. Berkeley: University of California Press.
  1955    Theory of Culture Change. Urbana/Chicago: University of Illinois Press.

# 14

## Institutional Dynamics and Development in the Tana Basin, Kenya

*Peter D. Little*

The study of river basin development and local institutions are important contributions of David Brokensha's work (Brokensha 1962; 1976; Brokensha and Nellis 1974; and Thomas and Brokensha 1985). His work both in the Volta (Ghana) and Tana (Kenya) basins have provided contexts for addressing the development concerns of local organizations and communities. This chapter builds on these dimensions of Brokensha's applied research by analyzing institutional dynamics and development in the Tana basin, Kenya. It pays particular attention to relationships between the major institution in the Tana basin, the Tana and Athi Rivers Development Authority (TARDA), and smaller institutions (e.g., water user and herder associations) representing thousands of smallholders in the region. The chapter argues that although TARDA is a regional institution, with regional and local development mandates, its structure and policies are national in orientation. This orientation places most of TARDA's plans in conflict with local institutions and inhibits meaningful local development.

Two recurrent themes highlight the discussion in this chapter. The first is the importance of historical specificity in the analysis of Tana Basin institutions, since these institutions often arose and, consequently changed, in response to particular historical circumstances. The second theme is that Tana institutions promote the interests of their members, which may complement or conflict with other institutional interests in the Tana basin. The ability of certain segments of the population, whether they be planners, rainfed farmers, irrigated farmers, or herders, to defend and support their economic interests depends on the strength of their representative institutions. Thus, those sectors of the Tana basin (e.g., the livestock sector) that have the weakest institutions have received the smallest share of development resources.

## Agroecology and Land Use in the Tana Basin

The Tana River originates in the highlands near Nairobi, flowing 708 kilometers in an easterly direction to the Indian Ocean. Its basin covers an area of approximately 62,210 square kilometers, which is approximately ten percent of Kenya's total land base, and encompasses a great diversity of agro-ecological zones and production systems (Ominde 1971; Saha 1982). These range from nomadic pastoralism and large-scale irrigation in the middle basin (arid rangelands) to low cost recession and flood water cultivation in the delta area (humid tropical lowlands) to intensive small-scale irrigation in the upper basin (highland zone).

The agroecological zones covered by the Tana basin are (based on Jaetzold and Schmidt 1983):

1. The coconut-cassava (annual rainfall in excess of 1000 mm) and cashewnut-cassava zones (800–1000 mm. annual rainfall) in the extreme southeasterly portion of the basin (comprising less than five percent of basin).
2. The livestock-millet and ranching zones in the area between Garsen and Mbalambala (400–650 mm. annual rainfall)—most of middle and upper Tana River and Garissa districts.
3. The cotton and sunflower-maize zones in lowland parts of Embu, Meru, and Kirinyaga districts, including the Mwea plains (650–800 mm. annual rainfall).
4. The coffee-tea zone of the upper Tana basin, including highland parts of Kiambu, Murang'a, Nyeri, Kirinyaga, and Embu districts (in excess of 1000 mm. annual rainfall).

A narrow band of riverine forest, frequently less than one kilometer in width, marks the river over most of its course. The vast majority of the basin, in excess of 70 percent of the territory, has annual precipitation below 700 mm, making agriculture marginal without irrigation or a form of recession cultivation.

Population densities and intensive agriculture tend to be concentrated in the extreme upper end of the basin. In the highest parts of the upper basin, population density exceeds 300 per square kilometer and intensive cultivation is practiced. Sprinkler and gravity flow irrigation is used in some of these areas to grow such high-value crops as coffee, green beans, and onions. Population density and agricultural intensification is very low throughout most of the middle and lower basin, except in a few areas along the river where investments in large-scale irrigation and settlement have taken place (e.g., the Bura area). For example, Tana River District, the largest administrative district in the basin, has a population density of only 3 per square kilometer and most of this is concentrated in a narrow band of settlements along the river. A form of extensive pastoralism is practiced over most of the district, as well as in neighboring Garissa District (see Ensminger 1984).

Adequate rainfall reduces the river's significance in determining settlement and production patterns in the upper basin. While the river is of considerable importance, rainfed cropping can be practiced in most of this area and where irrigation is practiced, such as at Kibirigwe, it is used to grow high-value crops as a supplement to rainfed agriculture. *Land is a scarcer and more valuable commodity than water in these areas.* The proliferation of urban centers (Murang'a, Nairobi, Nyeri, and Embu) and industry in the upper basin influence local economic activities there at least as much as the river.

As the river and its tributaries move out of the highlands and into the middle and lower portions of the basin, the importance of the river in the local economy greatly increases. By the time it enters Garissa and Tana River Districts, the river is a strong determinant of settlement patterns and local production. Recession cultivation and small-scale irrigation are practiced, and livestock production in the dry season depends on the water and vegetation of the riverine area. In the lower parts of the basin, from around Garsen to the shores of the Indian Ocean, the seasonal flooding of the river creates rich perennial pastures. These support up to 300,000 cattle which are essential for the welfare of some 10,000 herders, as well as for the restocking needs of several commercial ranches located outside the basin. The pastoral sectors of Tana River and Garissa Districts provide in most years up to 50 percent of the meat for consumption in Mombasa, Kenya's second largest city and its most important port (Ominde 1971:158). In these two districts, virtually all important settlements are in close proximity to the river.

The variety of local production systems is greater in the lower and middle than in the upper parts of the basin. From the delta to the Mbalambala area (middle Tana), agriculture is practiced by the Pokomo, Giriama, Korekore, and Malekote people in small settlements interspersed along the river, and by settled Somali in the vicinity of Garissa town. In addition, some pastoral families of the southern Orma (called the Chaffa) have begun to farm on seasonally inundated swamp lands around Garsen town. Small-scale irrigation, using pumps in many cases, and recession cultivation characterize the agricultural systems in these areas. The area cultivated by small-scale irrigation in Lower Tana District and the Garissa town area is approximately 215 hectares and 175 hectares, respectively (Merryman 1984:165; Kimani 1988). Although the area under recession cultivation/flood irrigation is unknown, it is likely to exceed that allocated to small-scale irrigation.

Pastoral livestock production covers the remaining estimated 95 percent of the territory of Tana River and Garissa Districts, including large parts of the delta where herder villages are dispersed among agricultural settlements. Seasonal livestock movements tend to be away from the river and delta during the wet season, while during the dry season cattle are heavily concentrated in the delta and along the river between Garissa and Garsen. Access to the Tana's water and riverine pastures allow herders and their animals to survive the long dry season, when risks of stock loss are very high. During an especially severe drought, such as that of 1984, livestock from as far as Wajir (a distance of more than 250 kilometers) converge on the lower Tana, where the concentration of cattle can be as great as anywhere in the country. Even in normal dry seasons, the density of cattle in the lower Tana may be among the highest in Kenya (see Kenya 1979).

## The Historical Context
## of Tana River Basin Planning

Historically, the agroecological diversity of the Tana basin has led to a very uneven pattern of investment and institutional development; in contrast to most other African basins, development activities and institutions have been concentrated more in the upper than in other parts of the basin. Because European settlers were attracted to the highlands of the upper Tana, with its excellent agricultural lands and plentiful water, this area received a disproportionate share of investment in transport, agriculture, and water development.

### Settler Institutions in the Colonial Era

The better agricultural lands around Nyeri, Kiambu and Thika in the upper Tana were alienated in the colonial period for European farmers, who were represented by several state-supported institutions, including the Kenya Farmers Association (KFA) and the Kenya Co-operative Creameries (KCC). As Leys (1974:36) points out:

> These arrangements called for an extensive set of institutions for managing their (settler) details. This was most notable in the agricultural sector, with its system of settler-controlled marketing and regulatory boards, production committees and land boards in every area of the highlands, and the quasi-company organizations which handled particular products, especially the Kenya Farmers' Association (KFA) (which both purchased grain and distributed seed and implements, and also built up a near-monopoly of grain milling), and the Kenya Cooperative Creameries (KCC), which controlled and handled the Europeans' diary output.

The concentration of development investment and institutional development in the upper Tana was established in the colonial period. The European farmers of the upper Tana had strong linkages with international capital and markets, and were able to attract foreign investment to the area (Swainson 1980:157). Because there were few European settlers and businessmen with interests in the middle and lower Tana, these areas lagged in almost every indicator of development, a trend that has continued to present. Many of the institutions operating in the upper Tana basin were opened up to Africans in the 1950s, when economic restrictions on African producers were lifted. These restrictions mainly included limitations on production of export crops and the ownership of certain crops. The KCC, the county councils, and producer cooperatives are among the more important institutions that became accessible to Africans, and that have played an important role in the post-independence development of the upper Tana.

## The African Land Development (ALDEV) Board and Other Government Institutions

The first government institution in the Tana basin specifically to promote the interests of African producers was ALDEV, the African Land Development Programme, which established irrigation schemes at Mwea and Hola. It also established the institutional framework for the National Irrigation Board (NIB), which after 1967 took over the management of these two schemes. While ALDEV's mandate was broader than the irrigation sector, its most enduring impact was in this sector. In addition to helping shape the institutional framework for government irrigation schemes in Kenya, it developed the most successful development project in the basin, the Mwea Irrigated Settlement Scheme. This scheme, which is discussed in considerable detail in Kimani (1988), provided the model for Kenya's medium and large-scale irrigation projects. Unfortunately, the irrigation model developed by ALDEV, while it apparently has proven successful in the Mwea case, has led to disastrous consequences elsewhere. The model called for a one year tenancy system, whereby farmers were leased plots on a year to year basis; a highly centralized management system, whereby almost all important decisions were made in Nairobi or by staff of the headquarters posted at the scheme; and rigorous production and marketing schedules that allowed farmers little flexibility. In remote areas of the country, such as at Hola, the centralized management system has resulted in considerable inefficiency. While there have been modifications in the management of government irrigation schemes since independence, the emphasis on centralized decision-making remains.

## The Importance of Historical Events

Several important historical events have shaped development activities and institutions in the Tana basin.[1] Among earlier events, the most important was the Mau Mau emergency in the 1950s, which forced the colonial state to consider more carefully the development of the African areas. The ALDEV organization clearly was a response to internal pressures to allocate resources to African farmers. Two other events that influenced the role of institutions in the Tana basin were the floods of 1961 and the prolonged drought of the 1960s and 1970s. In 1961, the entire lower Tana region was inundated with floods and isolated from the rest of the country, and emergency food relief had to be flown into the area. The event brought considerable attention and outside assistance to a part of the basin that had received virtually no development inputs to date.

Like the floods of 1961, the prolonged drought of the 1960s and 1970s resulted in further interest in the Tana basin, but in this case attention was focused on the Garissa area of the middle Tana. In the 1960s, several church-related organizations established small-scale irrigation schemes along the Tana near Garissa to provide opportunities for impoverished nomads. It should be noted that the impoverishment of herders at the time was due not only to drought, but also to prolonged fighting in northeastern Kenya (Merryman 1984). Nevertheless, the effect was the same—attention was focused on the

Tana area, and a number of outside institutions became involved in the region.

A fourth historical event that clearly influenced institutions in the Tana basin was the rise of the Amin regime in neighboring Uganda. When Amin began to consolidate his political base in the early 1970s, beginning a long period of political uncertainty and tyranny in the country, Kenya was more than 70 percent dependent on energy imported from Uganda. While development of hydropower in the Tana basin had begun as early as the mid-1960s, it was not until the 1970s that an accelerated energy program began. The risks of continuing to depend on Uganda as a source of electricity was an important factor in the rapid development of the Tana's hydropower sources. The dependence on imported hydropower was a national issue that was given priority over any concerns with regional and local development in the basin.

## The Tana and Athi Rivers Development Authority (TARDA)

The need to develop hydropower sources in the Tana basin rapidly required a more careful planning and monitoring of the area's water resources than had been the case in the past. The formation of TARDA (originally called TRDA)[2] in 1974 was partially to help plan for the integrated development of the basin's water resources, but more importantly it was to facilitate the development of hydropower. While it is likely that hydropower development would have been the most important activity of TARDA in its early years, the dependence on Ugandan energy was an important factor in ensuring the hydropower orientation. TARDA and the country's mandate was to develop energy sources in the Tana, and all other activities, such as irrigation and fisheries, were of very secondary importance. TARDA's bias toward hydropower development, even with the country's reduced dependence on imported energy, still very much influences its development agenda.

### *Lack of Integrated Planning*

The government of Kenya was concerned with the development of hydropower in the Tana, but not with river basin development or irrigation per se; nor with regional or local development. It has only been recently, with the realization that further expansion of rainfed agriculture in the country is limited, that there has been a national concern with irrigation development and, consequently, with the Tana basin; the Tana contains a large share (approximately 200,000 hectares) of Kenya's irrigable land.

The legislation that created TRDA (and later TARDA) allocated it responsibility for: (1) advising the government on all matters affecting the development of the area, including the apportionment of water resources; (2) devising a long-range development plan for the basin; (3) initiating a range of studies in the area; (4) coordinating "the various studies of, and schemes within, the Area so that human, water, animal, land and other resources are utilized to the best advantage"; (5) establishing a program of monitoring of the performance of projects within the basin; (6) ensuring close co-operation between all agencies concerned with the abstraction and use of water within the area; and (7) maintaining a liaison between the Government, the private sector and foreign agencies working in the basin (based on Kenya 1977 [revised 1982]:5–6). As the institution has matured and taken on its own identity, TARDA has broadened its activities to include more than just planning for hydropower. However, the energy sector still accounts for over 90 percent of the institution's annual budget. The institution itself has changed considerably since its inception, with a greater concern for the implementation of large, capital-intensive projects. TARDA's emergence as an implementing agency, which was not foreseen in its original or revised legislation, has been a significant change.

TARDA is supervised by an interministerial committee of government officials and private citizens, which in principle should help the authority to coordinate its activities with other relevant institutions (see TARDA 1982; 1986). In practice, however, the existence of interministerial committees rarely assures close coordination among different institutions, and the TARDA case is not an exception (discussed in greater detail below). One of the important functions of the interministerial committee is to allow TARDA to advise the different ministries on their activities in the basin, especially as they affect the allocation of water resources. The interministerial committee's record in this respect is mixed. In the case of irrigated agriculture, communication with the relevant institutions seems to have improved (at least in the case of national institutions), but with other ministries this does not seem to have been the case. For instance, TARDA does not seem to have coordinated its activities with the Ministry of Environment and Natural Resources. Several of TARDA's existing (e.g., the Masinga Dam) and proposed activities (e.g., the Tana Delta Irrigation Scheme and Kiambere Dam) have or will have deleterious effects on the environment, but the advice of the Ministry of Environment and Natural Resources has not been sought.

TARDA's governing committee is made up almost strictly of representatives of national-level institutions. The County Councils or Municipal councils or other local bodies in the basin are not represented on the committee. Nor are line ministries that represent local organizations found on the committee. For example, the Ministry of Cooperative Development, which in the upper Tana alone represents more than 50 agricultural cooperatives, is not represented on the committee; nor is the Ministry of Culture and Social Services, which represents local community development organizations and small-scale water user associations.

Integrated planning of the Tana basin has been hampered by the lack of a master plan. Although efforts toward producing a master plan began as early as the mid-1970s, with the work being carried out mainly by expatriate advisors, TARDA has yet to produce an integrated plan for the development of the basin. Without a master plan, TARDA has been unable to capitalize on the basin's rich diversity of human and physical resources. It continues to design and implement discrete, sector-specific activities, which do little to enhance the basin's local production systems and populations. That dam construction at Masinga and Kiambere in the Tana basin has been carried out with little attention to existing irrigation systems (including flood-based) in the lower Tana is evidence of the lack of integrated planning.

### Excessively Expensive and Complex Development Programs

The Tana basin has experienced some of the most expensive, donor-funded development "experiments" in Kenya. Most noteworthy is the World Bank-funded Bura Irrigation Scheme, which is among the most expensive irrigation projects in Africa with costs in excess of U.S.$25,000 per hectare. Less publicized are the very expensive donor projects (on a per hectare basis) at Minjila, Kibirigwe, and Mitunguu in the upper Tana. These projects are not replicable without excessive external subsidies, nor are they easily maintained on a recurrent basis by Kenyan institutions. These programs tax TARDA's managerial and financial capabilities when donor support is withdrawn, and help to maintain Kenyan dependence on foreign aid. In the Tana basin, even "small-scale" irrigation schemes have been fashioned according to donor preferences, and are inconsistent with local economic and institutional realities (cf. Kimani 1988).

## TARDA's Relationships with Other Institutions (Including Donors) in the Tana Basin

TARDA is a state parastatal, with regional responsibilities, that has its headquarters in Nairobi. By its very structure then, TARDA is likely to coordinate its activities more closely with national institutions, than with regional and local institutions. This, indeed, has been the case. Moreover, because there is no basin-wide master plan nor have basin-wide land and water use surveys been conducted, it is unlikely that the authority has a good understanding of the full range of institutions and land and water use systems in the basin. This latter factor may account, in part, for what seems to be an insensitivity on the part of TARDA to local institutions and local production systems.

This section shows that most inter-institutional collaboration has been at the national level, and that TARDA has not worked effectively with local institutions. The lack of recognition of local institutions has meant that most smallholders in the lower and middle basin have been marginalized by the development activities of TARDA.

### Power and Light Company

Given its emphasis on hydropower, it is not surprising that TARDA maintains its closest institutional linkages with this organization. The chairman of the Kenya Power and Light Company (KPLC) sits on the TARDA board, and TARDA works very closely with KPLC in the design and construction of hydropower schemes. TARDA coordinated much of the design and feasibility work for two of the three KPLC dams on the Tana. This accounted for the bulk of TARDA's work in its early years. It also constructed the Masinga dam, while the KPLC operates it; and TARDA is currently building the Kiambere Dam, which will also be operated by KPLC. The Masinga dam "protects"and regulates water for the three downstream dams built by KPLC—the Kamburu, Gitaru, and Kindaruma dams. TARDA and KPLC jointly have worked out a power price schedule on the Masinga dam to reflect KPLC's operating responsibilities. The sale of electricity generated at Masinga to KPLC is TARDA's major source of revenue at present. Unlike TARDA's relations with other institutions working in the Tana basin, the relationship with the KPLC is reinforced by mutually beneficial financial ties.

## Ministry of Agriculture (MOA)

Within the Ministry of Agriculture TARDA has worked closest with the Irrigation and Drainage Branch (IDB) (formerly the Small-Scale Irrigation Unit), assisting with planning, project identification, and feasibility studies. In working with IDB, TARDA has come closest to fulfilling its official mandate to advise institutions on water use activities in the basin and to assist them with planning and feasibility studies. TARDA carried out the initial feasibility studies for the Kibirigwe small-scale irrigation scheme, and then turned over implementation and management responsibilities of this project to the IDB. TARDA also was involved with the feasibility studies of the Lower Tana Village Irrigation Programme, which is another IDB scheme, but in this case the involvement was less extensive than at Kibirigwe.

Though TARDA seems to liaison well with IDB, the activities of the two institutions are not always complementary. For example, in the lower Tana TARDA's large-scale irrigation project (Delta Irrigation Scheme) is likely to make obsolete the IDB's Village Irrigation Programme (VIP). The TARDA project will compete for scarce labor with the village schemes, and will force the displacement of herders and farmers in the delta, who may resettle in the villages and compete for scarce water and irrigable land there. IDB is aware of the proposed TARDA scheme, but it has been unable to have an impact on TARDA's plans, except to ensure that the scheme's gravity-fed canal provides water to the VIP (for a description of the VIP, see Little 1988; Kimani 1988).

## District Development Committees (DDCs)

TARDA's record of dealing with the District Development Committees has been mixed. On the positive side, TARDA has completed (or is in the process of completing) several district-based resource inventories, which the DDC's can utilize for planning purposes. As of November 1986, TARDA had finished approximately five of these district profiles, and was working on additional ones. The staff at TARDA eventually hopes to have full coverage of all Districts in the Tana and Athi basins. The district reports provide good data on natural resource availability, land use potential, and climatic patterns.

On the negative side, TARDA has not always been sensitive to existing programs of the DDCs. The scale of funding for TARDA's programs are so much greater than those of the DDCs, the authority is unlikely to seek cooperation with DDCs unless it is absolutely necessary. In the case of the proposed Delta Irrigation Scheme, the DDC of the Tana River District did not participate at all in the planning of the scheme, even though the implementation of the project will greatly alter the district's economy and ecology. Communication between TARDA and the Tana River District DDC was so poor that the Member of Parliament (MP) of Tana River District had to approach TARDA directly (in Nairobi) to inquire about the project. In other cases, TARDA appears unaware of district-level projects and of the development priorities of the DDCs in the basin.

The lack of solid "linking" institutions[3] impedes TARDA's ties with local organizations and activities. Among institutions, the District Development Committees (DDCs) probably could best serve a "linking" function, but they are mainly represented by national ministries. The DDCs also suffer in other ways that inhibit their effectiveness. These include the fact that they are (1) new and fragile institutions that are very weak in the more remote districts of the basin (e.g., Tana River and Garissa Districts); (2) not well funded in many districts; (3) overloaded with other demands that would impair their ability to represent local interests vis-a-vis TARDA; and (4) they are so large and represent so many diverse interests that consensus is almost impossible.

## National Irrigation Board (NIB)

A member of the NIB sits on the TARDA interministerial committee. The activities of the two parastatals, however, have been managed almost totally independent of the other, although they are two of the largest institutional users of the basin. TARDA approached the NIB irrigation scheme at Bura very cautiously, and provided very little assistance in its planning. Similarly, TARDA has not sought NIB advice in the planning of the Delta irrigation scheme, nor is it likely to in the future.

Part of the lack of collaboration between TARDA and NIB may relate to the fact that two of NIB's major schemes on the Tana—Mwea and Hola—were begun almost 20 years prior to TARDA's establishment. Another reason may be TARDA's own desire to be involved in the implementation of large-scale irrigation projects, which until recently have been carried out by the NIB. The NIB has been under considerable pressure within the government to reform its irrigation program, and thus it is unlikely to be able to expand its program without considerable opposition. Disfavor with NIB is related to the parastatal's disastrous results at Bura in the middle Tana (Kimani 1988).

## Small-Scale Producer Organizations

TARDA has virtually no official contact with institutions at the local level, including cooperatives and water user associations (i.e., small-scale irrigation committees). Nor does TARDA collaborate with the national ministries, such as the Ministry of Cooperatives or Ministry of Culture and Social Affairs, representing these organizations. Among the different local institutions in the Tana basin, perhaps the weakest are those representing the interests of livestock producers—the company, cooperative and group ranches. Despite the importance of the livestock sector to the economy of the Tana basin, the interests of herders are often neglected in favor of large-scale irrigation and other interests, which are represented by stronger institutions. In the Tana basin there are six company (three) and group ranches (three) and one cooperative ranch, which are all located in Tana River District. Only the company and cooperative ranches are presently functioning, and even these are experiencing considerable economic and administrative difficulties.

Not surprisingly, the interests of herders have not been incorporated into TARDA's or other large organization's plans for the lower Tana. Herders have voiced their disapproval of TARDA's plans for the lower basin to the Tana River District DDC, but they are unlikely to succeed in altering TARDA's plans. As I noted earlier, TARDA does not view cooperation with DDCs as an important part of its development mandate.

Local water user associations in the lower Tana are more viable organizations than herder associations, but they also have received little recognition from planning agencies in the basin. The water user associations are involved with small-scale irrigation schemes, some of whom have received support from donors and non-government organizations (NGO). The associations are governed by a committee of elected officers (usually six members) that ensures:

- farmers do their own leveling of plots;
- farmers provide labor to help with the construction and maintenance of main and secondary canals;
- farmers contribute funds toward the purchase of fuel and spare parts; and
- water and land use conflicts are resolved in a fair manner.

In the lower Tana most of the small-scale irrigators are Pokomo, with the largest scheme being at Ngao (65 hectares) and the smallest one at Oda (20 hectares). Most farmers have irrigated plots of between 0.4 to 0.6 hectares. Rice is the most important crop on the irrigated perimeters, with more than 25 different varieties being grown (Budelman 1983:10). For most Pokomo farmers, irrigated production is only one component of a diversified production system that also includes flood recession cultivation, rainfed agriculture, and, in some cases, fishing. With the exception of rainfed farming, all other production activities are dependent on the river. In comparison to other locations, the areas at the lower end of the basin (the delta area) are most dependent on the river for flood recession cultivation. Here the villages attain food self-sufficiency in most years. Not only have they received little food relief assistance in recent years, including the drought of 1984, but also the out-migration of males, typical of many areas of the Tana basin, is relatively low. This may be evidence of a relatively stable domestic economy, but one that is very dependent on the river.

The agricultural activities of the lower Tana have already been affected by the reduction in flood levels at Garsen and Garissa, which has resulted from the construction of the Masinga and other dams in the upper basin. These investments were undertaken by TARDA in the 1970s and 1980s, with strong support from donors especially the World Bank. To our knowledge, the local communities were never advised about the effects that river regulation in the upper and middle Tana would have on their projects. Moreover, TARDA, with its predilection for capital-intensive projects, has begun to implement a large-scale irrigation project (of approximately 20,000 hectares) in the Tana delta that will replace much of the recession cultivation and small-scale irrigation in the area.

## Impacts on Local Production Systems

There are two types of activities of TARDA (and other large agencies operating in the Tana)—dam construction and large-scale irrigation—that have already drastically affected local production systems in the middle and lower Tana. High-frequency floods in the lower and middle Tana have been greatly reduced by the construction of a series of five hydropower dams, beginning in the 1960s. The last dam, the Kiambere, was completed in the late 1980s and required the relocation of more than 10,000 smallholders from the reservoir catchment. The smallholders that had to be removed from the Kiambere catchment were poorly informed about the relocation process by the government. TARDA placed an announcement in one of Kenya's English-speaking newspaper, *The Daily Nation*, indicating that the Kiambere reservoir was to begin being filled on 10 July 1987. The same advertisement also warned people living downstream of the dam that river fluctuations may be experienced during the filling exercise, which should take about six months. Based on discussions with local ecologists working in Kenya, the Kiambere dam is likely to further reduce high-frequency floods in the lower and middle Tana, making flood recession cultivation even more difficult if not impossible in certain locations.

Baseline information for the 1960s, the period prior to the construction of the first dam in the upper Tana, on flood recession and small-scale irrigated agriculture in the lower Tana is very sketchy. Interviews with farmers in the area indicate that it was not until the 1970s that the regulation of river flow began to really impact on local agriculture. Other evidence supports the position that small-scale irrigation and recession cultivation have become less reliable in recent years, although it is difficult to place the changes in a precise time frame. Alia et al. (1982), for example, show how communities have become increasingly dependent on pump-based irrigation, as a result of the decline in high-frequency floods (1982:27). The recent heavy involvement in wage labor migration by residents of the area may also be indicative of a declining agricultural system. In the early 1980s, it was found that almost half of the irrigated farmers in the lower Tana were absent because of commitments to wage employment outside the region (Alia et al. 1982:21). As indicated above, the communities of the lower delta area, where the practice of flood irrigation is still widespread, experience relatively low levels of outmigration by males.

Further investments in hydropower, without measures to ensure that flooding downstream is not eliminated, and large-scale irrigation, will increasingly marginalize small-scale farmers of the lower and middle Tana. The current Delta Irrigation Scheme, which has received financing from aid sources in Japan, is likely to eliminate those flood irrigation systems that have been maintained for centuries.

The elimination of high-frequency floods and the conversion of large segments of riverine land to capital-intensive irrigation has probably had (and will have in the future) a greater impact on local herders, than on small-scale farmers. Herders are especially vulnerable because the government, including TARDA, has the legal right to convert most of the region's rangelands to non-pastoral uses of land. In other areas of Kenya, such as the Maasai districts, herder associations ("group ranches") have been able to exert influence on development activities because they have some control over land-allocation decisions. By contrast, in the middle and lower parts of Tana River District, most of the land is state land, rather than trust (owned by the group) or private land, which means that the central government has total authority to allocate land as it deems appropriate, without compensation to herders. Legally herders in most parts of Tana River District are "squatters", and can be removed from the land without any legal recourse.

Large-scale irrigation investments, supported both by TARDA and NIB, have been made in pastoral areas without informing or compensating local herders. In discussing the serious environmental problems associated with the Bura Irrigation Scheme, Ledec notes that "the Orma were hardly even consulted about the Bura project, which took a portion [about 3,900 hectares] of their traditional grazing lands"(1984). As noted earlier, the effects of the current Delta Irrigation Scheme, implemented by TARDA, is likely to have an even more negative impact on local herders. The benefit/cost analysis for the Delta project, however, underscores this point by basing its calculations on an unrealistically low number of cattle (12,500),[4] in order to support the claim that irrigation is preferable economically to livestock production (Haskoning 1982:7).

If implemented as planned, the Delta project will jeopardize the entire livestock sector of the lower Tana and large parts of the middle Tana, by removing large segments of existing pasture as well as forcing herds to congregate and overuse the remaining rangelands. The delta is used by up to 10,000 herders during the critical dry-season period, and by a lesser number throughout the year. The pastoral system is also closely articulated with the local farming systems of the region, with mutual exchanges of products and flexible land tenure systems allowing both groups of producers to benefit. A realistic benefit/cost analysis, based on district, regional, and national accounting, would probably demonstrate that the strengthening of existing livestock and farming systems of the area would yield more favorable returns, than expensive, large-scale irrigated production in the delta (Little and Scudder 1986:16). The disastrous economic, social, and ecological experiences upriver at Bura reinforce this point.

## Summary

TARDA has not facilitated nor strengthened relationships among institutions in the Tana basin. While it is a regional development authority, it has done very little to promote the integrated development of the Tana basin. It has worked well with certain institutions, such as the Kenya Power and Electricity Company, but in most cases it has not collaborated with other organizations; nor has it served as an "umbrella" organization under which other groups could interact and coordinate activities.

TARDA has planned and implemented national development projects, where favorable benefit/cost ratios at the national level are more important than positive returns at regional or local levels. Its projects are also very expensive, which makes coordination with local institutions even more difficult. TARDA has shown some willingness to work with District Development Committees, but not in terms of soliciting their input in basin planning exercises. Other than the District Development Committees, there are really no other local institutions that could serve as effective "linking" institutions between local communities and TARDA. Under its present structure and portfolio of activities, TARDA is unlikely to increase its collaboration with local institutions in the basin and will likely continue to plan activities that jeopardize local production systems. Given its increased emphasis on the implementation of large-scale projects, TARDA increasingly is likely to enter into situations of potential conflict with local institutions and producers, and continue to fail to capitalize on the development potential (at considerably less financial cost) of these groups.

## Acknowledgments

This chapter is based upon research supported by the "Comparative Analysis of Institutional Experiences with River Basin Development in Africa" Project, sponsored by the Clark University/Institute for Development Anthropology Cooperative Agreement on Settlement and Natural Resource Systems Analysis. The latter is supported by a grant from the Office of Rural and Institutional Development, Science and Technology Bureau, USAID. I wish to acknowledge the assistance of Thayer Scudder, who served as director of the river basin development project and collaborated with me on the Tana field research. Appreciation is also extended to Gerald Karaska, Harry Schwarz, and Richard Perritt of Clark University, who provided editorial comments on an earlier version of this paper. In Kenya, generous advice, assistance from John Kimani and Shem Migot-Adolla, who accompanied the author during part of the field research, greatly facilitated fieldwork (see the former's own work on the Tana irrigation funded under the project, Kimani 1988). The views expressed in this chapter, are of course, strictly those of the author and should not be attributed to any of the above individuals or institutions.

## Notes

1. The advent of independence in 1963, of course had a significant effect on institutions in the Tana basin. This historical event is discussed earlier in the text in relation to upper Tana institutions, but because its occurrence was not specific to the Tana it is not dealt with in this section.

2. The original institution addressed development in the Tana basin only. In 1981 the TRDA was also given responsibility for the development of the Athi basin, and thus its title was changed to the Tana and Athi Development Authority (TARDA), to reflects its geographical coverage.

3. This term comes from a presentation by Eileen Berry at the Institute for Development Anthropology/Clark University river basin seminar in February 1987, Worcester, Massachusetts. It refers to an institution that facilitates linkages between a national agency (e.g. TARDA) and local organizations.

4. I would estimate that this is less than 25 percent of the cattle that graze in the designated project zone (based on interviews with government officials and livestock traders in the region, and available reports [Kenya 1979]).

## References Cited

Alia, P., S. E. Migot-Adholla, and G. Ruigu.
  1982   Evaluation of Small-Scale Irrigation Projects in Tana South, Coast Province. IDS Consultancy Report No. 10. University of Nairobi, Kenya.

Brokensha, David W.
  1962   Volta Resettlement, Ethnographic Notes of Southern Areas. Accra, Ghana: University of Ghana.

  1976   The Volta River Project. *In* Proceedings of the West Africa Conference. P. Paylore and R. Haney, eds. Pp. 119–123. Tucson, Arizona: University of Arizona Press.

Brokensha, David W. and John Nellis.
  1974   Administration in Kenya—A Study of the Rural Division of Mbeere. Part I. Journal of Administration Overseas. 13:510–513.

Budelman, A.
  1983   Primary Agricultural Research, Farmers Perform Field Trials—Experiences from the Lower Tana Basin, East Kenya. Unpublished report. Wageningen, Netherlands.

Ensminger, Jean.
  1984   Political Economy among the Pastoral Galole Orma: The Effects of Market Integration. unpublished PhD. dissertation. Department of Anthropology. Northwestern University, Evanston, Illinois.

Haskoning Consultants.
1982    Tana Delta Irrigation Project Feasibility Study. Volumes I–IX. Nairobi:
        TARDA.
Jaetzold, R. and H. Schmidt.
1983    Farm Management of Kenya. Vol. II/B. Central Kenya. Nairobi: Ministry
        of Agriculture.
Kenya, Republic of.
1977(revised 1982)   The Tana and Athi Rivers Development Authority Act. Chapter
        433. Nairobi: Government Printer.
1979    Kenya Livestock Density Map. Nairobi: Kenya Rangelands Ecological Mon-
        itoring Unit, Ministry of Tourism and Wildlife.
Kimani, John.
1988    River Basin Development: Case Studies Within Tana River Basin of Kenya.
        Binghamton, NY: Clark U/IDA Cooperative Agreement on Settlement and
        Resource Systems Analysis.
Ledec, George.
1984    Bura Irrigation Settlement Project. Mid-term Evaluation—Wildlife and
        Ecology Aspects. Washington, D.C.: The World Bank.
Leys, Colin.
1974    Underdevelopment in Kenya: The Political Economy of Neo-Colonialism.
        Berkeley: University of California Press.
Little, Peter D.
1988    Comparative Analysis of Institutional Experiences with River Basin De-
        velopment in Africa: The Case of the Tana Basin, Kenya. Binghamton, NY:
        Institute for Development Anthropology.
Little, Peter D. and Thayer Scudder.
1986    The Tana River Experience: Draft Interim Report. Binghamton, NY: Institute
        for Development Anthropology.
Merryman, J.
1984    Ecological Stress and Adaptive Response: The Kenya Somali in the Twentieth
        Century. unpublished Ph.D. dissertation. Department of Anthropology.
        Northwestern University. Evanston, Illinois.
Ominde, S.
1971    The Semi-Arid and Arid Lands of Kenya. *In* Studies in East African
        Geography and Development. S. Ominde, ed. Pp.146–161. Berkeley: Uni-
        versity of California Press.
Saha, S.
1982    Irrigation Planning in the Tana Basin of Kenya. Water Supply and Man-
        agement 6(3):261–279.
Swainson, N.
1980    The Development of Corporate Capitalism in Kenya 1918–1977. Berkeley:
        University of California Press.
TARDA (Tana and Athi Rivers Development Authority).
1982    Forward Planning Tana Basin (1982–1992). Nairobi: TARDA.
1986    Forward Planning (1986–1996). Nairobi: TARDA.
Thomas, Barbara P. and David W. Brokensha.
1985    The Institutional Aspects of African River Basin Development. *In* Problems
        and Issues in African River Basin Planning. Pp. 214–246. Worcester, MA:
        Clark University/Institute for Development Anthropology Cooperative
        Agreement on Settlement and Resource Systems Analysis.

# 15

## Development and Conservation of Natural Resources in Latin America

*Michael Painter*

This essay builds upon themes that have been hallmarks of David Bro-kensha's research: the study of social inequality and its decisive importance in shaping how people utilize natural resources in production. Brokensha's concern with issues of inequality, social justice, and the environment have figured prominently in his role as a founder and director of the Institute for Development Anthropology, and he has, of course, been decisive in contributing to IDA's success as a pioneer in increasing anthropological participation in development planning, implementation, and evaluation. More importantly, however, he has helped insure that the Institute is a place that promotes critical analysis of the experience gained through such applied work to contribute to a more profound understanding of the processes of development and underdevelopment generally. He has encouraged all of us to find ways of making the results of this analysis available in meaningful ways to local populations, in order that they might cease being dubious beneficiaries of policies, programs, and projects conceived and implemented by agencies whose interests and objectives are alien to their own, and begin to define in their own right how their human and natural resources are to be used. The following pages are respectfully dedicated to recalling these features of David Brokensha's life and work.

Recent research on natural resource management in Latin America makes clear the following points. First, environmental destruction associated with smallholding farmers is a consequence of their impoverishment relative to other social classes. Second, while development efforts have looked primarily at the natural resource management problems associated with smallholders, huge areas are degraded by wealthy corporate and individual interests. Generally, large-scale enterprises which are destructive have been granted land on concessionary terms by the state exercising sovereignty over the area in which they operate. This allows them to treat land as a low-cost input, and makes it more economical to extract the resource they want and move elsewhere rather than to husband the resource. Third, the same policies and practices which result in wealthy interests receiving land on concessionary terms are responsible for the impoverishment of smallholders, because they institutionalize and exacerbate unequal access to resources. Thus, the crucial issue underlying environmental destruction in Latin America is gross inequity in access to resources. To the degree that conservationists and developers fail to consider and address this issue, their activities will be at best palliatives that do not get at the crux of issues of environmental destruction or sustainable development, and at worst they may have long-term impacts of intensifying degradation and impoverishment.

Drawing upon cases from the lowland areas of Latin America, this paper will illustrate the social and economic processes that underlie environmental destruction and underdevelopment. On the basis of the evidence presented, it will argue that addressing these issues means dealing explicitly with the fact that both occur in complex societies joined to one another by global economy and ecology and characterized by social classes with fundamentally divergent interests. A given development or conservation activity will inevitably have different kinds of impacts on different sectors of a population. Which members of a population have their access to productive resources enhanced and which have it restricted by an activity is of profound importance in determining both development and conservation impacts. The crucial issues facing efforts to promote conservation and development are, on the one hand, which members of a local population are to be involved and under what sort of institutional arrangement, and, on the other, how to link local-level efforts in order to address national and international resource distribution issues that contribute to environmental destruction and underdevelopment.

## Themes in Studies of Resource Management

Over the past decade students of the development of tropical forests in Latin America have created a growing body of new information on processes of social, economic, and environmental change which challenges much of our previous understanding regarding the development of the region. Authors such as Dourojeanni (1984) and Moran (1987) have refined our appreciation of how local-level variation in soil types, topography, and rainfall define possibilities for developing different areas of the Amazon. Fearnside (1979; 1983), Goodland (1980; 1985), Uhl (1982) and others have examined many of the productive activities most commonly carried out as part of Amazonian development efforts and assessed the environmental consequences associated with them. Scudder (1981; 1984) and the World Bank (1985) have pointed out that populating the tropical forests and bringing them under agricultural production is not the same as developing them. For settlement to be part of a successful development strategy, issues such as market linkages, off-farm employment opportunities, and cash income, and the linkages between these variables and sustainable on-farm production must be addressed. This work also indicates that a combination of long-term involvement by sponsoring agencies and the empowerment of settlers to manage local affairs are critical ingredients of settlement success.

Previous studies have sought to consolidate our understanding of the lessons offered by attempts to develop the tropical forests of Latin America (Dozier 1969; Nelson 1973). In the process, they have provided valuable insights regarding the nature and scope of resource use in these areas. However, these studies treated economic growth and the establishment of sustainable production as separate issues rather than as aspects of the same overall development problem. This distinction remains an important one for national governments concerned about developing the resources of the Amazon, and interests concerned with conservation of the tropical forest environment. These two factions frequently adopt adversarial stances, and do not seriously discuss the importance of managing tropical forest resources in order to sustain economic growth over the long term.

## Agents of Environmental Destruction

A major weakness of research and planning related to natural resource management in Latin America has been a narrow sense of agency, which has led observers to extrapolate inappropriately from local-level situations. This is particularly apparent in discussions of environmental destruction by smallholders. The bulk of the social science literature on environmental destruction in Latin America focuses on the destructive practices associated with smallholder agriculture. Little attention has been given to the destruction associated with large-scale enterprises, or to the linkages of smallholder production with larger processes of social and economic change affecting the areas in which it occurs. This has resulted in analyses which legitimize efforts to blame the rural poor for environmental destruction and which justify policies and programs prejudicial to smallholders (Wood and Schmink 1979). In the long run, such efforts exacerbate the pressures underlying environmental destruction by failing to address the problems that promote destructive production behavior by smallholders and by ignoring the destruction associated with large and wealthy enterprises.

Environmental destruction by smallholders and large enterprises is linked by the issue of resource distribution. Smallholders and large enterprises co-exist within the same regions, so that the opportunities and constraints affecting one group have implications for the other. To the degree that smallholders must seek off-farm employment, they become a source of cheap wage labor for large enterprises, for example. Also, the policies which grant access to resources to large-scale enterprises on concessionary terms also deny or restrict access of smallholders to the same resources, increasing their relative disadvantage and the pressures on them to use destructive production techniques. Frequently, environmental destruction by smallholders is a direct consequence of being relegated to marginal areas while the best agricultural lands have been occupied by large enterprises (e.g. Painter 1987), or of being obliged to labor in a context in which they are subjected to pressures to forfeit or sell their holdings to others once production has been established (e.g. Foweraker 1981).

## Smallholders

Recent discussions of Amazonian development have cited smallholding settlers as the major agents of violence against Native American communities in the region (e.g. Vickers 1982; Whitten 1978), and of the environmental destruction associated with the introduction of unsustainable agricultural practices such as predatory burning and inadequate fallow cycles (e.g. Guppy 1984). At the same time, the bulk of research on smallholding farmers has emphasized that, while there is frequently considerable variation in individual knowledge and skill, they are rational users of productive resources and capable of quickly and drastically altering their behavior in order to respond to changing circumstances (e.g. Barlett 1980; Moran 1974). In this context, it is reasonable to ask why rational resource users would destroy the environment upon which they directly depend, and to look at the forces that shape the productive options that are available to small farmers. Four case studies, based upon research conducted in different areas of the Amazon illustrate the social and economic processes leading to destructive practices by smallholders.

Collins (1986) reviewed three cases in the Amazon basin in which smallholder production has been associated with environmental destruction, one along the Brazilian Transamazon highway, one in northeastern Ecuador, and the third in southern Peru. In each case, processes of impoverishment arising from the unfavorable position of the small farmer in relation to the regional and national society led to destructive patterns of resource use. In Brazil, this resulted from a combination of state incentives to encourage monocrop rice production to the exclusion of other activities, which were both technically inappropriate and poorly administered. This led to initially high levels of indebtedness and low rice yields, to which farmers responded by attempting to increase aggregate production by shortening fallow cycles, and by emphasizing cash crops. This strategy led to increased resource deterioration and indebtedness, and established a feedback relationship between indebtedness and declining land productivity. Eventually, those unable to pay their debts were bought out by wealthier interests who consolidated the smallholdings into larger units, and the smallholder population either went to work on these as laborers or moved deeper into the forest to try again.

In northeastern Ecuador, settlers were placed in debt from their arrival in the region by the cost of purchasing land and having it surveyed. They then could not obtain a clear title until they had repaid this debt, and in the absence of a clear title they could not receive credit. This created a pressure to maximize short-term profits through rapid conversion of forest to pasture, with no provision for the maintenance of soil fertility. Again, the result was the establishment of mutually reinforcing cycles of impoverishment and environmental destruction. Many farmers were forced to sell their land to wealthier individuals before they obtained a clear title, for which they received a very low price, and to move to a new area of the forest.

In southern Peru, a monopsonistic commercialization system, poor access to credit and agricultural inputs, and difficulties in obtaining land titles led to the establishment of a coffee production regimen characterized by low yields and poor quality. Smallholding settlers were unable to earn enough from coffee production to sever their ties with the farms in the highlands from which they had come. As a result a pattern of seasonal migration emerged in which family members move back and forth between the highlands and the tropical valley in an effort to attend to agricultural activities in each area. Family labor resources are insufficient for them to attend to anything beyond what is immediately necessary to realize a crop in either area. As a result, activities to manage soil and water and maintain the long-term productivity of both areas are neglected, and productivity has tended to decline. In the lowlands, the declining productivity has created a cycle where farmers exhaust the land in one, and then move deeper into the forest to begin anew.

The processes that lead to smallholder impoverishment do not occur in isolation, but are a product of resource competition with other interests. In eastern Bolivia, for example, smallholders are locked into an intense struggle for development resources in the form of access to markets, agricultural credit, transport facilities, and other services with large-scale commercial agricultural enterprises, lumber companies, and other interests. This competition appears as an inter-ethnic conflict between people who are native to the area, and migrants from Bolivia's highland and Andean valley regions. Efforts by smallholders to secure greater access to development resources are greeted with hostility and repressed by violence (Gill 1987; Painter 1988).

Because of their lack of access to development resources such as improved inputs, labor-saving technology, and transport and market facilities enjoyed by large commercial farms, the lumber industry, and other interests, smallholder farmers are unable to accumulate capital at the same time that other interests in the regional economy are accumulating capital rapidly. This situation initially manifests itself as one of relative impoverishment. On the one hand the price farmers receive for agricultural production has tended to decline steadily in relation to what they have had to pay for labor power. At the same time, prices for agricultural production have increased in relation to the costs of operating a tractor. The result is that large farmers, who are better able to mechanize production in the first place, and who enjoy much greater access to development resources made available by the state and by international donor agencies, have done much better than smallholders who are constrained by their own family labor resources and their inability to hire sufficient additional labor.

The smallholder is obliged to respond either by attempting to increase the aggregate production placed on the market, or to turn away from agriculture as a means of earning a living in favor of earning income off the farm. Both approaches have led to environmentally destructive production. Attempting to increase the aggregate production offered for sale is the approach that has been adopted by many settlers in the example from eastern Bolivia. Because their ability to increase production is constrained by their access to the resources to improve the productivity of their labor, smallholders achieve increased production by turning to more extensive production regimens, clearing large areas of forest and taking advantage of the flush of productivity that accompanies the initial removal of the forest cover. The impacts on the forest can be dramatic. Families practicing a production regimen that is similar to that recommended by the state agencies and non-governmental organizations working in the area to assist smallholders are able to clear a mean area of approximately 3.5 hectares of land each year. In the cases of comparably sized families who have adopted a more extensive strategy, the area of land cleared each year ranged from 9 to 35 hectares annually (Painter 1987:184; Painter et al. 1984).

## Large Enterprises

Vast environmental destruction has also been associated with the activities of large-scale corporate and individually owned enterprises, the most widely studied of which are cattle ranches. However, large-scale enterprises associated with environmental destruction, particularly in tropical forest areas, also include mining, industrial logging, and plantation forestry (e.g. Goodland 1980; 1985). In general, large-scale enterprises have become destructive when they have operated under conditions in which it has been more profitable to exploit the land until its productivity begins to decline and then move on than to husband natural resources in order to produce in the same area in a sustainable way.

Frequently, state policies equating economic growth with development, have created or encouraged such a situation. In Brazil during the mid-1960s, for example, the state sought to promote beef cattle production in the Amazon as part of a policy to promote the availability of cheap food for urban working classes and in response to a rapidly expanding international beef market. The state permitted a corporation to invest a substantial portion of its tax liability in Amazonian development projects. Enterprises established prior to 1966 were exempted from 50 percent of the taxes owed for 12 years, while enterprises established between 1966 and 1972 could receive exemptions of up to 100 percent. Qualifying firms could import equipment duty free, and were exempted from export duties for regional products such as timber. State governments provided their own inducements on top of those of the national government, usually in the form of land concessions, and livestock loans from international institutions such as the World Bank and the Inter-American Development Bank provided funds for special loans that could be mobilized for the Amazon. Under these incentives, the simple acquisition of land could be treated as a development cost and substantially written off, making it more profitable to continually acquire and exploit new land than sustainably to develop what one already had (Hecht 1985:670).

In a review of Brazil's Amazon development policy, Hall (1987) points out that, between 1975 and 1979, under the Second National Development Plan, 1.7 million hectares of land was sold in plots of 500–3000 hectares each to corporations and private businessmen. This was more than twice the amount of land that had been distributed to smallholding settlers prior to that time (1987:525–527). Also under the Second National Development Plan, the state approved 358 livestock projects involving £444 million in tax rebates in the Amazon region. Eleven percent (£47 million) went to the four largest ranches, which were owned by the Ometto group of Sao Paulo, the Centenco construction company, the Brazilian National Credit Bank, and Volkswagen, and over half of this amount went to the 560,000-hectare project of the Ometto group (pp.530–531).

Central America differs from South America in that states in the region have not explicitly linked expanding tropical forest production to the achievement of national development goals, and large amounts of state funds have not been used to promote tropical forest exploitation schemes (Collins and Painter 1986:5–6). However, Central American states have played a decisive role in promoting deforestation throughout the region. The promotion of expanded beef cattle production in response to a growing export market for beef in the U.S. and Western Europe through the concentration of resources for bank credits, technical assistance, and infrastructural development in support of this industry, and to the detriment of other types of agricultural activities, is an important and well-known area in which state policy has been detrimental to the sustained management of tropical forest resources (see, for example, JRB Associates 1982:66; Myers 1981; Nations and Komer 1983).

### Indirect Impacts

The construction of roads, oil pipelines, and hydropower facilities have also been responsible for widespread environmental destruction (e.g. Goodland 1980; 1985; ISTI 1980:27,34; Rudel 1983). Although they generate electricity to support productive activities in areas far removed from the sites where they are constructed, hydropower plants have had dramatic environmental impacts upon the areas where they are constructed. Brazil's hydropower projects in its Amazon Basin have disastrous consequences for Native American and Brazilian peasant populations, who have been forced to relocate because of inundation. The negative environmental impacts of these population movements have frequently been exacerbated by the refusal of the responsible national authorities and international donor agencies to make adequate provision for their relocation. In addition, hydropower facilities themselves have had vast, but, as yet, largely unmeasured environmental impacts. In addition to the economic loss associated with the failure to exploit the valuable timber resources that are flooded, the large amount of biological material contained in the reservoirs poses the possibility that these will become eutrophic, or even toxic to use (see Goodland 1980:20; 1985:7–9).

Conventional wisdom has held that road construction is an important step toward improving economic opportunities for smallholders in tropical forest areas (e.g. Nelson 1973; OAS 1984). Indeed, Wennergren and Whitaker (1976) have argued that opening roads and encouraging spontaneous settlement along them is the most cost-effective way for nations to develop their tropical forests. However, while such an approach has led to immediate, short-term economic growth, it is clear that road construction has been a major contributor to widespread deforestation, and that continued unchecked road building is a major obstacle to achieving sustainable tropical forest development.

Fearnside (1985), for example, has argued that a positive feedback relationship between road building and migration by settlers is one of the major forces currently driving deforestation in Brazil. Building new roads encourages more settlers to enter a region, while the resulting population growth justifies the construction of still more roads. Joly (1982:77) observed a similar dynamic in Panama. She noted that, while road construction is frequently justified in improving market access, a concomitant process is to facilitate entrance by large numbers of new settlers. ISTI (1980:27) concluded that the construction of the Pan-American Highway constitutes the single biggest threat to the tropical forests of Panama's Darién province. Drawing upon research conducted in eastern Ecuador, Rudel (1983) concluded that if establishing sustainable production systems through settlement is a development goal, road construction should follow settlement rather than precede it as an incentive for people to move into an area. While building roads into a new area does encourage settlement and rapid economic growth, Rudel found that it also encourages land speculation, poor matching of agricultural activity to soil conditions, and the establishment of unstable, predatory production systems. Stearman's (1985) observations in the Yapacaní settlement area of eastern Bolivia are similar. She found that the Yapacaní area grew dramatically after a road and bridge connecting it to regional urban centers were completed. However, this economic growth came at the cost of widespread land speculation, which led poorer peasants to sell their land and use the money to establish themselves elsewhere, usually in a new area of tropical forest. In recognition of the impact that roads have in accelerating the settlement and clearing of tropical forests, Glick and Betancourt (1983) recommended that road building be planned so as to direct settlement *away* from the Rio Plátano Biosphere Reserve in Honduras.

*Role of State Policy*

An additional difficulty has been that state policies have tended to define development in terms of narrow production goals or support to very specific economic interests (e.g. Goodland 1985:5; Ledec and Goodland 1989; Leonard 1987). Sustainability of production is frequently not a criterion in planning the allocation of state resources or in the formulation of policy, and environmental destruction is regarded as the inevitable price of economic growth. In this context, it is not necessary to build a variant of a "conspiracy theory" in which states are purposefully supporting economic oppression of the poor or facilitating the destruction of the environment upon which the common wellbeing depends in order to further the interests of narrowly defined economic groups in order to perceive that this is, in fact, the net result.

A hallmark of Brazil's policy toward Amazonian development has been that it has attempted to use the region for fundamentally contradictory purposes (Bakx 1987; Hall 1987). On the one hand, it has attempted to promote large-scale commercial agriculture through the sorts of incentives described above, largely in response to the need to generate export earnings and taking advantage of the expanding international beef market. In this case, the region is being mined as a resource in an effort to solve economic problems that are external to it. At the same time, and in the same areas, Brazil has attempted to use its Amazon territory as a "safety valve" to relieve social pressures in areas of the country experiencing land pressure, without addressing the underlying land distribution problems. Considerable frontier expansion has been driven by state subsidies for large-scale, export-oriented production of soybeans, sugar cane, and cattle in the Northeast and Center-South regions of the country. This has promoted a pattern of accumulation that has displaced many small farmers and compelled them to seek new lands in the Amazon. Through aggressive road construction, the state has sought to encourage this flow as a means of populating and asserting national sovereignty over the Amazon, and of avoiding addressing gross inequities in resource distribution in the migrants' home areas. At the same time that it encouraged settlement through road construction, however, Brazil declined to provide a means for settlers to secure title to their new landholding or to provide incentives for them to maintain and improve the productive potential of the land they have occupied. Investment focused on cattle ranching, the extraction of tropical forest products, and coffee, cocoa, and rubber production, all to supply export markets. The result has been that the inequities in resource distribution in other parts of the country that drove migration into the Amazon in the first place have been reproduced in this region as well.

In Peru, settlement of the tropical forests of the "high jungle"—on the eastern Andean slopes—has been used by the state as a means of attempting to relieve social and economic pressures in the nation's highland agricultural regions (Aramburú 1982). The first and second Belaúnde administrations (1963–1968 and 1980–1985) were particularly insistent upon expanding tropical forest production in lieu of addressing resource distribution issues elsewhere in the country, and as a means of promoting economic growth. The haste to make the tropical forest lowlands more accessible to settlers, cattle ranchers, timber companies, and other interests led to the construction of very expensive and poorly planned infrastructure which is not likely to survive for long on the steep slopes of the region without substantial continuing investment. In addition, large areas of land were earmarked for agriculture without regard for whether or not they were appropriate for that use. Furthermore, the state gave only begrudging recognition to the fact that much of the land to be incorporated into the tropical forest development projects was already occupied by Native American populations (Stocks 1987).

In Central America, state support for ranching has had numerous indirect impacts which have tended to reinforce regional agricultural trends, to the detriment of small farmers and the tropical forests. For example, Central America is heavily dependent upon small farmers (generally less than five hectares) for the bulk of its food production (Durham 1979; Nations 1980). Yet, while Central America's population is growing faster than that of any other part of the hemisphere, particularly in urban areas, agricultural productivity remains low. There is evidence to suggest that this is due to productivity gains in some areas being offset by low productivity lands in the frontier areas, between the expanding cattle ranches and the remaining tropical forest (see, for example, Conklin 1986:24).

## Implications for Conservation and Development

Anthropologists have long acted as advocates for broadly based local participation in both development and conservation contexts, and much of our applied work consists of attempting to create a context in which this participation can come about. Developers and conservationists have increasingly agreed in principle that local participation in project design and management is desirable for achieving their respective goals. As dialogue between developers and conservationists has broadened around the issue of how to promote economic growth on the basis of the sustainable use of natural resources, local participation has increasingly been recognized as essential. Conservationists have acquired a heightened appreciation that human beings are part of the environment they seek to protect, and that they have legitimate interests in utilizing the natural resources of the areas in which they live. Developers have learned that short-term economic growth which is achieved by depleting the resource base upon which long-term livelihood depends is of doubtful benefit. Building actions upon these improved understandings implies soliciting greater participation by those affected by conservation and development efforts in order to consider their immediate economic needs and to plan how they are to share in the benefits of conservation and development.

However, elements of the basic approaches of conservationists and developers to addressing their respective areas of concern remain obstacles to effective co-management of activities with members of local populations. Conservationists continue to view environmental destruction as a problem arising from how people use the environment, rather than recognizing that how humans exploit the environment is an outcome of the relationships between people, which define the value of particular resources in particular contexts and regulate access to those resources. As a result, they assume that their objectives may be achieved through some combination of education and improved technical remedies. In cases where these fail, the tendency is to fall back upon state-imposed regulation supported by strengthened law enforcement. For their part, developers continue to act as if local populations were homogeneous and empirically self-evident entities. When the differential impacts of their activities on members of a defined population are acknowledged, they are treated as a quantitative issue of wealthier members of the population getting "more" of the benefits. When members of a local population oppose an activity, or when it goes awry, developers seek solutions in improved communications with local people and in improved project design and management. That they may have communicated the benefits of their project perfectly well, and that these benefits may have conflicted in a fundamental way with the interests of a significant portion of the local population is rarely considered.

The challenges facing anthropologists concerned with promoting local participation in the interest of sustainable resource use and economic growth are several. First, we must sharpen our ability to conduct class-based analyses that place resource competition in an historical context, in order to identify and describe the social and economic underpinnings of natural resource degradation. Second, the recommendations we make need to be based upon an explicit understanding of the values we seek to promote through particular types of production regimes and institutional arrangements. While it may be comforting to pretend that our recommendations are value-free and emerge in a self-evident way from the data we gather, and while it may be necessary for the institutions for which we work to maintain this fiction, to forfeit a critical, anthropological perspective on our own work portends disaster for conservation and development objectives.

Ultimately, what we are talking about is who wins and who loses in the struggle for the resources upon which many depend to produce, and through their production, to survive and prosper. There are no "cut and dried" or "cookbook" answers here. As may be seen from the examples in the foregoing discussion, there is nothing inherent in smallholder production or in large-scale development which makes one or the other inevitably destructive. Rather, environmental destruction and economic underdevelopment are a consequence of relationships between people with diverse and conflicting economic interests. As social scientists, we hope that our recommendations are based upon a systematic analysis of empirical data. However, that same critical, scientific perspective demands that we recognize that our definition of the problem, which shapes how we collect our data, reflects a set of values and interests that we take with us to our work. As Redclift notes, for example:

> . . . the environment, whatever its geographic location, is socially constructed. The environment used by ramblers in the English Peak District, or hunters and gatherers in the Brazilian Amazon, is not merely *located* in different places; it means different things to those who use it. The environment is transformed by economic growth in a material sense but it is also continually transformed existentially, although we—the environment users—often remain unconscious of the fact (1987:3).

Thus, a third challenge is to recognize that it is not enough to promote local participation. In areas such as the Amazon, where smallholding settlers exist side-by-side with large lumber companies and multi-national automobile manufacturers, local participation quickly becomes a hollow concept unless we specify participation by whom and under what sorts of institutional arrangements. Only then do the issues of access to resources underlying underdevelopment and environmental destruction emerge, and only then can we examine the kind of world we wish to build through the exploitation and/or conservation of natural resources.

## Acknowledgments

This paper was prepared with support from the Cooperative Agreement on Settlement and Resource Systems Analysis of the Institute for Development Anthropology, Clark University, and the U.S. Agency for International Development. A previous version of the paper was presented to the Annual Meeting of the Society for Applied Anthropology, Tampa, Florida, April 21–24, 1988. The author thanks Jane Collins, Daniel Dworkin, Peter Little, and Katy Moran for helpful comments and suggestions. However, the views expressed are those of the author and do not necessarily reflect positions of any of the above-named people or institutions.

## References Cited

Aramburú, Carlos E.
   1982    Expansión de la frontera agraria y demográfica en la selva alta peruana. *In* Colonización en la Amazonía. C.E. Aramburú, E. Bedoya, and J. Recharte. Pp. 1–39. Lima: Centro de Investigación y Promoción Amazónica.

Bakx, Keith.
   1987    Planning Agrarian Reform: Amazonian Settlement Projects, 1970–86. Development and Change. 18(4):533–555.

Barlett, Peggy F.
   1980    Adaptive Strategies in Peasant Agricultural Production. Annual Review of Anthropology. 9:545–573.

Collins, Jane L.
   1986    Smallholder Settlement of Tropical South America: The Social Causes of Ecological Destruction. Human Organization. 45(1):1–10.

Collins, Jane L. and Michael Painter.
   1986    Settlement and Deforestation in Central America: A Discussion of Development Issues. Working Paper 31. Binghamton, NY: Institute for Development Anthropology.

Conklin, Frank S.
   1986    Panama: Agricultural Sector Assessment. Draft. Unpublished report prepared for USAID/Panama.

Dourojeanni, Marco.
   1984    Potencial y uso de los recursos naturales: consideraciones metodológicas. *In* Población y colonización en la alta Amazonía peruana. Consejo Nacional de Población and Centro de Investigación Amazónica, eds. Pp. 110–121. Lima: Consejo Nacional de Población y Centro de Investigación Amazónica.

Dozier, Craig L.
1969    Land Development and Colonization in Latin America. New York: Praeger Publishers.

Durham, William H.
1979    Scarcity and Survival in Central America: The Ecological Origins of the Soccer War. Stanford, CA: Stanford University Press.

Fearnside, Phillip M.
1979    The Development of the Amazon Rainforest: Priority Problems for the Formulation of Guidelines. Interciencia. 4(6):338–343.
1983    Development Alternatives in the Brazilian Amazon: An Ecological Evaluation. Interciencia. 8(2):65–78.
1985    Environmental Change and Deforestation in the Brazilian Amazon. *In* Change in the Amazon Basin. Vol.1. Man's Impact on Forests and Rivers. J. Hemming, ed. Pp. 70–89. Manchester, UK: University of Manchester Press.

Foweraker, Joe
1981    The Struggle for Land. Cambridge: Cambridge University Press.

Gill, Lesley
1987    Peasants, Entrepreneurs, and Social Change: Frontier Development in Lowland Bolivia. Boulder: Westview Press.

Glick, Dennis and Jorge Betancourt.
1983    The Rio Platano Biosphere Reserve: Unique Resource, Unique Alternative. Ambio. 12(3–4):168–173.

Goodland, Robert J.A.
1980    Environmental Ranking of Amazonian Development Projects in Brazil. Environmental Conservation. 7(1):9–26.
1985    Brazil's Environmental Progress in Amazonian Development. *In* Change in the Amazon Basin. Vol. 1. Man's Impact on Forests and Rivers. J. Hemming, ed. Pp. 5–35. Manchester: Manchester University Press.

Guppy, Nicolas.
1984    Tropical Deforestation: A Global View. Foreign Affairs. 62(4):928–965.

Hall, Anthony.
1987    Agrarian Crisis in Brazilian Amazonia: The Grande Carajás Programme. Journal of Development Studies. 23(4):522–552.

Hecht, Susana B.
1985    Environment, Development and Politics: Capital Accumulation and the Livestock Sector in Eastern Amazonia. World Development. 13(6):663–684.

International Science and Technology Institute (ISTI).
1980    Panamá: condiciones del medio ambiente y de los recursos naturales. Washington, DC: International Science and Technology Institute.

Joly, Luz Graciela.
1982    La migración de los interioranos hacia la Costa Abajo. *In* Colonización y destrucción de bosques en Panamá. S. Heckadon Moreno and A. McKay, eds. Pp. 63–80. Panamá, Panamá: Asociación Panameña de Antropología.

JRB Associates.
1982    Honduras: Country Environmental Profile. McLean, VA: JRB Associates.

Ledec, George and Robert J.A. Goodland.
1989    Epilogue: An Environmental Perspective on Tropical Land Settlement. *In* The Human Ecology of Tropical Land Settlement in Latin America. D. Schumann and W. Partridge, eds., Boulder, CO: Westview Press.

Leonard, H. Jeffrey.
1987    Natural Resources and Economic Development in Central America: A Regional Environmental Profile. New Brunswick, NJ: Transaction Books.

Moran, Emilio.
1974    The Adaptive Strategy of the Amazonian Caboclo. *In* Man in the Amazon. C. Wagley, ed. Pp. 136–159. Gainesville, FL: University of Florida Press.
1987    Monitoring Fertility Degradation of Agricultural Lands in the Lowland Tropics. *In* Lands at Risk in the Third World: Local-level Perspectives. P.D. Little and M.M Horowitz, eds. Pp. 69–91. Boulder, CO: Westview Press.

Myers, Norman.
1981    The Hamburger Connection: How Central America's Forests Become North America's Hamburgers. Ambio. 10(1):3–8.

Nations, James D.
1980    The Future of Middle America's Tropical Rainforests. Report to the Tinker Foundation and the Inter-American Foundation. unpublished draft.

Nations, J.D. and Daniel I. Komer.
1983    Rainforests and the Hamburger Society. Environment. 25(3):12–25.

Nelson, Michael.
1973    The Development of Tropical Lands: Policy Issues in Latin America. Baltimore, MD: Johns Hopkins University Press.

Organization of American States (OAS).
1984    Integrated Regional Development Planning: Guidelines and Case Studies from the OAS Experience. Washington, DC: Department of Regional Development, Secretariat for Economic and Social Affairs, Organization of American States.

Painter, Michael.
1987    Unequal Exchange: The Dynamics of Settler Impoverishment and Environmental Destruction in Lowland Bolivia. *In* Lands at Risk in the Third World: Local-level Perspectives. P.D. Little and M.M Horowitz, eds. Pp. 164–191. Boulder, CO: Westview Press.
1988    Competition and Conflict in the Bolivian Lowlands: Ethnicity and Social Class Formation. Paper presented to the invited session Conceptualizing Inequality: Class, Gender, and Ethnicity in the Andes. Annual Meeting of the American Anthropological Association. Phoenix.

Painter, Michael, Carlos A. Perez-Crespo, Martha Llanos Albornóz, Susan Hamilton, and William Partridge.
1984    New Lands Settlement and Regional Development: The Case of San Julian, Bolivia. Working Paper 15. Binghamton, NY: Institute for Development Anthropology.

Redclift, Michael.
1987    Sustainable Development: Exploring the Contradictions. London: Metheun and Co. Ltd.

Rudel, Thomas K.
1983    Roads, Speculators and Colonization in the Ecuadorian Amazon. Human Ecology. 11(4):385–403.

Scudder, Thayer.
  1981   The Development Potential of New Lands Settlement in the Tropics and
         Subtropics: A Global State-of-the-Art Evaluation with Specific Emphasis on
         Policy Implications. Binghamton, NY: Institute for Development Anthro-
         pology.
  1984   The Development Potential of New Lands Settlement in the Tropics and
         Subtropics: A Global State-of-the-Art Evaluation with Specific Emphasis on
         Policy Implications. Executive Summary. A.I.D. Program Discussion Paper
         No. 21. Washington, DC: U.S. Agency for International Development.
Stearman, Allyn MacLean.
  1985   Colonization in Santa Cruz, Bolivia: A Comparative Study of the Yapacaní
         and San Julián Projects. *In* Frontier Expansion in Amazonia. M. Schmink
         and C. Wood, eds. Pp. 231–260. Gainesville, FL: University of Florida
         Press.
Stocks, Anthony.
  1987   Tropical Forest Development in Peru. Development Anthropology Network.
         5(2):1–8.
Uhl, Christopher.
  1982   Recovery Following Disturbances of Different Intensities in the Amazon
         Rain Forest of Venezuela. Interciencia. 7(1):19–24.
Vickers, William T.
  1982   Development and Amazonian Indians: The Aguarico Case and Some General
         Principles. *In* The Dilemma of Amazonian Development. E. Moran, ed.
         Pp. 25–50. Boulder, CO: Westview Press.
Wennergren, E. Boyd and Morris D. Whitaker.
  1976   Investment in Access Roads and Spontaneous Colonization: Additional
         Evidence from Bolivia. Land Economics. 52(1):88–95.
Whitten, Norman.
  1978   Amazonian Ecuador: An Ethnic Interface in Ecological, Social, and Ideo-
         logical Perspectives. Copenhagen International Work Group for Indigenous
         Affairs. Document No. 34.
World Bank.
  1985   The Experience of the World Bank with Government-sponsored Land
         Settlement. Washington, DC: The World Bank.
Wood, Charles and Marianne Schmink.
  1979   Blaming the Victim: Small Farmer Production in the Amazon Colonization
         Project. Studies in Third World Societies. 7:77–93.

# 16

## "Big Men" and Cattle Licks in Oromoland, Kenya

*P.T.W. Baxter*

This essay is an attempt to set my understandings of an apparently isolated and very matter of fact piece of indigenous knowledge in its ethnographic and developmental contexts. That I have come to think that there is anything in the data which requires "understanding" follows from the many discursive conversations I have had over the years with David Brokensha which have directed my attention to the minutiae of daily life and of indigenous knowledge. These chats have been to me as enjoyable as salt is to Oromo livestock.

In the early nineteen fifties I carried out fieldwork among the Boran, one of the Oromo-speaking peoples of the Horn; I spent most of my time in Marsabit District in Northern Kenya. At that time the Boran were prosperous, self-sufficient pastoralists who subsisted almost entirely on the milk, blood, and meat which their herds supplied; they sold sheep and goats (and occasionally a bullock) to pay poll tax and fines levied for breaches of grazing regulations; to purchase cloth, blankets and household items such as enamel basins, mugs and tumblers, and supplementary foodstuffs such as sugar, tea, salt, and maize meal to vary their diet, and tobacco and coffee beans for their spiritual and social comfort. The pastoral life was arduous, but the people were largely self-sufficient and were still, or so it seemed, users of the encroaching market economy rather than its victims. A few younger sons joined the police or went to work as stockmen on European farms down country, but that was as much for the experience as for the wages. Boran recent sufferings and destitution make that period seem like a Golden Age.

Every family owned some cattle and sheep and goats, and an increasing number were acquiring herds of camels. In order to make best use of the sparse grazing, browse and water, a family usually divided its stock into distinct and territorially separated grazing units—one of milking cows, one of dry cows, one of milking camels and one of sheep and goats which run together. A very few exceptionally wealthy men had two or even three herds of milking cows, each in the care of a wife. According to the folk ideal, one of a set of brothers, or failing that close agnates, should be in charge of each unit according to seniority, that is the eldest with the milking cattle and the youngest with the sheep and goats. In practice, of course, this ideal was seldom achieved though almost invariably approximated; but we need not be concerned here with the ways in which the labor and stock of families were actually allocated (see Baxter 1966). For our present purposes it is sufficient to note certain consequences which followed from this particular style of animal husbandry. First, a family and its stock could well be distributed across an area as extensive as Wales. Secondly, the villages in which the milking cows were kept (*ola*) consisted mostly of older men, each with their wives and younger children; each elder was also the "father" (*aba*) or senior manager of the widely dispersed stock holdings of his family group.

A village of milking cattle, then, was also an assembly of elders, each of whom was, as it were, the center point of a set of specialized herding units; the members of any specialized unit were much more likely to visit the milking village than they were any of its satellite camps. The homestead of the milking herd was the place at which family plans were discussed and decisions made; the village of milking homesteads was the place where rituals were performed and the enduring moral point to which those who herded the dry stock in the satellite camps were attached. Milking villages and the dry stock may have been several days walk apart, but information and intelligence flowed readily between them. The members of a dry stock (*fora*) camp would be young childless couples, unmarried youths and girls and a more experienced man or two to advise. Camps moved frequently, especially following localized rainfall in the rainy season, whereas milking villages were much more settled; indeed, in the favored areas, such as the higher parts of Marsabit Mountain where the observations reported below were made, they were transhumant; villages moved down the Mountain to the plains in the rains and up again to the permanent wells for the dry season. If it did not rain in the plains, the milking villages remained where they were.

As cows matured they were brought up from the plains into the milking herds, where they normally remained, enjoying the richer grazing, until they ceased to bear calves. I was told that stock kept on Marsabit Mountain lost condition because there were no mineral springs (*hora*) for them to drink at, and because the richer mountain grazing could be too "strong". As a remedy, they were fed with *mulugdi* (Venturino 1973, uses the spelling *muludde*, his ear is probably better than mine. I cannot locate the word in any other Oromo dictionary). *Mulugdi* are chunks of coarse salt and congealed sand collected from the surface crust of the Chalbi desert, which is a vast dried salt lake to the northwest of Marsabit (Dixey 1948:3). The Chalbi becomes waterlogged after heavy rains, but, for most of the year, it is baked, white, shimmering flatness, relieved only by mirages, and firm enough for lorries to drive across. When the father of a herd thought his charges needed *mulugdi*, he could send word to young members of his family grazing near the Chalbi to bring some up, or send down a couple of members of his village family with some donkeys and goatskin sacks to fetch some up.

*Mulugdi* was freely available and collecting it was merely a rather tedious task. As I recall each homestead fetched its own supplies, though neighbors usually traveled together for the company. Negligible social planning or organized cooperation were required. Such small numbers of travelers would be welcome to spend the night at any camp or village, or could sleep safely and comfortably in the bush. The journey from Marsabit Mountain then did not require passage through the territory of hostile or unfriendly peoples.

I feel confident that no Boran would have denied *mulugdi* to a neighbor in need, but I do not recall ever hearing anyone beg it, and it would seem out of character for a father of a herd to have done so. *Mulugdi* was on sale in Marsabit's embryonic little market for non-Boran townsmen to purchase (though I neglected to note the price). Before being served to stock it was broken up and moistened; I did see sheep fed it on a discarded sleeping hide, but it was usually served in a trough. All stock clearly relished *mulugdi* and would continue to lick the trough long after the last crumb had been eaten. *Mulugdi* was a valued and essential, but free, element in the animal husbandry of a stock-owning family. Boran from Marsabit District did not trade *mulugdi* nor natron (*magardo*), but Boran to the north did exchange it with Konso for grain, cloth and metal goods. In the last century Boran from the Mega area, in what is now southern Ethiopia, traded salt from Sogida (Salt) and natron to as far away as the Benadir coast; but this long distance trade had long ceased (Pankhurst 1968:243, 436, 440; Abir 1970:133). The famous *amole*, or salt bars, which were traditional articles of exchange, and were still occasionally to be seen in markets in southern Ethiopia in the 1960s, have no connection with either the salt trade or the collection and distribution of cattle-lick (Pankhurst 1968:260–4).

I thought little about *mulugdi* then or later; it just seemed a common sense part of animal husbandry. Indeed I would probably not even have noted it, nor recalled it, but for the obvious pleasure people took in giving pleasure to their stock which, in turn, communicated itself to me. I had seen salt licks in the cattle fields and mineral blocks in the stalls of milking cows in England, and was vaguely aware that salt and mineral licks were widely used in stock management. I later learned that it was a common feature of animal husbandry across the world.[1]

I spent the academic year 1968–9 in the field among Arssi of Kofele District, Chilalo Province in Arussi Governorate in Ethiopia. The Arssi, like the Boran, are one of the several Oromo-speaking peoples who make up the Oromo nation; the two dialects are close and cultures similar. Arssi grew barley and kept stock. The eastern part of Kofele District and the western part of the neighboring district of Gedeb formed a complementary economic area; the Kofele segment mostly lies between 2485 and 2970 meters and the Gedeb segment mostly between 2000–2485 meters (see Kebede 1967). Generally speaking, cattle thrive better in Kofele during the dry season, because there is always water nearby, but better in Gedeb during the rains. Kofele produces cabbage, *ensete*[2] (False banana, *wuurki* in Oromo), bamboo for houses and stock pens, honey and other highland products; Gedeb produces more milk (and hence butter) and barley and a little flax as a cash crop. There are no mineral springs in either section. The Arssi were much more tied into the market economy than the Boran had been, and were much more restricted in their movements. All land was owned or tenanted and jealously guarded against intruders; most Arssi, in effect, were tenants of Arssi "big men" or Shoan landlords. But they still resided in clusters of agnates on land which they saw as lineage land, and all territory was still spoken of as "belonging" to particular specified lineages.[3] The day when homesteads could move freely with their herds, and any homestead had access to as much grazing as its herds could consume, was now only a folk memory. Pasture was in even shorter supply than stock and, like plow land, was guarded closely. But Arssi still asserted, as vehemently as ever Boran did, that they loved cattle and the dominant cultural ethos, as expressed in prayers, greetings, blessings, songs, and casual conversations, was a pastoral one. Most families from Kofele also maintained a homestead and land rights in eastern Gedeb, to which all or part of the family moved as good husbandry required. Arssi held very firmly indeed that cattle, small stock, horses, and mules, if they were to thrive, all needed regular access to mineral springs (*hora*) or to *boojji*, which is a salty mineral deposit similar to mulugdi, and which I shall describe more fully shortly.

I do not recall hearing the word *boojji* used in Kenya by Boran, but that may well be that I just did not note it. Certainly it was used, rather than *mulugdi*, in the market in Neghelli in Boran country in Ethiopia which I visited briefly in May 1969. (The price in the market there was 50% higher than it was in Kofele.) Father Leus of the Roman Catholic Mission at Yabello, which is in Borana in Ethiopia, includes *boji* in his recent dictionary (1988) but does not give *mulugdi*; whereas Father Venturino, in his Kenya-based Borana dictionary (1973), gives *muludde* but not *boojji*. Both Arssi and Boran, when I asked, said, rather dismissively, that the two substances were "the same" or "resembled each other" and served the same purpose. I do not think the differences are material here. Certainly, all stock have a passion for *boojji/mulugdi* and both Boran and Arssi, as I suspect all Oromo, enjoy feeding it to their stock.

With his first pay the small boy my wife and I employed about our compound in Kofele went to the market, and spent 10 cents on a heaped enamel bowl full of *boojji* for his beloved grandmother's few treasured sheep: my research assistant, Dadaafo Godaana, also bought *boojji* for his sheep, which were in the care of his father, and enjoyed taking me to see them enjoy it. When the late Adami Hussein's bedraggled horse, which was the apple of his eye, joined our compound, he gave it *boojji* to eat, which he had already bought in anticipation, even before grooming and drenching it. Horse and owner were clearly very happy.

I often saw *boojji* fed to stock in Kofele, where is was moistened and crumbled and evenly scattered on a clean patch of grass. The stock always licked and nibbled the grass and earth away until they left a shallow, bare depression. I was told that in areas which had a different type of soil, the *boojji*[4] needed to be mixed with a sort of red soil known as *hii'a*,[5] in the proportions of one basket of *boojji* to two of red soil. Arssi asserted that they had "always" given *boojji* to their stock and that they had "always" gone to great efforts to ensure a regular supply of it. One indication of the importance in which is was held is that Tutschek,[6] who compiled a dictionary of Oromo in the early 1840s in Munich, was given the word by his informants, who were freed slaves homesick in an alien land, which they translated for him as "a kind of eatable earth". This suggests that, for the informants, the earth was an essential ingredient. The use of *boojji* is certainly not recent. Yilma Deressa, an Oromo historian, argues that one of the attractions of the Rift Valley lakes (and places such as Ambo) for Oromo settlers in the sixteenth century, was the presence of mineral springs and mineral licks *bowji* (1966-7:216).[7]

Here I must divert for a moment and comment on the word *hora*, "mineral water", "source of mineral water", "hot spring": Gragg (1982) states that, in its primary meaning "hot spring water", the word has connections to both Arabic and Amharic. In Oromo, it is a "complex word" in the Empsonian sense, with a wide field of meanings, from the casually mundane to the holy, which merits a paper to itself. Briefly, as a noun *horin* it may mean cattle, money, wealth, possessions; indeed all desirable and enduring materials things. As a verb, in various forms, it may mean be rich, multiply, bear fruit, prosper, increase. *Hormata* are the reproductive parts of females and all other good things in life. In various forms it is used in blessings and as a response to prayers. It carries heavy charges of meaning. Water from *hora* is used in ritual purifications and, as Bartels puts it, "a *horra* means life in cattle and cattle is the life of the people"(1983:73). It is the *hora*, mineral water, that gives *boojji* its quality and its savor. But, as far as I could make out, *boojji* itself is simply a derivative and, in and as itself, does not have more than nutritional and medical properties. *Boojji* is just the name of a useful substance.

On dry Wednesdays there were usually a few *boojji* sellers at Kofele market—the most I noted was nine. On wet days there was no point in sellers coming, because *boojji* needs to be kept out of the rain so that its savor is not washed out. The going rates were 10 Ethiopian cents for a single heaped enamel bowl, or 50 Ethiopian cents for 20 heaped basins or flat basket lids plus two extra handfuls for goodwill; i.e. about three gallons for about 10 pence sterling or 20 American cents. In the market at Asasa town the administrative center for Gedeb and further from the sources of *boojji*, the rate was 20 tins for 50 cents; to my eye the tins looked smaller than the basins used in Kofele. At Allellu Market, only a kilometer or so from Shashamene, and only half as far from the sources, the price was only 5 cents a bowl. These few figures suggest that the selling price increased the further away from the sources, as would be expected. But it was mostly only townspeople and the poor who bought *boojji*; usually in Kofele a group of neighbors, who would also be close agnates, would get together to make up a caravan of pack horses and pack mules to go to Lake Shaalla, Lake

Abiata or Lake Langano to collect their own. Lake Shaalla was the nearest and most favored source of *boojji* for people from Kofele. Caravans from Kofele were usually small, just three or four leaders and two or three times that number of pack animals. Donkeys were rarely used, because they were slow and could only manage a half load. The driest months, March and April and September and October, were the times to travel, and then there was a flow of small local caravans and large caravans from Bale and Gedeb on the road. I lived alongside a major route and was in a good position to observe them. At trail junctions, such as the bridge over the River Webi, enterprising women set up charcoal braziers and sold boiled cabbage, barley cakes and coffee to the horse leaders and muleteers.

I visited two different *boojji* collecting points on Lake Shaalla Diika (Small Shaalla) on 2 May 1969, and one on Lake Shaalla Guddaa (Big Shaalla) on 24 May. The Small Shaalla collection points were on a goodish road, just below some hot springs and geysers which had become an attraction for tourists from Addis Ababa. *Shaalla* in Oromo means "pelican", with which the lake abounded and from which is took its name,[8] and the area had been scheduled as a Game Sanctuary. The rocks and pools were littered with hulled maize cobs, chicken bones, and eggshells left by picnicking tourists who had tried cooking in the boiling pools. The steam which arose was believed to have curative properties, and Ethiopians came from great distances to sit on logs over the jets of steam. Though *boojji* permeated with the mineral water was valued so highly, stock were not brought to drink the waters. Though, I was told, they did go to drink at the cooler mineral springs at Lakes Zwai and Langano.

One of the laborers employed at the site, which was on the shoreline of a shallow bay, pointed out the shelters used to store *boojji*, but stated he was not expecting many, if any, more customers as the rains had already started two days earlier. My companions then told me that Little Shaalla was only a small site anyhow and that the big one at Big Shaalla was much busier! The *boojji* was sand and soil over which the mineral water from the hot springs had spread out and seeped in. *Boojji* had to be collected after a longish spell of dry weather. It was first raked and scraped into small mounds about two feet high to dry (cf. Lovejoy, 1986:61), then into larger mounds, which were covered with dom palm mats to protect then from the rain. Most was sold directly from the heaps but, as the rains approached, any left unsold was carried in baskets by laborers to the shelters. Arssi stressed that *boojji* must always be protected from rain to prevent it being "destroyed", i.e. its savor and strength being washed out. In the market buyers tasted before they bought in order to check that the *boojji* had not lost its savor.

There were two collecting and selling points at Little Shaalla, both of which, I was told, were owned by absentee Amhara landlords. Amhara were the politically dominant ethnic group in Ethiopia, and Arssi expressed particular resentment at having to pay those whom they perceived as conquering and exploiting foreigners for that which God had given, as he had rain and grasses, to all men; or at any rate to all Oromo! The price was 50 Ethiopian cents a large gunny or hide sack. One sack made a mule or horse load. My very rough estimate is that one load would make about four 50 cent market lots of twenty basins each. The round trip from Kofele took four to seven days; so that the most that a man could make, for a week's exhausting work for himself and two pack animals would have been just about 50 pence or one American dollar! The local rural economy was a desperately poor one.

I was not able to visit the Big Shaalla sites until 24 May, by which time the season was over. The approach road was still firm but looked as if it would be a quagmire in the rains, which made it clear to me that, even if the *boojji* could have been kept dry in the rains, the caravan paths and the streams and rivers they crossed would only have been negotiable with difficulty. By contrast, the paths to the Chalbi in Marsabit would have usually been open for 11 months of the year.

The organization of a small *boojji* collecting caravan from Kofele was fairly simple and straightforward for a homestead, or set of neighbors, which had sufficient men and/or child-free women fit enough to undertake the walk (or who had access to saddle horses) and the requisite pack animals. Many poor homesteads did not have pack animals, or only had one, so they had to borrow and, in return, lead a second or third animal on behalf of a wealthier homestead. This was not perceived as exploitation, because a homestead which had fewer horses was not likely to have a large herd or flock, so would not need so much *boojji*! This light patronage was wrapped in the egalitarian idiom of agnatic kinship; during the journey, as at home or when herding, members treated each other as kinsmen, deferring in speech and in behavior only to age, generation and gender differences; no one was treated as an employee, servant, or client. The parties were a little more formally structured than those of the Boran to the Chalbi for *mulugdi*; because all land was owned and guarded and because Kofele could be cold at nights, a party aimed to overnight at homesteads where they would be known and made welcome, so they needed friends or affines en route. But a small caravan was still a small group of kinsmen-neighbors. No one could order anyone else about.

This contrasted with the caravans sent for *boojji* by Amhara landlords, which were made up of their tenants and laborers. To me, as they passed along the road, they were indistinguishable from Arssi caravans, but to Arssi they were constituted quite differently, because the members of landlord caravans had not come together as kinsmen but as clients or servants. Foolishly I never inquired where they overnighted.

There were only a few large Arssi landlords in Kofele; one did not exercise his rights as a landlord at all and behaved as nearly as possible like a traditional elder; another acted as much like an Amhara landlord as he could get away with; two others, who were outstanding innovators in many other ways, combined to send a lorry. But, in Gedeb and the neighboring Bale Province, there were several wealthy stock-owners and landholders, spoken of as "big men" *nama guddaa*, who were descendants of those preconquest "big men" who had survived the conquest of the Arssi by the Abyssinian armies of Menilik. These men had also often acquired titles to large tracts of land, the status of government recognized head-men of a major clan section (*balabat*) and, quite often, an honorific Imperial title. These men, as their ancestors had done, organized large caravans, often of seventy or more pack animals; I saw one of well over a hundred animals. Counting was not easy, the caravans straggled and at bottlenecks, such as the Webi River bridge, intermingled. The men, and they were always men on the large, long distance caravans, were clansmen of the "big men" who had organized the caravans, and who might, or might not, accompany the caravan themselves. The clansmen would also be the tenants, at least in law, of the "big men" but, I was assured, most of these "big men" still acted much as their grandfathers had done; that is, as "fathers" (*aba*) or traditional leaders (*haiyu*). They did not collect rent for pasture in cash nor kind and neither paid nor ordered men to accompany them. (One young, schooled *balabat* was an exception to this and behaved, as he was legally entitled to do, as much like an Amhara landlord as he dared.) I was told, on one hand, that one mark of a "big man" was that he could organize large caravans and, on the other, that one needed to be a "big man" in order to have the resources to organize the caravan. But, certainly, not all "big men" organized large caravans; to do so one needed junior clansmen to participate. After the conquest clansmen had been redesignated tenants, but prior to that they would have been free equals; some "big men" still behaved according to the preconquest ideal, others according to the colonial ideal of the armed settler (*neftanya*) landlord. I was not able to get data on the detailed social composition of any large caravan because they originated forty or more miles away from where I was living, and merely passed through Kofele.

But the point I want to make here seems clear enough: "big men" needed to be able to organize the labor of a number of poorer men, as well as to mobilize the homestead of other wealthy clansmen, because a caravan needed pack animals and leaders. To travel together in a caravan made for sociability and very welcome security. Arssi had never participated in an encompassing national "Peace" (*Nagaa*), such as Boran enjoyed (see Baxter 1965), and Gedeb and Bale was not safe nor secure, and so a large caravan supplied the safety that lay in numbers and the protection of a "big man's" name. But a long distance caravan had logistic as well as security problems; travelers could not rely for hospitality on friends or affines en route, and their numbers would have been more than most compounds could entertain. A "big man" had to rely on similar "big men" at appropriate stages along the caravan route, so that his men and pack animals could be fed, watered and be kept safe overnight. Arssi "big men" formed a loosely connected network across Arssi country, and even into the fringes of the national ruling elite, linked by affinity through the exchange marriage of sisters and by matrilineal kin ties. The most conspicuous attribute of "big men" was the number and span of their many marriages; indeed many could not be constrained to the Islamic maximum of four. In this respect "big men" were quite unlike even very wealthy ordinary men. To get a large, long distance caravan on the road, then, took stock-wealth, widespread and effective affinal connections, and organizational skills; organizing a caravan did not make one a "big man", one had to be a "big man" first in order to do it.

What Arssi stressed as the attributes of a "big man" were not so much his wealth, nor his wives, nor his power, but the social tact or knowledge of words which he required in order to get so many vociferously independent homestead to cooperate. Power and wealth, in themselves, were not sufficient to enable a "big man" to organize a caravan, simply because blatantly exercised power, indeed even the slightest appearance of being overbearing, would have dispersed the latent social power that wealth and the other attributes allowed.

The names of former "big men", of course, are remembered because they have had descendants who have become "big men"; but what was always recalled about the "big men" of old was their abilities as organizers of long distance caravans to Welayita and Wollamu for cloth, to Bale and beyond for salt,[9] and to the Rift Valley Lakes for *boojji* (see Baxter 1984:462). They were not remembered as cloth *traders*, not as salt *traders*, let alone as *boojji* traders; they were organizers not merchants. They are not honored in memory for their wealth nor their power but for their organizational skills, which they used, like they did their skill with "words", for the general benefit.[10] I am not suggesting that nineteenth century and turn of the century "big men" were just simple, public-spirited benefactors, but their organizational capabilities were represented to me, correctly I think, not as stemming from coercive power so much as from the abilities to manage men and to manage words.

This is not to say that power and wealth were not prerequisites; certainly no poor man could have made a name as a caravan organizer as he could, for example, as a warrior, but just that, in themselves, power and wealth were not sufficient; nor was the pursuit of wealth an end in itself. It is reasonable to assume that many wealthy and powerful men in the past, as in the present, were not able to organize their fellows at all, and thus become remembered as "big men"; indeed, they are only recalled at all in the genealogies of their immediate descendants. One could not be a "big man", as it were, in a little pool. In eastern Gedeb and in Bale in 1969, "big men" still had a role as organizers of *boojji* caravans, even though their roles as organizers of cloth and salt caravans had been usurped by traders with lorries. In Kofele, which was densely settled, secure and close to the sources of *boojji*, "big men" as organizers had become redundant.

As *boojji* is seen as an essential component of animal husbandry, and hence of Arssi identity as dedicated stock herders; so, the "big men" who organized its collection were represented to me as essential components of Arssi historical identity. But "big man" status cannot be adapted to other times and situations. The descendants of "big men" in Kofele, however wealthy and honored by the Ethiopian administration, could not be made into contemporary community leaders nor to be respected as "big men", simply because now they contributed nothing to the common weal. Whatever their coercive and economic powers, they were simply wealthy landlords and government headmen *balabats*.[11]

Finally, a postscript on indigenous knowledge or, perhaps, an epitaph for *boojji*. It must be clear that Arssi and Boran and, I think, most Oromo and, indeed, most inhabitants of Southern Ethiopia, hold that /*boojji* is essential to the wellbeing of stock that do not have access to mineral springs. Certainly non-Arssi in Kofele shared this belief, and I have mentioned that Amhara landlords organized caravans to collect *boojji* and that non-Arssi townsmen bought it in the markets. The official handbook of the Arussi Governorate, which was compiled by Amharas and Shoans, lists its mineral springs and sources of *boojji* among the natural resources of the Governorate (Defaye 1968:157).

I assumed that the Arssi and others knew what they were about and did not put themselves to great trouble for nothing. Most stockmen across the world have also thought salt and mineral licks good for their stock. As the *African Veterinary Handbook* put it: "it is essential to provide cattle kept on limited grazing with salt and mineral licks" (Mackenzie and Simpson 1953, 1971:214). Pratt and Gwynne have since put it very succinctly: "In most parts of East Africa livestock have a craving for salt, and there are numerous natural licks which have been used by wild and domestic animals for centuries. Few of these natural licks show the advantage when analyzed, and it has often been noticed that they are abandoned when animals have access to an introduced mineral mixture, well suited to the area"(1977). They also point out that licks are "a useful tool in grazing management" (Pratt and Gwynne 1977:199). This experienced pair of rangeland scientists also note that "most pastoralists are good stockmen", and that, "in certain localities one or the other food salts may be deficient. . . . a deficiency which will reveal itself in low fertility of breeding stock, weakness of the calves and slow growth of the young stock" (1977:152). These remarks might well have been made by Boran or Arssi.

The importance of *boojji* to the welfare of the stock seemed obvious to me, but I was quite incapable of even guessing in what its importance lay. I asked the Chilalo Agriculture Development Unit,[12] a sensitive Swedish-Ethiopian development organization that was working in the area, if they knew what *boojji* actually contributed to the welfare of the stock. They were, as always, most helpful; they had already had *boojji* analyzed and had concluded that it made no physical difference at all to the stock who could manage quite well without it. This view was not, of course, taken by the stockmen employed by the Development Unit and it was they, the workers at the very bottom of the hierarchy, on whom the stock depended for their day to day care. The stockmen were the only actually indispensable workers on the project. Like the old Buryat shepherds in the Siberian Karl Marx Collective described by Caroline Humphrey (1983:231), their traditional knowledge ("golden words") and skills were admired, but also devalued because their carriers were unschooled.

I found this "scientific" dismissal of *boojji* hard to accept. The Oromo, like any people anywhere at any time, I felt, might have been misled for centuries by the supposed mystical attributes of a medicine or a food, but *boojji* did not have any mystical qualities attributed to it. Neither its collection nor the way it was fed had any mystical overtones. Both Boran and Arssi were sharp-eyed, open-minded, experimentally oriented stockmen; if they asserted that stock deprived of water from mineral springs or *boojji* lost condition, I felt certain that they were likely to be right. In an inarticulate sort of way I felt that respect for indigenous knowledge was not just, "a courtesy to the people. . . . [but] an essential first step to successful development" (Brokensha et al. 1980:8) and should be heeded. So I took the question on to my friend Dr. Hugh Harding of the Veterinary Training School at Bishoftu. He suggested that *boojji* probably contained trace elements which could not then be discerned by laboratories in Ethiopia. He offered to take samples to FAO for analysis. I sent him specimens just as he was leaving so they would be fresh. But we then learned that the samples were classified as prospectors' mineral samples and hence would need an export certificate, which there was not time to obtain. When I came to leave I did not attempt to get permission to export samples, for a variety of reasons.

As far as I can ascertain *boojji* has still not been analyzed. I still find it hard to accept that, perhaps like some academic papers, it is merely a dummy, a comforter, a useless formula, a placebo, or just plain wrong. As least, so far at any rate, no one has suggested that *boojji* is harmful. But, of course, "truths" change, especially those concerned with diet and nutrition. I was brought up to believe as revealed truth what is now held to be self-evidently false; i.e. that a healthy human diet has as its basis full cream milk, farm-churned butter, home-cured fat bacon and ham, eggs, dark, rich dripping toast and suet dumplings that stuck to the ribs, and that white bread was purer than wholemeal. Similarly, cattle thrived on clean bedding, dry standings, sweet hay, deep pastures, and sweet air!

But of course, the scientific status of *boojji* is entirely irrelevant for us as anthropologists as are the scientific statuses of homoeopathic medicine, the cures of spiritual healers, or the biological consequences of the rules which define incestuous relationships or food prohibitions. Shared knowledge of such sorts is a community construction which is quite unconcerned with measurable "truth". The heartfelt, belly-warming responses (*garaa wollja-laachuu*) generated between human providers of *boojji* and its animal receivers have a value which is independent of the presence or absence of trace minerals. The consumption of *boojji* was an occasion for shared animal and human conviviality and joy. It is a cyclically repeated representation of the mutual dependencies of the stock of a homestead and the people of a homestead (*warra*). I have already noted the complex resonances of *horin* "productive (i.e. reproductive) stock, wealth"; *warra* "people, family" is an equally complex and resonant word. Here, the simple point is that, in proper times, you cannot have one without the other. Stockless individuals, whatever their genealogical connections, are not a *warra*. Stock join people. That I should have been concerned about the nutritional value of *boojji* only demonstrates my own ethnocentric, intellectual myopia, which led me to concentrate on the object, rather than the relationships which it generated.

Across the world those pastoral economies and cultures which have not already been destroyed are threatened with extinction and the arid zones with consequent degradation. One contributory reason for this ecological and human catastrophe is just that the powerful everywhere perceive livestock simply as a commodity, dull and inert like battery hens, mineral ore, stocks and shares or figures in a balance sheet. Whereas in truth livestock are active generators of social relationships, exemplars of truth and beauty and stimulators of the poetic imagination, of living memory and of the informed heart. Indigenous knowledge and practice, any more than "ethnographic facts", are not isolable snippets of useful knowledge which can be pulled up, or out, and just added to the world's store of intellectual bric-a-brac.

## Acknowledgments

I am indebted to Tim Ingold and Alula Pankhurst for references and to Ato Dadafo Godana for translation of Defaye's book on the Arussi.

## Notes

1. Ryder cites the description by Youatt (1840) of the stock management practices of the famous Spanish transhumant shepherds, which had "changed little over several hundred years . . . on arrival at the summer pasture the *mayoral* (shepherd in charge) spread salt on stones for the sheep to lick to guard against possible ill effects from the sudden change to rich herbage" (Youatt in Ryder 1983:432–3). Pratt and Gwynne (1976:162) note that East African sheep "make regular use of salt licks" and "it is generally agreed that cattle benefit from salt and mineral mixtures" (199). The *cure salee* was a regular part of the transhumant cycle in the Southern Sahara. In his masterly survey of salt production and trade in the central Sudan, Lovejoy summarizes the general animal husbandry practices as follows; "*Gari* [impure loose natron] was given to all livestock; donkeys, cattle and camels were fed the natron in their drinking water, while horses, sheep and goats were fed it with their food. *Gari* could be spread on the pastures for cattle. For horses, the *gari* was added to leaves . . . Sometimes ash was added. The *gari* was mixed with millet or guinea corn chaff as a food for sheep and goats." Lovejoy cites Lander, Bowdich and others to show that the practice was general from Agades to Asante (1986:29). Messing notes that the Amhara of the Ethiopian plateau follow Oromo practice, "Fully grown steers are fattened by feeding them a mineral salt, for two years, or when mineral springs (Oromo: *ambo*) exist by taking them to water there (Oromo: *hora*, lake). This is done also to increase the milk supply of cows. 'Rejuvenators', consisting of large pieces of mineral salt, are fed to them for this purpose" (1985:50). It is worth noting that Messing's Amhara informants used Oromo in this context. Sato records of the Rendille, who are neighbors of the Boran and share a common habitat: "Salts are indispensable nourishment for all livestock, and the lack of regular salt may result in a low resistance to lameness, trypanosomiasis, as well as producing a general decline in activity. Thus the Rendille intentionally lead their livestock, especially camels, to waterholes with brackish water as well as to salt licks. When watering camels, the Rendille also keep them feeding

on salt-shrubs such as *Dasysphaera prostrata* and *Salsola dendroides africana*. Salts are also supplied to camels on the way to waterholes (1980:17, 65)."

2. Convenient descriptions of *ensete* cultivation etc., are given in Smeds (1955) and Shack (1966), Chapter 3.

3. For thumbnail sketches of the political and economic situation in Kofele District at the time of the fieldwork, see Baxter (1980; 1983; 1984). The situations have, of course, radically changed since the Revolution.

4. I follow the spelling of Gragg's Oromo dictionary (1982) here. Gragg translates *boojji* as "salty sediment left after water evaporated (cows like to lick it)". Tutschek writes *bodji* which approximates more to the Arssi pronunciation than does *boojji*, he also gives *handjiro* and *goe* as sorts of "eatable earth", both of which looked something like grain. Leus (1988), a priest who is working in Boran, writes *boji*, "salty crust on the ground. . . . cattle, kudu etc., eat and lick it".

I have wondered if it might be *boojji* that is meant by *bogito*, rather than "sprouts", in the following song collected by Cerulli (1922:148):

"1.  abba farda collie                         5.  sombo gudda gala bai
     gababa botollie                               bode dina dura bai
     bogito nadita                                 mie dawaccisi
     bogite galta

1. master of the swift courser, 2. short, little, 3. thou eatest sprouts (*bogito*). 4. Thou wilt return a prisoner! 5. Come forth under the great sycamore! 6. Come forth before the lances of the enemies! 7. Come, gallop! *Notes*: This is a song of contempt of the shepherds for the horsemen who gallop passing near the flocks. *Bogito* (v. 3) is a green vegetable similar to the sprouts, also a food for the poor."

I cannot find the word *bogito* translated as "sprouts" in any dictionary or any other source, and I cannot think of any reason why shepherds should hold horsemen in contempt, or vice versa. Oromo are famed horsemen; in Jimma, for example, kings were named after their horses, and all Oromo are shepherds—it is not a specialized occupation. It seems more credible that the horses should eat *boojji* to give them strength than eat "sprouts"; this is even more likely if the next line is translated as "bring back prisoners of war", which it could well be. The last three lines also sound more like praise than contempt. The punning and sound parallelism are typical of Oromo poetry. Further, one has to travel in a party to collect both *boojji* and *boojia* "captives, booty".

5. This sounds like Leus' *Haya-i*, "a better quality, more salty (*boji*): good for the cattle".

6. See Pankhurst (1976) for an account of the Oromo young men who reached Munich via Cairo slave market, and the conditions under which they assisted the estimable Tutschek.

7. I have not got a copy of Yilma Deressa's work to hand, and rely here on notes that I made in the Institute of Ethiopian Studies in Addis Ababa.

8. Gragg gives *haad'a waaqoo* for pelican, literally "mother of god". I did not hear this nor have I located it in any other Oromo dictionary; it may be restricted to Leka Oromo. The word sounds as if it may be semi-serious, semi-jocular, rather like *gaala Waakat* "God's camel" for the praying mantis.

9. Braukamper (1980:253) notes the importance of *boojji* caravans in this area. McClellan (1986:181) notes that neighboring Gedo "could double the value of *ensete* by transporting it to neighboring Guji [also Oromo pastoralists] and exchanging it for butter, cotton, livestock or *bole* (an earth salt fed to cattle)". Since I first wrote

this paper I have been privileged to read a manuscript by Rev. van de Loo on the Guji Oromo which contains a wealth of ethnography. He notes that *duba* is a mixture of salt and sand given to cattle. "When the grass is growing again a mixture of salt, red lime, and water is given to the cattle in the long trough, *bidurru*." Guji organize caravans to undertake the dangerous and tiring journey to collect salt from Lake Abaya. Van de Loo cites songs in honor of the journey. Guji have a *halusisisa* ritual for the horses before the start of the journey. In one song a lover was rejected because he failed to bring salt for the cattle. One text notes that a woman who fails to prepare good food for her menfolk to take on the journey "risks a whipping". As in the Sudan, salt—for stock as for humans—was one item in a complex of trade goods and was not a specialized trade. Few, if any, African traders got rich from salt trading alone.

10. Interestingly, Abdul Sheriff (1987:169) cites an unpublished Ph.D. Thesis by Jackson (1972) to argue that Kamba ivory traders in the nineteenth century "constituted a 'small economic class' of powerful or prominent men. They did accumulate wealth to some extent in cattle, but Jackson was struck by the lack of emphasis placed on personal followings and clients."

11. Cf. Donham's account of Maale *balabats* who took on the lifestyle of their Amhara masters (Ch. 2, 1985).

12. See Nekby (1971) for a summary account of CADU and its activities.

## References Cited

Abir, M.
1970    Southern Ethiopia. *In* Pre-Colonial Trade. D. Birmingham and R. Gray, eds. Pp. 119–137. Oxford: Oxford University Press.

Bartels, Lambert.
1983    Oromo Religion: Myths and Rites of the Western Oromo of Ethiopia. An Attempt to Understand. Berlin: Collectanea Instituti Anthropos, Dietrich Reimer.

Baxter, P.T.W.
1965    Repetition in Certain Boran Ceremonies. *In* African Systems of Thought. M. Fortes and G. Dieterlin, eds. Pp. 64–78. London: Oxford University Press for International African Institute.

1966    Stock Management and the Diffusion of Property Rights. Proceedings of the Third International Conference of Ethiopian Studies. Pp. 116–127. Addis Ababa: Institute of Ethiopian Studies. Haile Selassie I. University.

1980    Always on the Outside Looking In: A View of the 1969 Ethiopian Elections from a Rural Constituency. Ethnos. 1–2:39–59.

1983    The Problem of the Oromo or the Problem for the Oromo. *In* Nationalism and Self-Determination in the Horn of Africa. I.M. Lewis, ed. Pp. 129–149. London: Ithaca Press.

1984    Butter for Barley and Barley for Cash: Petty Transactions and Small Transformations in the Arssi Market. *In* Proceedings of the Seventh International Conference of Ethiopian Studies. Sven Rubensen, ed. Pp. 459–472. Uppsala, Sweden and East Lansing, MI: Scandinavian Institute of African Studies and African Studies Center, Michigan State University.

Braukamper, Ulrich.
1980    Gesichte der Hadiya Sud-Athiopiens: von den Anfangen bis zur Revolution 1974. Wiesbaden, West Germany: Franz Steiner.

Brokensha, David, D.M. Warren, and Oswalt Werner, eds.
1980    Indigenous Knowledge Systems and Development. Lanham, MD: University
        Press of America.
Cerulli, Enrico.
1922    Folk Literature of the Galla of Southern Ethiopia. Vol. III. Cambridge,
        MA: Harvard African Studies.
Defaye, Dejazmatch Sailu.
1968    Arussi Population, Development and Community. Addis Ababa: Assela.
Deressa, Yilma.
1966-7  Imperial Ethiopian History in the Sixteenth Century. typescript. Addis
        Ababa.
Dixey, F.
1948    Geology of Northern Kenya. Geological Survey of Kenya No. 15. Nairobi:
        Government Printers.
Donham, Donald.
1985    Work and Power in Maale, Ethiopia. Ann Arbor, MI: University Microfilms
        Inc. Research Press.
Gragg, Gene.
1982    Oromo Dictionary. Monograph No. 12. East Lansing: African Studies
        Center. Michigan State University.
Humphrey, Caroline.
1983    Karl Marx Collective: Economy, Society and Religion in a Siberian Collective
        Farm. Cambridge: Cambridge University Press.
Jackson, K.A.
1972    An Ethno-Historical Study of the Oral Traditions of the Akamba of Kenya.
        Unpublished Ph.D. Dissertation. University of California, Los Angeles.
Kebede, Yilma.
1967    Chilalo Awraja. Ethiopian Geographical Journal. 5(1):25–36.
Leus, Ton.
1988    Borana-English Dictionary. typescript. Dadim, Ethiopia: Dadim Catholic
        Church.
Lovejoy, Paul E.
1986    Salt of the Desert Sun: A History of Salt Production and Trade in the
        Central Sudan. Cambridge: Cambridge University Press.
McClennan, Charles W.
1986    Coffee in Centre-Periphery Relations: Gedo in the Early Twentieth Century.
        In Southern Marches of Ethiopia. D. Donham and W. James, eds. Pp. 175–
        195. Cambridge: Cambridge University Press.
Mackenzie, P.Z. and Simpson, R.M.
1953 and 1971   The African Veterinary Handbook. London: Pitman.
Messing, Simon D.
1985    Highland Plateau Amhara of Ethiopia. New Haven, Conn: Human Relations
        Area Files Flex Books.
Nekby, Bengt.
1971    CADU: An Ethiopian Experiment in Developing Peasant Farming. Stock-
        holm: Prisma.
Pankhurst, Richard.
1968    Economic History of Ethiopia 1800–1935. Addis Ababa: Haile Selassie
        University Press.
1976    The Beginnings of Oromo Studies in Europe. Africa. XXXI(2):171–206.

Pratt, D.J. and Gwynne, M.D.
    1976    Rangeland Management and Ecology in East Africa. London: Hodder and Stoughton.

Ryder, M.L.
    1983    Sheep and Man. London: Duckworth.

Sato, Shun.
    1980    Pastoral Movements and the Subsistence Unit of the Rendille of Northern Kenya: With Special Reference to Camel Ecology. Senri Ethnological Studies 6:1–78.

Shack, William A.
    1966    The Gurage: A people of the Ensete Culture. London: Oxford University Press for International African Institute.

Sheriff, Abdul.
    1987    Slaves, Spices and Ivory in Zanzibar: Integration of an East African Commercial Empire into the World Economy, 1770–1873. London and Dar es Salaam, Tanzania: James Curry and Tanzania Publishing House.

Smeds, E.
    1955    The Ensete Planting Cultures of Eastern Sidamo, Ethiopia. Acta Geographica. XIII(4):1–39.

Tutschek, Charles.
    1844 and 1845    Dictionary of the Galla Language. unpublished manuscript.

Venturino, Bartolomeo.
    1973    Dizionario Borana-Italiano. Bologna, Italy: Editrica Missionaria Italiana.

# 17

## Patterns of Domestic Energy Utilization in Rural Kenya: An Agro-Ecological and Socioeconomic Assessment

*Patrick C. Fleuret*

This article focuses on domestic energy consumption in the Taita Hills, a rural agricultural area in southeastern Kenya. After presenting necessary background information on the research setting, income generation strategies, social organization, and the study communities, the article turns to three main questions: what are the main uses for and sources of domestic energy in Taita? What are rates of consumption, and how have people responded to scarcity? And finally, how do features of economic and social organization condition patterns of domestic energy consumption? A concluding section summarizes implications for policy and planning, and addresses as well some broader questions about the methodology and objectives of applied anthropology.

In adopting this approach, the article reflects some central themes in David Brokensha's approach to the anthropology of development. The main problem is one of rural resource management, a practical but vital dimension of life in rural Africa. The analysis builds on an assessment of people's behavior and perceptions, with an underlying recognition that much can be understood by viewing these within a broadly ecological frame of reference. Concepts and methodologies are straightforward but eclectic, meant to illuminate rather than overshadow empirical relationships. The most important relationships are revealed through multiple comparisons—across communities, agro-ecological zones, and socioeconomic strata—and some of the most significant relationships cannot be understood without addressing the sources and distribution of inequality within and among communities. Finally, the conclusions speak to two audiences: development planners and anthropologists. The former need to be reminded that rural problems are multiplex, and that in spite of this (or perhaps because of it?) the solutions that people find themselves are often the best. And the latter cannot forget that the ultimate value of their work is measured, at least partly, by the contribution it may make to policies and programs of rural development.

## Setting

The Taita people live in Taita-Taveta District, Coast Province, Kenya. The district's largest town, Voi, is located about 150 kilometers inland from the Indian Ocean along the main road connecting Kenya's capital city of Nairobi with the principal seaport of Mombasa. Most of the population of the district is located in the Taita Hills, an isolated cluster of hills surrounded by arid and largely unpopulated plains. Population densities in farming areas in the hills exceed 200 persons per square kilometer in places, as against two persons per square kilometer in the plains, or even less.

Only the foothills and plains immediately adjacent to the hills support a significant human population, and most of these are Taita who have migrated permanently to the lowlands within the last 30 years as a consequence of growing population densities and increasing competition for land within the hills.

From the surrounding plain, which lies at an altitude of about 300 meters, the Taita Hills rise to a maximum elevation of 2150 meters, with the majority of the population living in areas between 700 and 1700 meters above sea level. This is the most productive zone, favored in terms of soils, rainfall, and temperature; additionally, people located there are relatively well-placed to exploit the more specialized agricultural environments found in the higher elevations as well as the plains.

## Income Generation

In all zones the Taita agricultural cycle is oriented around the cultivation of the primary staple foods, maize and beans. Coffee and so-called European vegetables (such as tomatoes, cabbage, and lettuce) are widely grown in the higher elevations to earn cash. Agricultural cash-earning opportunities in the less-favored plains are fewer and less remunerative; the main crops are chilies, castor, honey, and cotton. The precise assortment of crops grown in the fields of any one household during a particular growing season is extremely variable, depending on family needs and inclinations, the amount of labor available (either within the household or hired externally), soils, drainage, availability of groundwater or irrigation water, exposure to sun and wind, presence or absence of trees, and the seasonal and locational vagaries of precipitation (see also A. Harris 1972; Nazzaro 1974).

Livestock holdings are also extremely variable across communities, households, and years. There is a rough association between the expense and risk of livestock ownership and their distribution. Labor constraints, seasonal shortages of grazing land, and the cash needs of young and growing families prevent many from maintaining large herds; in addition, well-educated and salaried men have alternative investment strategies.

Besides agriculture and livestock, wage employment constitutes an important third element in household income generation strategies. Options for wage employment among men and women are as diverse as options for crop production, varying widely in skills required, location, and remuneration. The income earned makes an extremely important contribution to household well-being through investment in children's education, household amenities, land, agricultural labor, and livestock.

Agriculture, livestock, and wage employment are the three main elements in Taita income generation strategies. As individuals, Taita pursue specific mixes of these that differ depending on needs, inclinations, skills, and opportunities; and the mix changes seasonally and over time. Throughout, women are principally active in agriculture and in managing small stock, while men are principally active in wage employment and in managing cattle. The result is that the array of income streams flowing into a household at any one time may be quite diverse, and is subject to significant variations over time.

## Social Organization

Taita social organization has been previously outlined by Prins (1952), Harris and Harris (1964), G. Harris (1962, 1978), Fleuret (1985), Maranga and Mathu (1986), and Mathu and Akotsi (1986). Social organization assumes significance at two distinct levels. The structural and ideational aspects of social organization at the community or supra-household level have some influence on access to and management of critical resources such as land, water, livestock, and labor. It is important to note, however, that the management and ownership of agricultural plots and other resources, particularly livestock, has been vested in individual men since at least the turn of the century. Indeed, the economic and jural independence of nuclear family households is a distinctive feature of Taita social organization. Within households, the organization of roles, responsibilities, and expectations among men, women, and children influence the application of individual and household resources in pursuit of an array of objectives which are often but not necessarily shared by all members of the household.

In the material following it will be seen that variations in agro-ecological location, material wealth, and household organization all have an influence on patterns of household domestic energy consumption.

## Research Communities

The data presented in this paper were collected during 1981–1982 in four contrasting communities. Three of these are agricultural communities. Msidunyi is located in a long-settled core area where population densities are high, soils are exhausted, and rates of migrant labor and out-migration are high. Commercial production is a relatively minor component of household income. Iparenyi is in a recently-settled area of higher agricultural potential, and commercial production of coffee and vegetables contributes significantly to household income. Bondeni is a newly settled plains area with marginal rainfall. Farm production is almost entirely for subsistence, although the area has received development assistance in cotton, legume and grain pro-

Table 17.1 - Sources of Domestic Energy in Four Taita Communities

| Purpose | Msidunyi | | Bondeni | | Iparenyi | | Mkonge | |
|---------|----------|------|---------|------|----------|------|--------|------|
| Source | # | (%) | # | (%) | # | (%) | # | (%) |
| **Cook Food:** | | | | | | | | |
| Firewood | 63 | (98) | 56 | (95) | 66 | (100) | 52 | (80) |
| Kerosene | 2 | (3) | 3 | (5) | 0 | (0) | 0 | (0) |
| Charcoal | 0 | (0) | 14 | (24) | 1 | (2) | 15 | (23) |
| Maize Cobs | 64 | (100) | 28 | (47) | 48 | (73) | 0 | (0) |
| Other | 0 | (0) | 0 | (0) | 46 | (70) | 16 | (25) |
| **Prepare Tea:** | | | | | | | | |
| Firewood | 63 | (98) | 55 | (93) | 66 | (100) | 48 | (74) |
| Kerosene | 7 | (11) | 4 | (7) | 0 | (0) | 0 | (0) |
| Charcoal | 0 | (0) | 12 | (20) | 0 | (0) | 12 | (18) |
| Maize Cobs | 63 | (98) | 21 | (36) | 33 | (50) | 0 | (0) |
| Other | 0 | (0) | 0 | (0) | 29 | (44) | 20 | (31) |
| **Heat Bathwater:** | | | | | | | | |
| Firewood | 64 | (100) | 57 | (97) | 64 | (97) | 51 | (78) |
| Charcoal | 0 | (0) | 7 | (12) | 0 | (0) | 13 | (20) |
| Maize Cobs | 64 | (100) | 4 | (7) | 41 | (62) | 0 | (0) |
| Other | 0 | (0) | 0 | (0) | 31 | (47) | 17 | (26) |
| **Warmth at Night:** | | | | | | | | |
| Firewood | 64 | (100) | 54 | (92) | 66 | (100) | 45 | (69) |
| Charcoal | 0 | (0) | 9 | (15) | 0 | (0) | 20 | (31) |
| Maize Cobs | 63 | (98) | 2 | (3) | 39 | (59) | 0 | (0) |
| Other | 0 | (0) | 0 | (0) | 39 | (59) | 18 | (28) |
| **Light for Reading:** | | | | | | | | |
| Koroboi | 59 | (92) | 32 | (54) | 27 | (41) | 49 | (75) |
| Wick Lamp | 44 | (69) | 46 | (78) | 48 | (73) | 16 | (25) |
| Pressure Lamp | 1 | (2) | 1 | (2) | 1 | (2) | 1 | (2) |

duction. The fourth community is Mkonge Estate, a labor camp on a major sisal estate, inhabited by landless and impoverished agricultural laborers who work for wages and have little or no opportunity to produce for their own consumption.

## Uses and Sources of Domestic Energy

The main uses of domestic energy include preparation of morning tea, preparation of the main meal, warmth at night, heating of bathwater, and light for conversation and reading in the evening. Table 17.1 summarizes the results of a survey of 255 households which reveals the frequency with which different fuels are used in four contrasting Taita communities.

### Food Preparation

In the agricultural communities, firewood is used almost universally as the main fuel for food preparation because it is relatively inexpensive and provides a slow, even heat. But there are important variations seasonally. At the time this survey was conducted, maize was being harvested, and so maize cobs appear as an important source of fuel. Iparenyi households also burned significant quantities of dried maize stalks (reflected in the "Other" category); these are usually fed to cattle in Msidunyi, where alternative fodders are scarce, but in Iparenyi there is a relative abundance of good grazing land still available. Workers at Mkonge find firewood procurement a difficult task due to their labor obligations and local scarcity, so they use this fuel less frequently than people in the agricultural communities. They compensate by burning sisal stalks, which make a poor fuel but are freely available. Both plains communities—Bondeni and Mkonge—use charcoal for food preparation, but for different reasons. Many Bondeni households earn extra cash by preparing and selling charcoal in the bush (an activity which is officially proscribed), and so they have ready access to this fuel. Many sisal estate households use charcoal simply because it is available in local shops and convenient. A few households occasionally use kerosene for cooking food, which is an extravagance.

### Tea Preparation

Patterns of energy use in tea preparation closely parallel the patterns associated with food preparation, although a few more households use kerosene. It is easier and quicker to heat tea with a kerosene stove than with firewood, although few households can afford the expense. In comparison to food preparation, rather fewer households use maize cobs and other crop residues to prepare tea because these materials are neither easy to set alight nor particularly hot-burning.

### Bathwater, Warmth at Night

Patterns of energy use for these purposes are exactly alike. Firewood and crop residues predominate, although charcoal is used where it is available. Very few Bondeni households use maize cobs for these purposes in comparison to the highland agricultural communities, which reflects relative availability— people in Bondeni harvest lesser quantities of maize and the cobs are fully utilized in cooking. Moreover, nights in the plains are warmer than in the hill communities.

### Illumination

Pressure lamps provide the best light and consume kerosene most efficiently, but are relatively expensive, so few households in any community can use them. Commercial hurricane wick lamps are far less expensive and provide acceptable light, so they are used by a large number of households in all communities. Tiny *korobois*, which are locally-made lamps with a soldered metal base and an unenclosed fabric wick, are very inexpensive but produce an inefficient, smoky flame that offers weak illumination. Exclusive use of a *koroboi* is the mark of a poor household.

Table 17.2 - Perceptions of Difficulty in Collecting Firewood in
Four Taita Communities

| Collecting Firewood is: | Msidunyi | | Bondeni | | Iparenyi | | Mkonge | |
|---|---|---|---|---|---|---|---|---|
| | # | % | # | % | # | % | # | % |
| Hard Work: | 61 | (95) | 46 | (78) | 62 | (94) | 63 | (97) |
| Easy Work: | 2 | ( 3) | 4 | ( 7) | 3 | ( 5) | 0 | ( 0) |
| No Response: | 1 | ( 2) | 9 | (15) | 1 | ( 2) | 2 | ( 3) |
| Total: | 65 | (100) | 59 | (100) | 66 | (101) | 65 | (100) |

Table 17.3 - Variation in Frequency of Daily Cooking Fires in
Four Taita Communities

| | Msidunyi | Bondeni | Iparenyi | Mkonge |
|---|---|---|---|---|
| Average Number of Daily Fires: | 2.5 | 3.3 | 3.0 | 3.0 |

## Firewood Scarcity: Perception and Response

Firewood remains the fuel of choice, because it is relatively inexpensive and relatively well-suited to most purposes. But growing populations in the Taita Hills engender ever-greater pressure on this limited resource. To assess the effects of scarcity, the survey collected several types of complementary information which are summarized below.

### Difficulty of Collection

Women in each community were asked to comment on the difficulty of firewood collection. This obviously subjective assessment varied across communities in a revealing pattern, as illustrated in Table 17.2.

Most women in all communities view firewood collection as hard work, not a surprising result. But far fewer are concerned about the work of firewood collection in Bondeni, which is in the bushy plains where firewood is easy to gather. This relative unconcern with firewood is also reflected in the comparatively large number of women in Bondeni who felt the question deserved no answer at all.

### Effect on Food Preparation

The relative difficulty of collecting firewood should be reflected in patterns of utilization. One clear result of scarcity, as shown in Table 17.3, is that fewer cooking fires are built.

Table 17.4 - Perceptions of Change in the Availability of
Firewood in Four Taita Communities

| Collecting Firewood is: | Msidunyi # | % | Bondeni # | % | Iparenyi # | % | Mkonge # | % |
|---|---|---|---|---|---|---|---|---|
| Now Harder: | 60 | (94) | 51 | (88) | 46 | (70) | 65 | (100) |
| Now Easier: | 0 | ( 0) | 5 | ( 9) | 8 | (12) | 0 | ( 0) |
| The Same: | 4 | ( 6) | 2 | ( 3) | 12 | (18) | 0 | ( 0) |
| Total: | 64 | (100) | 58 | (100) | 66 | (101) | 65 | (100) |

Table 17.5 - Variation in Frequency of Tree Planting in Four
Taita Communities

| | Msidunyi # % | Bondeni # % | Iparenyi # % | Mkonge # % |
|---|---|---|---|---|
| Households Planting Trees: | 56 (88) | 32 (54) | 39 (59) | 8 (12) |

In Bondeni, where firewood collection is generally not thought a problem, women light fires more often than elsewhere. In Msidunyi, where firewood is a severe problem, fires are built less frequently than in the other communities, and far less frequently than in Bondeni. Most often people forego the evening fire, choosing instead to eat cold leftovers from earlier in the day.

### Perceptions of Change

Apart from the absolute difficulty of firewood collection, it is necessary to know something about perceptions of change in firewood availability, since relative perceptions are often an important influence on behavior. The same women in each community were asked to compare the task of firewood collection in the present and past (see Table 17.4).

All women on the sisal estate thought firewood collection has become more burdensome, which reflects both genuine scarcity and an absence of low-cost alternatives. The majority of women in the agricultural communities also felt firewood collection is now more difficult, but the proportion was highest by far in Msidunyi. This perception of changing availability has had a clear effect on behavior, as illustrated below.

### Tree Planting

Households in all four communities had planted trees. Planted trees are used for a multiplicity of purposes, including firewood, charcoal, fruit, fodder, and building materials (principally poles). As Table 17.5 shows, there were

Table 17.6 - Sources of Firewood in Four Taita Communities

| Source: | Msidunyi # | Msidunyi % | Bondeni # | Bondeni % | Iparenyi # | Iparenyi % | Mkonge # | Mkonge % |
|---|---|---|---|---|---|---|---|---|
| Bush | 61 | (95) | 52 | (88) | 50 | (76) | 49 | (75) |
| Farm | 62 | (97) | 5 | ( 8) | 35 | (53) | 3 | ( 5) |
| Purchase | 5 | ( 8) | 2 | ( 3) | 26 | (39) | 22 | (34) |

important variations among the four communities in the frequency with which trees had been planted by individual households.

Far more Msidunyi households have planted trees than in the other communities, a reflection of both absolute and relative scarcity. Only a handful of Mkonge households have planted trees; usually these are leafy trees which provide shade for people and fodder for domestic goats. No sisal estate dweller has any right to the land occupied, which is a disincentive to investment in trees.

*Sources of Firewood*

Patterns of relative scarcity, together with differential patterns of tree-planting, are responsible for further variation in how and where people obtain firewood (see Table 17.6). A very large number of Msidunyi households obtain firewood from their own farm plots, which reflects the higher frequency of tree-planting in that community. Firewood is also frequently obtained from farms in Iparenyi, where tree-planting is relatively common—a response to profligate land clearance in the decades of initial settlement. By contrast, firewood purchasing is comparatively common in both Iparenyi and Mkonge, but for different reasons. In Iparenyi, which is a prosperous agricultural community, many women choose to purchase firewood to save themselves an arduous task. The people who provide firewood are women from poor households who have few and inadequate sources of cash income. In Mkonge, women purchase firewood—which is brought there on trucks by traders—primarily because it is cheaper than other fuels; great scarcity in the vicinity of the estate makes this option relatively attractive. A few people (local Taita) have access to farm plots and can gather a little firewood there; others harvest firewood illegally wherever they find it.

In the three agricultural communities, where people usually collect their own firewood, the survey recorded the local names of the trees and woody shrubs that were actually being used as fuel at the time of the survey. In each community about two dozen different trees and shrubs were found in the homes. Also recorded were the names of preferred trees and shrubs. Not surprisingly, there was often a difference between the fuel sources people preferred to use and those that were actually in their homes. In Msidunyi, fully 68 percent of the households were utilizing non-preferred fuels, as against 58 percent in Bondeni and 50 percent in Iparenyi. It seems clear that relative scarcity constrains people to use less desirable fuels, which may be difficult to harvest, smoky, smelly, or quick-burning.

## Rates of Consumption

Energy consumption rates were measured for a small sub-sample of households, selected to represent variation in size, wealth, and location. Four energy sources were investigated: firewood, charcoal, kerosene, and maize cobs. At the beginning of the one-week survey period, the quantity of each fuel present in the households was measured (firewood, charcoal, and cobs in kilograms, kerosene in liters). Each day during the survey period, research assistants visited each household to measure the additional quantities of fuel brought there that day. At the close of the survey, fuel stocks remaining in the household were measured. In terms of consumption per day or per capita, use of charcoal and kerosene was extremely low, and the results are not considered here. Use of maize cobs was somewhat higher, but in overall terms did not deviate from patterns of consumption of firewood. Firewood was by far the most important fuel consumed in quantitative terms. Figure 17.1 illustrates rates of firewood consumption among the sample households.

Daily firewood consumption averaged between 5 and 16 kilograms per household. In general, larger household sizes are associated with greater consumption, but this really only pertains to households with over seven or eight members. Thus there is a threshold effect in firewood consumption. Small- to mid-size households use about the same amount of firewood, implying that it takes nearly as much energy to cook for and heat three or four people as it does to provide for the needs of seven or eight people. Larger households however require more fuel.

Per capita firewood consumption averaged between 1.0 and 4.5 kilograms during the one-week survey period. Per capita consumption is inversely related to household size, implying that there are efficiencies associated with cooking for—and warming—larger numbers of people. From the perspective of the women involved, belonging to a large household is efficient in another sense, for this means the chore of firewood collection can very likely be shared among several grown or adolescent women.

## Effects of Economic Variation

In Taita as elsewhere in East Africa there is a great deal of variation in relative wealth among households in rural farming communities. This is caused chiefly by variation in employment opportunities, and to some extent as well by access to rewarding cash crops. Relative wealth also plays a role in patterns of domestic energy consumption. Greater wealth brings greater convenience, in that people may use fuels other than firewood, and they may also escape from the drudgery of firewood collection. To illustrate, Table 17.7 shows how differences in wealth accompany differences in patterns of domestic energy utilization. During the period of research, relative household wealth was measured by two independent indices: one based on possession

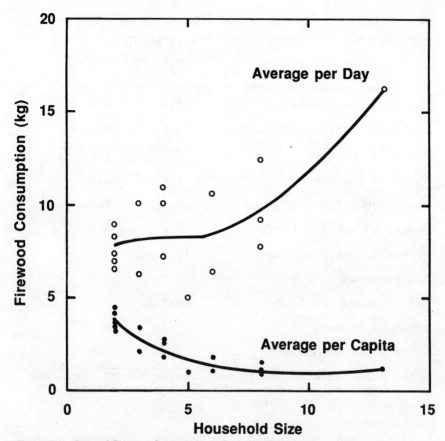

Figure 17.1 – Rates of Firewood Consumption in Taita Households

of consumer durables, and one based on details of house construction. Both indices have proven useful in the East African context (cf. Castro, Hakansson, and Brokensha 1981). Both yielded similar results in this analysis, so only the data based on the house construction index are presented here.[1]

This table shows clearly that households with greater wealth have access to a broader array of energy sources, to more efficient energy sources, and to more convenient energy sources. Rural energy scarcity hits first and hardest at poor households, who have the fewest alternative sources available to them. Similarly, most conceivable domestic energy innovations will be more accessible to the wealthy.

## Effects of Social Organization

We have already seen that household size has an important influence on rates of domestic energy consumption. Other more subtle features of household

Table 17.7 - Household Wealth and Energy Utilization

| | Mean Score House Construction Index | |
|---|---|---|
| | YES | NO |
| Use kerosene for tea? | 9.4 | 4.6 |
| Use kerosene for food? | 8.4 | 4.8 |
| Use cobs for tea? | 5.5 | 4.2 |
| Use cobs for food? | 5.4 | 3.6 |
| Use koroboi for light? | 3.8 | 6.6 |
| Use wick lamp for light? | 5.9 | 2.6 |
| Pressure lamp for light? | 11.0 | 4.8 |
| Get firewood from bush? | 4.7 | 6.8 |
| Get firewood from farm? | 5.7 | 4.0 |
| Purchase firewood? | 7.9 | 4.3 |
| Plant trees for fodder? | 6.4 | 4.5 |

Note: A higher score indicates greater wealth. Analysis of variance showed each of the differences listed here to be significant (P <.05)

organization also influence patterns of domestic energy utilization. Three aspects of household organization are considered below: the family development cycle, structural linkages to other households, and marital status.

*Family Development Cycle*

In Taita it is relatively easy to distinguish three stages in the family development cycle: young families, with resident children aged 12 years or younger; established families, whose children are older than 12 as well as younger; and mature families, with few resident children. These family stages are associated with several aspects of energy utilization, as illustrated in Table 17.8.

Older, mature families are content to let firelight serve for illumination; these days, the children of younger families need better sources of light for school work and social meetings. Only younger families use flashlights to any great degree, this being a relatively recent innovation that is looked upon with some disdain by older people. As families grow older, the likelihood increases that they will have planted trees on their farm plots; and as the

Table 17.8 - Family Stages and Aspects of Domestic Energy
Utilization

| Energy Utilization | Percent of Households* | | |
| --- | --- | --- | --- |
| | Young | Established | Mature |
| Use firelight for light: | 14 | 12 | 31 |
| Use flashlights: | 14 | 3 | 3 |
| Get firewood from farm: | 42 | 49 | 67 |
| Have planted trees: | 56 | 64 | 78 |
| Planted fodder trees: | 17 | 34 | 14 |

\* Each of these proportions is derived from raw counts that
were assessed by means of chi square tests and which proved
significant (p <.05).

trees mature, they are increasingly likely to provide a source of firewood.
Hence mature households are most likely to have planted trees and get
firewood from their farms, and young families are least likely to do so.
Fodder trees, by contrast, are planted mainly by established families. Younger
families have not had the opportunity to accumulate the herds of livestock
that make fodder trees desirable, while mature households have assigned
most their animals to younger political clients and potential heirs, and have
no great need for supplementary sources of fodder.

## Household Linkages and Marital Status

Most Taita households are nuclear households, physically separate from
the nearby residences of kinsfolk and neighbors. In some of these households
the household head is a man, physically present. In others the household
head is a woman, and her husband is absent working. In either case physical
separation is mirrored in economic independence. Some Taita households
are merged with the family of the household head's mother; this matrilateral
extension happens most frequently when the head of household is a woman
who has never been married, but it also happens sometimes when a woman
has been divorced and very occasionally when she has been widowed. Other
Taita households are merged with the family of the household head's father.
This patrilateral extension happens often when a male household head is
absent working but has not set up an independent household, but may be
observed under other circumstances as well. Whether these extended households are linked through the mother's family or the father's family, there is
a parallel merging of economic resources. These patterns of association have
some implications for patterns of domestic energy use, as illustrated in Table
17.9.

The extended households—whether matrilateral or patrilateral—have access
to a broader and more convenient range of energy sources than do the
independent households. This results from several related factors. First,
extended households generally have greater adult labor availability than

Table 17.9 - Household Linkages and Marital Status in Relation
to Domestic Energy Utilization

| | Percent of Households* | | |
|---|---|---|---|
| | Independent Households | Extended Households Matrilateral | Patrilateral |
| Use residues for tea: | 13 | 30 | 36 |
| Use koroboi for light: | 65 | 50 | 27 |
| Use wick lamp for light: | 67 | 90 | 91 |

* Each of these proportions is derived from raw counts that were
assessed by means of chi square tests and which proved significant
(p <.05).

independent households; maize production in particular is eased, leading to
a greater availability of maize residues. Moreover, the general absence of a
mature, active male in either type of extended household implies that livestock
holdings will be minimal; consequently, crop residues can be burned as fuel
that would otherwise be provided to animals as fodder. Second, extended
households often have greater cash availability than independent households.
In the case of patrilateral extended households, this is because the absentee
wage-earner usually sends substantial sums of money home at regular intervals.
In the case of matrilateral extended households, this is because the unmarried
female head of household is usually engaged in some non-subsistence activity
(vegetable production, nursery-school teaching, letter-writing, carrying water
and firewood for wealthier households) that brings in extra cash. Moreover,
the absence of a young or middle-aged adult male in these households reduces
the drain on household resources associated with drinking, idiosyncratic
purchases of personal accouterments, and the like. This frees up resources
for the purchase of many household conveniences, including wick lamps and
kerosene.

## Conclusions

From a practical or policy perspective, the material presented here sheds
light on several aspects of rural energy consumption that tend to be overlooked.
First, there is a great deal of variability in patterns of domestic energy
utilization. This variability has a seasonal component, an agro-ecological
component, an economic component, and a social organizational component.
The result is that the severity of the problem of provisioning households
with domestic energy is unevenly distributed across rural society, a fact
which needs to be reflected in planned programs of economic development.
Planned solutions tend to offer monolithic, "optimal" solutions to problems
that are multi-faceted, and which will admit no single, best resolution for
all involved. Second, Taita villagers themselves are working out suitable
responses to rural energy shortage, largely by investing in multi-purpose
trees. This is an affordable, technologically-appropriate approach that combines

simplicity with flexibility; moreover, the risk of loss is low, and the potential benefit substantial. Most planned schemes of development—and those dealing with alternative energy solutions in particular—must unfortunately be described in just the opposite terms. In the realm of rural energy, as in many others, outside experts could learn much simply by taking a close look at what people are doing on their own.

From the perspective of applied anthropology, this essay offers a number of lessons. First, the research design is comparative across contrasting communities, and many interesting findings would not have come to light had the approach been otherwise. But in anthropology generally, statements lauding the comparative approach are far easier to find than research efforts employing it. Apart from providing a rich source of empirical variation, comparison strengthens one's position when faced by doubtful "experts", and lends analytic rigor to explanations by taking into account many location-specific factors. Second, the research design incorporates perspectives derived from what anthropologists call participant observation, as well as the quantitative results of a fairly large survey. There are obvious complementarities here, which again are honored too often in the breach. Applied anthropologists in particular are frequently guilty of pursuing one approach to the exclusion of the other, which weakens their individual contributions at the same time as it stifles the development of the sub-discipline. Third, the analytic approach used here makes use of modest probability-based statistical techniques which allow one to demonstrate that one's anthropological findings—in all likelihood—have an empirical foundation. This too is an advantage in circumstances where the logical beauty of anthropological inference may be unappreciated. Finally, the analysis strives to be holistic, by treating people's perceptions as well as their behavior, and by assessing economic, agro-ecological, and social organizational aspects of community life. No great sophistication is reached in any of these areas of analysis, but the overall argument is nevertheless strengthened through overlapping and complementary conclusions. Too many applied anthropologists weaken their observations by offering exquisite analyses that are as narrowly based as those prepared by any technical specialist.

## Acknowledgments

This research was done as part of a broader research program assessing the agricultural and socioeconomic causes of variation in child nutrition in Taita-Taveta District during the period 1981–1985. Financial support was provided by the U.S. National Institutes of Health. Institutional support was provided by the Social Process Research Institute (University of California, Santa Barbara) and the Population Studies Research Institute (University of Nairobi). The assistance of these organizations is gratefully acknowledged.

## Notes

1. House construction scores ranged from 1 to 20, and the overall mean was 4.9. The base (zero score) for the scoring system is considered to be a three-room house

with wattle-daub walls, a thatched roof, no wooden or glass windows, and an earth floor. A typical three-point house might possess several wooden windows. A typical six-point house might possess as well a partial or complete roof of zinc-plated corrugated iron sheets. A typical nine-point house might have in addition a partially-cemented floor or plastered interior walls.

# References Cited

Castro, Alfonso P., Thomas Hakansson, and David Brokensha.
1981    Indicators of Rural Inequality. World Development. 9(5):401–427.

Fleuret, Patrick.
1985    The Social Organization of Water Control in the Taita Hills, Kenya. American Ethnologist. 12(1):103–118.

Harris, Alfred.
1972    Some Aspects of Agriculture in Taita. *In* Population Growth: Some Anthropological Implications. Brian Spooner, ed. Pp. 180–189. Cambridge, MA: Massachusetts Institute of Technology Press.

Harris, Grace.
1962    Taita Bridewealth and Affinal Relationships. *In* Marriage in Tribal Societies. M. Fortes, ed. Pp. 55–87. Cambridge: Cambridge University Press.
1978    Casting Out Anger. Cambridge: Cambridge University Press.

Harris, Alfred and Grace Harris.
1964    Property and the Cycle of Domestic Groups in Taita. *In* The Family Estate in Africa. R.F. Gray and P.H. Gulliver, eds. Pp. 117–154. Boston: Boston University Press.

Maranga, J. and G. Mathu.
1986    Social Customs. *In* Taita-Taveta District Socio-Cultural Profile. R. Soper, ed. Pp. 133–147. Nairobi: Ministry of Planning and National Development, and the Institute for African Studies, University of Nairobi.

Mathu, G. and M. Akotsi.
1986    Social Organization. *In* Taita-Taveta District Socio-Cultural Profile. R. Soper, ed. Pp. 148–153. Nairobi: Ministry of Planning and National Development, and the Institute for African Studies, University of Nairobi.

Nazzaro, Andrew.
1974    Changing Use of the Resource Base among the Taita of Kenya. unpublished PhD. dissertation. Department of Geography. Michigan State University.

Prins, A.H.J.
1952    The Coastal Tribes of the North-Eastern Bantu. London: International African Institute.

# 18

## Sacred Groves and Social Change in Kirinyaga, Kenya

### Peter Castro

This paper is inspired by two themes prominent in the work of David Brokensha. The first is the importance of religion in African social change. Brokensha's (1966) seminal study of Larteh, Ghana, showed how the introduction of Christianity profoundly influenced sociocultural changes associated with urbanization and colonialism. His recent works on Mbeere, Kenya, have described changes in the ritual uses of trees and plants (Riley and Brokensha 1988a; 1988b).

The second theme is the necessity of understanding community resource management systems. Brokensha has been a pioneer in identifying the development implications of indigenous technical knowledge (for example, see Brokensha et al. 1980). He has also written about the impact of economic inequality, colonialism, and national institutions and policies on local resource use, including common property regimes (Brokensha 1987a; 1987b; Riley and Brokensha 1988a; 1988b; Little and Brokensha 1987; Brokensha and Castro 1984, 1987; Castro and Brokensha 1987a; 1987b).

The present study examines changes in the perception and use of sacred groves among the Ndia and Gichugu Kikuyu of Kirinyaga District, Kenya. Its purpose is to analyze the linkages between religious conversion, wider processes of sociocultural change, and modifications in a particular form of common property resource regime. Sacred groves were once symbols of local cultural cohesion. Their decline in the twentieth century has been indicative of the socioeconomic divisions which have emerged in Kikuyu society. Although the paper focuses on Kirinyaga, some comparative information is included from other parts of central Kenya.

Sacred groves throughout the world have often been studied as ethnographic curiosities, rather than as a distinct and locally important common property resource. Fortunately, there is a growing appreciation, especially in Asia, of sacred groves and forests as valuable cultural and environmental resources (for example, see Gagdil and Vartak 1977; 1981a; 1981b; Messerschmidt 1986; Worjal 1985;). Sacred groves and forests not only serve as indigenous nature reserves, they also have deep cultural and historical meanings for the local society. However, as the present case study has shown, the groves, like other forms of common property resources (see Oakerson 1986), are subject to drastic changes in tenure and use.

## Sacred Groves as Symbols of Precolonial Unity

Kirinyaga is located on the southern slopes of Mount Kenya (see Castro 1987, for a detailed account of the district). This generally fertile district is the homeland of the Ndia and Gichugu Kikuyu. In precolonial times they were similar to other acephalous farming and herding peoples of central Kenya (Middleton and Kershaw 1965; Ambler 1988). Their traditional social organization centered around kinship and neighborhood groups, with age- and generation-sets being significant local sodalities.

The Kikuyu customarily used selected groves, scattered throughout the countryside, as places of neighborhood worship and sacrifice (Routledge and Routledge 1910; Beech 1913a; 1913b; Hobley 1967; Kenyatta 1938; Leakey 1977a; Middleton and Kershaw 1965). In Kirinyaga, H. S. K. Mwaniki (1974:258–59, 282) was told, "Every ridge had at least one of these groves", and, "Every locality had a sacred grove, like a church, for . . . sacrifices". Indeed, the extent of local or neighborhood identity was almost defined by shared worship at a particular grove. Around 200 sacred groves were recorded in Kirinyaga during early the 1930s (EPRB n.d.: "List of Sacred Groves").

Renowned "medicine men" or "prophets" had particular sacred groves associated with them, though no exclusive ownership was apparently implied (Hobley 1967:40). For the most part, the sacred groves constituted a form of collective property. Some groves were managed by the elders of particular descent groups, since the trees were located on their holdings. In many cases the groves were under the control of the elders from the "ruling" moiety or generation set. It needs to be emphasized that descent groups and generation sets were not entirely distinct entities, since there was considerable overlap in personnel (Castro 1987).

The sacred trees were centers of public ritual during rites for influencing rainfall, sacrifices to stop epidemics, prayers of thanksgiving, dances, and other situations involving the entire community. An elder from Nduini in Inoi, Ndia, recalled a ceremony:

> Irungu [name of generation set] . . . met when there was no rain. They offered a sheep or goat as sacrifice. When they completed the slaughtering, rain would automatically fall. The slaughtered goat was eaten by Irungu, not taken home. If they were unable to finish it, they burnt it to ashes.

Rites of passage ceremonies—for circumcision and elderhood—also took place in the groves (EPRB n.d.: "List of Sacred Groves"; NTTC, DC, South Nyeri, Jan. 1926, "Itwika Goats"). These rites were very important for neighborhoods because they cut across descent group ties (Lambert 1956). The age-grade ceremonies were spaced every few years. Less frequent was the ceremonial transfer of power from one generation set to another. This happened once every generation—roughly every 30 years or so (Castro 1987). This event was held in each locality's own sacred grove, but celebrations were coordinated from ridge to ridge in Ndia and Gichugu (Mwaniki 1974:280).

The groves were often located on hilltops and ridges, and they varied in size and composition. Colin Maher (1938:153) observed in Kirinyaga during the late 1930s that groves ranged from "a tenth of an acre to two or three acres". They frequently consisted of several tall trees with spreading branches, plus an understorey of smaller trees, woody shrubs, and bush. The Kikuyu preferred "huge trees" because they resembled the abode of Ngai [God] (Kenyatta 1962:227). Some of the "giant" trees were more than 30 meters high. A single tree within a grove often formed the focal point of ceremonies. Large wild figs with spreading branches were the sacred tree par excellence: *Ficus natalensis* (*mugumo*), and to a lesser extent, *Ficus walkfieldii* (*muumbo*) in moist northern and central Kirinyaga; and *Ficus capensis* (*mukuyu*) in the drier southern lowlands. However, not every fig tree was sacred, nor were figs always found in the groves (see Maher 1938:153).

Louis S. B. Leakey (1977b:1084–89) wrote that each generation-set in southern Kikuyu established its own sacred trees. However, it appeared that sacred groves in Kirinyaga were usually inherited from one generation to the next (Mwaniki 1974:282). Except for taking cuttings to propagate new sacred trees, most groves were inviolable. Any clearing or cutting was regarded as, ". . . sacrilege and treated as a serious anti-social act requiring expiation" (Lambert 1950:21fn.). Elders in present-day Ndia confirmed the sanctions against disturbing the groves: "No one was to disturb a grove", and, "The leaf could not be picked from such a tree". Drought, epidemics, and other calamities were frequently attributed to illicit cutting (Saberwal 1970). A person who encroached on a sacred grove had to pay a goat to the generational elders, plus face the wrath of neighbors and kinsmen.

Some of contemporary Kirinyaga's most beautiful trees owe their survival to their reputation as shrines and ceremonial sites. For example, along the Gakoigo-Ithareni road in Nduini, Inoi, is a small grove dominated by a tall *mururi* (*Trichilia emetica*) tree with a thick bole. People said it used to be surrounded by "lots of bush", but nowadays the tree has a thin understorey of *mukindu* (*Phoenix reclinata*) and woody shrubs. Over the years maize has been planted closer and closer to the *mururi*. An elderly resident of that area recalled the tree's colorful history:

> Years ago Kikuyu warriors used to measure their strength by throwing clubs and spears over this tree. Then, some people, the old men called Irungu, saw it wise to pray to God here.

God is said to have spoken to the Kikuyu through a prophet who climbed the tree in precolonial times. Another elder from the area stated,

Githuku, a well-known seer, told people to come to the tree. After they gathered, he climbed the tree. Ngai [God] spoke through him, and he came down to say what he had been told. First, Ngai said people different from us [Kikuyus] would come, and they would have different skin color from us. Also, when the newcomers arrived, they would not stay a long time. If the people saw a place called Kiamucue being built with metal sheets, they would know the strangers were ready to return to their own country . . . [And] at the time when they would leave, the power of Irungu would be finished.

The old man who retold the prophecy claimed it had been accurate. For example, corrugated metal sheets appeared at Kiamucue around the time of the Mau Mau Emergency, while independence happened near the end of Irungu generation. Other accounts say that the prophets mentioned the coming of "an iron snake"—an obvious reference to the railway. For many people, the *mururi* tree was regarded as an important link with their precolonial past.

Jomo Kenyatta (1962:240), who later became President of Kenya, wrote that sacred groves were a "key institution"of Kikuyu culture, marking

. . . their unity as a people, their family integrity (for their fathers sacrificed around it), their close contact with the soil, the rain and the rest of Nature, and . . . their most vital communion with the High God. . . .

Perhaps the most important aspect of the sacred groves was their role as a focal point for the shared concerns of the local community—the loosely organized collection of families that were in daily interaction with one another. These people did not identify themselves as member of a "tribe" per se, but as neighbors who possessed common values and problems.

### Colonialism and Sociocultural Change

Kirinyaga was brought under colonial control in 1904, nearly a decade after Great Britain established the East Africa Protectorate. Colonialism undermined the indigenous sociocultural system which supported the sacred groves. Some groves in southern and western Kikuyuland were lost through land appropriation by the colonial administration and white settlers (Kenyatta 1962; Sorrenson 1968). In Kenyatta's (1962:240) Kiambu "neighborhood", for example, only one sacred tree survived on unalienated ground. The other trees were cleared by Europeans who claimed the land. Cuttings were reportedly taken from some sacred trees situated on land alienated by white settlers (Lambert 1950:22fn.). They were planted inside the Kikuyu country, providing some spiritual continuity for a people undergoing dislocation and forced socioeconomic change.

Relatively few sacred trees were lost through land appropriation in Kirinyaga. European land speculators and colonists had been denied access to the district (Castro 1987:85; 141–44). Nevertheless, the Ndia and Gichugu lost several ceremonial sites when the upper slopes and summit of Mount

Kenya were alienated in 1911 as a government forest reserve (Castro 1987:729–35). For the most part, the decline of sacred groves in Kirinyaga came about through subtle processes of political, cultural, and socioeconomic change.

The erosion of the generation-set system diminished the cultural significance of the sacred groves. The colonial government regarded customary Kikuyu political organization as too diffuse to be used for administrative purposes (Dundas 1915:239–49), and established a formal political hierarchy. Government-appointed chiefs, councilors, and other functionaries supplanted the traditional authority of the "ruling" moiety. Some matters, particularly matrimonial or domestic affairs, were allowed to remain under the control of the local generation set. Nevertheless, the scope and force of customary authority waned under colonial rule. By the 1930s, the influence of the "ruling" Irungu generation set was so weak that its representatives had to appeal to the Local Native Council, a colonial-created body, to enforce payment of traditional fees (ELNC 27–28 Nov. 1934:4; 3–4 May 1938:10).

Religious conversion, mainly to Christianity but also to Islam, reduced the ideological and popular basis of support for the groves. The Ndia and Gichugu became acquainted with Islam through caravan traders and wage labor migration to the coast (Stigand 1913:254; Orde-Browne 1925:206). An informant from Inoi, Ndia, recalled,

> When people went to the coast, some of them became Muslims. They came back here and influenced others [to convert to Islam]. Before there were only a few here, then their numbers increased.

Despite a spurt of conversions in the first years of colonial rule, Islam was soon overtaken by Christianity as the major source of religious change. The Church Missionary Society (CMS) established stations at Kabare, Gichugu, in 1910 and Mutira, Ndia, in 1912. Other Christian churches eventually sought converts in Kirinyaga, including the Roman Catholic Church and Salvation Army (KSAR 1933:15; EDAR 1934:14).

Religious conversion was gradually accompanied by a process of socio-cultural differentiation. Missionaries encouraged the Kikuyu to adopt a "package" of western culture. For example, the Church Missionary Society started the first schools and provided the first public health care in the southern Mount Kenya area (Crawford 1913). In addition, missionaries promoted many aspects of western material culture. Photographs taken by the Anglican missionaries who opened Embu mission in 1910 showed neophytes wearing khaki clothing. Photographs included in Father Cagnolo's (1933) account of Consolata Mission activities in Nyeri District showed Kikuyu children being taught to eat with plates and spoons while sitting at a table. The missionaries also fervently opposed indigenous customs which went against their moral values, especially infanticide, polygyny, bridewealth, and, eventually, clitoridectomy (Castro 1987). By the early 1920s, a distinct "mission" community, identifiable from "pagan elements", had emerged in Kirinyaga (KSAR 1928:19).

The sustained presence of missionaries, particularly at the CMS stations, was an important factor in the development of the Christian community. Except for brief periods, Kabare mission was operated by Rev. W. J. Rampley and family between 1918 and 1931 (EPRB 1945:182). Rampley and other missionaries not only provided spiritual guidance, but also influenced the political and social outlook of their neophytes. The Kabare congregation had nearly 2,000 members by 1928 (Rosberg and Nottingham 1970:120). The other missions and stations had smaller, though growing, followings. The schools run by the missions attracted people to the new religions. The Kikuyu increasingly valued formal education as a means for socioeconomic advancement in colonial society.

Religious conversion was also connected to political change. The missions, especially the CMS, were active in the new political institutions (KSAR 1931:6–7). Christian neophytes were represented in the local tribunal (*kiama*) and district council. Friction developed between "pagan and mission elements" in parts of the district, especially Ndia, and many local elections for council and tribunal posts were hotly contested (KSAR 1928:19; 1931:3).

Other related processes of socioeconomic change influenced events in Kirinyaga (see Castro 1987). The clearing of land increased in response to demographic pressures and the commercialization of agriculture. Much of the population growth derived from Kiambu and Nyeri Kikuyus who immigrated into the district. There was also tendency for land tenure to become individualized, though descent groups often resisted this change. Economic differentiation apparently became more pronounced, especially as some families started adopting western consumption patterns. Kikuyu "cultural nationalism" steadily developed as a local political force, with the anti-colonial Kikuyu Central Association establishing a branch in Ndia.

Thus, deep sociocultural fissions emerged among the people of Kirinyaga. They were no longer united by shared values and customs. A young man from Kerugoya succinctly summarized the impact of religious change:

> Before as Kikuyus we worshiped one God, Ngai, who stayed on Mount Kenya. Ngai united the people. Today, some say "Allah" or "God of Moses", and others worship idols . . . People do not share the same customs.

New forms of political organization had eroded traditional authority. Demographic and economic factors also contributed to the process of sociocultural differentiation. These profound changes would be reflected in the controversies that eventually engulfed the sacred groves.

## Challenges to the Groves

Although colonial administrators often viewed the sacred groves as ethnographic curiosities (Beech 1913a; 1913b; Dundas 1915; Lambert 1956), many missionaries considered them symbols of savagery and darkness. For example, Father C. Cagnolo (1933:27) of the Roman Catholic mission in Nyeri called the groves "temples of the Kikuyu paganism". He compared the sacrifices held in them to those carried out by "the Druids of Gallia". Some elderly Christians in Kirinyaga recalled being told by missionaries that the sacred groves were "bad" places.

The sacred groves eventually became targets for missionaries and neophytes attempting to root out "pagan superstitions". One of the first recorded challenges in southern Mount Kenya area took place in 1911. An Italian priest from the Consolata Roman Catholic Mission desecrated sacred groves in Nyeri (NDPR 1911, "The Work of Missions"). The district commissioner noted that the priest's activities were "unpopular" with local inhabitants. It was unclear from colonial records whether the priest had any Kikuyu accomplices. However, Father Cagnolo (1933:28), another Nyeri missionary, years later described some early neophytes, "who having long before rejected the old beliefs, dared to fell some of the [sacred] trees with the purpose of making good firewood". They reportedly, ". . . did not end the year alive, but paid dearly for their boldness".

Such assaults on the sacred groves apparently were not common in the first two decades of colonial rule. Early colonial records and other accounts suggested that the groves largely remained untouched. For example, Major G. Orde-Browne, an administrator in Embu between 1909 and 1916, recorded that people had "considerable respect" for the groves, ". . . no trees being felled and no one living within them".

The threat of such violence may have influenced some early converts to leave the sacred groves alone. But many neophytes apparently felt little need to tamper with such an important cultural symbol. Orde-Browne (1925:205–206) points out that conversions often were "nominal". Despite the introduction of the new religious beliefs and practices, many spheres of local social life continued to be guided by the "habit rationality" of precolonial society (c.f. Erasmus 1977:357; Castro 1987:284–301).

By the early 1920s, the sacred groves and the ceremonies associated with them again faced a challenged from Christians. This time the CMS led the campaign, with most of the controversy initially centered around the traditional handing-over ceremony (*ituika*) between the generational moieties. As was mentioned, the *ituika* ceremony was one of the most important rites held in the groves. The last transfer of power had taken place during the 1890s, prior to the onset of colonial rule. The ceremony was supposed to happen about every 30-plus years. The process was usually long and complex, involving "gifts" or payments of livestock and honey beer from the incoming moiety to the outgoing generation set. Ndia and Gichugu coordinated their ceremonies, beginning them in the lowlands and moving upward ridge by ridge (Dundas 1915; Mwaniki 1974:269). All families were expected to participate.

Officials in Nyeri, which then included Kirinyaga in the district, reported that preparations began for the transfer from Mwangi to Irungu moieties in 1912 (SNAR 1916:5–6). In parts of western and southern Kikuyuland colonial officials attempted to halt the ceremonies, regarding them as "seditious" (see Benson 1964; Kenyatta 1938:196–97). But administrators in southern Mount Kenya apparently did not try to interfere with the process.

In fact, district commissioners in South Nyeri and Embu strongly encouraged the Africans to carry out the traditional ceremony (see NTTC, South Nyeri DC, 4 July 1925; EDAR 1932:9–14; Lambert 1956:40–60; Saberwal 1970).

Controversy arose in the early 1920s when many CMS neophytes, particularly "mission boys" from Kirinyaga, refused to pay the customary *ituika* fee (NDPR 1922, "Extract from Minutes of the Provincial Council Meeting Held at Fort Hall, 21 October"). The CMS adherents had "conscientious objections" to the payments, arguing that it was part of a "repugnant" pagan ceremony (SNAR 1925:10; NDPR, DC South Nyeri "Itwika Goats", 16 July 1925; NTTC, Ag. CNC Kikuyu to CS Kenya, 20 Jan. 1926). They feared the goats were used as a sacrifice to a "heathen Evil Spirit" (NTTC, DC South Nyeri Jan. 1926). The matter was discussed several times by the Nyeri Advisory and Local Native Councils during 1925 and 1926 (NDPR "Minutes, Advisory Council" 30 Jan. 1925; SLNC "Minutes" 6 July 1925, 2 Nov. 1926). It was decided by councilors that the fee had to be paid, but the goats belonging to Christians could not be sacrificed. Instead, they could only be used for meat. District administrators agreed to oversee the slaughter of goats to ensure enforcement of the resolution.

CMS converts who were members of the South Nyeri Council voted against the resolution, and they protested to the Chief Native Commissioner and other senior officials. A Kikuyu mission teacher led the dissidents (NTTC, Ag. CNC to CS, 20 Jan. 1926). However, according to official accounts, CMS missionaries Rev. Rampley at Kabare and Rev. H. J. Butcher at Mutira (who resided at the station between 1921 and 1926) "abetted" or "inspired" the protests (NDPR, DC South Nyeri, "Itwika Goats", 16 July 1925; NTTC, Ag. CNC to CS, 20 Jan. 1926; NTTC, DC South Nyeri, Jan. 1926; SNAR 1926:78).

Many of the colonial officials were critical of the CMS missionaries and followers. Arthur Champion, the South Nyeri District Commissioner, attacked the notion that the sacrifice was to an "Evil Spirit". He claimed it was directed toward "the good God who lives on Kirinyaga [Mount Kenya]", a deity similar to the God of "Moses" (NTTC, DC South Nyeri Jan. 1926). Champion wrote that the native Kikuyu "idea" was "a beautiful one", possessing "the best Christian principles" (NTTC, DC South Nyeri Jan. 1926). C. F. Watkins, the Acting Chief Native Commissioner, worried that nonpayment would split the Kikuyu into two groups, "the qualified ruling Rika" [generation set] and "disenfranchised" Christians (NTTC, Ag. CNC to CS, 20 Jan. 1926; also see SNAR 1926:78).

The controversy temporarily declined. Government pressures to end the affair, as well as the rise of the hotly contested "female circumcision" and land issues, probably influenced the course of events. *Ituika* ceremonies started in Ndia and Gichugu about 1931 and continued through 1933 (ELNC 27–28 Nov. 1938:6; EDAR 1933:16). They coincided with another conflict over the sanctity of the groves. There were reports of clearing by Christians, and elderly informants recalled zealous neophytes who challenged tradition. However, district records indicated that not every accusation about the destruction of sacred trees had merit (EDAR 1933:5). "Pagan" elders apparently manipulated traditions about the clearing of sacred or ritually impure grounds in order "to annoy individuals". For example,

. . . individuals were prevented from opening up new cultivation because of the death of a dog near the site. The elders admitted that this had been done in the past and that such action really was unsupported by law or custom (EDAR 1933:5).

The CMS "agitated" against prosecution for any desecration, and several lawsuits were initiated in the native courts.

Unable to resolve the conflict in the tribunals, the sacred grove issue was brought before the Local Native Council at Embu in 1933 (Kirinyaga had been transferred from South Nyeri that year). It ordered the registration of all "places of worship", including sacred groves, in Kirinyaga and Embu (NAAR 1933:12). This proposal was resisted by the CMS, but it eventually relented (EDIR Sept. 1933:2). Places of worship now were protected by the Council, with violators subject to prosecution. In Ndia, 117 sacred groves were registered, while 85 groves were preserved in Gichugu. Another 15 groves were registered in Gichugu, but these could be opened for cultivation by order of local elders. All of the Kirinyaga sites were set aside for use in the generation set handing-over ceremonies.

With the sacred groves now registered and protected by the Council, the controversy died down. The Embu District Commissioner reported that "all denominations" welcomed the solution and apparently abided by it (EDAR 1933:12). Thus, the sacred groves, once the embodiment of local identity and unity, had become a symbol of the new sociocultural heterogeneity. They were no longer sufficiently protected by custom and peer pressure. Instead, their preservation now depended on powers delegated to the Embu Council under Section 8 (g) of the Native Authority Ordinance.

It was probably not a coincidence that the District Commissioner reported that the obligation of Christian subscriptions to the *ituika* ceremony was "settled amicably" (EDAR 1933:16). No mention was made of the specific agreement.

The formal protection of the sacred groves in the 1930s did not halt their declining religious, political, and cultural significance. Continued religious conversion, the introduction of mass public education, the disintegration of the generation- and age-sets, the privatisation of land during the Mau Mau Emergency, and the widening of economic inequality among households reduced even further the sociocultural solidarity that had once sustained the trees (Castro 1987).

In the mid-1950s, a district official noted that the Irungu elders did "little beyond" preserving the sacred groves. Provisions were made by the Land Consolidation Advisory Boards to protect the trees during privatisation (EDAR 1957:6). Some "preliminary" discussions were held about the transfer of control from Irungu to Mwangi moieties before the State of Emergency in 1952 (EDAR 1957:6). However, interest waned by the end of the decade

(EDAR 1959: 12). The generation sets were nearly moribund as Kenya became independent in 1963.

Nowadays, groves are not used for ceremonies. An elder remarked, "People have churches. They don't offer sacrifices under trees any more. The *muratina* [*Kigelia africanum*] has shed its leaf". Some informants pointed out that many groves and their surrounding bush were severely cut back after land tenure reform. Provisions made for the protection of the groves apparently lapsed. "The owner of the land can do whatever he likes to the tree", an old man explained. But respect for tradition has caused many landowners, including devout Christians, to preserve some groves. Another informant suggested that people still "fear" the sacred groves, suspecting misfortune if they harm the trees. The "fear" of criticism from, and "backbiting" by, neighbors also made quite a few property owner maintain the trees. The groves or trees also often provide practical benefits: catchment protection, windbreaks, shade, seeds, and useful products such as firewood. Hence, community sentiment and utilitarian concerns have continued to protect some sacred groves.

## The Sacred Groves in Perspective

The role of common property resource regimes in Third World rural development has attracted considerable attention in recent years (for example, see NRC 1986). Ironically, the trend in many parts of the world is for them, including sacred groves, to disappear or disintegrate. This pattern is often related to processes, events, or ideas associated with, or related to, the development process itself. In colonial Kirinyaga, the introduction of new belief systems, political hierarchy, and economic stratification eroded the old bonds of sociocultural unity. Deep fissions emerged among a people who no longer shared values and customs. These new ideological and sociocultural commitments led a small number of neophytes to rebel against tradition. Although the district administration actually attempted to preserve the groves, the social forces set in motion by colonialism undermined the cultural roles and importance of the trees.

Despite their diminished status, many of the trees remained protected today by community sentiment and respect for the past. Their preservation sometimes involved utilitarian concerns such as catchment protection, providing shade, or furnishing useful products. Although the sacred groves are a relic of a past society, they are, to quote Bernard Riley and David Brokensha (1988:200), ". . . environmentally desirable and a pleasing reminder of one aspect of . . . traditional life."

## Acknowledgments

I am grateful for the generous support I received in preparing this paper. In particular, I would like to thank the following people and institutions: in Kirinyaga, Cyrus Kibingo, George Muriithi, John Guthuri Gichobi, Albert

Gichoki, and the Kerugoya School for the Deaf; the Kenya National Archives staff in Nairobi and the Library for Special Collections, Syracuse University; and David Brokensha, Denise Castro, Miriam Chaiken, Ann Fleuret, and Tom Conelly. Financial support for field research was provided by the National Science Foundation (NSF BN81-15930), the Intercultural Studies Foundation, and the University of California, Santa Barbara. I am responsible for all opinions and conclusions.

## References Cited

Ambler, Charles.
    1988    Kenyan Communities in the Age of Imperialism. New Haven: Yale University Press.

Beech, M.
    1913a    The Sacred Fig-tree of the A'Kikuyu of East Africa. Man. 13:4–6.
    1913b    A Ceremony of a Mugumu or Sacred Fig-tree of the A'Kikuyu of East Africa. Man. 13:86–89.

Benson, T.
    1964    Kikuyu-English Dictionary. London: Oxford University Press.

Brokensha, David W.
    1966    Social Change at Larteh, Ghana. London: Oxford University Press.
    1987a    Inequality in Rural Africa: Fallers Reconsidered. Manchester Papers in Development. III:1–21.
    1987b    Development Anthropology and Natural Resource Management. L'Uomo. 11:225–250.

Brokensha, David W. and A. H. Peter Castro.
    1984    Fuelwood, Agro-Forestry and Natural Resource Management. Binghamton, NY: IDA Working Paper No. 12.
    1987    Common Property Resources. Rome: Food and Agriculture Organization.

Brokensha, David W. D.M. Warren, and Oswald Werner, eds.
    1980    Indigenous Knowledge Systems and Development. Lanham, MD: University Press of America.

Cagnolo, C.
    1933    The Akikuyu. Nyeri: Catholic Mission Press.

Castro, Alphonso H. P.
    1987    Facing Kirinyaga: A Socioeconomic History of Resource Use and Forestry Intervention in Southern Mount Kenya. unpublished Ph.D. dissertation. Dept. of Anthropology. University of California, Santa Barbara.

Castro, Alphonso H. P. and David W. Brokensha
    1987a    Institutions and Food Security: Implications for Forestry Development. Rome: Food and Agriculture Organization.
    1987b    Landholding Systems and Agrarian Change. Rome: Food and Agriculture Organization.

Crawford, E. May.
    1913    By the Equator's Snowy Peaks. London: Church Missionary Society.

Dundas, Charles.
    1915    The Organization and Laws of Some Bantu Tribes in East Africa. Journal of the Royal Anthropological Society. 45:234–306.

EDAR.
1931 to 1934 Embu District Annual Report. (Kenyan National Archives).

EDIR.
1933 Embu District Intelligence Report. July. (Kenya National Archives).

ELNC.
various dates Embu District Local Native Council Minutes. (Embu District Council Archives).

EPRB.
various dates Embu District Political Record Book. (Kenyan National Archives).

Erasmus, Charles.
1977 In Search of the Common Good. New York: The Free Press.

Gagdil, M. and V. Vartak.
1977 The Sacred Groves of Western Ghats in India. Economic Botany. 30:152–160.

1981a Studies on Sacred Groves among the Western Ghats from Maharashtra to Goa: Role of Beliefs and Folklore. *In* Glimpses of Indian Ethnobotany. S. Jain, ed. Pp. 272–78. New Delhi: Oxford and IBH Publishing.

1981b Sacred Groves of Maharashtra: An Inventory. *In* Glimpses of Indian Ethnobotany. S. Jain, ed. Pp. 279–294. New Delhi: Oxford and IBH Publishing.

Hobley, C. W.
1967 Bantu Beliefs and Magic. 2nd. ed. London: Cass (originally published 1922, 2nd. edition in 1937).

Kenyatta, Jomo.
1938 Facing Mount Kenya. London: Secker and Warburg.

1962 Facing Mount Kenya. New York: Vintage.

KSAR.
1928, 1931, 1933 Kerugoya Sub-District Annual Report. (Kenyan National Archives).

Lambert. H.E.
1950 The Systems of Land Tenure in the Kikuyu Land Unit. Cape Town: School of African Studies, Communications No. 22.

1956 Kikuyu Social and Political Institutions. London: Oxford University.

Leakey, L.S.B.
1977a The Southern Kikuyu before 1903. Vol. 1. New York: Academic Press.

1977b The Southern Kikuyu before 1903. Vol. 3. New York: Academic Press.

Little, Peter D. And David W. Brokensha.
1987 Local Institutions, Tenure and Resource Management in East Africa. *In* Conservation in Africa. D. Anderson and R. Grove, eds. Cambridge: Cambridge University Press.

Maher, Colin.
1938 Soil Erosion and Land Utilisation in the Embu Reserve, Part I. Nairobi: Department of Agriculture.

Messerschmidt, Donald.
1986 People and Resources in Nepal: Customary Resource Management Systems of the Upper Kali Gandaki. *In* Proceedings of the Conference on Common Property Resource Management. National Research Council. Pp. 455–480. Washington, D.C.: National Academy Press.

Middleton, John and Greet Kershaw.
1965 The Kikuyu and Kamba. London: International African Institute.

Mwaniki, H.S.K.
1974   Embu Historical Text. Nairobi: East African Literature Bureau.
National Research Council (NRC).
1986   Proceedings of the Conference on Common Property Resource Management. Washington, D. C.: National Academy Press.
NDPR.
various dates   Nyeri District Political Records. (Kenyan National Archives).
NTTC.
various dates   Native Tribes and Their Customs, Vol. 1 (Kenyan National Archives).
Oakerson, Ronald J.
1986   A Model for the Analysis of Common Property Problems. *In* Proceedings of the Conference on Common Property Resource Management. National Research Council. Pp. 13–30. Washington, DC: National Academy Press.
Orde-Browne, G.
1925   The Vanishing Tribes of Kenya. London: Seeley and Service.
Riley, Bernard and David W. Brokensha.
1988a   The Mbeere in Kenya. Vol. 1. Lanham, MD: University Press of America.
1988b   The Mbeere in Kenya. Vol. 2. Lanham, MD: University Press of America.
Rosberg, Carl G. and John Nottingham.
1970   The Myth of "Mau Mau". New York: Meridian Books.
Routledge, W. Scorsby and K. Routledge.
1910   With a Prehistoric People. London: Arnold.
Saberwal, Satish C.
1970   The Traditional Political System of the Embu of Central Kenya. Nairobi: East African Publishing House.
SLNC.
various dates   South Nyeri Local Native Council Minutes. (Kenyan National Archives).
SNAR.
various dates   South Nyeri District Annual Report. (Kenyan National Archives).
Stigand, C.H.
1913   The Land of Zinj. London: Constable.
Sorrenson, M.
1968   Origins of European Settlement in Kenya. Nairobi: Oxford University Press.
Worjal, S.
1985   The Potential of Sacred Groves as Nature Reserves in India. unpublished M.A. thesis. College of Environmental Science and Forestry. State University of New York, Syracuse.

# About the Editors
# and Contributors

**P.T.W. Baxter** lectures in Social Anthropology in the University of Manchester, Manchester, England. He has carried out field research in Uganda, Kenya, Ethiopia, and Ghana, and has a particular interest in pastoral peoples.

**Manuel L. Carlos** is currently Professor of Anthropology and Research Associate of the Center for Chicano Studies as the University of California, Santa Barbara. He has been a senior Postdoctoral Fellow of the Tinker Foundation and a Postdoctoral Fellow of the Social Science Research Council. He has published on development problems, the U.S.-Mexican border, ethnic stratification and ethnic relations in Mexico and the U.S. Southwest, and on local-level politics, development and state-society relations in Mexico. In 1971, he published *Politics and Development in Rural Mexico* (N.Y. Praeger). His most recent work is a book he is completing, *Peasant Political Brokers and the Mexican State, the Mexicali Valley 1934–1982*, (in process). His latest field research is a study of land tenure classes, development, and the state in Queretaro, Mexico's municipios (counties), 1934–1988. The study was initiated in 1988 and is being conducted in collaboration with the University of Queretaro, Mexico.

**Peter Castro** is an Assistant Professor of Anthropology at Syracuse University. He has been a consultant for the United States Agency for International Development, the Food and Agriculture Organization of the United Nations, and CARE on topics such as community forestry, land tenure, farm credit, refugee livelihood, and social science methodology. He has carried out fieldwork in Kenya and Somalia, and he is currently Editor of the African Publication Series for the Foreign and Comparative Studies Program in the Maxwell School of Citizenship and Public Affairs.

**Miriam S. Chaiken** is an Assistant Professor of Anthropology at Indiana University of Pennsylvania, and a graduate of the University of California at Santa Barbara. She has conducted applied anthropological research both in the Philippines (1980–81) and in Kenya (1984–1987) and served as a consultant to UNICEF, the Rockefeller Foundation, and the International Labour Organization. Her research interests include nutrition intervention design, new lands settlement, and women and development.

**W. Thomas Conelly** is an Assistant Professor of Anthropology at Indiana University of Pennsylvania. His dissertation research (1980–81) focused on upland farming systems and the development potential of shifting cultivation on the island of Palawan in the Philippines. In 1984–85, as a Rockefeller Foundation Social Science Research Fellow, he participated in an Integrated Pest management program in Kenya which included studies of indigenous pest management and intercropping techniques. During 1986–87 he worked for the University of Missouri, Columbia and Winrock International as anthropologist on an interdisciplinary farming systems project (Small Ruminant CRSP) investigating smallholder crop-livestock management strategies in Kenya. In 1988–89 he was Visiting Assisting Professor of Anthropology and Environmental Studies at Oberlin College. He has published an article on forest collecting in the

Philippines in *Economic Botany* and several book chapters on pest control and livestock management in Kenya.

**James F. Eder** is Professor of Anthropology at Arizona State University. He has conducted eight years of fieldwork in the Philippines, principally on Palawan Island, where he has two long-term research projects. The first, the subject of this paper here, concerns the interplay over time of economic development and social differentiation in a frontier farming community; the second concerns the consequences of incorporation into wider socioeconomic systems for the Batak, a forest-dwelling foraging people. He is the author of *Who Shall Succeed? Agricultural Development and Social Inequality on a Philippine Frontier* (Cambridge University Press 1982) and *On the Road to Tribal Extinction: Depopulation, Deculturation, and Adaptive Well-Being Among the Batak of the Philippines* (University of California Press 1987).

**Anne K. Fleuret** holds a Ph.D. in Cultural Anthropology from the University of California, Santa Barbara, and has taught at California State University Los Angeles, The American University, and the University of Nairobi. Her fieldwork in Tanzania (1975–1977) and Kenya (1981–present) supported by NSF, SSRC, and NIH has examined relationships among food production, distribution, and consumption and their nutritional outcomes. Publications include articles in journals such as Human Ecology and Human Organization, as well as numerous book chapters. She is currently completing a book-length manuscript on the socioeconomic determinants of nutritional status in rural Kenya.

**Patrick C. Fleuret** is head of the social sciences branch in USAID's Regional Economic Development Services Office for East and Southern Africa, located in Nairobi, Kenya. He has conducted long-term field research on marketing and social change in Tanzania (1975–1977) and on the agricultural and socioeconomic determinants of child nutrition in Kenya (1981–1982). He has worked for shorter periods of time in 13 countries throughout the region, focusing on policy and institutional issues arising in programs of agricultural and rural development. His professional publications are concerned with the social causes and consequences of agricultural changes in Africa.

**Jack Glazier** is Professor of Anthropology and Chairman of the Department at Oberlin College. He has done fieldwork in East Africa among the Mbeere people of Kenya, where he first met David Brokensha. His African interests and publications are extensive, including land tenure and social change, social structure, symbolism, and folklore. In recent years, he has turned his attention to the anthropological and ethnohistorical study of American Jews, and he has published on such topics as Ashkenazic-Sephardic relations, identity and social change, and the problem of the anthropologist working in his own community.

**Thomas Hakansson** has a Ph.D. in Cultural Anthropology and is a teacher and researcher at the Department of Cultural Anthropology, Uppsala University. His regional specialization is sub-Saharan Africa and he has done fieldwork in Kenya among the Gusii 1982–83 and 1985, and among the Rabai 1985–86. His main interests are family organization, gender relations, social and economic change, and political economy and evolution. He is the author of: *Bridewealth, Women and Land: Social Change among the Gusii of Kenya* (1988); Environment, Bridewealth, and Family Structure in Eastern Africa: A Comparative Study of House Property Systems, in *Ethnology* (1989), and other articles on family organization, bridewealth, and socio-economic inequality.

**Barry S. Hewlett** is an Assistant Professor of Anthropology at Tulane University in New Orleans. He first conducted research with African Pygmies in 1973 and has made numerous field trips since that time. His primary research interests include cultural transmission, the father-child relationship, demography and biosocial perspectives on human behavior. He has published book chapters on the father-child relationship and published articles on cultural transmission, demography and human growth in such journals as *American Anthropologist, Man* and the *New England Journal of Medicine*.

**Michael M Horowitz**, Professor of Anthropology at State University of New York at Binghamton and Director of the Institute for Development Anthropology, has carried out research among farming and pastoral peoples in Senegal, Niger, Mali, Burkina Faso, the Sudan, Zaire, Rwanda, Zimbabwe, Tunisia, Jamaica, and Martinique. He has been an advisor and consultant to the United Nations Development Programme, the U.N. Environment Programme, the U.N. Sudano-Sahelian Office, the Food and Agricultural Organization, the World Bank, the Agency for International Development, the Overseas Liaison Committee of the American Council on Education, the Overseas Development Council, the Board on Science and Technology for International Development of the National Academy of Sciences, and the U.S. Congress Office of Technology Assessment. In 1974–1975 he served as regional anthropologist and director of applied social science research for USAID's Regional Economic Development Services Office for West Africa, and from 1979 to 1984 he was senior social science advisor to USAID's office of Evaluation. He received the Ph.D. in anthropology from Columbia University.

**Dolores Koenig** is Assistant Professor and Coordinator of the M.A. Program in Applied Anthropology at the American University in Washington, D.C., and also works as a freelance international development consultant. She has worked in various Francophone African countries, with special emphasis on Mali. Her interests include gender, farm level economic development, and settlement and resettlement in conjunction with river basin development.

**Peter D. Little** received his Ph.D. in 1983 from Indiana University. He is a Senior Research Associate at the Institute for Development Anthropology (IDA) and an adjunct faculty member at SUNY-Binghamton. He has served as consultant to the United Nations, the World Bank, the Agency for International Development, and the Office of Technology Assessment of the U.S. Congress, and is a member of the Advisory Board for the Africa Program of Oxfam America. He has carried out research on pastoral ecology and production systems, regional marketing, and irrigated agriculture in Kenya and Pakistan, and is currently conducting research on livestock and milk marketing in Somalia. He coedited *Lands at Risk in the Third World* (Westview 1987) and *Anthropology of Development and Change in East Africa* (Westview 1988) and has published widely in edited books and professional journals, including *Africa, American Ethnologist, Human Ecology,* and *Human Organization*.

**Randall C. Luce** is currently the Corporate Relations Assistant with Interchurch Medical Assistance (IMA). IMA solicits donations of medical supplies for use in hospitals affiliated with it's member agencies. He has worked with PVOs for the past four years. His research interests include development, local politics, and race and ethnicity.

**Josette Murphy** is the Senior Monitoring and Evaluation Specialist for Agriculture in the Africa Region, the World Bank. Previous affiliations include the International Service for National Agricultural Research (ISNAR), the United States Agency for International Development (USAID), and Purdue University. Her interests focus on agricultural development, particularly its institutional and managerial dimensions as well as its sociological aspects. Her publications include two books and a number of technical documents on monitoring and evaluation methodologies, as well as impact evaluations and agricultural sector assessments on agricultural research and extension programs. She holds a Ph.D. in Cultural Anthropology from the University of California-Santa Barbara, and undergraduate degrees in history and in biology.

**Michael Painter** is a Research Associate at the Institute for Development Anthropology and an Adjunct Assistant Professor in the Department of Anthropology of the State University of New York at Binghamton. He has conducted research on natural resource management, and food and agricultural policy in Peru, Bolivia, and Ecuador, and he has taught and written extensively on these topics.

**Thomas M. Painter** received his doctorate in sociology and development anthropology from the State University of New York, Binghamton. He is affiliated with the Department of Anthropology, Hunter College, City University of New York, where he has taught and serves as Associate Editor for the journal *Human Ecology*. Previously, he was a Program Associate at the Social Science Research Council where he staffed the Project on African Agriculture, and a Research Associate at the Institute for Development Anthropology, where he managed projects in West Africa. He has published a number of articles and book chapters on migration, agriculture, and rural development in West Africa, has co-edited, with Michael M Horowitz, *Anthropology and Rural Development in West Africa* (Westview 1986), and is currently writing a book on the political economy of peasant migrations and agrarian change in Niger and the larger West African regional economy.

**Bernard Riley** was born and received his first university education in England. He spent several years in the Colonial Education Service in Tanganyika (now Tanzania), followed by a period of teaching in Rhodesia (Zimbabwe). He came to the USA. in 1959, on a Fulbright Scholarship, and received his Ph.D. at Indiana University, followed later by a Masters in Library Science from UCLA. He collaborated with David Brokensha in a longitudinal study of social and ecological change in Mbeere, Kenya, and co-authored many articles and a two-volume book with Brokensha. Now retired, Riley taught Geography, and Environmental Studies, at the University of California (first at Berkeley, then at Santa Barbara) from 1966 until 1989.

**Thayer Scudder** is Professor of anthropology at the California Institute of Technology, Pasadena, and director of the Institute for Development Anthropology, Binghamton, New York. Educated at Harvard University, since 1956 he has pursued research interests related to new land settlement, river basin development, and long-term community studies. His publications deal particularly with the Kariba Dam Project in Central Africa, and with dam relocation and new land settlement worldwide. He has worked as a consultant for the World Bank, USAID, and other organizations on projects in Africa, Asia, and the Middle East. Currently he is revising for publication a book-length report prepared for USAID on the experience with river basin development in Africa.

**Monica Udvardy** is a graduate student in the Department of Cultural Anthropology, University of Uppsala, Sweden. She is currently completing her Ph.D. dissertation entitled *Gender and the Culture of Fertility among the Giriama of Kenya*, Based on fieldwork in 1983 and 1984–1986. Her research interests and publications concern expressions of gender in society and culture; both applied and symbolic aspects of ethnomedicine; AIDS and anthropology; and women in development. Her regional area of focus is East Africa.

# Index